COMEDIA
Series editor: David Morley

Looka Yonder!

Looka Yonder!

The imaginary America of populist culture

Duncan Webster

R

A Comedia book published by
Routledge
London and New York

A Comedia book
First published in 1988 by
Routledge
11 New Fetter Lane, London EC4P 4EE
29 West 35th Street, New York NY 10001

Printed and bound in Great Britain by
Butler & Tanner Ltd, Frome and London

British Library Cataloguing in Publication Data

Webster, Duncan
    Looka yonder!: the imaginary America
    of populist culture.
    1. United States—Popular culture—
    History—20th century
    I. Title
    306'.1   E169.1

    ISBN 0-415-00715-1
    ISBN 0-415-00716-X Pb

Library of Congress Cataloging in Publication Data

Webster, Duncan, 1958–
    Looka yonder!: the imaginary America of populist culture/Duncan
    Webster.
        p. cm. — (A Comedia book)
    Bibliography: p.
    Includes index.
    ISBN 0-415-00715-1
    ISBN 0-415-00716-X Pb
    1. United States—Popular culture—History.   2. Populism—United
States—History.   I. Title.
E169.1.W318   1988
973—dc 19

Contents

Acknowledgements vi

Introduction: Looka yonder! 1

1 Family fields: the farming narrative 27

2 Country images: from Steinbeck's Okies to Hollywood's heartland 56

3 Sam Shepard's cowboy mouth: representing masculinity 85

4 'Things fall apart': loss in recent American fiction 115

5 American crime: 'Debts no honest man could pay' 135

6 'Are you ready for the country?': tradition and American music 157

7 The long reaction: 'Americanization' and cultural criticism 174

Conclusion: President Rambo's poodle 209

Notes 248

Index 263

Acknowledgements

There are several people to thank. I am grateful, as ever, to my family for their support and encouragement, and to my flatmates, Craig Dickson and Basil Whybray, for putting up with my typing. I would also like to thank David Morley for useful criticisms and patient editing.

Friends have given their usual interest and support: I'm grateful to Gabriel Firth, Susy Firth, Rebecca Kidd, David Imrie, Duncan Hadfield, Darcy Sullivan, Richard Johnson, and Rachel Cooper. More specifically, thanks to Joe Cushley for conversations on music and loans of records, Barry Taylor for discussions of crime fiction, and Tim Stevens for regular bulletins from North Carolina. Finally, this book is dedicated to Yvonne Tasker, in expectation of much argument and some agreement.

Introduction:
Looka yonder!

A few years ago a Texas company, Braniff Airlines ... used for an
advertising slogan: 'If you've got it, flaunt it.'
 'If you've got it, flaunt it.' The spirit of the American Southwest
speaks. Down in Texas, they have a clear notion of God: He loves the
strongest man in town. In such a theology, the Lord approves of the
productive process and those who thrive on it. He has a soft spot for the
rich. At their worst, the rich must still have luck, and luck is the power
to know when to take a big chance. There, between Calvin and Nietzsche,
sits Texas and Maggie Thatcher.[1]

Norman Mailer's observation, made in a commentary on the British
General Election in 1983, places Mrs Thatcher through the 'spirit of
the American Southwest'. It links an imaginary America within the
US – all the mythic reverberations of Texas – with an imaginary
America within Britain, the entrepreneurial culture that Thatcherism
sought to produce from a top hat of tax cuts, privatization, and an
onslaught on the Welfare State, which came with an appeal to Britain's
past ('Victorian values') but was more obviously influenced by a
wistful gaze at America. If one of the important contexts for this book
is the populist vision shared by Reagan and Mrs Thatcher, another
context is also suggested by Mailer's comment, images of America in
popular culture. For another bridge between Texas and British life,
besides Mailer's ingenious linking of Calvin, Nietzsche, and Thatcher,
is the popularity of *Dallas*. The success of this Texan saga has also
produced anxiety about its effect on British national culture, the
threat to British television being often expressed as 'wall-to-wall
Dallas'. The book concludes with these pleasures and threats, and
the way that they invent an 'America' through British consumption,
and this is a persistent theme throughout this work. This is not to
suggest, however, that Americans have an unmediated and uninflected
access to a homogeneous culture. The main part of this work will
examine the contradictions and struggles over meanings and traditions
within the United States.

1

These contradictions are located by looking at the historical flash-points of American populism – the 1890s, the 1930s, and the Reaganite 1980s – and by examining a wide range of cultural works in the light of these contexts. The first two chapters concern the American farmer, moving from early agrarian images to contemporary films and fiction responding to the farm crisis of the 1980s. If agriculture today presents a series of economic problems and political embarrassments, around such topics as free trade versus protectionism or western food surpluses versus Third World famine, my discussion focuses on a different context, the historical and cultural echoes of foreclosure, debt, and suicide in America's farming communities. Chapter 1 begins with the current concern for the American farmer, a concern that can be seen in films, music, fiction, and political campaigns. The issue of the loss of the family farm links themes of labour, gender, and property, and these themes are traced from early American literature and political rhetoric up to the populist agitation and regionalist fiction of the late nineteenth century. Chapter 2 picks up the agrarian narrative in a new context, the South of the poor white tenant farmers captured in the writing of the 1930s and the images of New Deal America. It concludes by returning to recent films and fiction and, especially, to the ambivalent response that this work produces in metropolitan critics who worry that the new ruralism is a form of 'hick chic'.

The close link between America's cultural and political rhetoric and ideas of the land means that the farm crisis touches more people than the estimated 3 per cent of the population living on farms. This struggle is not only about the survival of smallscale agriculture, it's also a struggle over the traditions, myths, and symbols clustered around the image of the independent farmer. This contest over meanings opens up the idea of 'Americanness' and testifies to a conflict within American populism, fought out on the terrain of tradition. The economy under Reagan has seen the suffering of one of America's central symbols, the family farmer, and this raises the possibility of retrieving conservative and populist themes from the right and mobilizing them in an oppositional way.

These struggles look back to earlier periods of rural poverty and protest, particularly the 1890s and 1930s, and these moments of populist discontent will be discussed later in this introduction. Along-side this sense of period, there also exists a strong sense of place, a kind of geography of authenticity: the West, the Midwest, the South. These landscapes also provide the backdrop for a representation of women that challenges both the symbol of the male independent farmer and feminist ideas of what 'progressive' images of women might be. The farm wives and women country singers in recent films are placed firmly within the family, but they are also identified through their work. The effect of this is an overlapping of the radical and the conservative, a productive tension between wife and worker. This issue is central to my argument and, complementing this discussion of farming and femininity, Chapter 3 looks at another way of linking landscape and gender, investigating the contradictory representations of masculinity in the work of Sam Shepard.

Chapter 3 is something of an exception, being the only chapter devoted to a single writer. The importance of Shepard lies partly in his range of work, crossing drama, film, writing, and acting, and with a continual use of jazz, rock, or country music. If this makes him central to any discussion of recent American culture, his concern with the repertoire of American masculinity (the cowboy, the farmer, the criminal, the drifter, the musician) is particularly significant. His work unravels the marriage of farm and family discussed in the previous chapters, as faith in the land is seen to be a mirage. Masculinity in his plays is not seen as an essentialist attribute but as shaped by culture, but this culture is problematically American, partly celebrated, partly criticized. The typical landscape for this questioning is the desert, but that classic Western terrain is also littered with the detritus of a modern pop culture. Shepard's combination of populist and popular cultures can be glimpsed in Stanley Kauffmann's description of Shepard's characters in *Curse of the Starving Class*: 'They are something like John Steinbeck's Okies seen by Donald Barthelme.'[2] From the populist classic, Steinbeck's *The Grapes of Wrath* (1939), to the postmodernist playfulness of Barthelme's fiction, for example, *Snow White* (1967), the comment captures the peculiarity of Shepard's writing, the populist themes and settings and their modern treatment.

Chapter 4 discusses new American fiction (Jayne Anne Phillips, Bobbie Ann Mason, Raymond Carver, Richard Ford, Tobias Wolff, Frederick Barthelme, Elizabeth Tallent, and others). This fiction can be seen as part of the revival of the American short story and also as the return of regional voices, for several writers overlap with the work discussed in Chapter 2. But for British readers, the important introduction to these writers was through *Granta*'s 'Dirty Realism' issue. Bill Buford prefaced that collection by pointing out the differences between this fiction and American novels of the 1960s and 1970s. Neither epic nor playfully metafictional this is prose 'devoted to the local details, the nuances, the little disturbances in language and gesture': 'unadorned, unfurnished, low-rent tragedies'. Characters are from 'Kentucky or Alabama or Oregon, but, mainly, they could just about be from anywhere'.[3] Buford highlights the way that this fiction has moved away from the cities and campuses and suburbs to uncover forgotten regions and characters. In this the writers revive important traditions but within the context of an economic recession where, after Vietnam and after anti-war activism, politics has been relocated to the everyday. There is an ambivalent sense of place evoked by characters from Kentucky or Alabama who 'could just about be from anywhere'; a transformed regionalism testifying to the relationship between the local and national popular culture. A South that is watching MTV is a long way from the world of Faulkner. One possibly misleading aspect of this description of 'Dirty Realism' is the stress on characters being working class. This is true to an extent but, like the tendency in British reviews of this fiction to fix its social location as 'bluecollar' or 'petit bourgeois' or whatever, it overlooks the range of these writers. They include computer operators as well as cowboys, car salesmen as well as English professors, waitresses and research students. This American writing suggests a kind of affective democracy, with feelings of anxiety cutting across economic setting. A sense of loss is general, although pinned down to specifics, relationships and jobs, for example, and this sense and its literary and political implications, seems to be at the heart of this fiction.

This sense of loss seems to me to be as central to populism as the loss of the family farm. There is a feeling that life is out of your control – it's being decided and determined elsewhere by the economy or in the realm of the political – combined with a distrust of political discourse. This is seen even more clearly in the works discussed in Chapter 5, novels, plays, and films about the blurring of crime and 'normal' economic activity. The focus here is on language, the rhythmic, foul-mouthed, demotic dialogue heard in the films of Martin Scorsese, the plays of David Mamet, and the novels of George V. Higgins and Elmore Leonard. This language ties together issues of exclusion, masculinity, and communities of work (whether legal or illegal or on the border between these). As opposed to the earlier agrarian settings, Chapter 5 deals with specifically urban lives. However, within the city we recognize similar themes of masculinity and work, as well as uncovering communities based on ethnic identity, criminal activity, or professional codes (cops, lawyers). So similar questions about the politics of place and the place of politics are raised either side of the city/country division. In both cases politics is something that occurs out there; something that happens *to* you. Or, in some novels, politics is something known so well and so cynically that it belongs to a small world of deals and fixing. Either way it's possible to argue that the strongest expression of populist themes is not Farm Aid nor Reagan's appeal to tradition, but the evidence of a massive disillusion with politics. The decisive Republican victory in 1980 should not lead us to overlook the millions of Americans who did not vote. With only 55 per cent of the electorate going to the polls, Reagan won with just 28 per cent of the eligible vote.

Populism as a political discourse pretends to be outside or above 'politics'. One could think of the Southern demagogues, from Huey Long in the 1930s to George Wallace, giving a voice and an often worrying form to discontent, while presenting themselves as an alternative to accepted political rhetoric. But American politics contains many examples of mainstream attempts to appropriate this populist alternative. One could think here of the ways in which presidents have rhetorically distanced themselves from Washington (Lyndon Johnson, Carter, Reagan). But the works in Chapter 5 focus specifically on one of the major themes of modern populism – 'Law and Order' – opening up a gap between political rhetoric and the language and reality of those in the front line (police, criminals, lawyers). There is a scene in Scorsese's film, *Taxi Driver*, where Robert De Niro, playing Bickle the Vietnam veteran now driving taxis in New York, gets the chance to talk politics, to speak to a politician and, supposedly, shape campaign policies. De Niro's language spirals away from what can be recognized as an 'issue' into a description of the squalor, crime, and alienation of his world. The candidate tries to translate this into a 'law and order' issue, but the gap between the two men's language is evident, and is underlined by the physical separation of the men, the way they are seated in the taxi. In that scene populist rhetoric is forced to confront its raw material (De Niro's description of the streets), and is seen to be inadequate. De Niro builds up to the film's final explosion of violence, initially directed at the political candidate but displaced on to the pimps who he kills. The film shows an ironic retrieval of De Niro's violence, with the newspapers painting his killings as heroic. Some critics, missing the irony, have described *Taxi Driver* as an 'arty' variant on the vigilante movie, but Scorsese's art is precisely engaged in opening up the contradictions behind that populist hero, the vigilante, revealing the language and the feelings that the newspapers and 'law and order' rhetoric gloss over.

Chapter 6 covers American music, specifically the re-emergence of an interest in country music by rock audiences, and the American guitar bands of the mid-1980s, heralded by some British writers as marking a return to authenticity in a period of pop shallowness. Music is another area where struggles take place over the meanings of tradition. Bruce Springsteen is a central figure here, especially his attempt to create a patriotism against conservatism, linking pride in his country with extensive criticism of its policies. Springsteen mediates his love of America through smaller units – regions, cities, the idea of the hometown. While his music attempts to unify disparate traditions, he has used his fame not so much to unify his audiences as to particularize them, to specify, when playing live, local issues and identities. It is no accident that Reagan's attempt to appropriate his work was a strategic appeal to Springsteen's territory made in a speech in Hammontown, New Jersey, in September 1984. Reagan said:

> 'America's future rests in a thousand dreams inside your hearts. It rests in the message of hope in songs of a man so many young Americans admire: New Jersey's own Bruce Springsteen. And helping you make those dreams come true is what this job of mine is all about.'

Springsteen's response was given to an audience rather than to the press. Introducing 'Johnny 99' he said, 'The president was mentioning my name the other day and I kinda got to wondering what his favorite album musta been. I don't think it was the *Nebraska* album. I don't think he's been listening to this one ...', and then playing a song that opens with the closure of an auto plant and then moves through arbitrary violence to arbitrary justice.[4]

Some significant oppositions emerge from this exchange: the specific narrative of 'Johnny 99' versus Reagan's generalized American dreams; Reagan's stress on the future versus a trend in music to look back, exploring the past and reclaiming various musical traditions, not in a clichéd return to roots but in a rediscovery of influences and histories that foreground the heterogeneity and plurality of the US, replacing a monolithic America with the local accents and details of regions and traditions. I see this theme of tradition as part of an active salvaging of the past, forging continuities or bringing new combinations out of inspired bricolage. This re-emergence of traditions is discussed in a framework of responses from British writers and musicians, and this leads into the final part of the book, an analysis of the theme of 'Americanization'. A number of histories feed into or frame the works discussed in the following chapters, giving not only political contexts but also political weight, the weight of appropriated traditions, to my examples. These will be briefly introduced here to map out some of the central themes and contradictions of American populism.

Reagan country

Reagan's appeal has always had a powerful populist component with his rhetoric building on patriotism, religion, and ideas of the frontier spirit. William Adams has analysed an example from Reagan's 1984 election campaign, a 'manipulation of romantic pastoralism' which is linked to the idea of a geography of authenticity. A campaign photo in *Time*'s special election issue showed the president 'standing beneath an enormous mural of "Reagan Country" – a classic pastoral landscape of rolling hills, farms, river and pond, etc. – a figural representation of the values the president pushed so relentlessly during the campaign: hard work, moral virtue, independence'. This pastoral image was one of the 'principal symbolic vehicles' in Reagan's television advertising and in the film of his life shown at the Dallas Republican convention. Adams continues: 'America had wandered, he told us, and the symbolism of traditional rural life became a way of telling us what we had left behind.'[5] It is easy to caricature this image but cartoons of the cowboy president miss what is going on in these photos and speeches. These country signifiers shouldn't be pinned down to Reagan's B-movies; they summon up influential traditions and associations. Unless we understand the function of 'Reagan country' we will miss the significance of opposition which is contesting this conservative pastoralism on its own symbolic and geographical terrain. Reagan promises a future as harmonious as this idealized rural past, but this image has been opposed by images of the hard reality of the present farm crisis as well as by more radical retrievals of the struggles of the 1930s.

Sam Shepard's Cavale, acted by Patti Smith and based on her own messianic fusion of rock and poetry, said in *Cowboy Mouth* in 1974 that people wanted a 'street angel': 'They want a saint with a cowboy mouth.' Six years later they got Ronald Reagan. Or, to put it another way: 'The worst nightmares of the American left appear to have come true. Like the beast of the apocalypse, Reaganism has slouched out of the Sunbelt, devouring liberal senators and Great Society programmes its path.'[6] Norman Mailer writing about Barry Goldwater provides a good starting point for understanding these nightmares and the emergence of the new right. Mailer attended the 1964 Republican convention with his usual good eye for a fight, in this case the struggle between West and East, new money and old. One of the many precedents for the 'Reagan country' image is the cover of *Life* discussed by Mailer. Goldwater manipulates the imagery of the West:

wearing a pearl-gray Stetson and clean, pressed, faded blue work shirt and Levi's while his companion, a Palomino named Sunny, stood with one of the Senator's hands on his bridle, the other laid over the vein of his nose. It was Hopalong Cassidy all baby fat removed, it gave promise of the campaign to come: the image of Kennedy was now to be combated by Sheriff B. Morris Goldwater, the Silver Gun of the West. It was one of those pictures worth ten thousand speeches – it gave promise of delivering a million votes.[7]

However powerful the image, Mailer points out that the accompanying article warned that the new money, in Ohio, Illinois, Texas, Los Angeles, San Francisco, could not match the old money's political power and connections. Mailer describes the Goldwater delegates, men from the Midwest and the West, as 'a Wasp Mafia where the grapes of wrath were stored', suggesting both the politics of *ressentiment* and the ambivalent nature of American populism. For the reference to the grapes of wrath may suggest, in this context, Steinbeck's Okies, but their radicalism has been transformed into the hate-filled conservatism of Goldwater. Mailer sees this constituency as being formed by the 'Wagnerian drama of the Wasp'; a drama whose characters are those left behind in the small town, feeling that they have missed out on the pleasures of the city and also that they lack the heroism of their settler ancestors. There is 'no hatred like hatred for the East in the hearts of those who were left behind'. They feel vaguely snubbed, 'because the Establishment of the East rarely rejects, it merely yields or ignores, it promises to attend your daughter's party and somehow does not quite show up'. The feeling at the convention was that this time, 'the Eastern Establishment was not going to win again, this time Main Street was going to take Wall Street'. Mailer compares the Goldwater supporters with the Beat Generation – in both cases the press had overlooked the subterranean currents of American social life. Mailer mirrors the right's paranoia, describing this 'underground generation of the Right' as 'a frustrated posse, a convention of hangmen who subscribe to the principle that the executioner has his rights as well'.[8]

Mailer's convention report, 'In the red light', suggests Steinbeck through its references to Okies and the grapes of wrath only to replace that picture of heroic populism with the world of another novel, also set in California and published in the same year as *The Grapes of Wrath* (1939). The first epigraph of the piece comes from Nathanael West's *The Day of the Locust*, a novel which ends with the apocalyptic scenario of dispossessed Midwesterners rioting outside the Californian Pleasure Dome. Mailer's description of the California delegation draws on West's vision:

> Most of the California delegation looked like fat state troopers or prison guards or well-established ranchers. A few were thin and looked like Robert Mitchum playing the mad reverend in *Night of the Hunter*. One or two were skinny as Okies, and looked like the kind of skinny wild-eyed gas-station attendant who works in a small town, and gets his picture in the paper because he has just committed murder with a jack handle. Yes,

the skinny men in the California delegation leered out wildly. They looked like they were sitting on a body – the corpse of Jew Eastern Negritudes – and when the show was over, they were gonna to eat it. That was it – half the faces in the California delegation looked like geeks. They had had it and now they were ready to put fire to the big tent.[9]

By 1968 when Mailer covers the Republican convention in Miami, he sees the party as bound to choose Nixon: in 1964 they 'had been able to be insane for a little while ... now they were looking for a leader to bring America back to them, their lost America, Jesusland'. Reagan's 1968 candidacy, however, contains echoes of 1964: 'Reagan's men had straight hair cropped short, soldiers and state troopers for Ronnie.'[10] What has proved central to Reagan's subsequent political career has been his ability to combine an appeal to the 'madness' of the Goldwater constituency – the geeks setting fire to the big tent – with the evocation of 'lost America, Jesusland'. It's a combination that other writers have found in California, like the California of Joan Didion's remark, the place where 'a belief in the literal interpretation of Genesis has slipped imperceptibly into a belief in the literal interpretation of *Double Indemnity*'.[11] Writers discussed later, such as Raymond Carver or Bobbie Ann Mason, deal with these points where popular culture meets tradition in a more sympathetic light.

However, what emerges from Mailer's commentary is a theme that will be discussed later, the contradictions of American conservatism. What Mailer observed was the birth of the new right and that raises a question that returns us to California, the issue of how the new right managed to move from the periphery to the centre, or how they managed to shift that centre decidedly rightwards.

California *Uber Alles*

If Reagan's entry into politics came through Hollywood and McCarthyism, through his involvement in the Screen Actors Guild, it was not until 1964 that he emerged as a prominent spokesman for the right. In the closing days of the Goldwater campaign his speech, 'A Time for Choosing', was nationally televised. Its theme was one that he would return to throughout his career: 'Either we accept the responsibility for our own destiny, or we abandon the American Revolution and confess that an intellectual belief in a far-distant capital can plan our lives for us better than we can plan them ourselves.' A traditional conservative message, self-help versus the state, is given a populist form with the suspicion of the intellect and the theme of emotional, political, and geographical distance from

Washington, 'a far-distant capital'. Goldwater proved a turning point for Reagan and for the right generally. Californian conservatives persuaded Reagan to run for governor in 1966; wishing to avoid another Goldwater failure it was agreed to soften ultraconservative positions, and the campaign was managed by the political consultants Spencer-Roberts, who were identified with arch-Easterner and Goldwater opponent, Nelson Rockefeller.[12]

The new right learned from the Goldwater campaign that their economic convictions could prove an electoral liability, but the campaign's organization was significant in their emergence as contenders for national power. Goldwater's financial independence, the campaign's autonomy from the Eastern establishment, was premised on the effects of the postwar boom which built up Los Angeles, Houston, and Denver as financial centres, fuelled by the military spending funnelled into the West and South. There is an important continuity: 'Goldwater was bankrolled by many of the same "angels" who would later elevate Reagan.' Mike Davis also points out a crucial innovation of 1964, the use of mailing lists and mail contributions in funding. This 'revolutionary step forward' liberated the new right from the Eastern establishment, 'providing the resources for it to survive and grow as a network of institutionalized single-issue movements and multipurpose umbrella groups'.[13] I'll return to this theme, after briefly discussing the geographical location of the right.

Mike Davis discusses the prefigurative quality of Californian politics: 'Berkeley, Watts, Delano literally and symbolically heralded the movements of the sixties and early seventies, while Orange County was celebrated as both birthplace and promised land of the New Right.' As the suburbs reacted against the campus and the ghetto, California 'offered a model laboratory for contriving united fronts of middle-class and white working-class backlash against integrated housing (1964–5), abolition of the death penalty (1965, 1976), the rights of farm labour (1972), school busing (1979) and property taxes (1978)'. The tax revolt in California is seen as the 'missing link between the New Right and a new majority', providing Reagan with an example that he extended into his 'fiscal neo-populism', which in turn has had an effect in Britain, strengthening the Thatcherite vision of prosperity through tax cuts.[14] Wider economic and demographic factors are involved in the geography of the right. In 1980, the year of Reagan's success, 'for the first time in American history, the population centre of the United States was located west of the Mississippi River'.[15] Because Reagan is identified as 'cowboy' rather than 'yankee', and as a product of the sunbelt, his victory was seen 'not merely as a triumph of Republicans over Democrats but as a power-shift from the Eastern Establishment to the country's Southern

Rim'.[16] This shift must also be seen in terms of the economy. A Vietnam war boom boosted industry in the South and the recessions of 1971 and 1974 led to 'capital flight from the unionized Northeast to the relatively "union-free" environments' of the South and Southwest. 'The seventies thus witnessed the most rapid and large-scale shift in economic power in American history.' Southern California's boom resumed 'after a short aerospace depression at the end of the sixties, and both Los Angeles and Houston began to flex their new muscles as international financial centres'.[17] It is this history that has shaped the rise of the right, and which underlies the Western nature of Reagan's image.

The new right: conservative contradictions

Gillian Peele has usefully distinguished between neo-conservatives, the new right, and the religious right, and although both crossovers and alliances exist, there is also potential for division between these groups.[18] A commitment to conservative thought and supply-side economics does not necessarily suggest support for campaigns against homosexuality, abortion, or pornography. There is also a considerable distance between conservative New York Jewish intellectuals, whose ideas were formed through earlier arguments with the Communist Party and through a reaction to the 1960s, and Southern televangelists. An important factor in the 'newness' of the new right has already been mentioned, the way reaction has been marketed around single issues and direct mail funding. Ironically, the Democrats were partly responsible for this expansion, through Congress's 1974 'Watergate reforms' of campaign financing, limiting the maximum an individual could donate. Instead of making election campaigns more open and democratic, they shifted power from 'traditional partisan structures ... to corporate-dominated Political Action Committees (PACs) and the proprietors of direct mail technology'. The PACs are a key element of the new politics, linking corporate interest groups to 'mass single-issue constituencies' with the traditional party being bypassed by the use of direct mail. The names of contributors, stored on computers, can be retrieved for electioneering. The new right have been able to link many single-issue campaigns through these methods, and one of the key figures of direct mail technology, Richard Viguerie, an ex-Goldwater supporter and admirer of McCarthy, gloated that 'the liberals are eight to ten years behind us in developing the technology of politics'.[19] This technological supremacy provides the odd spectacle of computerized Creationists, using new technology to oppose Darwin.

The new right's loyalty is to single-issue campaigns rather than to the Republicans as a party. Richard Viguerie said in 1976 that the Republicans would be as difficult to sell as the Edsel or Typhoid Mary: 'The Republican Party is like a disabled tank on the bridge impeding the troops from crossing to the other side. You've got to take that tank and throw it in the river.' He even declared the party to be dead and sought the vice-presidential nomination of the American Independent Party.[20] The third party idea has been shelved because of Reagan's appeal to the populist right, and because of their success in setting the political agenda. Gillian Peele has suggested that the Republicans have 'been tilted towards a radical populism which, while still liable to be held in check by other elements in the party, is nevertheless going to be a dominant feature of the GOP for some years to come'.[21] As single-issue movements expanded, 'an unprecedented panoply of inter-locking organizations and constituencies' appeared, ranging from law and order groups and the gun lobby, to the 'new cold war' hawks, and politicized fundamentalism, the Moral Majority, and others. The most effective mobilization centred on 'white suburban family life', movements reacting to a great extent to the successes of the women's movement, and challenging the Equal Rights Amendment, gay rights, and abortion. These issues penetrated blue-collar communities understandably not so receptive to conservative economic philosophy. Viguerie said in 1981:

> It was the social issues that got us this far, and that's what will take us into the future. We never really won until we began stressing issues like busing, abortion, school prayer and gun control. We talked about the sanctity of free enterprise, and about the Communist onslaught until we were blue in the face. But we didn't start winning majorities until we got down to gut level issues.[22]

Davis suggests that as the economy has divided the working class, with prosperity or poverty depending on such issues as what industry you work in or where you were born, 'social' issues have become central and family, home, neighbourhood, and race displace class solidarity.[23]

The appeal of the new right is built on contradictions. Reagan himself has been said to 'speak for old values in current accents. Like the nation, of which he is such a representative figure, he is a contradiction in terms – a hero of the consumer culture preaching the Protestant ethic.'[24] Reagan's first administration was described as 'not just a regime rent by contradictions, it is a regime built around an *impossibilism*. It is the political Woodstock of American capitalism, aspiring to an impossible unification of the interests of all the socially privileged strata of American society.'[25] If early Reaganomics was the right's Woodstock, then the farm crisis might be seen as a mini ideological Altamont. The right is losing populism to its opposition, and its appeal to rural America is revealed as complicity with agribusiness and little aid to the small farmer. What is at stake, in a struggle that precedes Reagan and will outlast him, is the meaning of American conservative thought and the question of who has the right to American traditions.

We started with Norman Mailer on Barry Goldwater, and this question of conservatism and tradition returns us to that piece. Mailer has often used conservatism against capitalism, writing, for example, about the contradictions between the needs of business and a consumer culture and tradition. Besides quoting West's *The Day of the Locust*, his coverage of the Goldwater phenomenon is punctuated by epigraphs from Edmund Burke as a way of opening up the tension between classic conservatism and the 1964 right. (Another interesting reference here is David Mamet's play, *Edmond*, discussed in Chapter 5, as Mamet's significantly named Edmond Burke enters the world of the new right's nightmares, leaving his wife for a world of violence and prostitution, finally embracing violence as the only thing that makes sense of this world.) There are, however, some strange similarities between Mailer and Goldwater, both of them having a rather Manichean view of the world, and both being exponents, in very different ways, of what Richard Hofstadter has called 'the paranoid style'. Hofstadter argues that while America has no monopoly on 'the paranoid style', as proved by Fascism and Stalin's purges, it does regularly throw up minority movements fuelled by conspiracy theories. He works back through history to argue his case, quoting first Senator McCarthy speaking in 1951, then a manifesto signed by several of the leaders of the Populist party attacking the international conspiracy of the gold standard advocates in 1895, then a Texas newspaper article of 1855 warning of a Catholic conspiracy, finally an extract from a sermon preached in Massachusetts in 1798 about the plotting of the Illuminati.[26]

There is a problem with this stress on conspiracy theories. Hofstadter tends to lump together left and right, democratic and authoritarian movements, eliding their differences in order to defend a liberal centre. But Hofstadter's essays on the paranoid style and on the pseudo-conservative dissent of McCarthy and Goldwater are still very productive discussions of a contradictory conservatism. He used the term pseudo-conservative to describe what we can now see as the emergence of the new right, in order to characterize those who 'although they believe themselves to be conservatives and usually employ the rhetoric of conservatism, show signs of a serious and restless dissatisfaction with American life, traditions, and institutions'.

13

In later essays he considers Goldwater's achievement, seeing his capture of the Republican nomination as 'the triumphal moment of pseudo-conservatism in American politics'. (This, of course, was written before Reagan's victory.) He sees Goldwater as 'a "conservative" whose whole political life has been spent urging a sharp break with the past', and whose moment as a party leader 'was marked by a repudiation of our traditional political ways'. Hence, 'if we are in search of tradition-breakers we are most likely to find them among the ideological conservatives'. Goldwater was proud of his moral rather than political campaign, making a virtue of such self-destructive episodes as his attack on poverty programmes delivered in Appalachia. Hofstadter comments: 'He wanted to drive the politics out of politics.' This relates to two themes already mentioned: the distrust of politics, and the rhetoric directed against the East, such as Goldwater's own comment, 'this country would be better off if we could just saw off the Eastern Seaboard and let it float out to sea'.[27] As Hofstadter's pseudo-conservatives turned into the new right, they moved from the margins to the political centre, carrying their ideological contradictions with them.

To be identified with capitalism and tradition simultaneously is a precarious position, and speaking 'old values in current accents' can sound schizophrenic. Alan Wolfe has pointed out that Ray Kroc, a leading financier of the new right, is typical of this conservative paradox. He 'not only invented the McDonald's hamburger chain, which has done more to destroy the "natural" functions of the family than a generation of radical feminists, but also developed the replacement of real grass by synthetic turf for the baseball team he owns'.[28] The conservative stance on the environment highlights the problems the new right has with the notion of actually conserving anything. James Watt, when Secretary of the Interior, proposed, for example, that no new land should be acquired for the national parks, and that the permanent ban on future mining and drilling leases in the remaining eight million acres of American wilderness might be changed, as he wished to 'use our resources rather than keep them locked up'. In 1977 he had headed Denver's Mountain States Legal Foundation which fought federal regulations on the environment. As part of the 'Sagebrush Rebellion', a movement of western conservatives, he has argued that conservation is unpatriotic, designed to weaken the US rather than protect its environment. He gave a classic statement of the populism of the West to a congressional hearing in 1979:

'We in the West believe that in too many instances our States are being treated like colonies. 'Foreigners' – bureaucrats who seem to be out of control – are making the decisions affecting the land, water, and resources which are the foundation of wealth for the West and indeed in many respects, the Nation.'[29]

Watt's claim resembles other populist complaints, polemics from the 1890s or the 1980s where Western farmers have criticized the distant, 'foreign' government and Eastern banks. But these moments have produced a radical critique of dominant capitalist forms (not capitalism as such but the trusts in the 1890s and corporate agribusiness in the 1980s), rather than arguing like Watt for the unbridled exploitation of natural resources. The ambivalence of populism is seen in this shared rhetoric, and the 1980s farm crisis highlights this with anti-Semitic pamphlets circulating in the farm belt but also with the surprising amount of support that white farmers have shown for Jesse Jackson's radical vision. Populism is a slippery concept, applied to American farmers and to Russian intellectuals, to Peronism as well as Thatcherism. This makes it a close relative to nationalism which has fuelled liberation movements as well as moments of reaction. Populist rhetoric tends to draw on nationalism (in the American context, the idea of national virtues, of American industries being sneakily undercut by the Japanese, and so on), while Tom Nairn has suggested that nationalism necessarily resorts to populism. He describes nationalism as 'The Modern Janus', an image that echoes Lenin's comment on populism: 'the populist, in matters of theory, is ... a Janus, looking with one face to the past and the other to the future'.[30] If that image contains a political judgement, the look into the past being a sign of political reaction, it also describes one of populism's key strategies – the mobilization of history and tradition.

Populism and the past

The investigations into the Reagan administration and the Iran-Contra scandal demonstrate a range of issues through the choice of a name for the affair: Irangate, Contragate, Iranamok, Iranscam. Whether concern focuses on trading arms for hostages or on the illegal continuation of the war against Nicaragua, whether blame settles on the Presidential style or on the administration's policies, Reagan's seeming media invulnerability has ended. His gift has been to make the problems of the present disappear by flanking them with a reassuring vision of the past and a dream of a benign future. An anecdote from the Irangate coverage provides an ironic commentary on this marriage between Hollywood and populism. The former White House National Security Adviser, Robert McFarlane, who resigned in December 1986 and under the pressure of the Iran scandal attempted suicide, revealed that one of the many gifts sent to him by sympathizers was the Frank Capra film *It's a Wonderful Life*. In this populist classic James Stewart is saved from suicide by being shown how his small town would have degenerated if he had not lived. The juxtaposition of Capra's celebration of small town values and the scandal of the Irangate revelations seems to precisely encapsulate the unravelling of Reagan's appeal.

Capra belongs to a classic period of populist cinema, the Western and small town narratives that stretch from the New Deal through to the 1950s. And if Reagan's rhetoric draws themes from this body of work, so do the farming films of the 1980s, which look back to this cinematic period and, in some cases, turn back to an earlier historical period for their narratives of strong rural women confronting a harsh economy (for example, *Places in the Heart* or *The Dollmaker*). Jeffrey Richards' *Visions of Yesterday*, a study of populist films, argues that populist radicalism was killed off by Roosevelt's New Deal: 'The implementation of this "New Deal" meant the end of populism.' Roosevelt is seen as 'the New York aristocrat, who presided over the death and burial of the populist ethic', because the New Deal, rather than 'glorifying the individual', extended government control across wide ranges of the social and the economic fields.[31] As a response to this, Richards sees populism becoming nostalgia for a lost, less complex America, with its terrain changing from rural protest to small town good neighbourliness; no longer third party radicalism but, precisely, Capra's *It's a Wonderful Life*. While Richards captures the small town values of the films, his interpretation of history should be challenged. The New Deal is not the death of populism but one of the significant sources of our images of rural poverty and protest. Equally the 1930s saw an increased interest in the 1890s as a decade of agrarian protest and populism, for example, the publication of C. Vann Woodward's study of the populist leader from Georgia, *Tom Watson: Agrarian Rebel* (1938) and John D. Hicks' history, *The Populist Revolt* (1930).[32] The most important misreading in Richards' account is the suggestion that populism is individualist and thus eclipsed by state intervention. We can challenge this by turning to the struggles of the late nineteenth century.

Two quotations may set the scene, the first from the novelist Willa Cather, the second from the historian of the frontier, Frederick Jackson Turner:

And the farmer is always swindled, no matter by whom the offences come. The crash may start in Wall Street, but it ends in the hillside farms and on the prairie. No matter where the lightning strikes, it blackens the soil at last.[33]

On the prairies of Kansas stands the Populist, a survival of the pioneer, striving to adjust present conditions to his old ideals.[34]

Mary Elizabeth Lease, the Kansas populist, suggested that farmers should 'raise less corn and more hell', and their struggles in the 1890s have been seen by a modern historian as 'the last substantial effort at structural alteration of hierarchical economic forms in modern America'.[35] This moment of rural protest is the most radical and organized expression of American populism and, just as 1980s populism looks back to the 1930s, and as the 1930s looked back to the 1890s, so the 1890s movement itself also depended on a mobilization of the past. What we see is a tradition modified and partly created by the needs of the 1890s, a radical (re)vision of American history.

The populists demonstrated their awareness of the cultural politics of tradition, and the potency of certain dates within the national culture, through their choice of historically loaded days for their conventions, holding Farmers Alliance conventions on the Fourth of July, appropriating Independence Day as 'Alliance Day' and, in 1892 at the St Louis convention, choosing Washington's birthday to announce the formation of the People's Party.[36] They also looked back to Jeffersonian agrarianism and the Jacksonian attack on the Bank of the United States. General Weaver, the Populist presidential candidate in 1892, appealed in his campaign to the ideals of Jefferson and Jackson: 'The rugged utterances of these statesmen ring out today like a startling impeachment of our time.' Richard Hofstadter quotes Weaver and comments on the parallels between the Jacksonian era and the populists, seeing a similar criticism of monopoly in both, with 'the same fear of the regulation of financial affairs from a single, presumably sinister centre' in both movements, 'Wall Street, Lombard Street, and the House of Rothschild' replacing the Bank of the United States as this centre.[37] We have already seen Hofstadter's inclusion of the populists as part of his discussion of 'the paranoid style', but the stress on conspiracy theories leads him to overlook historical and political differences. It is important to see the populists' rhetoric as a strategic mobilization of the past rather than nostalgia. The farmers' demands were not a version of pastoral, nor a wish to return to any 'Adamic "natural" pre-capitalist economy'; apart from the settling of their land they had never known anything but capitalist production for distant markets.[38]

Richards was quoted earlier suggesting that populism was an individualist ideology, but this overlooks the co-operative ideals of the 1890s agrarian movement and also the farmers' demands on the state. The American pioneers settled the West with considerable state support, economic and military, as seen in the Homestead Act and the wars against the Indians.[39] The populists' demands were made on the state rather than against it, arguing for state regulation of the emergent corporate capitalism. The Granger movement in the 1870s and the populists in the 1890s proposed regulation of the railroads not as a pastoral response to technology, 'The Machine in the Garden', but as an argument for democratic control over necessary means of transportation: 'Public functions should never be permitted to be controlled by private corporations ... there is a growing feeling that our government must own railways, or be owned by railway corporations'.[40] This not only challenges Richards' argument about the state intervention of the New Deal being a break with earlier populism, it also qualifies Hofstadter's argument about the continuity from Jefferson and Jackson to the populists. As Lawrence Goodwyn has argued, when proposing government ownership of the railroads the 'Populists did not find it helpful to invoke Jeffersonian injunctions about "the government that governs least".' He continues: 'Nor was Jacksonian preoccupation with hard money a notable aid in advancing greenback monetary analysis. Nostalgia for lost agrarian Edens, Jacksonian or otherwise, was therefore in short supply on third party hustings. Rather, the politics of the industrial age received the focus of attention.'[41]

Goodwyn questions Hofstadter's characterization of the populist movement, taking issue with his view of the farmers as anti-urban paranoids trapped in an agrarian myth, and seeing Hofstadter's misreading of the populist revolt as stemming from his concentration on 'the shadow movement' of the campaign for free silver rather than on the Farmers Alliance and the People's Party.[42] Goodwyn sees the farmers as having confronted the central economic and political questions of their period, demonstrating an awareness of their present rather than an idealization of an agrarian past. Goodwyn's narrative reveals a very different story, a gathering of 'democratic momentum' that began 'on the Southern frontier, then swept eastward across Texas and the other states of the Old Confederacy and thence to the Western Plains'. This was a politicization of farmers, a fifteen-year-long radicalization based around the co-operative ideals of the Farmers Alliance, leading up to the formation of the People's Party ('Texans had led the farmers to the Alliance, Kansans led the Alliance to the People's Party').[43] The 'financial question' was central to this movement, raising the issues of what constituted money (gold, gold and silver, paper) and who could issue it (the government or private bankers), and addressing the conflict between the nation's producer-debtors and banker-creditors which, after the Civil War, worsened the plight of the farmers and led to the argument between 'hard money' advocates (the 'goldbugs') and those who proposed a flexible currency (the 'greenbackers'). Here is where what Goodwyn terms 'the shadow movement' appears – the campaign for the remonetization of silver (silver had been demonetized in 1873, hence the rhetoric about 'the crime of '73') which challenged the gold standard but not the doctrine of 'hard money'.[44] The silver campaign meant that some states developed a populism that diverged from the Alliance and People's Party platforms. These developments transformed a popular radical movement leading it into conventional two-party electoral politics, as the silver Democrats nominated William Jennings Bryan as their presidential candidate in 1896, and after fierce debate the People's Party decided to endorse him. 'Free silver' replaced the critique of monopoly, and fusion took over from radicalism.

Bryan's famous 'Cross of Gold' speech at the Democratic convention in 1896 marks the end of the radical populist vision, while still drawing on its themes. This moment of incorporation centres on the question of monetary reform, with the 'greenbacker' challenge discarded for support for silver and opposition to the gold standard: 'You shall not press down upon the brow of labor this crown of thorns, you shall not crucify mankind upon a cross of gold.' This argument leads Bryan back to the economic and moral priority of agriculture. The cities may be in favour of the gold standard, but 'the great cities rest upon our broad and fertile prairies'. Cities depend upon farms; the relation of country to city is that of base to superstructure. And country means the mythical resonance of the West. Bryan said that he was not speaking against 'those who live upon the Atlantic coast', but 'the pioneers away out there', pointing to the West, 'are as deserving of the consideration of our party as any people in this country. It is for these that we speak.' Another element of the populist repertoire alluded to and diluted by Bryan is an argument about work and value. Bryan suggests that 'the definition of a businessman' is too limited: the employee is as much a businessman as his employer; the country lawyer is as much a businessman as the 'corporation counsel'; the farmer is as much a businessman as 'the man who goes upon a board of trade and bets upon the price of grain'; miners are as much businessmen as 'the few financial magnates who, in a back room, corner the money of the world. We come to speak for this broader class of businessmen.'[45] This is a significant reversal of the populists' definition of workers, making a similar point but making it sound less radical. We will now turn to the populist theme of 'producerism', one of the key contexts for my argument.

Workers and millionaires: the 1890s

Goodwyn discusses the Great Southwest Strike of 1886, when the notorious railroad magnate and 'robber baron' Jay Gould tried to crush the union, the Knights of Labor, and a strike spread through Texas leading to bitter conflict. William Lamb, president of the county Farmers Alliance, argued for farmers to support the strikers. 'Alliance radicalism – Populism – began' with his demand and his dream of a farmer–labour coalition.

> His argument reflected a new conception about the farmers' place in American society. The farmer as producer-entrepreneur and small capitalist – the 'hardy yeoman' of a thousand pastoral descriptions – is nowhere visible in Lamb's view. This traditional portrait, dating from a simple Jeffersonian era and still lingering in the social tradition of the Grange, was patently out of place to a man who saw society dominated by manufacturers and their 'agents'.

The 'farmer of the new industrial age was a worker', thus 'the organized farmers of the Alliance should join forces with the organized workers of the Knights of Labor'.[46] It was this radical vision that generated the description of the strikebreaking organization, the Pinkertons, as a 'hireling standing army', a phrase from the Populist platform of 1892. Goodwyn acknowledges the problems that this project faced, seeing the Texan coalition as misleading, for 'few of the reigning cultural obstacles were present'. In Texas or Kansas there was a shared set of cultural assumptions between worker and farmer, but outside 'certain homogeneous locales in the West' problems arose. How were the populists to recruit 'a Slavic steelworker in Pittsburgh, a "patriotic" Republican farmer in Michigan, or a black sharecropper in South Carolina'?[47] Goodwyn discusses these obstacles, particularly the persistence of Civil War allegiances. However, without underestimating the radical break with earlier images of the farmer, the traditional image persists in populist rhetoric. Up to the present there is a tension in representations of the farmers' lives between their specific struggles and a timeless pastoral (in terms of the arguments already considered, between Hofstadter's 'agrarian myth' and Goodwyn's populist politics). The two intersect around the role 'producerism' plays in populist rhetoric.

The populists' definition of workers divided the world between 'producers and parasites, workers and predators, "the robbers and the robbed". In this conception farmers, urban workers, and small businessmen fell on the one side, bankers, middlemen, and monopolists on the other.'[48] This idea of production rests not on Marx and the theory of surplus value but on the Bible. Adam's curse is turned into the source of human dignity: ' "In the sweat of thy face shalt thou eat bread." This decree was uttered 6,000 years ago. It is as immutable as time itself.... The idler is a drone; he shirks the immutable decree of Deity; he feeds upon the labor of others; he is a parasite upon society; he is a robber.'[49] The farmer is central to this rhetoric, uniting the mythic resonance of the pioneer settler with the virtues of husbandry and with the independence of the property-owning. Populism radicalized this rhetoric, as the first national plat-form of the People's Party (Omaha 1892) stated: 'Wealth belongs to him who creates it, and every dollar taken from industry without an equivalent is robbery. "If any will not work, neither shall he eat." The interests of rural and civic labor are the same; their enemies are identical.'[50] And one of the most impressive attempts to build on these common interests was the effort to achieve an alliance between blacks and whites in the South.

Henry George's influential *Progress and Poverty* provided the terms for the later populists: 'It is not the storekeeper who is the cause of the farmer, but the farmer who brings the storekeeper. It is not the growth of the city that develops the country, but the development of the country that makes the city grow.' The priority of agriculture is given even more resonance through the cultural potency of the frontier in America. Henry George suggested that the democratic and republican features of American society stemmed from 'unfenced land'. This 'public domain', he argued, was an important fact in the consciousness of urban workers, suggesting the available alternative to the city, and it also acted as an Americanizing experience, being 'the transmuting force which has turned the thriftless, unambitious European peasant into the self-reliant farmer'.[51] It is an argument that was taken up by Frederick Jackson Turner, who marked the official closure of the frontier with his 1893 paper, 'The Significance of the Frontier in American History'. He argued that the frontier experience was the key to understanding American development, an interpret-ation that he applied to the populists, seeing them as in the tradition of the pioneers.[52] As with the context of the new right discussed earlier, the connection between geography and politics is seen as crucial.

During Henry George's 1886 campaign to be mayor of New York, the United Labor party split between socialists and those who followed George's central plank of the Single Tax. George's remark is of interest in comprehending the 'enemy' of populism: 'There is in reality no conflict between labor and capital; the conflict is between labor and monopoly.'[53] This was a line followed by the later populists, although the movement also involved socialists. Another influential figure, Edward Bellamy, author of *Looking Backward*, who moved from the Nationalist party to an involvement with populism, stated that it was the new capitalists, the plutocrats of the late nineteenth century, who were the revolutionaries. Nationalism appealed to the constituency that populism would later capture, the Midwestern farmers, and Bellamy's 1890 speech belongs to the strategy I discussed earlier, the attempt to oppose conservatism and capitalism.

> 'We are the true conservative party,' [he argued], 'because we are devoted to the maintenance of republican institutions against the revolution now being effected by the money power. We propose no revolution, but that the people shall resist a revolution. We oppose those who are overthrowing the republic. Let no mistake be made here. We are not revolutionists but counterrevolutionists.'[54]

The late nineteenth century saw an extraordinary concentration of American capital: the annual number of corporate consolidations increased towards the end of the century, with 69 in 1897, 303 in 1898, and 1,208 in 1899. By 1900 there were 73 trusts, each having a capitalization of over ten million dollars, two-thirds of them having been formed between 1897 and 1900.[55] The merger movement and the rise of the trusts is the background for the populist attack on monopoly. That attack was sharpened by the farmers' dependence on the railroads. It was also, in populist rhetoric, grounded on an agrarian suspicion of finance capitalism. Both politically and symbolically, the farmer stood opposed to the financier; the growth of real products was juxtaposed with money making money via city speculation on the commodity exchanges. This is a theme that continues after the 1890s into the farmers' protests of the 1930s and 1980s. Fiorello LaGuardia fought in the 1920s for aid for the rural and urban poor, and in 1933 he spoke in Congress for federal aid to be given to the farmers. Using the farmer versus speculator opposition, he said: 'what chance has the farmer when the demand is controlled by manicured-finger men in Chicago and New York dealing in agriculture by means of the ticker tape ...?' He talked of the farmers' debts and bankruptcies: 'if foreclosures continue, there will be no individual ownership of land. Then what? Can insurance companies and saving banks till the soil and produce food for the Nation?'[56] The farmer is replaced by the faceless company and bank, just as populist rhetoric foretold, and just as the recent country films maintain. The farmer is represented as caught between two arbitrary forces, the potential violence of nature (floods, droughts, etc.) and, on the other hand, the railroads and the city markets.

The populists were not alone in their critique of monopoly. Turn-of-the-century America saw the rise of investigative journalism, the 'muckrakers', the emergence of the naturalist novel, and various critical representations of wealth. William Dean Howells' centrality in nineteenth-century American literature rests not just on his realist fiction but also on his role as editor, critic, friend, and patron of young writers. As editor of the *Atlantic Monthly* he accepted in March 1881 an article by Henry Demarest Lloyd, 'The story of a great monopoly', an indictment of Standard Oil. Lloyd followed this with other attacks, *Lords of Industry*, a collection of criticisms of the trusts, and *Wealth Against Commonwealth*. As such 'muckraking' journalism boosted circulations, magazines began to specialize in these exposés. And works like Lincoln Steffens' *Shame of the Cities*, Thomas Lawson's *Frenzied Finance*, and Ida Tarbell's *History of the Standard Oil Company*, can be put alongside the populists' critique of monopoly, leading to the reformist tendencies of the Progressive Era. Naturalist novels combined social criticism with a literary theory that stressed research and a segmentation of the social and economic worlds: the new world of consumerism in Dreiser's *Sister Carrie*, or of speculation in his *The Financier*, the Chicago stockyards in Upton Sinclair's *The Jungle*, and Frank Norris' 'epic of wheat', *The Octopus* and *The Pit*, two volumes of a proposed trilogy. The spectacle of the conspicuously wealthy was analysed in different ways by Thorstein Veblen in his *Theory of the Leisure Class* and by Henry James in his fiction and in works like *The American Scene*. If they analysed the display of wealth in houses at Newport, art collections, and so on, J. A. Hobson's *Imperialism*, although not solely concerned with the United States, argued that the millionaires of the turn of the century were also the cause of America's new militarist imperialism, the consolidation of capital leading to a search for new markets and the American involvement in Asia, the Caribbean, and Central America.

Turn-of-the-century America offered writers a world of brutal contrasts: on one side the millionaires, the plutocrats, the 'lords of industry', on the other, the sweated immigrant workers, the urban unemployed, the debt-ridden farmer. Within the criticisms of this spectacle of wealth, one can see entangled the old and new styles of capitalism, the individual figures, the robber barons, the millionaires, and the new corporate world of the trusts. Ignatius Donnelly used a negative agrarian image in his populist argument: 'In short, the most utterly useless, destructive and damnable crop a country can grow is – millionaires.'[57]

America: consumption and criticism

Chapter 7 and my Conclusion investigate the way that an 'imaginary America' is created in a British context. This means that we turn from themes of work to ideas of consumption and pleasure, but continue with the centrality of gender in this discussion. The 1980s offer a strange parallel to the conspicuous consumption and the spectacle of wealth discussed in the last section. George Michael, for example, spoke in an interview about Wham's success:

> Glamour is seen in this country as *America*. We just picked up on the normal traits of stardom, and as my musical angle has always had an American side, the two things fitted. England suddenly became like *Miami Vice* in the rain, and that combined with the quality of what we were doing. It all fitted together very nicely, though I didn't plan it that way.[58]

Other elements of populist politics and culture will feature in this later section, but the politics of American culture as seen, heard, read, used, and sold in Britain is the most important theme, and the *pleasures* of that culture as well. That, personally, is where this book started and that, politically, is where it concludes.

A major concern is the way that rhetoric about the United States combined with an idea of a lost or threatened England (the rural past, the organic community, minority culture, the working-class community) has been a persistent stumbling block for the left. Political analysis is blunted as questions of power become entangled in a discourse of 'Americanization', and opposition to foreign policies collapses into arguments about 'cultural imperialism'. Thus opposition to the bombing raids on Libya draws confusingly on criticism of *Rambo*; Reagan's B-movies are referred to rather than his governorship of California or his long involvement with the new right. Britain's status as a power relative to the United States means that popular culture and military policy become metaphors for each other: cheeseburgers and cruise missiles, TV cops and US bases, Hollywood and Nicaragua are blurred together whether people are mourning lost empires or lost working-class militancy.

A tangled tradition leads from Matthew Arnold to the Leavises detours via Orwell and Hoggart and ends up still active in figures like Paul Weller, arguing that the main threat to British culture is 'Americanization'. Just as left and right, feminists and pro-family moralists, can agree, for different reasons, on such topics as the pernicious influence of television, 'video nasties', and pornography, so equally bizarre alliances of conservatives, socialists, cultural critics, and musicians, use America as a symbol to displace contemporary problems of British identity. In fact, the parallel between the 'moral

24

panic' and 'Americanization' is a close one, as seen in the campaign against American horror comics in the 1950s. This highlights some of the dangers of the appeal to 'national culture' and to the threat of cultural colonization. Even if 'America' is functioning rhetorically in opposition to the United States' foreign or military policies, its use carries unacceptable notions of 'Englishness' and implies, because of the tradition behind it, an irrelevant and offensive critique of what the tradition would call 'mass culture'.

Obviously neither America nor popular culture should be uncritically celebrated. But my argument is not against criticism but against the identification of America and popular culture which leads to both being seen as monolithic, innocent of contradictions and complexity. The fragmentation of both, the plurality of positions means that young American blacks can forge rap and hip hop from pieces of white television, film, and rock culture, mixing it with black musical traditions and European electro. Similar strategies allow the potent combination of criticism of America with pleasure in American styles and traditions. It is possible to speak American without tears (to borrow Elvis Costello's phrase) because there are so many languages to choose from or create. American culture also offers a way of talking about popular culture without separating it from 'high' culture. Frederick Jackson Turner's frontier thesis, mentioned earlier, argued that America was marked by the fact that it had developed not with the European notion of fixed borders but with a moving frontier. Culturally, there are frontiers rather than borders as well; it's easier to move across genres, forms, and across the high/popular division. Greil Marcus wrote that in *Mystery Train* he was dealing with 'rock 'n' roll not as youth culture, or counter culture, but simply as American culture'; and that possibility (in the next chapter the possibility of moving between early American literature and, say, country music) broadens any discussion of cultural politics.[59] American culture offers both continuity and heterogeneity, through a plurality of traditions and through a continual tension between an idea of 'America' and the specificity of the local.

I don't want, however, to reinforce simple binary divisions between America and Britain/Europe. Another element that undermines the view of America as monolithic is the play between it and European culture. European émigrés go to Hollywood and the thrillers they make are later hailed by French critics as *film noir*, out of a French reappraisal of Hollywood comes the New Wave, and Godard's *Breathless* is later remade with the plot turned inside out by Jim McBride in Hollywood. The young American film director, Jim Jarmusch, has talked about how he found out about American directors through European ones, Godard teaching him about Nicholas Ray and Sam

Fuller, Fassbinder putting him on to Sirk. But this section will close with a writer mentioned in the previous section, Henry James, whose work explored the promise of this interplay between America and Europe. His fiction investigated such figures as the American millionaire, the tourist, and the journalist, but we will close with some remarks from one of his critical essays. James was often tempted to deal with culture in Arnold's terms: the rise of mass reading publics, the flood of bad writing and sensational journalism, the minority marooned within a vulgarized culture, and the philistines at the gates. And in this set of stock responses America was, and still is, seen as everybody's future, as if popular culture was an invasion rather than something generated by industrialization.

In a piece written in 1898, James starts with the mass American reading public and the emergence of the bestseller. These new conditions produce not alarm but a 'delicious rest from the oppressive *a priori*'. He points out that the American public is not unique but only a larger and more intense example of what was happening in other industrial nations. He talks of the 'homogeneous' nature of the American public but later admits the possibility of a range of readers and a variety of styles and genres for different audiences. Potential divisions within the mass homogeneous culture undermine those very terms, preventing James from making 'extravagantly general' predictions and returning him to the critic's sport and pleasure, the cast-off *a priori*, the release from 'the cramped posture of foregone conclusions and narrow rules'. And he warns against foregone conclusions, the substitution of prejudices for criticism, against monolithic views, and in a remark that should be inscribed at the heart of cultural studies, he writes: 'There will be no real amusement if we are positively prepared to be stupid.'[60]

1 Family fields:
the farming narrative

Playboy: You sound a bit fatalistic.
Dylan: I'm not fatalistic. Bank tellers are fatalistic. Clerks are fatalistic.
I'm a farmer. Who ever heard of a fatalistic farmer? I'm not fatalistic. I
smoke a lot of cigarettes, but that doesn't make me fatalistic.[1]

Bob Dylan's Live Aid comments in July 1985 caused the idea of
hardship to boomerang embarrassingly back into the heartland.
Playing with Keith Richards and Ronnie Wood, Dylan suggested
that some of the money – 'just one or two millions' – should go to
help the farmers of the Midwest. Suddenly 'they', the objects of
charity, as in the Band Aid song 'Do They Know It's Chistmas?'
were much closer to home, in fact were identified with 'home', with
a certain kind of American community that has historically been seen
as the central storehouse for national values and virtues. While nobody
would suggest that the farmers' suffering is on the same scale as
Ethiopia's, Dylan's plea was answered by Farm Aid in September
1985, a rock and country benefit for America's farmers. There has
been another Farm Aid concert in July 1986, and films and records
testify to the fact that the farm crisis has touched a cultural nerve.
    An event from May 1985 can introduce some of the issues to be
considered: the testimony given before a congressional subcommittee
by Jessica Lange, Sissy Spacek, and Jane Fonda arguing for more
federal aid for the stricken farmers. All had played farm wives in
recent films, and Sally Field, whose role in the Depression era *Places
in the Heart* has obvious echoes in the current situation, sent a
statement that was read by Jane Fonda. A group of women from the
farming communities were also there, members of an organization
called WIFE (Women Involved in Farm Economics). The actresses
spoke not only of their films and what they had learned of hardship
among the farmers while researching their roles, but also of their
family histories. Jessica Lange's father had lost his land during the
Depression and Sissy Spacek's father had been a New Deal agricultural agent in Texas. The allusions to family history included not

just experience of agricultural problems, the films themselves were given historical precedents by Jane Fonda, as she spoke of her father's love of the role of Tom Joad in John Ford's *The Grapes of Wrath* (1940).

Henry Fonda testifies to a tradition of populist films, demonstrating the power of stars to accumulate a political resonance across their roles. In his case, and staying within the Ford canon, these include not only Steinbeck's Tom Joad but also *The Young Mr Lincoln* (1939), and the definitive lawman, Wyatt Earp in *My Darling Clementine* (1946).[2] So the traditions that informed the actresses' protest fuse history (the Depression, the New Deal), cultural history, and family memories. This meeting of family, culture, and history around the mythic and economic significance of the land structures this chapter and the following one. Other issues raised by the event will also be addressed: the possible contradiction of Hollywood stars speaking for small-scale farmers; the significance of women speaking for one of America's male icons, the independent farmer; the odd connection glimpsed in that acronym, WIFE, of women using a conservative gender position to produce an oppositional argument.

In the November 1986 mid-term elections which saw the Republicans losing control of the Senate, the campaigns were characterized by Ronald Reagan's failed attempt to graft his personal popularity on to campaigning that was dominated by local issues. Observers have suggested that the electioneering marked a low point in US politics, with contests centred on television slots and 'negative advertising', challenging the opponent's record rather than presenting an alternative. It is interesting to see what the Democratic Congressional Campaign Committee chose for their one generic advertisement. The public across the Midwest saw on their screens an empty farmhouse with the voiceover: 'It wasn't just a farm. It was a family. Vote Democrat.' Although the farm crisis was not the only issue of economic hardship which swung several states away from Reagan's revolution, it was an important issue and one with a resonance outside the farm belt. Not just a farm but a family, the slogan raises the crucial issue of gender in this context, and the links between farming and families will be discussed across a range of cultural works.

Agrarian notions have always been central to American culture, and the connection between narrative and agriculture, between telling and tilling America, was forged early and shows remarkable cultural persistence. So although this chapter is mainly concerned with writing up to the turn of the century, and the following chapter with writing from the 1930s and then the films and fiction of the 1980s, both of them will move between past and present, popular culture and populist history. Country music has been transformed by moves from the country to the city, and has often taken such economically enforced journeys as its subject. But what is significant in American popular culture is that the plight of the farmers has spread beyond its obvious home in country (Merle Haggard's recent 'Amber Waves of Grain', for example). Even with MTV and the hegemony of stadium rock, much American music keeps a strong sense of place or of local music traditions. This helps explain the appearance of stickers on guitars proclaiming 'Save the Family Farm' or 'Farmers are the Backbone of America'. The farm crisis has provoked concern in bands who attempt to fuse country and rock traditions (Jason and the Scorchers, for example), but it has also reached figures with the chart standing and mainstream appeal of John Cougar Mellancamp (as seen in his 'Scarecrow' album and in his organizational role at the Farm Aid concert) thus underlining the mythic potency of the farmer.

The visibility of the issue in popular culture highlights the difference between America and Britain around the concept of the land. A British rock star might buy a trout farm but he is unlikely to feel that the farmer is a mythical figure. Where English culture indulges in pastoral nostalgia or in dreams of the organic community, the comparison with America would reveal the resonance of the frontier experience and, due to the vastness of the country, the complicity between geography and history in the farmer's cultural centrality. There is a vast difference between the connotations of the settler's homestead and, for example, English culture critics mourning the demise of the wheelwright's shop. But one topic links an international populism to American populist histories, bridging Live Aid and Farm Aid, and that is overproduction.

In *The River*, one of the films to be discussed later, Mel Gibson, a Tennessee farmer, is forced by his farm's financial state to take a temporary factory job, which he finds out to his dismay involves breaking a strike. One of his reluctant fellow strikebreakers is a black man amazed to find farmers working in a city factory. He asks Mel Gibson how people can still be hungry when the farmers grow so much food. In the film it's a throwaway line but since 'overproduction' is often the term used against farmers' protests it has behind it a certain history. For the politicized farmers of the 1880s and 1890s, and their spokesmen and women in the Farmers Alliance and the Populist Party, it was essential to challenge the argument of overproduction, a view held by conservative economists that made the farmers' hardship their own fault. So people transformed the concept by talking of the 'overproduction of poverty, barefooted women, political thieves and many liars'. Discussion of hardship was confined to comparisons between states, as when a dairy farmer called John Otis pointed out in January 1890 that in western Kansas farmers were 'burning corn for fuel, while coal miners and their families in another section of our land are famishing for food'. Polk, president of the National Alliance, declared in 1890 that he had shown statistics of hardship, from all over the country, to the politicians in Washington who had told him that the cause was overproduction. Polk said that if they had stepped out on to Washington's cold November streets, they would have seen children picking pieces of coal out of ash piles and going through garbage in search of food: 'As long as a single cry for bread is heard, it is underproduction and underconsumption.'[3] In a speech in July 1894, Governor Lewelling of Kansas mocked the conservative theory, saying that 'a good Republican friend' of his had surprised him by telling him that:

> the reason there were hungry people in Kansas and the United States, was because there was too much bread. He said the reason there were so many people going poorly clad, was because there was too much cloth and too many garments made for the people to wear. Now, I confess, I can't understand that philosophy, but he can, and he explained it and I leave you to find out from him what the theory is.[4]

These themes of the 1890s are picked up again during the hardship of the 1930s, as in Fiorello LaGuardia's Congressional speech seeking federal aid for the farmers. Some, he said, feared overproduction but, 'Only after all of the people of the country are properly and sufficiently fed, the remainder, if any, can be called a surplus.'[5] More famously, one of the best known portrayals of rural poverty and dispossession, John Steinbeck's *The Grapes of Wrath*, uses a description of the destruction of food to build up to the line, 'In the souls of the people the grapes of wrath are filling and growing heavy, growing heavy for the vintage.' Steinbeck writes of oranges being dumped in order to keep the price up. People come to take the free fruit but it is sprayed with kerosene for commercial reasons: 'How would they buy oranges at twenty cents a dozen if they could drive out and pick them up?' With a million people hungry fruit is deliberately ruined:

> And the smell of rot fills the country.
> Burn coffee for fuel in the ships. Burn corn to keep warm, it makes a hot fire. Dump potatoes in the rivers and place guards along the banks to keep the hungry people from fishing them out. Slaughter the pigs and bury them, and let the putrescence drip down into the earth.

This crime 'goes beyond denunciation. There is a sorrow here that weeping cannot symbolize. There is a failure here that topples all our success.' That this misery stems from America's natural abundance poisons the national dream and makes a mockery of America's long-standing boast of feeding the world. The passage ends with the people watching kerosene being sprayed on oranges, watching potatoes float down rivers, listening to pigs being slaughtered and covered in quicklime, watching fruit rot.[6] The New Deal promoted the voluntary curtailment of crops backed up by government subsidies as a way out of the farmers' hardship. Steinbeck suggests a more radical solution, redistributing food and changing the economic system that, to return to my original reference to *The River*, allows hunger while producing so much food. That simple questioning is now heard on an international scale as the Western response to the Ethiopian and Sudanese famines (Live Aid, Band Aid, etc.) has led people to point out the juxtaposition of EEC grain mountains and African hunger.

The simple question of how there can be at the same time famine and too much food, comes up against the complexity of agriculture within the international economy of competing trade blocs. It is certainly easier to map out the cultural response to the farm crisis than it is to endorse the proffered solutions of either protectionism and subsidy or the reform of subsidy and the hegemony of the market. It is now possible to detect set scenes in films generated by the crisis (the meeting with the bank manager, the natural disaster, the farm auction) and some evocative symbols in songs or articles about the farm belt – the crosses outside the courthouse representing lost farms, for example. But there's a tension between a dramatic image, say, a farmer's suicide, and complex economic causality. This tension is seen in the films occasionally toying with an idea that the farmer is partly to blame. There are also political ambiguities, stemming from the basic ambivalence of populism. The Democrats may have benefited in 1986, and some farmers' organizations may call on traditions of radical protest, but this rural discontent can also be recruited for the extreme right through anti-Semitic conspiracy theories which build on a populist demonology of Jewish Eastern bankers.

There is also the question of reception, raised across these chapters by the relation between regional writers and metropolitan critics. However, it is worth considering here the problem of how much a British audience knows about the American farm crisis. Interestingly, more information has been available here through the coverage of popular culture (interviews with rock singers, reviews of films) than through conventional news channels. In British newspapers the farm crisis has tended to be discussed, at least before coverage of the 1986 mid-term elections, on the financial pages in terms of the pressures for protectionism within the US. Where the farmers have crossed over into longer features or articles (and this shapes Hollywood's response to the farm crisis as well), natural disaster has played the main part in transforming American farmers from economic issue to 'human interest' for British readers or viewers. The heatwave in the

South in the summer of 1986, for example, prompted some lengthy features. Obviously these familiar images of drought and disaster were felt to be more exportable, as it were, than the Midwest's farm crisis. Although this crisis is mediated culturally it also lacks, for a British audience, work with mass appeal. However, the slump in oil prices in the mid-1980s and the consequent loss of jobs (150,000 jobs lost in Houston in three years, for example) received several newspaper features, partly one suspects because of the popularity of *Dallas*. With no such obvious hook to hang a story on the American farmers have been largely overlooked by the British media. However, in the United States their struggles have had a high media visibility, and the crisis has generated a rhetoric that sees the loss of the family farm as part of the dismantling of America. The United States, which since the turn of the century has boasted of being able to feed the world, has in mid-1986, for the first time in two decades, been importing more agricultural produce than it exports. Even before the Democrats' victories in 1986 farm subsidies stood at a record high, and since their successes demands for protectionism may increase, challenging the Reagan administration's stand on free trade. But instead of seeing the crisis within a strictly economic or a narrowly political context, we must ask why the loss of the family farm speaks to such a wide audience in America. As farmers' debts overwhelm families they bring down not only rural banks and local businesses, they also threaten very central themes in American culture.

In an interesting article on the symbolism of the farm crisis, William Adams discusses the non-economic meanings generated by the loss of small, family farms. 'From the very outset,' he argues, 'and with surprising constancy and certainty, we have pinned our sense of self and worth to the figures of farm and family.' The American farmer has not only supplied food for the nation, 'he has also given us a fair portion of the symbolic materials out of which our political culture has been constructed – a contribution no less worthy of note than carrots, potatoes, and peas'. The crisis is not just an affair of subsidies and land values and credit, it's also 'nothing less than a drama of political culture and imagination in crisis'.[7] The family fields are a fertile intersection of politics, culture, and myth.

Work, property, and protest

The family farm represents a crucial linkage of work and ownership. Wanting to overcome the division between mental and manual labour, one of the aims of American Transcendentalism, Emerson argued that while not overstating 'this doctrine of labour', and not insisting that every man should be a farmer 'any more than that every man should be a lexicographer', it was still true that the 'husbandman's is the oldest and most universal profession'. If a man does not seem suited for any particular alternative, farming 'may be preferred'. I have already suggested the role that *producerism* plays in later populist rhetoric, and Emerson's argument seems to anticipate this by seeing farming as representative work, the most obvious meeting of nature and human labour.

> But the doctrine of the Farm is merely this, that every man ought to stand in primary relations with the work of the world; ought to do it himself, and not to suffer the accident of his having a purse in his pocket, or his having been bred to some dishonorable and injurious craft, to sever him from those duties; and for this reason, that labor is God's education; that he only is a sincere learner, he only can become a master, who learns the secrets of labor, and who by real cunning extorts from nature its sceptre.[8]

As with the later populists one notices that work is the source not only of value but of virtue as well. It is, in this rhetoric, doubly supported by a biblical injunction and by an American ideal of democracy.

This notion of virtuous labour also raises questions of gender. As mentioned earlier, when Hollywood actresses went to Washington to publicize the plight of the farmers, they were accompanied by women from the farming communities, members of the organization WIFE (Women Involved in Farm Economics). If that acronym suggests a contemporary possibility for a radical protest to be expressed from a conservative position, with the archaic figure of the husbandman, etymology links farming and the family, husbandry and the husband, around the idea of home. These examples are linguistic clues to the specificity of the family farm in terms of the gendered division of labour and the relation of home and work. In an article that takes a critical look at the current popularity of rural themes, Ann Hulpbert sees recent films as giving a spuriously updated feminist gloss to the figure of the farm wife, and this and other themes from her article will be discussed in Chapter 2. I will argue that there is an interesting two-way movement in the rural films, combining 'progressive' images of women with 'conservative' themes of an essential Americanness tied to the family and to the soil. This stems not only from Hollywood liberalism but also from the basic political ambivalence at the heart of the American populist tradition. It also testifies to the way that the defence of the family farm produces representations of the family that rescue the family from the conflict between a feminist critique and a conservative backlash, re-ordering the relation between husband, wife and children while maintaining gender roles. What these films suggest is that for the family to still work as a concept, it is now necessary to show the family literally working. This takes us back to farming, gender, and the division of labour.

> The family exists for work. It exists to keep itself alive. It is a cooperative economic unit. The father does one set of tasks; the mother another; the children still a third, with the sons and daughters serving apprenticeship to their father and mother respectively.[9]

The above comes from Agee's classic study of tenant farmers in the South of the late 1930s, *Let Us Now Praise Famous Men*. Leaving aside for the moment the important difference between the tenant farmer and farmers who own their property, Agee's characterization of the family as a 'cooperative economic unit' seems to echo within recent films. It is this which reinforces the family unit while challenging the conventional ideology of the family. The shift in the nineteenth century from agricultural to industrial production was accompanied by transformations that reworked the gendered division of labour around a new relation between home and workplace. With industrialization and factory production there came new forms of socialized work which split the family into those who sold labour and those who bought goods, mapping out new social and economic territories through a division of home and workplace. Instead of the family model of earlier agricultural production where members were interdependent workers, they are now assigned to the newly discrete spheres of production and consumption. In terms of structure and ideology it could be argued that authority passes from the family patriarch to the factory owners, but this needs some significant qualifications. A contradiction emerges between the needs of ideology and industry, for a patriarchal image persists, constructing men as providers and earners of the family wage and women as guardians of the domestic sphere and as that historically new entity, the consumer. However, industry still drew on women's labour and, of course, families still needed women's income. Capitalism benefits from this contradiction which divides workers and constructs women as a reserve labour force whose 'proper' place is elsewhere. This 'proper' place, the home, is the site of the unacknowledged labour of women, what has been called the invisible work of childcare, housework, all the unwaged services that support and reproduce the labour force.[10]

If the fragmentation of the family as a productive unit brings a segregation of work along gender lines, this only builds on what is already a division of labour in traditional agricultural economies. In the Agee passage, for example, we see that sons and daughters are apprenticed to both sex roles and divided labour. The representation of gender in the works discussed in this chapter is significant not because of nostalgia for some pre-industrial family harmony, although that accounts for some of their appeal in the 1980s, but for the continuity of work shown whether that work is divided between men and women or shared. But if work unites these representations, property divides them. The family for Agee's sharecroppers is a co-operative unit from necessity, for reasons of survival, while the family farm in recent films ties the family to property, to the fathers who farmed the land before and the sons who will inherit the land. The threat to property through auctions and foreclosures is also a threat to family history and to the male line. Some types of agriculture retain pre-capitalist features and it is this persistence that explains some of the political ambivalences of agrarian culture. John Fekete's Marxist account of American literary theory traces the transformation of an influential group of 1930s Southern poets, teachers, and critics from the Agrarians to the New Critics, from schemes to put people back on the land to ways of reading the words on a page. Fekete examines their pastoral critique of industrialism, suggesting that the Agrarians privileged agriculture as a way of combining a radical attack on the industrial and monopoly developments of American capitalism with a conservative and racist stand, enabling them to reject industry while supporting capitalist property relations. Fekete points to the reverse of this conservative pastoral in a footnote concerning the Southern Tenant Farmers Union. Here we see a radical organization of 1930s sharecroppers, demonstrating against the cultural grain the possibility for racial divisions to be crossed through the solidarity of the landless, the dispossessed rather than the propertied.[11] But there are problems with a class analysis of American agrarian movements. This returns us to the opening of this section: farming as a link between work and ownership, generating ideologies of producerism *and* of individualism.

Steinbeck's *The Grapes of Wrath* predicts a shift, along existing ideological grooves, from individual to collective expressions of dis-possession. Hence the importance of populism rather than 'un-Amer-ican' socialism and the significance of 'Okie' migrant workers rather than the Chinese, Japanese, Mexican, and Filipino workers who preceded them, against all of whom racism could always be mobilized if they threatened to become organized. Apart from being undeniably American, they brought families with them to California rather than coming alone, bringing as well a different set of expectations and a different ideological background. Steinbeck's article in the *Nation* in 1936 (written after *In Dubious Battle* and before *The Grapes of Wrath*) saw a greater potential for resistance in these refugees from the dust bowl. Rather than being from 'a peon class', they have either 'owned small farms or been farm hands in the early American sense, in which the "hand" is a member of the employing family. They have one fixed idea, and that is to acquire land and settle on it.'[12] They are less easily intimidated because of their attachment to land, and so property is paradoxically the basis of radicalism rather than conservatism. Steinbeck also suggests that there are very different classes of farmers in California. There is the small farmer whose sympathies in disputes might well be on the workers' side, but there is also 'the speculative farmer,' like A. J. Chandler, publisher of the Los Angeles *Times*, or Herbert Hoover or William Randolph Hearst. Allied to these absentee owners with their large holdings, there are 'the big incorporated farms owned by their stockholders and farmed by instructed managers, and a large number of bank farms, acquired by foreclosure and operated by superintendents' taking orders from the bank. Steinbeck remarks that the Bank of America is 'very nearly the largest farm owner and operator in the state of California'.[13] These different types of farmers belonged to different political organizations, the small farmer often belonging to the Grange while the speculative farmer would belong to the Associated Farmers of California, with its close links to the State Chamber of Commerce, and its resistance to attempts to organize the migrant farm workers.

Steinbeck describes a situation in its political specificity: the propertyless with their memories of and desire for land; the small, independent farmer threatened less by farm workers than by the larger owners; the rich owners who resemble the negative images of nineteenth-century populism – speculative, plutocratic (the infamous Hearst), absentee, incorporated farms run by managers, farms taken into ownership by banks. These kinds of distinctions are vital in understanding agrarian politics, reminding us of the economic and symbolic differences between the family farm and agribusiness. The question here is of styles of ownership and the future of agriculture: who owns American land, the family or the corporation or the bank? Lawrence Goodwyn's history of 'the Agrarian Revolt' of the 1880s and 1890s questions the value of class as a simple interpretive tool: 'offhand "class analysis", when applied to the agrarian revolt in America, will merely succeed in rendering the populist experience invisible'. There are obvious differences in ownership and in 'property-consciousness' between 'rich landowners, smallholders, and landless laborers' but 'these distinctions create more problems than they solve when applied to the agrarian revolt'. Goodwyn challenges the assumption that landowners can be seen as automatically politically reactionary: 'The condition of being "landed" or "landless" does not, *a priori*, predetermine one's potential for "progressive" political action: circumstances surrounding the ownership or non-ownership of land are centrally relevant, too.' And the Populist movement was a creation of both 'landed *and* landless people'. The movement's platform argued for the landless, seeing those demands as progressive for small landowners as well: 'from beginning to end, the chief Populist theoreticians – "landowners" all – stood in economic terms with the propertyless rural and urban people of America'.[14] Apart from these moments of actual agrarian challenges, there are also potent traditions and associations that make the farmer's property a different matter from, say, the urban landlord's, and the works discussed in this chapter tend to draw both on a historical moment and on these cultural traditions.

The debate raised by the real and the fictional farmers in the 1980s centres on the difference between owners, the families, or the banks or the corporations. Agribusiness has been attacked on many grounds, ecological and economic, but its farming practices are usually defended through its supposed efficiency. Goodwyn undermines this defence by turning to the history of the increasing centralization of land ownership. The context of his argument is the reforms of agricultural credit which Goodwyn sees as having, in the early years of this century, been biased in favour of large-scale interests and against the small farmer.

> Purely in terms of land-ownership patterns, 'agri-business' began to emerge in rural America as early as the 1920s, not, as some have suggested, because large-scale corporate farming proved its 'efficiency' in the period 1940 to 1970. In essence, 'agri-business' came into existence before it even had the opportunity to prove or disprove its 'efficiency'. In many ways, land centralization in American agriculture was a decades-long product of farm credit policies acceptable to the American banking community.

Goodwyn returns to the point, arguing that ownership had been concentrated before corporate farming could prove its 'economies of scale': 'It was simply a matter of capital and the power of those having capital to prevent remedial democratic legislation.'[15] The power that the family farmer has in films and fiction concerning the current closure of farms and the consequent concentration of land in the hands of corporate farming, is the power of tradition. We can now turn to an early representation of the family farmer, a text that helped to establish this tradition.

Founding farmers

'American literature, as the voice of our national consciousness, begins in 1782 with the first publication in England of *Letters from an American Farmer*.' Crèvecoeur's book certainly addresses this idea of beginning, asking the question, 'What, then, is the American, this new man?'[16] Crèvecoeur's 'American Farmer', Farmer James, combines a narrative stance of simplicity ('you well know that I am neither a philosopher, politician, divine, or naturalist, but a simple farmer'), with a social ideal ('good, substantial, independent American farmers – an appellation which will be the most fortunate one a man of my class can possess so long as our civil government continues to shed blessings on our husbandry').[17] He answers the question about American identity by saying 'we are a race of cultivators', and this marks the founding farmers of America off from a European past characterized by antiquity and a more rigid social structure: 'I had rather admire the ample barn of one of our opulent farmers, who himself felled the first tree in his plantation and was the first founder of his settlement, than study the dimensions of the temple of Ceres.' And he would rather watch this 'industrious farmer throughout all the stages of his labours' than 'examine how modern Italian convents can be supported without doing anything but singing and praying'.[18] But this differentiation occurs within America as well. Crèvecoeur's fertile, peaceful middle colonies of New York and Pennsylvania are distinguished from the slave-holding South and the wildness of the frontier. The latter represents the emigrant's nightmare, not virgin land but a degeneration into savagery.

The narrator's journeys away from the middle colonies map out what Stephen Fender has called 'a moral geography in which a region is judged by how well it cultivates its environment', with each excursion involving Farmer James in 'an experiment to determine the true relationship between soil and society'.[19] Crèvecoeur's analysis is influenced by the French Physiocrats, whose economic philosophy saw agriculture as the only source of real values, but this intellectual context foreshadows later populist rhetoric and the producerism that opposes the true workers – with farmers being the truest of the true, as it were – to the urban world of speculation and finance capitalism. Such oppositions appear in *Letters from an American Farmer*, which defines the independent farmer's other as the American zeal for litigation and the consequent value of lawyers, whose trade in language and paper has parallels with the later figure of the speculator. Equally, the slave-owning states deviate not only from humanity but also from the natural sign of humanity, labour. They are characterized by luxury and founded on the work of their slaves, not on the book's ideal small farmer.

This ideal centres on property which separates the independent farmer from the European peasant: 'I therefore rest satisfied and thank God that my lot is to be an American farmer instead of a Russian boor or an Hungarian peasant.' Farmer James links moments of 'paternal ecstasy' with his child, his love of home, and 'the bright idea of property, of exclusive right, of independence', in the family fields.

> Precious soil, I say to myself, by what singular custom of law is it that thou wast made to constitute the riches of the freeholder? What would we American farmers be without the distinct possession of that soil.... No wonder we should thus cherish its possession; no wonder that so many Europeans who have never been able to say that such portion of land was theirs cross the Atlantic to realize that happiness.[20]

Crèvecoeur deliberately avoids the pleasant prospect of 'our American fields' in the instructive 'History of Andrew, the Hebridean', preferring to celebrate the immigrant rather than the settled farmers, in order to underline the theme of the new beginning. 'I had rather attend on the shore to welcome the poor European when he arrives', so to observe 'his first moments of embarrassment', 'his primary difficulties', 'his first thoughts and feelings, the first essays of an industry, which hitherto has been suppressed'.

> I wish to see men cut down the first trees, erect their new buildings, till their first fields, reap their first crops, and say for the first time in their lives, 'This is our own grain, raised from American soil; on it we shall feed and grow fat and convert the rest into gold and silver.'[21]

The book gestures through its title to political rhetoric. Thus Garry Wills writing on Jefferson:

> When Jefferson referred to himself as a farmer, he was not indulging false modesty. 'Letters of a Farmer' was a basic literary form in his time – the voice of an independent and reflective man, of the Country Party in England; in America, of John Dickinson attacking the Stamp Act or Richard Henry Lee attacking the Constitution.[22]

Adams, in the article quoted earlier, sees Crèvecoeur's agrarian vision as a moral and political training, forming character and civil liberties. Here, again, Crèvecoeur suggests Thomas Jefferson. Nature linked via property and farming to independence is also a theme of Jefferson's *Notes on the State of Virginia*, which sees husbandry as the privileged setting for virtue and self-reliance and this is reflected both in his policies and in his philosophy. Adams discusses the peculiarly American nature of this, even though there is obviously a long European tradition of pastoral images and writing. The European tradition lacks the history of the frontier.

Jefferson and Crèvecoeur thus shared a particular narrative focus and ground: the virtuous husbandman, appropriating and developing his land and mastering, in the process, the code of moral and political virtue. It is a narrative that is in some sense uniquely American: where else but in this vast and (in 1780) apparently endless continent could this fascination with land, appropriation, and husbandry become a ruling figure of political language and imagination; where else could 'nature' be taken with such unequivocal and literal seriousness?[23]

The idea of America as virgin land was one of the ways in which Native American culture was made invisible, through taking farming and settled land as the only signs of culture. Adams also sees the idea of unsettled land as a screen on which American political thought projected various debates, adapting such fundamental liberal notions as the link between the autonomous self and property. But after these Lockean beginnings, the agrarian tradition continued in American political rhetoric, most obviously in the mid-nineteenth-century 'land for the landless' agitation and the homestead movement. Adams discusses this theme in the speeches of Lincoln, in the 'Free Soil' platform of the Republican Party in 1860 and in the Homestead Act of 1862. The West is seen here as a 'safety valve' to supplement the transformed and industrialized East, and to ease the new urban tensions. Although there were obvious discrepancies between the rhetoric and the actual results of the Homestead Act, Adams sees this as a continuation of the agrarian tradition in its liberal form, which he distinguishes from the Southern agrarians like George Fitzhugh who constructed an alternative pastoral that acted as an apology for slavery rather than an argument for independence.[24]

One of the peculiarities of this history, a history of rhetoric, of political thought, of literary representations, but also of migration, settlement, and so on, lies in the intersection of the *timeless* and the *specific*; almost mythic figures of virtuous husbandry stand in the shadows of periods of economic and regional crisis, to return in a rhetoric that mixes the images of pastoral with the direct action of protest. And as we will see, some critical discomfort is generated by this combination of the idyllic and the realistic. But before looking at the cultural products of this history, the narrative of actual protest needs to be traced. The frontier historian, Frederick Jackson Turner, one of Adams' 'liberal agrarians', saw American history as shaped by the frontier experience, and saw populism within a tradition of American renewal on the shifting frontier line. He suggested that demands for credit could be traced back from the 'recent Populist agitation' to early colonial times; the 'demand for an expansion of the currency has marked each area of Western advance'. Turner saw the past as a clue to his contemporaries, the Populists: 'If the reader would see a picture of the representative Kansas Populist, let him examine the family portraits of the Ohio farmers in the middle of the century.' Looking back along the tradition of the Puritan farmer, Turner linked the Populists to early New England radicalism, suggesting that the spirit of this agitation could be traced as far back as Cromwell's army.[25] The appeal of this tradition is in seeing a line unfold up to the present, up to the American Agricultural Movement's tractors blocking Washington in 1977, up to the farm crisis of the 1980s.

History is, however, not so univocal. Fred Shannon's helpful *American Farmers' Movements* charts rural protest from the 1600s to the 1930s, but what emerges is not the continuous cultural tradition but specific grievances rooted in time and place, often evident in the names of movements, like the Kentucky Night Riders of the early 1900s and their violent opposition to the fixing of tobacco prices. A larger picture emerges with the farmers' situation after the Civil War, linked not so much to Turner's frontier thesis as to the power of the emergent trusts and to the financial situation. Farmers were faced with low prices for their produce but high prices for essential purchases, tight credit, transportation problems, and powerful middlemen (the produce exchanges, the grain elevator operators, the meat packers, and so on). Shannon points out that most of the tactics adopted by industry during depressions were impossible for farmers. The farmer could not cut back on labour, as his labour force was usually his own family; half-grown crops could not be abandoned when the market for them dropped; and unlike the industrial monopolies, farmers had no organization to restrict output and maintain prices. The prices quoted on the exchanges were much higher than those actually received by the farmers of the South, the West, and the Midwest. And problems with credit and high interest rates and with transportation charges prompted the discontent of the 1870s, 1880s, and 1890s. Resentment about the railroads is highlighted by Goodwyn:

the system ... made it possible for large elevator companies to transport grain from Chicago all the way to England for less money than it cost a Dakota farmer to send his wheat to the grain mills in near-by Minneapolis. A number of railroads also forced shippers – grain dealers as well as individual farmers – to pay freight costs equal to the rail line's most distant terminal, even should they wish to ship only over a lesser portion of the line.[26]

Attempts to bring the railroads under control can be seen in the Granger movement of the 1870s with their temporary and local 'Granger' legislation fixing maximum rates, and more broadly, in the anti-monopoly rhetoric and proposals of the Farmers Alliance and the Populists. Monetary reform was linked to agrarian protest through first the greenback movement in the 1870s and then in the Populists' proposals, and in the 'Free Silver' campaign which finally split the party and led to their incorporation into the Democrats in the 1890s. The problems farmers had with getting adequate credit were given a further twist in the South by the pressures of the crop lien system. The store owner would advance groceries and other supplies, charging a higher rate for the goods, to sharecroppers and tenants, who would then be tied to one store with their crop mortgaged to the owner. As the year's accumulated debt often exceeded the income from a year's cotton crop, the humiliating cycle of dependency would be extended for another year.[27]

The two clearest examples of populist politics are the almost contemporary agrarian movements in Russia and America. One difference between these moments of rural protest focuses on the role of intellectuals. Instead of Russia's urban intelligentsia bringing political agitation to a peasantry, the 'ideologists of the North American movements were drawn from the farming community itself. They were a *local*, not a national or cosmopolitan intelligentsia.'[28] Although there are qualifications one might make, the interest of some socialist writers in the populist movement, for example, this makes a useful point. Goodwyn's account of the agrarian revolt stresses that populism needed not only 'hard times' but also, more importantly, a political culture. Its organizational base was the Farmers Alliance and their 'powerful mechanism of mass recruitment – the world's first large-scale working class cooperative'. Joining this was a political education in itself, as opposition to the scheme clarified the farmers' sense of the concentration of economic power, but this education was reinforced through the 40,000 lecturers in the Alliance lecturing system. The strength of opposition to this experiment in economic co-operation led the movement to realize the need for their own institutional voice – the People's Party. The democratic nature of this voice and the power of radical ideas can be seen in the fact that there were over 1,000 Populist journals circulating in the 1890s.[29] But apart from the movement's 'organic intellectuals', there is also the involvement, with varying degrees of political awareness, of novelists with a more problematic relation both to their roots and to their readership. The next section will discuss some fiction dealing with the farming communities.

'Nebraska is distinctly declassé': regional fiction

The cultural promise held out by America was gradually displaced on to the West by many nineteenth-century writers. If the East was still trapped in European standards and forms, the West promised a more vital and vernacular writing, a national culture that would look to the democratic potential of the people rather than to the traditions of Europe. Intellectuals from the West and the Midwest were romanticized, as with Turner writing about William Dean Howells: 'Farmer boys walked behind the plow with their book in hand and sometimes forgot to turn at the end of the furrow; even rare boys, who, like the young Howells, "limped bare foot by his father's side with his eyes on the cow and his mind on Cervantes and Shakespeare".' And Howells used his position as editor and critic to promote both realism and writers he considered western, like Hamlin Garland. In an introduction to Garland's *Main-Travelled Roads* (1891), Howells wrote: 'If any one is still at a loss to account for that uprising of the farmers in the West which is the translation of the Peasants' War into modern and republican terms, let him read *Main-Travelled Roads* and he will begin to understand.'[30]

Garland, out of the writers considered here, was the closest to the political context sketched above. He spoke on behalf of the single tax, met its prophet, Henry George, and became a campaign speaker for the People's Party of Iowa, also writing a novel, *A Spoil of Office*, based on the Populist campaign. In his writing the political moment of rural discontent meets the turn-of-the-century literary idea of regionalism. He left Dakota for Boston in 1884 but described his visits home in the later 1880s as something of a literary awakening, writing in his autobiography, *A Son of the Middle Border*:

> All that day I had studied the land. . . . The lack of color, of charm in the lives of the people anguished me. I wondered why I had never before noticed the futility of woman's life on the farm. I asked myself, 'Why have these stern facts never been put into our literature as they have been used in Russia and England? Why has this land no storytellers like those who have made Massachusetts and New England illustrious?'

Could farming be given the same scrutiny as the urban world? 'Other writers are telling the truth about the city . . . and it appears to me that the time has come to tell the truth about the barn yard's daily grind.'[31] The 'Six Mississippi Stories' of *Main-Travelled Roads* stand as this attempt.

They deal with such issues as land speculation and the situation of the tenant farmer ('Under the Lion's Paw') but the story I will focus on is one that revolves around the idea of the writer's return to the farm: 'Up the Coulé: A Story of Wisconsin'. The dramatist, Howard McLane, returns home with a vague feeling of having neglected his family; 'a new play to be produced, or a new yachting trip, or a tour of Europe' has always caused the visit to be postponed. The drudgery of the farm contrasts with Howard's new style, as he and his brother Grant look at each other, the passage emphasizing Howard's elegant cuffs, collar, and shirt, the 'jewel of his necktie', and Grant standing 'ankle-deep in muck', resenting the 'gleam of Howard's white hands'. Grant later asks about the theatre: 'I s'pose you fellers make a pile of money.' Howard says that it is like gambling, you can make 1,000 dollars one week, and lose it the next. This attempt to stress the risky nature of his work is likely, however, to sound more like speculation to Grant, who replies, 'I wish I was in somethin' that paid better than farmin'. Anything under God's heaven is better 'n farmin'.' Howard's guilt increases as he discovers how hard things have been in his absence, while Grant places Howard as a writer, and according to a producerist logic, alongside the plutocrat and the metropolitan idle: 'We fellers on the farm have to earn a livin' for ourselves and you fellers that don't work. I don't blame you. I'd do it if I could.'[32]

The world of labour clashes with that of literature when Howard dresses the next morning in his casual, country clothes which are first misread by his mother as 'a special suit put on for her benefit', and then mocked by Grant. The clothes have been made according to a city tailor's idea of 'the country' but an idea of 'the real country' is introduced when Howard offers to help with the haymaking. After more comments about Howard's soft, white hands, Grant adds that he will ruin his 'fine clothes'. 'They're made for this kind of thing', Howard replies unwisely, for Grant then asks him the price of his outfit, saying he must get the same. Grant continues with his sarcasm: 'Singular we think the country's goin' to hell, we fellers, in a two-dollar suit, wadin' around in the mud or sweatin' around in the hay-field, while you fellers lay around New York and smoke and wear good clothes and toady to millionaires?' Howard, used to a world of culture, of poets and 'brilliant women', walks away angry, 'shoved aside, by a man in a stained hickory shirt and patched overalls, and that man his brother!' Now alone he surveys the landscape, admiring its beauty but noting also the monotonous signs of work, trying to negotiate a position which would recognize both. ' "The poet who writes of milking the cows does it from the hammock, looking on," Howard soliloquized', while he watches the flies swarm around the cows. After hearing the grievances of local farmers later, he thinks 'of the infinite tragedy of these lives which the world loves to call "peaceful and pastoral" '. The juxtaposition of an aesthetic view (the beautiful landscape, the pastoral life) and the rigours of rural life is resolved by realism, the literary form that denies its literary nature, reproducing the real rather than the poet lounging in a hammock admiring beauty. The story reverses Garland's insight that the realist or naturalist treatment of the city could be extended to the country, as Grant's wife complains of the drudgery of the farm and dreams of escape to the city. The perspective of pastoral is turned around, for her the city is the place of romance and the country is the realistic site of labour. She does not realize, Howard thinks, that the city is also the setting for the struggle for existence, the terrain of the realist or naturalist novel. The story closes with Howard confessing that he has neglected his family, and has been too busy with plays, pictures, his yacht. He is reconciled with Grant but if he is not too late to revive his sense of the family, Grant tells him it is too late to help with the farm.[33]

The tragedy here, and the word is used several times in the story, is the inevitable poverty of the farmer, as seen in Grant's final pessimism. The book's introduction suggests that Garland's career can be seen in these same terms, as 'an American tragedy', a decline into sentimentality as the 'bitter realism' of his early work gave way to the 'complacent romanticizing' of his later novels.[34] Realism is the key in both tragedies and in fact they mirror each other around this concept; the story concerns a shift from a pastoral, nostalgic view of the land to a contemporary realist depiction of its hardship, while the literary career reverses this perspective, moving from realism to romance. The story highlights its theme of realism and its choice of a realist style through having a writer as a protagonist. Howard's mixture of aestheticism (the beauties of nature, the pastoral setting) and personal guilt (his wealth, his ten-year absence) reinforces the mud, the flies, the two-dollar suits, the sweat, and the tedium, the literary signs of realism. Urban ideas of the country as a retreat from a busy world are mocked, and just as Howard's tailor ('Breckstein, on Fifth Avenue and Twentieth Street') has his country outfits satirized by Grant, so the narrative subverts the standard romance of the soil and its notion of the dignity of agricultural labour. But the romance/realism opposition is never that fixed in the agrarian context, and this can be seen by moving from Garland's Mississippi stories to Willa Cather's Nebraska novels.

Although Cather's work is set in the time and place of the farmers' agitation of the 1880s and 1890s, the agrarian politics that appears is closer to a modern understanding of populism than to the demands of the People's Party. Some of her early stories touch on the opposition between the prairie farmers and the Wall Street speculators, but the sentiments of 'Neighbour Rosicky' (a story written in 1928 but set earlier), are more typical. Rosicky, the Bohemian immigrant who has worked in London and New York, remembers hearing through the Bohemian newspapers about the Czech farming communities in the West. His journey West was his last migration, and now he looks back at the end of his life and worries about the future of his farm. He thinks his son might go and work at the stockyards, not realizing the importance of the land: 'To be a landless man was to be a wage-earner, a slave, all your life; to have nothing, to be nothing.' It is a line that echoes Crèvecoeur's early representation of the independent property-owner, but this independence is given a further modern twist. With farming, 'what you had was your own. You didn't have to choose between bosses and strikers, and go wrong either way.'[35] Instead of the alliances between farmers and workers promoted by the 1890s populists, Cather separates the farmer from the industrial world, suggesting both the agrarian tradition and the more modern version of populism that argues that class politics can be transcended. Cather had worked as an associate editor on *McLure's Magazine* in New York in the early 1900s, which brought her into close contact with the world of investigative journalism, 'muckraking' in the phrase of the time, and naturalism. Her own fiction is opposed to these committed reports or social Darwinist panoramas. Rosicky's anxiety about his son going to the stockyards suggests an earlier narrative of the immigrant's experience, Upton Sinclair's *The Jungle*, which viewed the Chicago stockyards through the lens of a socialist naturalism. Cather follows Rosicky away from this urban world toward the land.

Garland was quoted above as realizing that the land he had grown up in had received no real literary representation. Similar regionalist sentiments can be found in Cather's article, 'My first novels (there were two)'. She dismisses *Alexander's Bridge* (1912) as a false start, marked by literary influences and conventions. She turned to a more personal project based on childhood memories of Nebraska neighbours. This became *O Pioneers!* (1913), which she saw as a 'book for myself' rather than one fitting prevailing literary trends: 'The "novel of the soil" had not then come into fashion in this country. The drawing-room was considered the proper setting for a novel, and the only characters worth reading about were smart people or clever people.' If the novel did not belong to this dominant idea of the literary, associated with Edith Wharton and Henry James, it also seemed likely to offend notions of the popular. Cather says that she did not expect that people

> would see anything in a slow-moving story, without 'action', without 'humour', without a 'hero'; a story concerned entirely with heavy farming people, with cornfields and pasture lands and pig yards – set in Nebraska, of all places! As everyone knows, Nebraska is distinctly declassé as a literary background; its very name throws the delicately attuned critic into a clammy shiver of embarrassment. Kansas is almost as unpromising. Colorado, on the contrary, is considered quite possible. Wyoming really has some class, of its own kind, like well-cut riding breeches. But a New York critic voiced a very general opinion when he said: 'I simply don't care a damn what happens in Nebraska, no matter who writes about it.'[36]

Not only was the novel set in Nebraska but the characters were Swedes; Cather adds that their contemporary literary fate was to appear in humorous sketches, stressing their physical strength and inability to pronounce the letter 'j'.

Several things are left out of this account: there is, for example, no mention in Cather's sketch of her literary context of the opposite to the genteel tradition of James and Wharton, the alternative to the drawing-room novel – naturalism. Also this description of childhood memories and personal writing suggests a naturalness that the composition denies, overlooking the existence of several earlier stories which Cather revised into the novel. The passage may be somewhat evasive but it outlines the relation between a regional setting and a metropolitan literary culture, a relation which is still problematic. Echoes of that New York critic can still be heard today in phrases like 'hick chic', and this will be analysed later in Chapter 2 and in Chapter 4.

Cather's idea of place is peculiarly complex, a fact highlighted by opening *O Pioneers!* First, the title, taken from Whitman, celebrant of America and the West; then Cather's poem 'Prairie Spring' which pits the 'sharp desire' of youth against 'the flat land'; then an epigraph from Mickiewicz's *Pan Tadeusz*, 'Those fields, colored by various grain!'; finally, a dedication – 'To the memory of Sarah Orne Jewett in whose beautiful and delicate work there is the perfection that endures.' Whitman's phrase points to the experience and myth of the pioneers but Cather then decentres this, placing women rather than men at the heart of the experience. Rather than simply celebrating the prairies her poem also suggests the stifling nature of the lives there. The use of a line from a Polish poet has a double effect: it displaces the idea of the pioneering experience as one of 'Americanization', and in a parallel with the new centrality of women Cather sees the settling of the West as an immigrant venture. Secondly, as

A. S. Byatt has pointed out, the line from *Pan Tadeusz* emphasizes 'both her sense that she, like Mickiewicz and Virgil, was writing national epic, and her sense of the European origin of her cultural roots, of continuities, as well as gaps, between the Old World and the New'.[37] Sarah Orne Jewett's *The Country of the Pointed Firs* (1896) was singled out by Cather as being, along with *The Scarlet Letter* and *Huckleberry Finn*, one of the few American works that would last. Jewett was both friend and influence, and her admiration of Flaubert and her use of New England as the setting of her fiction, give another context, one involving several other American women writers, that of late-nineteenth-century regionalism, or local colourism.

The title, epigraphs, and dedication suggest different ways of representing Nebraska, all of which go beyond Cather's own opposition between her personal biography and an unsympathetic literary context seen earlier. Cather suggests that the move from her first novel to *O Pioneers!* was a shedding of literary influence and a rediscovery of personal and regional truth, but it has also been seen as the opposite, a betrayal of her early short stories and a romanticization of Nebraska. Robert Edson Lee's *From West to East* argues that the Western experience has always been diluted, censored, or rewritten for Eastern consumption. The journey from West to East is also one from realism to pastoral. Lee admires Cather's early short fiction for its account of the miseries of the immigrant settlers, but sees *O Pioneers!* as a break with that honesty, a novel 'written by an outsider, a dispassionate peopling of Nebraska with the peasants of Millet'. To please her Eastern friends – he includes Sarah Orne Jewett here – 'she chose the rosy tints of romanticism, which inhibit all of her later writings about the West'. Her novel is 'an idyll or a pastorale', substituting beauty for history. 'She has polished and tamed a land and its people out of all recognition. She did this, she had to do this in self-defense; who cared, after all, about Nebraska? She had come, by 1913, to write from the point of view of the East, substituting artifice for truth.'[38]

The problem here would seem to be that Lee identifies realism with truth, the early stories being seen as unvarnished, without artifice. In fact, the melodrama of a short story like 'On the Divide' (1896) with its brutalized settlers is as 'literary' as any of her novels.[39] It is clear that the mood of Cather's fiction changes as she becomes more distant, both geographically and in time, from Nebraska but that transformation should not be seen as romanticism replacing realism or, in Lee's strong formulation, reality itself. If we look at the openings of *O Pioneers!* and its sister novel *My Antonia* (also set in nineteenth-century Nebraska), the land is seen as indifferent rather than brutal.

But the great fact was the land itself, which seemed to overwhelm the little beginnings of human society that struggled in its sombre wastes.

Of all the bewildering things about a new country, the absence of human landmarks is one of the most depressing and disheartening.[40]

There was nothing but land: not a country at all, but the material out of which countries are made.

Between that earth and that sky I felt erased, blotted out. I did not say my prayers that night: here, I felt, what would be would be.[41]

The land refuses to be a conventional landscape, something that could be framed and viewed. What the novels show is not the romanticizing of Nebraska but the humanizing of it. Agriculture writes with the plough on this giant blankness. And the blankness gives Cather a chance to retain an ambivalent attitude to the land: it's both a refusal of human meaning and also the potential for it. This ambivalence is founded in Cather's own feelings about Nebraska, combining nostalgia with a gratitude for having escaped the enormity of the land and the smallness of the towns.

Nebraska had an interesting relation to the Populist agitation of the 1880s and 1890s, developing its 'shadow movement' that led to William Jennings Bryan and fusion with the Democrats, as discussed in my Introduction. But Cather makes this kind of organized politics marginal; it's as if politics is a kind of male luxury, rhetoric a masculine frippery – something that is seen in *O Pioneers!* with Lou's bluster about William Jennings Bryan and the West making itself heard.[42] As opposed to this language of demands, Cather develops the claims of desire. It is desire that links the potential of the country (agricultural potential as well as an idea of its growing importance) to the youth of those who can see it: 'A pioneer should have imagination, should be able to enjoy the idea of things more than the things themselves.'[43] It is also desire that deconstructs the realism/romance opposition, linking dreams to material effects.

The representation of land is connected to the representation of women. In Garland's world we saw the toll that the routines of the farm exacted from women, whereas a critical view of Cather's work might argue that, in a series of linked evasions, the country is romanticized, the hardship of agricultural labour is played down in a glossy romance of the soil, and that the female protagonists tend towards earth-mother figures, connecting crops and children in 'natural' images of fecundity, natural because women are seen as controlled by the rhythms of nature not by the codes of culture. Alexandra Bergson avoids making this description in *O Pioneers!*; her success is partly due to a faith in the land, an ability to love it, but it mainly stems from her astute agricultural sense, putting in alfalfa and planting wheat instead of corn. Her economic astuteness prevents her being overtaken by the fixity and naturalness of myth. *My Antonia* ends with a triumph of fecundity but the mythic dimension of Antonia is always seen through Jim's eyes, drawing attention to the male observation that shapes Antonia's story. *My Antonia* also contains other representations that resist a sentimentalized vision of maternity. There's Lena, controlling both her sexual and financial destinies, rejecting the confines of domesticity and motherhood, while Tiny's experiences in the Yukon also disrupt any single interpretation of women in the novel. Some final points can be drawn from the section of the novel which gives, as it were, a group portrait of its women, 'The Hired Girls'.

Whitman, writing about 'The women of the West', declared that he was not as satisfied with the women of Kansas City and Denver as with the men. The women seemed to lack the originality of the men, remaining true to the codes of 'gentility'; 'their ambition evidently is to copy their eastern sisters'. 'Something far different and in advance must appear,' Whitman says, 'to tally and complete the superb masculinity of the West, and maintain and continue it.'[44] Cather achieves some of Whitman's hopes while subverting his assumptions. He opposes the ideal women of the West to the existing ladies, but women are still there to complete masculinity, to maintain and continue it. In other words, he seems to want a more vigorous lady. In 'The Hired Girls', Antonia, Lena, and others have moved to Black Hawk from their families' farms. The section gives a picture of autonomous women, women defined by each other rather than by their relations to men. They have moved to town to work, and their sexual and social independence is linked to financial independence. While their escape from the family context is seen to be the basis of their pleasure, they remain dutifully connected to their families, but more from a sense of economic solidarity than from conventional notions of a nineteenth-century woman's duty. Jim remembers them as always helping to pay for ploughs, reapers, and livestock for the family farm. While the section celebrates the body, it does not reduce this to sexuality. Instead their ease and pleasure in physicality is linked to work, their early labour on their parents' farms, their newfound wages. In this they are distinguished from the Black Hawk ladies, confined in respectability and, as Cather notes, alienated from the physical worlds of work, sexuality, even sport. This opposition of the hired girls and the respectable ladies fulfils Whitman's hopes but challenges his central notion.

It is explicitly the immigrants who are contrasted to the Americans; it is Bohemian and Scandinavian women who embody Whitman's ideal of the Western woman and the Americans who continue to adhere to the respectable code of the lady. These women develop a group identity which does not revolve around maintaining and complementing Western masculinity, and which challenges ideas of the West or the frontier or the pioneering experience as 'Americanization'. This returns us to the tension between the epigraphs and title of *O Pioneers!* but it also intervenes in a denser cultural history. The pioneer normally is a figure confirming both masculinity and Americanness. We have already seen this with Crèvecoeur's Andrew the Hebridean, and his transformation from European peasant to American farmer. It's also a notion that is central to Frederick Jackson Turner's frontier thesis: 'In the crucible of the frontier the immigrants were Americanized, liberated, and fused into a mixed race, English in neither nationality nor characteristics.' Again: 'They were American pioneers, not outlying fragments of New England, of Germany, or of Norway.'[45] Cather's great achievement is to undermine this myth, investigating the poignant juxtapositions of 'historyless' landscapes and the residual continuities of the immigrants' culture. Her Nebraska fiction displaces the male American pioneer to focus on the work and desires of Swedish, Norwegian, or Bohemian women.

Frank Norris proposed a trilogy which would be 'the epic of wheat': its production, *The Octopus, A Story of California* (1901); its distribution, *The Pit, A Story of Chicago* (1903); and its consumption, *The Wolf, A Story of Europe.* He completed the first two volumes, covering a Californian conflict between wheat growers and the railroad trust, and a narrative of speculation in the Chicago wheat pit, before he died in 1902. He went to California in 1899 to research *The Octopus*, especially the Mussel Slough incident of 1880, a violent clash in the San Joaquin valley which compressed many of the contemporary grievances about the railroads into one dramatic event.[46] If the novel focuses on one of the central themes of the populists of the period, the power of the railroad trust, it also returns to the problem encountered in Garland and Cather, the need to transcend the realism/romance opposition that consistently structures the agrarian narrative. As with Garland's story, Norris foregrounds this problem by having a writer as a main character, Presley, the poet. Presley's ambition is to write the epic of the West, 'one single, mighty song, the song of the West'. However, the farmers' struggles sabotage this vision, undermining 'that huge, romantic West that he saw in his imagination' with the reality of the conflict between the San Joaquin farmers and the Pacific and Southwestern Railroad. 'The romance seemed complete up to that point. There it broke, there it failed, there it became realism, grim, unlovely, unyielding.' The contradiction within Presley's aesthetic between the desire to be true and the wish to be epic, reflects Norris's own problems as well as the opposition that runs through the American agrarian tradition, with conflicting images of the farmer, the honest yeoman of pastoral versus the historical actuality of debt, sweat, labour, and political organization. Presley wants to write the poem of the ranch but the prose of the railroad shatters his romance. He feels he is on the side of the people but their problems challenge his poetic vision: 'He searched for the true romance and, in the end, found grain rates and unjust freight tariffs' (pp. 464–5, 13–14, 15, 16).

Norris reworks his material in order to replace a populist vision (grain rates and freight tariffs) with a naturalist one. The novel displays a kind of vertigo before size and force, and this reaction slowly resolves the conflict between the farmers and the railroad, through a mystical response to nature and the economy in which the facts of human labour disappear. Farming is seen as a mystical and sexual union between man and nature, with the land seen in terms of fecundity and fertility, and ploughing seen as sexual penetration. The wheat is presented as a natural force, a matter of reproduction not production, the labour of childbirth rather than agricultural labour. It is the scale of the farming described that leads Norris to these purple passages and primal passions, as he concentrates on large ranches, celebrating their size. Alongside his mystification of agriculture there is also an awareness of the transformation of the rural economy. The novel's Californian ranchers have telephones and ticker-tapes; agriculture is not separated from the modern capitalist economy, a residual and virtuous oasis, it is a part of an international world of markets (pp. 94–6, 128, 44). Cedarquist, the novel's industrialist, talks of a general transformation which could provide a lesson for the farmers: 'The key word of this nineteenth century has been production. The great word of the twentieth century will be – listen to me, you youngsters – markets.' The search for new markets points towards Asia, echoing ideas of American 'Manifest Destiny' in a context of the late nineteenth century, the closing of the frontier, the war in Cuba, and the emergence of the United States as a world power. Populist discontent is resolved through an imperialism generated by the struggle for markets, with ideas of racial superiority playing their part: 'the whole East is disintegrating before the Anglo-Saxon'. Magnus Derrick, the Californian rancher, embraces this vision as the liberation of the farmer from the speculator, the middleman, and the trust, as wheat could be shipped direct to Asia avoiding Chicago. So farmers, instead of arguing for democratic control over public services like railroads, instead of offering a populist challenge to the emergent corporate world, should become a part of it, 'organizing into one gigantic trust themselves'. Californian wheat would flood 'the Orient in a golden torrent. It was the new era' (pp. 216–17, 226, 227). The novel's conflict is both political and aesthetic: realism versus romance, and farmers versus the railroad. Norris adopts various strategies to transcend these oppositions: the winning of new markets, for example, avoids the populist arguments by turning to Asia, providing an epic vision which draws on both romance and realism; and, most importantly, the mystification of both the wheat and the railroads around ideas of energy and force. As the conflict between the farmers and the railroad reaches violence both Presley and Norris rise to the epic possibility: 'the last fight between the trust and the people, the direct, brutal grapple of armed men, the law defied, the government ignored – behold, here it was close at hand' (p. 364). But this is exceptional in paying attention to the agents of the conflict, elsewhere the human dimension is diminished via a cult of power and energy. I have already suggested the way that Norris depicts agriculture as a mystical and sexual awakening rather than a product of human labour. As the wheat comes up, stretching towards the far horizon, it is seen as miraculous, a natural rebirth: 'There it was. The wheat! The wheat!' It is 'a mighty force, the strength of nations, the life of the world' (p. 276): 'it was over this that the railroad, the ranchers ... were wrangling. *As if human agency could affect this colossal power!* What were these heated, tiny squabbles, this feverish, small bustle of mankind, this minute swarming of the human insect, to the great, majestic, silent ocean of the wheat itself!' (p. 316, emphasis added). It may have been human agency that settled and irrigated the land, ploughed it, planted the wheat, and so on, but people become more and more irrelevant to the book. Men, life, death, all are seen as 'naught'; there is only 'FORCE', 'FORCE that made the wheat grow, FORCE that garnered it from the soil to give place to the succeeding crop' (p. 446). In such passages one sees the fascinatingly unstable nature of naturalism's intellectual repertoire: its interest in science suddenly plunges into mysticism; its project of demystification (for example, its links with 'muckraking' journalism) becomes the opposite as social forces dissolve into FORCE. The novel does not so much conclude as transcend; the people have become a 'little, isolated group of human insects', '*But the WHEAT remained*' (p. 458). What has happened to those brutal facts, those stubborn grievances, that so undermined Presley's romance of the West?

Norris describes the official railway map of California and the network of red lines marked Pacific and Southwestern Railroad. These lines are seen as 'a veritable system of blood circulation' but also 'tentacles' clutching outlying towns; they are both 'ruddy arteries' and bloodsuckers, draining the country's 'lifeblood' in order to feed the centre, 'a gigantic parasite fattening upon the lifeblood of an entire commonwealth'. Here is the octopus, a popular cartoon image for the railroad trust, displaying the grip of wealth over commonwealth. Even here, in the critical and central image, contradictions emerge. Metaphors are mixed, blood circulating, tentacles gripping, vampires or parasites draining blood. But the railroads were the lifeblood of the West, and opponents of them were not opposing transport or machinery, both of which they depended on, but ownership and monopoly. The railroad may shatter Presley's romance of the West, but it was essential for the farmers. Their argument was that something built with federal and local support should be at least regulated, if not taken into public ownership. However, Norris uses the natural images to transform the railroad into something like the wheat, a natural force beyond human control. Presley meets the railroad magnate, Shelgrim, towards the end of the novel. In this interview Norris conflates the mysteries of the wheat with those of finance, in a vertiginous surrender to ideas of force, higher laws, and size. The early octopus/bloodstream/parasite image gives way to an image that is still organic. Shelgrim tells Presley that railroads are neither made nor controlled, they grow – 'railroads build themselves'.

Shelgrim gives the poet a lesson in economics that is also a lesson in fatalism:

> Where there is a demand sooner or later there will be a supply. Mr. Derrick, does he grow his wheat? The wheat grows itself. What does he count for? Does he supply the force? What do I count for? Do I build the railroad? You are dealing with forces, young man, when you speak of wheat and the railroads, not with men. There is the wheat, the supply. It must be carried to feed the people. There is the demand. The wheat is one force, the railroad another, and there is the law that governs them – supply and demand. Men have only little to do in the whole business. Complications may arise, conditions that bear hard on the individual – crush him maybe – *but the wheat will be carried to feed the people* as inevitably as it will grow.

The language is familiar, contemporary: one is crushed by forces or rescued by the market. The economy is a distant, uncontrollable area as mysterious as nature: 'Can anyone stop the wheat? Well, then, no more can I stop the road.' Instead of objecting that the conflict was not about the railroad's existence but about its rates and its claim to public lands, Presley is hypnotized by this common indifference of nature, trusts, and machines. Having naturalized the man-made, he proceeds to mechanize nature: 'Nature was, then, a gigantic engine, a vast cyclopean power, huge, terrible, a leviathan with a heart of steel' (pp. 205, 405, 406).

While Presley is overwhelmed by rhetoric, the novel's villain, the railroad agent Behrman, is literally crushed by the wheat. As he watches the loading of a ship he falls into the hold and is slowly drowned by an avalanche of wheat (pp. 452–3). It is the classic rural revenge on the agent of urban finance; one that is echoed in Peter Weir's film, *Witness*, where urban violence and corruption follow Harrison Ford to the isolated, pastoral world of the Amish community, where one of the gunmen dies, suffocated by grain.

2 Country images: from Steinbeck's Okies to Hollywood's heartland

This chapter moves from Southern poverty in the 1930s to Hollywood's recent responses to the farm crisis, concluding with recent fiction dealing with the transformations of the American country. The contexts outlined in the previous chapter provide a framework for this discussion, and similar oppositions appear between, for example, regional fiction and metropolitan critics. As with the fiction from the turn of the century, the problem is whether to see the rural world as one of idyllic pastoral or as a world of work and hardship, and part of this cultural ambivalence stems from those contradictions within the American dream, the poor whites. Carolyn Chute's *The Beans of Egypt, Maine* provides a contemporary example. Part of the attention that this powerful novel received stemmed from what Ann Hulbert described, rather patronizingly, as 'the rarity of the real hick writer'. Chute's life is seen to authenticate the rural voice of her fiction: she was married at sixteen, a grandmother at thirty-seven, her second husband is illiterate and she lives on a Maine back road, similar to the world of her novel. Whatever frisson this gives urban intellectuals, Chute claims a more political intention for her representation: 'I want whoever reads my book to care about the working poor', she said to the *New York Times Book Review*, as either 'people blame all the country's ills on them or they don't see them'.[1] Once seen they are recognized in very different ways, as reviewers' comments demonstrate: 'A literary Diane Arbus' (*Vogue*); 'There are layers here, plumbed by few since Faulkner, and a portrait of a woman as dehumanized and brutalized, yet alive, as the women of Alice Walker's *The Colour Purple*' (*Publishers' Weekly*); 'Powerful, immediate, passionate ... the kind of writer English critics may choke on – their loss rather than ours' (Pat Barker, author of *Union Street*); 'The most powerful voice yet heard from the depths of Reagan's America' (*The Publisher*). These quotations taken from the novel's cover show how the story of Earlene's involvement with the Bean family brings various contradictions into focus.

We can leave to one side the question of whether English critics see the novel in a different way to Americans, for the issue here is cultural distance, and in that geography of assumptions New York is as far from Chute's Maine as London is. Rather than romance versus realism, the quotations above offer the grotesque versus the authentic. On the one hand, *Vogue* reaches, understandably, to the photographs of Diane Arbus, a comparison suggesting the 'freakish' nature of the rural poor, but the novel is also heard as a voice from the depths of Reagan's America, 'immediate, passionate' rather than ironic, voyeuristic. A clue to the usual habitat of this opposition is given by *Publishers' Weekly*: the comparison with Alice Walker perhaps registers a certain surprise that these brutalized characters are white rather than black, but the references to Walker and Faulkner point us away from Maine, point us South.

White trash aesthetics: representing Southern poverty

The contradiction that emerged from reactions to Carolyn Chute was summed up in another context by Flannery O'Connor: 'Any fiction that comes out of the South is going to be called grotesque by Northern readers – unless it is really grotesque. Then – it is going to be called photographic realism.'[2] The South is a terrain of conflicting representations, most obviously around the perspectives of black and white writers, but even in those representations where blacks are largely invisible, a struggle takes place. The best-known romance of the region is, of course, the mystified plantation of aristocratic elegance, belles and faithful darkies, a world that is gallant but doomed. There is also the mountain South, the Appalachians providing local colourists with either deprivation or idyll; nobility, pride, independence or incest, feuding and criminality. That kind of contradiction appears wherever Southern poverty does, and Sylvia Jenkins Cook's study of the fictional treatment of the Southern poor white focuses on the history of an ambivalent image that mixes deprivation with 'sloth, absurd folly, and random violence'.[3] 'White trash' or 'plain folk', 'sturdy yeomen' or 'good old boys', the South intensifies the oppositions that I have traced through other agrarian narratives. Another question is also heard, not so much how to represent the South but who is it represented for? Cook's work examines the way that an established comic and grotesque figure – she gives the date of the first comic picture of the Southern poor white as 1728 – clashes with other, political and aesthetic, imperatives.[4] She suggests that the term poor white was transformed from being somehow oxymoronic, freakish through going against the supposedly self-evident status of whites, to being symbolic. The Depression and the 1930s provided a changed context for the production and reception of images of white poverty: 'the poor white had transcended the local limits of his culture and had become a symbol for the distress and failure of the nation'.[5] Another commentator looking at films and fiction talks of the 'weird bifurcation of Dixies' during the 1930s along the romance/realism divide, the Old South bathed in nostalgia, the New South of economic hardship 'wallowing in misery and yankee pity'.[6]

A rural South emerged in fiction that was not idyllic but was either 'realistic' or 'symbolic'; sometimes seen as in need of government help, elsewhere as a repository of virtues of proud independence. Ellen Glasgow argued that the South in a period of transition needed a literary programme of 'blood and irony'. Jack Temple Kirby writes of her understanding and sympathy for 'the yeomanry and the "trash"': 'Ordinary whites – not planters and plutocrats – were the soul of the culture and the wave of the future. They heroically restored destroyed farms, waged grueling war with creditors and railroads, and rose to political authority as populists.'[7] Besides Glasgow's work, for example *Barren Ground* (1925), the twenties saw other novels dealing with sharecropping or with small-scale farming, several of them focusing on the burden of the poor white woman: Edith Summers Kelley's *Weeds* (1923), Elizabeth Madox Roberts' *The Time of Man* (1926), and Dorothy Scarborough's Texan world, *In the Land of Cotton* (1923). Such self-explanatory titles continue: Jack Bethea, *Cotton* (1928), Henry Kroll's *Cabin in the Cotton* (1931).[8] If the titles point to the land as a problem (*Weeds, Barren Ground*) or as the site of economic necessity, cotton rather than, say, the very different connotations of a title like *The Country of the Pointed Firs*, the novels offer various solutions, with several suggesting the need for more modern farming techniques.

It was Ellen Glasgow who coined the phrase 'the Southern Gothic School', meaning it disapprovingly and referring, in 1935, to Faulkner and Caldwell. Erskine Caldwell's *Tobacco Road* (1932), successful as a novel, play, and film, and *God's Little Acre* (1933), which has proved to be the bestselling version of the South, exceeding even *Gone With the Wind*, revitalized grotesque images of the poor white. With such success, realism becomes a fraught term for many Southerners, not an aesthetic issue but a political one which involves a Southern anxiety about Northern readers. Southern defensiveness became aggressive in the writings of the Agrarians, a group of poets, critics, novelists, and historians. John Donald Wade argued an Agrarian challenge to Caldwell, his response focusing on an uneasy relation between New York critics and rural writers, which we have already seen in Cather's comments and in responses to Carolyn Chute. Caldwell's rural fiction depicted just the sort of people, Wade wrote, that 'sophisticated New Yorkers and would-be New Yorkers – the major part of the book-buying population of America – can at once most envy and marvel over and deplore', thus satisfying 'the current vogue for primitivism and constant vogue of metropolitan complacency'.[9] What the North may see as realism, the South could see as voyeurism. Following Mencken's polemic against the philistinism of the South, 'The Sahara of the Bozart' (1920), and the 1925 'Scopes Monkey Trial' in Tennessee when a young teacher was convicted for teaching Darwinism, a satirical approach to white Southern culture gained momentum, emphasizing hillbilly violence, backwardness, and the extremes of country religion. The novels of T. S. Stribling took an ironic look at Tennessee (for example, *Teeftallow*, 1926), and Robert Penn Warren accused him of 'hick-baiting'. Mencken's invective was taken up by W. J. Cash's *The Mind of the South* (1941), a hillbilly masterpiece of 'the visceral, mindless South'.[10] Against this critical view the Agrarians reassembled a reactionary pastoral.

The Agrarians evolved into the New Critics, a crucial grouping in the history of the professionalization of literary criticism. Faced with the social dislocation arising from the industrialization of the South, these writers looked back to ideas of the land rather than to the deprivation of contemporary agricultural workers. A perceived need to defend the South led to their manifesto, *I'll Take My Stand*, published in 1930 by 'Twelve Southerners'. John Crowe Ransom's contribution to that volume gives a sense of their position: 'Reconstructed but unregenerate'. In Ransom's writing farming was seen as the best labour due to its 'contact with the elemental soil', the appeal is to an organic ideal in order to criticize features of capitalism while supporting its property relations. John Fekete points out that most Agrarian articles appeared in Northern publications (*Hound and Horn, New Republic, The American Review*), which suggests a mobilization of ideas about the South for national conservatism rather than authentic regionalism. Fekete discusses Ransom's articles such as 'The state and the land' and 'Happy farmers', which argued that the land could be used as a safety-valve to ease the misery of urban, industrial workers. Subsistence farming rather than commercial farming would provide a chance for many to get back to the organic rhythms of a pastoral life. Fekete sees this as presupposing state intervention, pointing to an accommodation between 'the neocapitalist state' and the Agrarian tradition.[11] If the Agrarians not only rendered blacks either passive or invisible but also avoided discussing actual agrarian struggles – the world of populism rather than pastoral – this attempt to appropriate the rural South for a reactionary position is mirrored by similar attempts of the left.

In *From Tobacco Road to Route 66*, Cook discusses the problems of radical writers faced with the cultural weight of images of the poor white as comic, grotesque, idle, and so on. She looks at the way that the journal *New Masses* discovered that 'to go left meant to go South', an announcement made in the May Day issue in 1929 and prompted by strikes of Southern textile workers. The strikes offered violent examples of class conflict together with a classic Marxist transformation of feudal, agrarian workers into an industrial proletariat, as most of the workers had been farmers or sharecroppers before working in the mills. Yet their culture and the ways in which they had been traditionally represented set up a tension between comic, irrational hillbilly and world historical subject, 'between Southern tradition and Marxist metamorphosis, between reactionary poor white and revolutionary hero'. The strike in Gastonia in North Carolina inspired at least six novels and Cook discusses the problems encountered by their writers. The radical novelists had to deal 'not only with the poor white as he had just revealed himself in the strike but with the *idea* of the poor white as a long-established literary personality'. What would a writer do with the conservatism of poor white culture around questions of race and gender? Cook picks up the latter point in her discussion of three Gastonia novels which have poor white mountain women as their protagonists.[12] What is significant here is the idea of tradition as obstacle, and the difficulty of writing within an established context of representations and assumptions.

After the committed *New Masses* audience, Southern deprivation touched a wider, liberal concern in the later 1930s, due mainly to the explosion of New Deal cultural, especially documentary, programmes. The Farm Security Administration sent out photographers and Southern hardship was soon represented in books combining photographs and text. More and more magazines featured articles on and images of the plight of rural America, and Southern poverty became, as Cook says, 'a journalistic institution'. The work that many would now identify with this context is *Let Us Now Praise Famous Men*; Walker Evans' photos are now recognized as classics of the genre. The book however is very self-conscious about this liberal context and about its possible reception, with James Agee's experimental text deliberately sabotaging many of the usual readings. In the summer of 1936 Evans and Agee went to Alabama to document the life of an average white family of tenant farmers, and their first refusal was of this idea of the *one* representative family, and thus the book concerned itself with 'Three Tenant Families'. They were commissioned by the businessman's magazine, *Fortune*, but this original article was never published; Harper Brothers were going to publish the expanded work but, after a long interval, the material was rejected. It was finally published in 1941 by Houghton Mifflin, five years after they had lived with the tenant families, and it was a commercial disaster, only becoming successful on its release after Agee's death in 1961.[13]

Agee's real project was 'to recognize the stature of a portion of unimagined existence, and to contrive techniques proper to its recording, communication, analysis, and defense'.[14] The text deliberately misleads with its epigraphs from *Lear* and from the *Communist Manifesto*, but it is brutally clear about its original purpose. Agee writes that it seemed 'curious, not to say obscene and thoroughly terrifying', that it could occur to people,

> to pry intimately into the lives of an undefended and appallingly damaged group of human beings, an ignorant and helpless rural family, for the purpose of parading the nakedness, disadvantage and humiliation of these people before another group of human beings, in the name of science, of 'honest journalism' (whatever that paradox may mean), of humanity, of social fearfulness, for money, and for a reputation for crusading and for unbias which, when skillfully enough qualified, is exchangeable at any bank for money.

Also curious, he adds, that the people commissioned for this, himself and Evans, both shared an attitude that 'from the first and inevitably they counted their employers, and that Government likewise to which one of them was bonded, among their most dangerous enemies' (p. 7). (The government reference alludes to Evans and the Farm Security Administration.)

By focusing on the 'unimagined existence' Agee seems to mean what is lost in conventional literary and documentary expression of Southern poverty. The book stresses the 'immeasurable weight in actual existence', the non-fictionality as it were, of its farmers, with Agee adding that he would prefer if it were possible to dispense with writing, to present these lives through objects:

> It would be photographs; the rest would be fragments of cloth, bits of cotton, lumps of earth, records of speech, pieces of wood and iron, phials of odors, plates of food and of excrement. Booksellers would consider it quite a novelty; critics would murmur, yes, but is it art; and I could trust a majority of you to use it as you would a parlor game. (pp. 12–13)

Agee's response to this problem of writing and his bitter awareness of the text's probable audience is an experimental shifting of styles, veering between the 'poetic' and the 'factual'. The sheer length of descriptions of possessions, decorations, clothing, and so on, move beyond sociological detail or an appeal to the pathos of cheap objects, to something more like the *nouveau roman*, a kind of fantasy of objectivity where writing could become an inventory of things. Elsewhere his prose can burst into somewhat awkward lyricism.

Always there is the sense that what he and Evans are doing with the Woods, the Ricketts, the Gudgers, is somehow horrifying in terms of the inequality of cultural power. He turns on the assumptions of his readers, not to displace guilt but to lay bare the workings of this context:

> However ... this is a book about 'sharecroppers', and is written for all those who have a soft place in their hearts for the laughter and tears inherent in poverty viewed at a distance, and especially for those who can afford the retail price; in the hope that the reader will be edified, and may feel kindly disposed toward any well-thought-out liberal efforts to rectify the unpleasant situation down South, and will somewhat better and more guiltily appreciate the next good meal he eats; and in the hope, too, that he will recommend this little book to really sympathetic friends, in order that our publishers may at least cover their investment and that (just the merest perhaps) some kindly thought may be turned our way, and a little of your money fall to poor little us. (pp. 14–15)

The word sharecroppers is in inverted commas to signal an unease about the way that Southern poverty was becoming almost fetishized. Agee says that throughout the South he heard 'sharecropper' used in a precise sense as a type of tenant, except when talking to 'new dealers, communists, and various casts of liberal'. But in the North, 'and particularly in the seaboard north, where most of the writing and printing and reading of the United States is carried on, sharecropper has, through the agencies of print and the lectured word, become the generic term' (p. 455). Similarly, this reformist focus on Southern tenants is rejected, Agee seeing this as just one among many upheavals caused by the 1930s crisis in the world economy, and seeing a focus on the economic as possibly overlooking other disadvantages less easy to reform.

> I understand that this particular subject of tenantry is becoming more and more stylish as a focus of 'reform', and in view of the people who will suffer and be betrayed at the hands of such 'reformers', there could never be enough effort to pry their eyes open even a little wider. (p. 208)

The political importance of Agee's text is, however, more its attitude to representation rather than reform or revolution. Its value lies in its self-consciousness about reading and writing and cultural traditions.

He is, in a way, a forerunner of the New Journalists of the 1960s and 1970s, making his desires, his anger, his guilt, part of the story, also giving the reader details of how the story was got. He feels that it would be as bad, 'to simplify or eliminate myself from this picture as to simplify or invent character, places or atmospheres' (p. 240). He feels that he is violating these lives: 'It is not going to be easy to look into their eyes' (p. 189). Of course, the reason why we can now look into their eyes is Walker Evans' camera. Agee writes of the revolutionary importance of the camera but he also analyses in painful detail the mixtures of shame, trust, and willingness to please that the Ricketts display when asked to pose. Agee apologizes for the intrusion but he stresses the difference between his project and more conventional literary impositions ('If I were going to use these lives of yours for "Art" . . .') (pp. 363–6, 366). The text does not only reject 'Art': it challenges any notion of the 'naturalness' of journalism; it complicates any reading of Southern agricultural workers as either 'victims' or potential revolutionary force; it also refuses the vocabulary and assumptions of liberal, reformist responses. It gives great importance to nature and to a human sensory relation to the land but scoffs at easy pastoral. Writing of the meagre lunch had by the families during cotton picking, Agee adds:

> It is of course no parallel in heartiness and variety to the proud and enormous meals which farm wives of the wheat country prepare for harvest hands, and which are so very zestfully regarded by some belated Virgilians as common to what they like to call the American Scene. (p. 341)

These refusals of easy appropriations of the book's material help explain its failure in 1941 and its classic status now. But we can now turn to an opposite achievement, one of the best-known representations of the poor white, Steinbeck's *The Grapes of Wrath*.

Steinbeck's novel presents America in a state of transition, most obviously in its descriptions of packed used cars taking to Highway 66:

> the path of a people in flight, refugees from dust and shrinking land, from the thunder of tractors and shrinking ownership, from the desert's slow northward invasion, from the twisting winds that howl up out of Texas, from the floods that bring no richness to the land and steal what little richness is there. From all of these the people are in flight, and they come into 66 from the tributary side roads, from the wagon tracks and the rutted country roads. 66 is the mother road, the road of flight.[15]

Cook argues that this flight is also Steinbeck's away from the novelist's problems with the Southern poor white. She argues that he had 'to move the poor whites not only to the periphery of their geographic location in the South' but also away from the process of industrialization there.[16] She sees Steinbeck as retreating from the project of the proletarian novel; a retreat that may partly account for the novel becoming a bestseller. She analyses the way that the Okies and their Westward migration summon up more attractive cultural traditions (the pioneer, the frontier) than the North Carolina mill workers. Also, she suggests that the novel's opening dust storms add an element of natural tragedy or supernatural fate to the uprooting of the Joads, eliding questions of guilt and responsibility. One sees a kind of strategic 'Americanism' within the book and Cook places this in a context of attempts to retrieve Americanism for the left (Earl Browder's 1936 presidential campaign slogan was 'Communism is Twentieth-Century Americanism'). Within Cook's argument, the trip to California is seen as a way of shedding two centuries worth of images of the poor white as comic, grotesque, or disreputable.[17] It is significant that the character closest to these images, the lecherous, vicious, complaining, childlike Grampa, dies on the journey.

One way of rephrasing Cook's discussion would be to see Steinbeck moving from a Marxist to a Populist perspective, the text's own shift being reinforced by the famous film. Steinbeck tries to balance reformism and revolution, in the alternation between the chapters' narrative and the interspersed general analysis, transporting his characters from individualistic to collectivist ideologies and hoping that he can take his readers along with them. *The Grapes of Wrath* draws on agrarian myths and on the pioneer experience to underline its historical ironies rather than to soften its critique. The dispossession of the Joads establishes a motif that dominates the recent threatened farm movies, the farmer seen as squeezed between the forces of nature and the pressures of banks, with both of these seen as arbitrary, mysterious, and unaccountable. However, unlike Norris's mystification of force, this parallel is used partly to explain the peculiarities of the crisis in the dust bowl, partly to explore the farmers' reactions. If Hollywood tends to use nature as an alibi for the economy, a less contentious cause of deprivation, Steinbeck uses the similarity to capture the bewilderment of the dispossessed. Early in the novel, the land's owners, or spokesmen for them, tell the tenant farmers that they will have to leave the land. The tenant system no longer works: 'One man on a tractor can take the place of twelve or fourteen families.' The tenants press their claim to the land: grandfathers settled it, fathers farmed it, borrowing money in bad years until the bank ended up owning it. Against family history and human investment there is legal title, leaving a feeling of a dehumanized economy: 'The bank isn't like a man.' The bank is 'something more than men.... Men made it, but they can't control it.' A feeling of resistance – 'Grampa killed Indians, Pa killed snakes for the land. Maybe we can kill banks' – gives way to puzzled impotence (pp. 38–9).

As the tractors arrive so does some of the novel's least impressive writing, with Steinbeck expanding the idea of dehumanization and descending into a trite contrast between machinery and land. The tractors are 'monsters' smashing their way across the country, 'through fences, through dooryards, in and out of gullies in straight lines'. Their drivers belong to the realm of the inorganic; a man at the controls 'did not look like a man: gloved, goggled, rubber dust-mask over nose and mouth, he was a part of the monster, a robot in the seat'. He is cut off from the soil: 'He could not see the land as it was, he could not smell the land as it smelled'; his feet touch iron pedals rather than warm earth. Insulated from the organic, 'He loved the land no more than the bank loved the land.' Steinbeck's description generates into anti-mechanical fantasies, for example, the seeders viewed as 'twelve curved iron penes erected in the foundry, orgasms set by gears, raping methodically, raping without passion'. Instead of an argument about farming techniques and land exhaustion, there is sentimentality: 'The land bore under iron, and under iron gradually died; for it was not loved or hated, it had no prayers or curses' (pp. 40–1). However, Steinbeck's analysis returns to the more interesting idea of the difficulty of making the causes of dispossession visible or answerable. The farmers feel that there is no point in fighting the tractor drivers – they are only replaceable workers. Behind them is the bank, but they realize that the chain does not stop there as it stretches back East – 'But where does it stop? Who can we shoot?' One tenant describes the frustration, 'It's not like lightning or earthquakes. We've got a bad thing made by men, and by God that's something we can change' (p. 44). It may be made by men but the corporate chain of command means that it is difficult to confront. Muley describes how the person who evicted him said that it wasn't his fault:

> 'Well,' I says, 'whose fault is it! I'll go an' I'll nut the fella'.' 'It's the Shawnee Lan' an' Cattle Company. I jus' got orders.' 'Who's the Shawnee Lan' an' Cattle Company?' 'It ain't nobody. It's a company.' (p. 53)

Muley still roams the land while the farmers are displaced from fields to the road: 'Place where folks live is them folks. They ain't whole, out lonely on the road in a piled-up car' (p. 58). The descriptions of this exodus focus on the selling off of a past, of family history, memories, a way of life.

The used cars head for California where jobs are advertised and where the families hope to make a new start. This dream dissolves in the face of unemployment, starvation wages, the conditions in the camps for the migrant workers, and harassment by local law officers. Steinbeck gives a compressed history of California, beginning with the American squatters taking the land from Mexicans. As their farms prosper so profit replaces an immediate relation to the land, until the owners 'were no longer farmers at all, but little shopkeepers of crops, little manufacturers who must sell before they can make'. The small farmer is squeezed out, 'the business men had the farms, and the farms grew larger, but there were fewer of them'. As farming becomes more like industry, the labour is done by imported workers, Chinese, Japanese, Mexicans, Filipinos. Racism could always be mobilized against these workers while ownership becomes even more concentrated, 'farms grew larger and the owners fewer'. Steinbeck evokes an organic and pastoral world against this emergent agribusiness: 'They farmed on paper and they forgot the land, the smell, the feel of it...' Then the dispossessed arrive, 'from Kansas, Oklahoma, Texas, New Mexico, from Nevada and Arkansas, families, tribes, dusted out, tractored out'. They have a different background to previous migrant workers: 'We ain't foreign. Seven generations back Americans, and beyond that Irish, Scotch, English, German. One of our folks in the Revolution, an' they was lots of our folks in the Civil War – both sides. Americans' (pp. 245–7). The text tries to mobilize support for the Okies through organic myths of the soil and through Americanism, resistance being thus made more acceptable.

The novel is a populist gamble, strategically mobilizing conservative ideas for a radical message. Interestingly, after the shift from the proletarian novel to the populist one, there is a further transformation. Class analysis is replaced with notions of 'the people', but the representative voice is possibly no longer a male one. Ma recites the family history: ' "We're the Joads. We don't look up to nobody. Grampa's grampa, he fit in the Revolution. We was farm people till the debt" ' (p. 326). It seems to be suggested that women are the ones to keep this history alive. Ma talks of the different relation that men and women have to crisis, and it appears that women are not only, as Pa grumbles, 'takin' over the fambly', but also becoming the voice of the people. They conserve memories and tradition and maintain continuity, a task which also serves as an act of resistance.

> 'Man, he lives in jerks – baby born an' a man dies, an' that's a jerk – gets a farm an' loses his farm, an' that's a jerk. Woman, it's all one flow, like a stream, little eddies, little waterfalls, but the river, it goes right on. Woman looks at it like that. We ain't gonna die out. People is goin' on – changin' a little, maybe, but goin' right on.' (p. 448)

In this, as in many other themes, *The Grapes of Wrath* establishes elements that become central in the 1980s in Hollywood's response to the farm crisis.

Stars and barns: celluloid and the soil

The relation between regional fiction and metropolitan criticism has been touched on at several points above, so far from the point of view of the regions. The perspective is reversed by turning to Ann Hulbert's *New Republic* article, headlined 'Fiction and films are living off the fad of the land'. She begins with a 1980s 'taste for rusticity', 'rural chic'. The image to aspire to in the magazines is that of 'a fancy, well-pressed hayseed', and there is 'a bumper crop of regional fiction and earthy movies'. She distinguishes between 'hick chic' ('a craving among the quiche crowd for pure country vistas and prettified country values'), and 'hick shock' ('the fall-out from recent decades of change in rural America'). She quotes Jonathan Yardley's coinage of 'hick chic' in the spring of 1985 in the *Washington Post*, and his complaint about a modish appropriation of the rural. As she says, that fashion has recently been satirized in Albert Brooks' film of yuppies trying to live out *Easy Rider, Lost in America*, and in Ann Beattie's novel *Love Always*, which revolves around a Vermont magazine called *Country Daze*.[18]

The piece draws on Hofstadter (see my discussion of him in the Introduction), to outline a 'populist romanticism' with its view of a rural golden age snuffed out by commerce. Here longstanding cultural traditions meet recent movements, those elements of the counter-culture who moved back to the land in the 1960s and 1970s, and the contemporary ecology movement. This provides the framework for a range of works from Garrison Keillor's successful radio show, 'A Prairie Home Companion' and the tongue-in-cheek nostalgia of his *Lake Wobegon Days*, to Hollywood, to new fiction and, one could add, to the trend for 'authenticity' and 'roots' in rock music and the revival of country. In William Adams' discussion of the threatened farm movies, they are placed in the contexts of the farm crisis and the tradition of the agrarian narrative, the latter explaining the interest caused by the plight of the farm belt at a time when the United States is far from being 'a nation of cultivators'. The films fit neatly into the tradition, as farming is portrayed as a virtuous life, its labour producing not only food but also 'moral simplicity' and independence. Family farms are menaced by corporate interests aided by corrupt politicians; banks having encouraged expansion now press hard on debts: 'the institutions are indifferent to a fate they have in some respects arranged, masking their complicity with vague allusions to "the free market" and the inevitability of change.'[19] Hulbert takes a more cynical look at the family farms of *Country*, *The River*, *Places in the Heart*; linking those issue films to the revival of the Western, mentioning not only Kasdan's *Silverado* and Clint Eastwood's *Pale Rider* but also the fact that 'the actor in the White House gets his best reviews in rustic settings – out on the ranch, with hat and horse or chainsaw'.[20]

In March 1987 reports about Michael Dukakis, Governor of Massachussetts, and a candidate for the Democratic presidential nomination, suggested that his political sophistication might have failed him in Iowa. In what seems an amusing clash of yuppie and heartland values, he floated the idea that the answer to the farm belt's problems might be for farmers to turn to more fashionable crops – endives and mushrooms. It is that kind of clash of values that Hulbert zeroes in on. The films, she argues, endorse 'the well-worn populist little good guys vs. big bad guys conspiracy theory of history'. But they then add 'a dollop of contemporary liberal cultural values – precisely the values that not so long ago inspired an anti-rural trend in the media'. Previously cinematic rural America has been the site for random redneck violence and small town bigotry (for example, *Deliverance* or *Easy Rider*).[21] Hulbert focuses on this new liberal concern for the country, especially on the testimony of actresses (including Jane Fonda, whose contribution to work inspired by the farm crisis was a television film, *The Dollmaker*) to the House Democratic Caucus Task Force on Agriculture.

The fact of being actresses and stars is felt to invalidate their testimony. They are accused of evading the conflict between 'their Hollywood poses and values and the hick story', and of presenting themselves 'as spokeswomen for simple rustic virtues, as if their screen experience made that perfectly possible'. There's something odd here: a writer accuses actresses of being patronizing while she herself refers to films about the farm crisis as 'the hick story'; she also ignores the fact that the actresses spoke out not only because of their roles (Fonda, 'As actresses whose work is to identify with what is most human, we cannot confine ourselves to the screen while the cruel and unusual punishment of farmers grinds on'), but also because of what they had learned during their research (would Hulbert also object to a journalist writing a supportive piece from the farm belt?), and because of family background (Jessica Lange's father lost his land in the Depression, Sissy Spacek's father was a New Deal agricultural agent in Texas, and Jane Fonda, the only one born into 'Hollywood poses and values', referred to her father's role as Tom Joad in John Ford's populist classic *The Grapes of Wrath*). Hulbert seems to feel that those in show business have no right to criticize agribusiness, and also that both the stars' statements and their films present a problematic liberalism. She cites Fonda's claim that the Reagan administration wanted to 'subsidize silos for MX missiles but not for family farmers', and Lange's suggestion that the farm crisis will be remembered 'alongside the memory of the American Indian, the memory of Vietnam, and all our other memories that are intimately related through greed and arrogant disregard'. Hulbert wonders what the farmers 'who staunchly supported Reagan would make' of such statements. Whatever they thought, the swing to the Democrats in the mid-term elections showed that the farm crisis had eroded support for Reagan in 1986.[22]

Hulbert considers *Country* and *The River* as cliché-ridden attempts at a 'hybrid of Hollywood and hick'. In both a family farm is suddenly in deep financial trouble, partly due to 'the ravages of nature' (in *Country*, a cyclone, in *The River*, a flood), 'but above all to the heartlessness of the credit system'. She sees the politics of both as an agrarian fantasy of 'a city slickers' conspiracy', but adding 'more up-to-date, liberal sentiments' in their sexual politics. Spacek and Lange are singled out 'as superwomen – they don't merely cook and raise kids, they manage the farm's accounts, they fix machines'. This feminist twist to 'the tradition of the strong farm wife – a central but hardly liberated figure in rural life – looks less authentic, not more'. The themes of community are found to be equally contrived; both films stage 'a gathering of usually gruff farmers who suddenly speak up in unison for a beleaguered family in their midst'. Something of an exception is made for *Places In the Heart* and for Peter Weir's *Witness*, both of which have 'registered a few tremors of "hick shock"', problematizing their vision of the rural community by including racism and religion. They inch towards a more realistic view of rural America, a view that is built on no golden age but on a recognition that the American farmer has operated in a market economy for over a century, as part of 'a fast-changing commercial order' rather than as an oasis of old-fashioned values. Of course, *Witness* sees the rural world precisely as an oasis, the Amish community living in a kind of time capsule environment, a refusal of the present rather than a reassuring continuity.[23] Continuing this move towards more ambivalent notions of community, the article turns to a selection of novels by Bobbie Ann Mason, Douglas Unger, Larry McMurtry, Louise Erdrich, Jayne Anne Phillips, and Carolyn Chute, finding in this fiction a more demythicized and unromantic view of a rural world in transition. One notices in this 'fiction versus Hollywood' argument the continuing power of the romance/realism opposition in discussions of agrarian narratives.

The argument is not just structured by ideas of realism and

romanticism, a notion of authenticity plays a part as well. We have already seen a distrust of the fashionable, 'hick chic', and of the actresses' commitment, and this becomes more intense: 'Hollywood stars can manically accumulate roles and stacks of money – and proclaim the enduring importance of more authentic, earthy values'; 'the stars blur the issue, wielding their rakes for the spotlight and huge sums'. There is an opposition between the false values of the film stars' earnings and genuine agricultural work; an opposition that obviously goes beyond the fact that they are not *really* farmers – after all an actor playing an accountant is similarly inauthentic – but which stems from the idea of farming as the most genuine labour. The theme heard through populist rhetoric and seen earlier in Garland's story of the dramatist and the farmer, occurs rather surprisingly in an article otherwise opposed to the populist. Hulbert notices that work is not elided in these films and she suggests that it is glamorized instead: 'The film stars join the novelists in playing up the physical travails, for there's romanticism in rigor these days.' This romanticism of the muscular is linked to contemporary style: 'Everyone is proud to display the external signs of physical exertion. ... Many are also eager to earn the rugged look by pounding their bodies into shape.' She links the fashion for working out to a revival of the work ethic which has, as it were, put muscles back into pastoral: 'sweat, usually in the background of arcadia, now glistens in the foreground – and the land's allure only grows.'[24] Sweat is to populism what blood is to nationalism, an almost mystical fluid that preserves tradition, but the visibility of work in these films is not so much linked to the work ethic but to questions of gender.

What Hulbert discusses is connected to a new ordering of masculinity and visual pleasure in the cinema (a topic discussed in the next chapter and in this book's conclusion), where masculinity is celebrated but as a spectacle beyond the unquestioned virility of older images of masculinity (the cowboy, for example). She is right to see a vogue for sweat and muscles but she misses the interesting feature of this in the farm movies. For the farmer is already a privileged symbol of the masculine in American culture, a representative of pioneer virtues of independence and strength. So something of a contradiction opens up with Mel Gibson in *The River* and Sam Shepard in *Country*. Here masculinity is something both assumed and to be looked at. Interestingly, masculinity changes from something to be looked at as *spectacle* to something to be looked at as a *problem*. You get a sense of this in Mark Rydell's comment about directing Mel Gibson in *The River*, 'in this case I think he overcame that gorgeous face he has'. Both Gibson and *Country*'s Sam Shepard create the sort of problem Hulbert points to (glamour versus authenticity), but in a way that, probably unconsciously, enhances the films which deal with a crisis of masculinity. Men representing male glamour play farmers representing classic, American masculinity. The economy has undermined these masculine virtues of independence, while the stars draw attention to the topic of masculinity.

Gil (Shepard) tells Jewell (Lange) that he's not having his wife working as a waitress for tips, his pride, as she points out, being more important than the grocery bills. Rather than discuss their problems, Gil goes out drinking, he fights with his son, he hits his wife. It is Jewell who rallies the farmers to a collective resistance. Similarly, in *The River*, Sissy Spacek says to Mel Gibson as he refuses help during a flood, 'You stupid goddamn farmer', again challenging a male sense of pride that is intensified by the myth of the independent farmer. If the farmer welds male pride to an idea of independence, we see another feature overlooked by Hulbert. Instead of clichés of community these films show a difficult transition from individualist ideologies to collective action. The doubly representative masculinity of Shepard and Gibson is seen to be at a loss, powerless. The films hint at the economic base of masculine virtues: if men aren't supposed to cry, aren't supposed to be powerless, what happens when the bills come in and you can't pay, or when the bank writes to say you have thirty days to pay back your loans, or when the auctioneer is about to sell off your farm machinery? Reports from the farming states in the mid-1980s have shown the effects of conservatism in crisis: people either blaming themselves for their problems (the farm crisis has apparently produced a high rate of suicides) or turning to conspiracy theories, some disturbingly anti-Semitic, others blaming more realistic combinations of government, banks, and corporate agribusiness. The films have a narrative and ideological duty to defer the crisis, or at least to postpone the loss of the farm.

In *Country* Gil is at first confrontational, telling the banker that farming isn't a business but a way of life; than he becomes puzzled and angry, complaining that the banks had encouraged them to expand; finally he is almost passive in the face of the loss of the farm. Jewell tries to organize a collective response from other farmers in difficulty. She is transformed by the crisis but Hulbert's talk of liberal, feminist updates seems a mistake. During the film Jewell is seen cooking, caring for her children, doing the accounts, working on the farm. This is not a 'superwoman' image but, as I argued earlier, a way of demonstrating a continuity of work within a specific context, the peculiar relation between farming, gender, and the division of labour. The family farm identifies work and family, and therefore helps to reveal domestic labour as part of a world of productive and reproductive work. It is this sense of keeping the family going that leads Jewell to fight back against both Gil and the bank. It is essentially an extension, as well as a transformation, of her conventional task of maintaining the family. Her action is thus both conservative and radical, and it wins them a deferral as well as bringing Gil back into the family. The threat to the family farm transforms family relations as it challenges masculine conservatism and radicalizes Jewell for a goal that is literally conservative.

The River is an uneasy combination of nature photography, genre values (the Western, especially), and committed issue film. It does, however, bring out in an interesting way the weakness of individualist solutions, and again the transition to collective action is partly motivated by Sissy Spacek. The farmer is once more squeezed between natural disaster and pressure from the bank, the latter being pressured itself by the large corporation. The film's notion of 'community' is complicated by the image of independent masculinity and by the inclusion of an industrial scene. Mel Gibson goes to work briefly in the city and realizes, after having committed himself to the job, that he is helping to break a strike. Although the strikers are pictured as violent, it is the strikebreakers who feel guilty. Mel Gibson has chosen an individual route out of his difficulties but that has led him to cross a picket line. When he himself needs solidarity, farmers turn out to help him control the flood, but Joe Wade, the film's corporate villain, hires unemployed help to dismantle their levee. As the water starts running through, Mel Gibson struggles against it alone, almost an allegorical figure of the individual faced with corporate power; but he is joined first by Sissy Spacek, then by his son, the other farmers, and the unemployed. It's an odd scene in that it seems both sentimentally optimistic and aware of eventual failure.

The scenes of solidarity, however fragile, seen in the two films were described by Hulbert as inauthentic and contrived. In fact, both films contain effective scenes of disrupted auctions of farming machinery, farmers chanting 'no sale', refusing to help to sell fellow farmers out. These have not only a basis in the present but also a tradition of farmers taking direct action. Through Iowa and extending into Minnesota, in the early 1930s, farmers used the tactic of the 'penny sales': when a sheriff put a bankrupt farmer's possessions up for sale, his friends prevented other people bidding and then bid for everything at ridiculously low prices, afterwards returning them to their friend as a permanent loan.[25] When Gil and Jewell's possessions are being valued, Jewell's father asks for a harness to be left out of the valuation as it belonged to his father. In the end it is auctioned but Gil and Jewell's son buys it back before the auction is halted. A moment of family history intersects with a larger history, a family possession retaining its meaning in a scene of dispossession. Such moments are the subject of the final section of this chapter but first other films with rural settings will be mentioned.

Places In the Heart directed by Robert Benton, draws on his own family history of the 1880s, being a fictionalized account of his great-grandmother's life shifted to the years of Benton's childhood, the Depression of the 1930s. Sally Field plays the wife of a sheriff who is killed in an accidental shooting, to keep her home she raises a crop of cotton, helped by a black vagrant, by her son, and by her blind lodger. They win out against the usual twin pressures of nature and the bank, but the Klan finally breaks up their community. Watching Sally Field the viewer may remember her role in *Norma Rae*, an example of the way that stars accumulate associations across films. Sissy Spacek and Jessica Lange help to link the figure of the farm wife to the country singer: Spacek played Loretta Lynn in *Coalminer's Daughter*, while Lange played Patsy Cline in *Sweet Dreams*. Both films belong to a cinematic re-appraisal of country post-*Nashville*, where the music is no longer seen through its sometimes tacky surroundings but as rooted in a Southern working class culture, Bruce Beresford's *Tender Mercies* with Robert Duvall being another fine example. Sam Shepard is discussed in the next chapter but it's worth pointing out that Ed Harris, who provides *Places in the Heart*'s subplot, also performed in Shepard's play *Fool For Love* and acts opposite Jessica Lange in *Sweet Dreams*. There is a chain of country connotations which performers bring with them from film to film; memories of other roles provide viewers paradoxically with a sense of authenticity.

There are more maverick pictures of rural America such as Louis Malle's *Alamo Bay*, a sort of displaced farm movie of threatened livelihoods, refused loans, and repossessed equipment in a Texan fishing community. This presents a more problematic picture than some of the other rural films, as it pits local white fishermen against Vietnamese immigrants. James Foley's *At Close Range* is also different as it uses its rural Pennsylvania setting for a crime story, with Sean Penn's teenage gang stealing expensive agricultural equipment, partly to impress Penn's criminal father, played in a hypnotic performance by Christopher Walken. Here the agrarian narrative of rustic virtue is overshadowed by the corruption normally associated with the city, and family ties need to be broken not preserved.

From family farm to mobile home

I discuss recent fiction in a later chapter but as a conclusion here some emblematic moments from recent short stories and novels will provide a condensed vision of a world in transition. Bobbie Ann Mason's collection, *Shiloh and Other Stories*, brings a variety of cultural, social, and geographical shifts into focus. People move from South to North: 'One day I was listening to Hank Williams and shelling corn for the chickens and the next day I was expected to know what wines went with what.'[26] Northern boyfriends are invited back to rural Kentucky, introducing a new self-consciousness:

> After supper, Nancy showed Jack the farm. As they walked through the fields, Nancy felt that he was seeing peaceful landscapes – arrangements of picturesque cows, an old red barn. She had never thought of the place this way before; it reminded her of prints in a dime store. (p. 184)

Couples who have been farming all their lives, sell up their land and livestock and buy campers and head to Florida.

In 'Old Things', Cleo has her daughter and grandchildren staying; having sold the farm on the death of her husband Cleo moved to town, selling off their possessions and starting anew. Having surrounded herself with 'modern' furniture, she finds out from her daughter that she is culturally out of step. While being socially more conservative than her daughter, and worrying about the latter's marriage, she finds her daughter turning to the past not as a repository of conservative values or traditions but as 'antique': 'Everybody's going back to old-timey stuff. Furniture like yours is out of style' (p. 87). To 'keep up with the times', you must buy what is called either 'junk' or 'antiques', depending on which generation you are. So Cleo and her friend Rita Jean go to 'trade day' at the stockyard.

> Most of the traders at the stockyard are farmers who trade in second-hand goods on the side. Cleo is shocked to realize this, though she knows nobody can make a living on a farm these days. She recognizes some of the farmers, behind their folding tables of dusty old objects. Even at the time of Jake's death, feeding the cows was costing almost as much as the milk brought. She cannot imagine Jake in a camper, peddling some old junk from the barn. That would kill him if the heart attack hadn't.
>
> Cleo and Rita Jean drift from table to table, touching Depression glass, crystal goblets, cracked china, cast-off egg beaters and mixers, rusted farm implements, and greasy wooden boxes stuffed with buttons and papers. (p. 91)

Here the farm has become the cultural equivalent of the family attic. In another story a restaurant recycles tools of labour as visual decoration, part of a transition from old to new South.

We ate at a place where you choose your food from pictures on a wall, then wait at a numbered table for the food to appear. On another wall was a framed arrangement of farm tools against red felt. Other objects – saw handles, scythes, pulleys – were mounted on wood like fish trophies. I could hardly eat for looking at the tools. I was wondering what my father's old tit-cups and dehorning shears would look like on the wall of a restaurant. (p. 129)

Mason's fiction of the South in transition is shaped by the persistence of memory, the confusion of values, the overlapping of cultures in a world where tradition rubs shoulders with, and is re-invented by, popular culture. *Leaving the Land* by Douglas Unger is probably the most ambitious recent agrarian narrative, covering the changes in a South Dakota farming family. It is apt that a novel dealing so much with the memory of work, and in itself an impressive work of memory, was in its writing, as Ted Solotaroff informs us, a first novel worked on, reworked, put aside in disappointment, reworked again, and encouraged as so much recent fiction has been by Raymond Carver.[27]

The setting shifts between the Hogan family farm and the small town of Nowell, and jumps in time from Marge Hogan's marriage to Jim Vogel, a lawyer working for the novel's representative of agribusiness, the Nowell-Safebuy, to Kurt, their son, returning to Nowell after its economy has collapsed and most people have left, Marge being an exception. The novel interweaves small town discontent with large historical events, within the complex relation between family farmers, Nowell-Safebuy, and the government. Family history has an almost mythic quality; the distance from Ben Hogan to his grandson Kurt seems vast. The Hogan farm 'had a tight board house that had once been a railroad station'. Ben had 'moved that house on rollers eighteen miles from the town of Nowell'.[28] And then built a barn with logs he cut himself in the Black Hills. Things change with the bombing of Pearl Harbor. With the entry of the United States into the war, the state intervenes in farming, setting priorities. Ben Hogan can either raise sugar beet or turkeys; he could, of course, continue with his corn but he would get no government subsidies and a very low priority with transportation. The choice of turkeys leaves one literary route firmly closed – descriptions of the birds as either grotesque or stupid bar any agrarian romanticism (one cannot imagine, following Norris, the turkeys! the turkeys!). The country is almost defined as that which denies the romantic, crushing Marge's dreams of escape and of love: on the first night of her honeymoon, in the bathroom with her diaphragm and jelly, 'the whole process reminding her of greasing down a tractor bearing and shoving it home with two fingers' (p. 117). The farmer's life is expressed through politics not pastoral, as Ben argues with his neighbours in the Nowell Farmers' Organization, an activist splinter group of the Farmers' Union. Hogan is disappointed by the price offered by Nowell-Safebuy, reckoning that they could get a better deal in Omaha. He tries to bypass Nowell-Safebuy but the truck is intercepted and he quits raising turkeys. There is no market for his wheat and as other farmers get into trouble, Nowell-Safebuy buys them out. After a life on the land, the Hogans are amazed to hear Jim's talk about the company's vision of the future of agriculture: 'new miracle grains, new miracle fungicides, new miracle ten-ton tractors and planting techniques', hormones that will produce turkeys weighing over a hundred pounds.

Kurt's return switches us to first-person narration, as he comes back to a practically deserted town where coyotes roam freely at night, where rubbish swirls through the streets, and where the major industry, the Nowell-Safebuy turkey plant stands gutted and empty. He remembers when Safebuy had threatened to turn into a 'huge vertical farm' and he thinks of Buster Hill, its manager who died in the streets of the town that he had put on 'the map within the national system of Safebuy supermarts, raising a million Safebuy turkeys per year, writing out the paychecks for a thousand farmers and workers who took care of them'. After Hill's death, his successor Sam Carlson continued 'an industry-wide program of vertical integration', continuing to contract with farmers to buy turkeys a season ahead for a fixed price, so the farmers could borrow from the bank on the strength of the contract. Crisis hits this system with a national turkey surplus and, more pressingly for the farmer, the price of grain rises steeply. Farmers grow desperate as every day they keep their crop alive, they lose money. The novel gives us the retrospective story: the farmers' organizations and arguments; their decision to break their contracts with Nowell-Safebuy; their complaints about the company buying up family farms; finally, their horrific gesture of a mass destruction of their birds. The arguments become intense in Kurt's home as his mother still sides with the farmers and his father must act for the company. Carlson tries to make up for the drop in turkey prices with an increase in volume at the plant: 'six thousand turkeys a day slaughtered, plucked, processed, packed a dozen different ways'. The rains in August add to the high cost of grain: 'Times were hard. But according to the small farmers, times had always been hard' (pp. 151, 153–4, 169–70).

The turkey plant takes two years to shut down as expenses rise, prices are low, and volume declines.

The Nowell-Safebuy completely restructured its system of farms. The logical extreme of vertical integration was direct ownership of the land. When the smoke finally cleared from the N.F.O. protests and the violent upheavals in local farm credit during hard times for farmers, the Nowell-Safebuy began to buy land.

Kurt gives an example: Ben Reary's farm was overextended and he couldn't get the First Bank of Belle Fourche 'to extend his loans or to refinance, couldn't get president David Whitcomb to give him what farmers called the guts and hide loan, "the loan it takes the banker a barrowload of guts to give and everyone involved stands to lose his hide"'. Sam Carlson visits Reary's farm and inspects his 'long steel outbuildings' in which he keeps 'ten thousand White Holland hybrid turkeys in tier upon tier of wire cages'. It's important to stress the toughness of the novel here; the family farm is purely a matter of *ownership*, not some kind of small-scale, free-range alternative to agribusiness methods. Carlson watches Reary push the buttons on his new Harvestore silo, 'like a huge thermos bottle standing between his turkey barns, which let loose its measured doses of dry, vacuum-packed feed with a powerful inrush of air'. The description continues with the whoosh of the feeder, the food moving down the troughs, the noise of the turkeys, feathers fluttering across the barn, beaks clattering against the troughs. Reary shows off his cornfields, 400 acres which produce enough for his silo.

He showed off his tractor, as big as a small house, his discs and harrows and seeders as wide as a two-lane highway, which were costing him thousands of dollars per quarter just in interest. Sam Carlson produced a sheaf of papers, dozens of forms, prospectuses, statistical graphs, even a health insurance plan.

He offers to pay off all Reary's loans, buy his turkeys, buildings and equipment, and give him several thousand dollars 'to count as equity for the work of two generations'. He would still live and work there, 'as "unit farm manager" to work turkeys for the Nowell-Safebuy, just like the plant workers in town'. Reary tries to sell elsewhere but, 'That next harvest, Ben Reary and many other small farmers raised turkeys for wages' (pp. 177–9).

One of the advantages of this unsentimental, unromantic view of Reary's loss is that Carlson's policy is seen as just that, not a conspiracy but part of the received economic wisdom. That wisdom is later shaken. Kurt says that Carlson should have known, should have heard of 'the Bates Rubber Company's fiasco in northwest Colorado'.

Bates bought up hundreds of thousands of acres of wheat and grazing land, pumping millions of investment dollars into the most modern cattle feeders, into a fleet of tractors powerful enough to level mountains and into a new crossbreed of cattle that could grow to weights of up to two thousand pounds in eighteen months with the aid of growth hormones.

Farming is no longer juxtaposed with the world of Eastern finance capital:

Everything was beautifully described in color brochures printed by the thousands for stockbrokerage firms in the East, including graphed projections of vast profits symbolically represented to the potential investor by line drawings of a series of even fatter steers growing across the page.

But Bates ends up having to hire one and a half times as many unit farm managers as there had been family farmers, for no real increase in production. The way of life versus business opposition re-emerges with deadpan irony as Bates discovers 'after intensive sociological research' that whereas family farmers would work eighteen hours a day just to 'hold on to the land', unit farm managers 'punched their time clocks after eight hours and drove home. Production dropped.' Soon the Bates Land and Cattle Company began losing millions. Here the book shows a rare flicker of anger:

Leading agrieconomists in the East, most of them men who had never so much as once experienced the realities of scraping barnyard manure off their boots, suddenly stopped talking about the benefits of vertical integration. They sat discoursing around a brand-new topic called 'farm unit management problems'.

The same story unfolds slowly in Nowell, with two hundred workers laid off at the turkey plant (p. 180).

The turkey plant moves towards shutdown and the NFO tries to raise money through federal loan programmes to form a turkey farming co-operative, and buy the processing plant and machinery.

After a history-making court decision in the dairy industry set a legal precedent, the federal government decided its loans to farm cooperatives could not be used to purchase means of production such as processing plants. Such cooperative ownership of processing was called 'socialist agricultural policy' by editorials in many newspapers.

The Nowell-Safebuy has other plans, wanting to move the machinery to a small town in Minnesota, 'much nearer main arteries of trans-portation'. And they have plans for the country around Nowell. To help to control the production of grain, Congress 'decided to pay subsidies to farmers for not growing crops'. Sam Carlson's final decisions as general manager included putting 'all land purchases here on long-term financing. Then he announced a plan for the conversion of all Nowell-Safebuy real estate in this country into wheat farms.'

> Much of the land could sit idle that way, federal wheat allotment subsidies paying the interest on the bank loans the Nowell-Safebuy had used to buy farms. Many years later, with the new technologies of chisel-plowing, with aerial seeding, with new pesticides and herbicides slowly sifting earthward in pungent yellow clouds under the drone of airplanes, with tractors as big as houses, with discs and harrows wider than any farmer here would have imagined possible, nearly as wide as a four-lane highway, two hired men eventually farmed the same number of acres it had once taken twenty families to farm.

The turkey plant shuts and vast, eighteen-wheeler trucks take away the dismantled machinery, leaving only a 'storm of ancient factory dust and bits of white feathers' in the deserted yards. The 'For Sale' signs start going up then, gradually, as people can no longer find buyers for the houses and they just leave (pp. 193–4).

The value of an unromanticized and detailed account like this story of an industry and a town falling apart is enhanced by the novel's investigation of local attempts to make sense of these events. In the largely deserted town café (ex)farmers still argue about vertical integration and what they should have done. Occasionally the outside world intrudes, air force men drop into the café after a shift underground in one of the prairie missile silos. But mainly it is a shattered town trying to make sense of its recent past. Kurt is a neutral witness to the collapse, a literal collapse in the case of many of the buildings, of his hometown. The public library still exists and it strikes him 'that a historian of the future might best describe this town by what books have never been read here' (p. 197). This detached view from someone who has come back unwillingly, provides a more productive framework for the town's decline than any easy rhetoric about 'community', and it gives a greater weight to some of the final moments of Nowell. At the height of the town's panic, after the bank closed, when almost everyone had lost their jobs, and just as people start to leave secretively, leaving behind unsold houses and unpaid debts, many of the people left turn to the Reverend Ott for the church's response. He knows that they expect and want fire, brimstone, and accusation, and leaves his sickbed for a desperate congregation convinced 'that somehow they had brought disaster upon themselves'. Kurt recounts that the minister produced a newspaper and said, 'I'm going to read to you from the only faith this country's got left.' He slowly reads through the farm prices ('October turkeys ... twenty-six, that's down two cents. Hard winter wheat ... two dollars and seven cents this December'), then pauses. Saying, 'This is what the Lord says', he turns to the Bible and reads: *'every one that thirsteth, come ye to the waters, and he that hath no money, come ye, buy and eat; yea, come, buy wine and milk without money and without price.'* A week later he is dead and the church is finally sold to Great Westward Sugar, Inc. (pp. 223–5).

Kurt comments that the town found a temporary resource in 'antiques'. A 'random car full of curiosity seekers passed through town' every now and then and people would stop to explore the old, abandoned houses. 'A chimney from a kerosene lamp was treated with similar awe and reverence as an arrowhead or a flint knifeblade of the Sioux.' They picked up 'countless old bottles, tools, furniture, knick-knacks. They inspected them, exclaimed over their treasures, carried armloads of booty to their cars.' The café owner would then walk out, claiming the objects were his: 'He figured he averaged about fifteen dollars a car this way' (pp. 195–6). This resembles the uneasy relation to the past seen above in Bobbie Ann Mason's stories, but it also has an immediate context in the scene of the post-funeral auction after the death of Kurt's grandfather. He describes a frenzied carrying away of equipment, a dismantling of the past. Pieces of his grand-father's life, representing a whole history of labour and the slow building-up of a farm, lie piled up in front of his house. Marge thinks that it is better that neighbours end up with her father's things than for them to be never used. But she then sees a man struggling out of the barn with 'a load of tack and harness', carrying so much that he looks two feet taller, 'a kind of weird giant with a bale of tangled leather for his head'. She sees her bridle among the load and argues with the man. Kurt tries to help her, suddenly seeing a new severity in his mother's face: 'something showing in it that I had never seen before – like the faces of old tintypes of my family where the inflexible cast to the mouth, the deep lines around harsh, distant eyes tell of hardship, scant food, the deaths of children'. The man deliberately drops the bridle without looking back:

> It was a work of remarkable beauty, brown and white horsehair braided into a diamond pattern, the reins at least six feet long, fluted Spanish silver bells woven into the cheek straps and two large, dark green onyx jewels set into silver dollars where the headband joined that part that fastened behind a horse's ears.

This object finally unlocks Marge's grief and loss and she turns and hugs Kurt (pp. 187–8, 189–90).

Thinking over the incident with the harness, Kurt wonders what

Don Hinkle would do with all of it, as he no longer has a team. As in Mason's Southern restaurant, the useful is turned into the decorative. Kurt pictures him hanging it around the farmhouse, decorations displayed with 'scattered implements in one corner of the dining room', just as his grandfather's house had 'antique implements arranged' around it, 'like so many exhibits in a museum'.

I imagined a set of horse collars and harness hung over the heating stove. I thought of bell straps hung up so they would jangle in a summer breeze. In my mind, I heard an old man's voice spinning tales and outright lies about that harness, stories of just how it was when he was a young man out there horse farming, *gee hawing* and slogging through sod-covered earth sowing homestead wheat with that very same tack hanging right there on his walls.

Here is the nearest the novel comes to the agrarian scene, the honest yeoman, and it is explicitly located as fiction. But why take the harness, why invent this tradition, and especially, why should a farmer create this fantasy past? Kurt finally thinks he understands: '*Ownership was not to be confused with heritage.* That harness would hang for years as decoration, until Don Hinkle eventually sold his farm or died. Then it would all be stolen back again from him' (pp. 191–2, emphasis added). The Nowell-Safebuy may end up owning most of the land but nobody possesses the heritage.

Kurt's move on to his grandfather's farm leads to a powerful meditation on the work of farming which takes the opposition between tradition and agribusiness popular in other representations and makes it problematic. As with the earlier descriptions of the turkeys, agricultural labour is seen in close-up not framed by notions of the dignity of labour or the virtues of husbandry or the authenticity of proximity to nature and the soil. Kurt's work includes castrating lambs and scraping scabs off their gums. Sore mouth disease is, understandably, not a common feature of pastoral. Viewed from Kurt's perspective the tractor 'as big as a house' seen on the horizon may still be imagined as 'a bright red mechanical insect' but it is judged in a totally different way to Steinbeck's juxtaposition of families and dehumanizing machinery. The tractor is part of the Nowell-Safebuy's new wheat-farming operation, on land that once belonged to a family farmer but is now 'part of forty thousand acres of wheatland' farmed 'with maybe a half-dozen employees'. It is seeded in the fall, sprayed by planes in the spring. The Nowell-Safebuy

maybe sent a tractor out like that one, once in a summer, to sweep the weeds off fallow land. Then just waited. That was all. Waited for the combine crews to harvest all the grain, working their way up north all the way from Texas. Doing it that way, it was possible to take this one state and raise enough grain to feed the entire Indian subcontinent with a bare minimum of human toil. And, like my father, I believed it was right that way.

His father, the lawyer, his mother, the farmer's daughter: Kurt's parents rework a classic populist opposition within a family. Kurt sees the wheat operation as just 'so much more efficient than what I was doing. The point was food, quantities of food.' Why value sweat and hard labour when farming can look so easy? With

> that tractor driver in his air-conditioned cab, that wonderful machine crawling across the face of the same earth it would have taken my ancestors forty years to plow. What matter if a whole style of life was gone? What matter if the earth no longer served a single family, a small parcel of immortality for the common man? All that was lost to me, as lost as a cherry orchard in which people no longer knew the meaning of cherries, as lost as the unwritten language of a long-expired race of men. All that mattered was food, the wheat on the hill, the hay in the meadow, the mutton under my boot. Whatever method could raise them best and most efficiently would win the prizes of the earth. There was little beauty to it, in my mind. There was only sweat, and maybe a certain sense of unspeakable smallness in my soul in that of all the generations behind me, of all the lost tribes of my forefathers who had dug potatoes, milked cows, sown grain, picked fruit from primeval gardens, it had all come down to me in a knowledge I only wished to lose. (pp. 247–8)

It would be a mistake to read Kurt's voice as necessarily the voice of the author. The novel's representation of agribusiness and its frequent mentions of hormones used in farming possibly qualifies this endorsement of efficiency over tradition. The point is the power of Kurt's voice, the authority of one who knowing the traditions also calls them into question. So as Kurt and Marge visit the Belle Fourche Safebuy to stock up for Christmas, the supermarket's abundance is seen from the point of view of memories of a pinched life of work. Consumption allows labour to be forgotten, and this is a mystification in which Kurt and his mother are willingly complicit. Above the freezer the slogans of the chain that closed the Nowell turkey plant say 'Merry Christmas from Safebuy' and 'All America Loves Safebuy Turkeys'. And rows of birds condense and deny the history that the rest of the novel has examined:

> I looked at them, inspecting their labels, most of them Safebuy brand from Minnesota, most of them injected with oils and marked 'self-basting', most of them with a bright red plastic button that popped up erectly out of the breast when the bird was roasted. (pp. 266–7)

The passage can be read ironically but that it is to read against the challenge of Kurt's feelings, a challenge to easy pastoral, to traditions, to the self-evidence of the agrarian tradition.

The novel ends with Kurt on his grandfather's farm, wondering what to do with this inheritance of memory and tradition. He thinks of his grandfather 'out in the first spring sun *gee-hawing* to his team, pushing his horses to drag a single plowshare a half acre a day through thick clay sod'. He thinks of the others still alive, dispossessed farmers, his mother, all witnesses to the slow death of a way of life. He knows why they still hold on, the power of their memories.

> It was like a secret now, an all-but-unobtainable secret once a wisdom strong enough to move whole tribes across mountains, whole nations across oceans, my own grandfather across half a continent in a Model T Ford that stuck in reverse gear on the journey so he had to back up the last two hundred miles. Then he found the house we were in, a seldom used line station for the railroad that he put on log rollers and hitched to his team, moving it inch by inch eighteen miles to this piece of dry prairie he could call his own. It was the knowledge of his generation that if at first you don't succeed at life, you can always learn to plow. I thought, *There must be other secrets now and I don't know them.* (pp. 276–7)

Another Marge narrates a final scene of dispossession in Raymond Carver's short story 'The Bridle'. She runs a motel in Arizona with her husband Harley and the story opens with 'an old station wagon with Minnesota plates' pulling in:

> These people looked whipped. There are clothes hanging inside; suitcases, boxes, and such piled in back. From what Harley and I put together later, that's all they had left after the bank in Minnesota took their house, their pickup, their tractor, the farm implements, and a few cows.

Harley calls them the Swedes (shades of Cather's pioneers) and asks what the man does. When Marge says, 'He's a farmer', Harley replies 'There's not much to farm around here.' The family are called Holits and their failure belongs to the world of Carver's losers rather than to the agrarian tradition. Marge sees them unloading their boxes and cases and watches Holits carry in 'something that has straps hanging from it. It takes a minute, but then I figure out it's a bridle.' What at first looks like a rural reminder is later revealed to be the cause of their failure. (Holits bought a racehorse and ran through their money paying for it, keeping it and, above all, betting on it.)

When they finally leave for an unknown destination, Marge goes to clear out their unit. She finds the bridle left in a corner, and wonders if it was forgotten or left behind deliberately. The story closes with a brilliantly compressed passage, using the bridle as a symbol for determined, driven as well as drifting, lives. At the end of Carver's story it stands for both a rural life left behind and for the failure of that life, as well as for the pressures of their current existence. At the end of this chapter it reminds us of other bridles, other losses (*Country*, *Leaving the Land*, Mason's fiction), of ways of life transformed and lost, farmers entering mills and factories, Okies setting out for California in a used car, echoes of change heard through history, films, fiction, country music.

'Bridle', I say. I hold it up to the window and look at it in the light. It's not fancy, it's just an old dark leather bridle. I don't know much about them. But I know that one part of it fits in the mouth. That part's called the bit. It's made of steel. Reins go over the head and up to where they're held on the neck between the fingers. The rider pulls the reins this way and that, and the horse turns. It's simple. The bit's heavy and cold. If you had to wear this thing between your teeth, I guess you'd catch on in a hurry. When you felt it pull, you'd know it was time. You'd know you were going somewhere.[29]

3 Sam Shepard's cowboy mouth:
representing masculinity

When *Paris, Texas* was released in 1984, Sam Shepard, overcoming his usual distrust of publicity and the press, gave several interviews to British magazines. Chris Peachment concluded his *Time Out* interview with an anecdote about a woman journalist from a continental newspaper seeking to talk with Shepard. Her interpreter was 'one of those New York intellectuals whose trademark is an extreme pomposity of language which makes the short hairs on your neck stand up. Watching Shepard, you can see his hackles rising.' The problems of the proposed interview were aggravated by not having a tape recorder, a lack which the translator tries to justify in an 'incredibly verbose' way. Peachment observes the scene leading up to Shepard's reaction. The New York intellectual talks on:

> but if the poor fool had ever stepped outside Manhattan and watched a horse, he would have spotted an extraordinary transformation come over Shepard. He lowers his head and looks with apparent concentration at his cowboy boots. His nostrils flare. His eyes narrow and peer out sideways at the man, for all the world like a bad horse, watching the approach of a rider smelling of fear.

The story ends with Shepard saying no to the interview: 'Fine thing to watch, that, a man who can't stand bullshit.'[1] Shepard here is not so much revealed as mythicized. Nature is opposed to culture as hackles rise, nostrils flare, and eyes narrow, and the West is opposed to both the Old World of the continental journalist and the Manhattan world of the intellectual. The horse simile combines with the cowboy boots to juxtapose the laconic style of the cowboy and the pompous and pretentious verbosity of the city, a peculiarly American style prompted by European incomprehension. There is even a tradition into which the anecdote could slot: the Easterner or the European out West, where the tenderfoot is undermined by the cowboy's knowledge.

Populist images of the intellectual are generally negative: urban, rootless, pretentious, and in populism's more virulent, small-town conspiracy theories, Jewish and un-American. American populism's central notion of honest work raises the uneasy question of writing's relation to other forms of labour. Writers may celebrate the authenticity of agricultural labour or focus on its numbingly repetitive nature, but either way writing seems an *escape* from this work, a utopian practice that fuses toil and pleasure. In Shepard's *True West*, Lee needles his brother Austin about his job as a Hollywood scriptwriter, saying he is 'paid to dream'. Austin protests that it is not that easy, 'There's a lot of work involved', to which Lee replies: 'what's the toughest part? Deciding whether to jog or play tennis?'[2] Writing and work are raised as an issue by Shepard when the editors of *Theatre Quarterly* ask him if he thought of playwriting as his 'real job', once his plays were performed in the mid-1960s. Shepard says that he never thought of it as a job, 'because it was something that made me feel more relaxed', whereas jobs were 'something that made you feel less alive – you know, the thing of working ten hours a day cleaning horseshit out of a stable'.[3] Writing here is seen as an escape from the oppressive routines of work, and Shepard also refers to writing as 'play', probably influenced by 1960s theories of art and theatre and critiques of 'one dimensional' alienated society. He began writing plays in 'the hope of extending the sensation of *play* (as in 'kid') on into adult life. If 'play' becomes 'labor', why play?'[4]

Shepard's career certainly follows a recognizable pattern: from country to city, from 'work' to 'play'. He has described his childhood on an avocado ranch in California: 'it was a real nice place actually. It was like a little greenhouse that had been converted into a house, and it had livestock and horses and chickens and stuff like that. Plus about 65 avocado trees.' He 'really liked being in contact with animals and the whole agricultural thing', at one time thinking of becoming a vet. 'And I had a chance actually to manage a sheep ranch, but I didn't take it. I wanted to do something like that, working with animals.' He even had 'the grand champion yearling ram at the Los Angeles County Fair one fair. I did. It was a great ram.' He moved to New York, partly under the influence of the Beats, living on the Lower East Side and starting to write plays. He worked at the Village Gate, seeing some of the best of American jazz.[5] However, both sides of this city/country contrast are more complex than this sketch of pastoral simplicity and urban sophistication might suggest. Rural adolescence also contains memories of amphetamines and joyriding, while New York is not celebrated in itself but precisely as a place where people from outside the city were drifting to and creating a culture. Shepard recalls the mid-1960s on the Lower East Side: 'I mean nobody knew what was happening, but there was a sense that something was going on. People were arriving from Texas and Arkansas in the middle of New York City, and a community was being established. It was a very exciting time.'[6] The journey from champion rams to meeting Nina Simone is reflected in the landscape of Shepard's work, a landscape where populist themes of the land and a popular culture of the image are fused together.

Sam Shepard's career ranges across several cultural forms. He is one of the best living American dramatists; he is a powerful film actor (Terence Malick's *Days of Heaven, The Right Stuff*, acting opposite Jessica Lange in *Frances* and *Country*, and acting in *Fool for Love*, his own play turned into a film by Robert Altman); his involvement with music stretches from drumming with the Holy Modal Rounders to his role as observer with Dylan's 1975 Rolling Thunder Revue and his participation in *Renaldo and Clara*, and, perhaps more importantly, to the numerous jazz, rock, and country references that punctuate and shape his plays. The mixture of writing and performance brings together text and life to form Shepard's image, constructed partly from his work and partly by the media. His life echoes in the autobiographical elements in his plays and in prose like *Motel Chronicles* and *Hawk Moon*, and his writing seems to spill over into his life. We've already seen in the showdown between cowboy and intellectual that opened this chapter, how Shepard is written about in a way that identifies him almost completely with the world of his plays, as a kind of thinking person's John Wayne. His work and life may conspire to form this image but his writing also reflects on this image-making process. *The Tooth of Crime* is Shepard's sustained investigation of a modern condition where images compete and overlap, with the struggle set in the arena of rock music. Spalding Gray, who played Hoss in the play, discussed in an interview how he had become something of a star through acting in a play about stardom, in a role that shifted his interest from theatre to performance. He tells an amusing story of Shepard coming to one of his solo performances and inviting him to go to a Lou Reed concert. Gray says that driving in 'this huge, Bronco Ford truck, with him driving in his cowboy hat, it suddenly hit me that this was a style match between Hoss and Crow'. A match building on their identities 'as Spalding Gray, the performer, and ... Sam Shepard, the playwright', which becomes literal when Gray accepts Shepard's challenge to a game of pool. Remembering the game, Gray sees it as bringing the play back to life with its central image duel between Hoss and Crow: 'I'm not saying one was Hoss and one was Crow but it was definitely two styles coming together – the Western cowboy man and the East Coast salt-tweed man.'[7] The anecdote suggests another way of seeing Shepard's image and the concern with images in his work, rather than seeing Shepard as *natural* (the flaring nostrils and anti-intellectualism of the opening story) one might more profitably look at his self-consciousness about images, with Shepard reflecting on American myths and performing them rather than embodying them.

Cowboy Mouth, the play that Shepard wrote with Patti Smith and performed with her in 1971, dramatizes their life together in the Chelsea Hotel, with Shepard even commenting on the guilt of having left his wife and child. But rather than being just an autobiographical account of their relationship, the play revolves around images of rock music and stardom and the brief lives of American singers and French poets. That is to say, that rather than being self-dramatizing, the play is about their need for heroes and their relation as writers and performers to those heroes. Similarly, Patti Smith's poem 'Sam Shepard: 9 Random Years (7 + 2)' mixes events from Shepard's life with themes from his work in a way which simultaneously mythicizes Shepard and reveals his relation to American myths.

The poem blends together cars, guitars, horses, cowboys, and artists in an American celebration of 'the poetry of Speed'. In '1964' Patti Smith captures a turning-point: *'December 30.* Sam Shepard wrote his first play *Cowboys* in true pioneer style ... on the back of used Tootsie Roll wrappers.'[8] Cowboys, pioneers, and Tootsie Rolls: one of the fascinations of Shepard's work is this kind of collision between traditional American figures and contemporary pop or junk culture. One of the bridges that links the cowboy to the rock star, or the mustang as horse to the Mustang as car, is the theme of masculinity. Shepard links this question of masculinity to 'Americanness' in his work and in his image, across both writing and performance. Masculinity is the often unspoken assumption behind many populist themes of work, independence, and the strength of 'the people', hence the interesting twist that some of the works discussed in the previous chapter give to these themes by linking them to women rather than men. In Shepard's work masculinity connects the American West to popular culture and to literary tradition, a problematic connection for many critics.

Bonnie Marranca suggests that one of the most problematic features of Shepard's work is his 'consistent refusal or inability ... to create female characters whose imaginative range matches that of the males'. Women are 'the background of the plays' while men 'take risks, face challenges, experience existential crises'. Marranca continues: 'For a young man Shepard's portrayal of women is as outdated as the frontier ethic he celebrates.' The plays always define women through their relation to men, never expressing a woman's point of view. 'Shepard has no apparent interest in the relations of men and women, preferring instead to write about male experience. He writes as if he is unaware of what has been happening between men and women in the last decade.'[9] Autonomous women in his work find their freedom through male images and escape routes, like Cavale in *Cowboy Mouth* created through Patti Smith's obsession with rock music and (male) outlaws and poets, or Emma in *Curse of the Starving Class*, who breaks out of the family via a masculine mix of Westerns (riding and shooting up a bar) and the Beats (going on the road, driving down to Mexico). Marranca connects this reactionary portrayal of women to the frontier ethic and the cowboy image, expressing surprise that Shepard's youth hasn't forced him to transform this ethic. This is a point that needs to be reversed, but the role of the cowboy in shaping masculinity in the plays needs to be pursued.

Marranca sees the cowboy as representing 'a longing for heroes and heroic deeds' which is central to the myth of the West, to Shepard's work, and to America's self-image. Even Henry Kissinger has compared himself to a cowboy.[10] That particular comparison is taken up by Florence Falk in her essay, 'Men without women: the Shepard landscape', which opens with Kissinger's remark about acting alone and resembling a cowboy, a remark made in an interview with Oriana Fallaci. Falk points out that the lone cowboy 'moves straight to the heartland fantasy of America'; but asks why Kissinger would draw on this fantasy, which he later described as his worst mistake in dealing with the media, when interviewed by 'an especially provocative woman journalist'. She suggests that it is because the cowboy image 'glorifies the male'. It

> costumes him in unfeeling masculinity (his horse, a kind of pedestal) to display virility and hint at imminent violence; places him in the open spaces and tells him they are his (even the sunset he rides into); tells him like an obliging woman, a woman who knows her place (in contrast to Oriana Fallaci who refuses to be so consigned), that the landscape has been swept free of rules, regulations, and commitments.

So the cowboy *is* masculinity in Shepard's work; in the plays, 'the cowboy is the reigning male; consequently, *any* female is, perforce, marginalized'.[11]

Marranca and Falk's arguments about the cowboy and sexual politics are linked to an earlier point in Marranca's essay, concerning the politics of the West. 'The spirit of the American West, its triumph of individualism, unlimited potential, transcendent beauty, and disdain of regulation is the soul of Shepard's work.' Marranca adds: 'It is also the same philosophy that put Ronald Reagan in the White House ... the frontier ethic turns ugly when set in global, even national perspective'. Alongside this frontier ethic, 'and its concomitant isolationism, oppressive view of women, retreat from group concerns', there is Shepard's other side, 'sixties-style radical politics with its dread of the "system", its pastoral ideals, and persistent criticism of the American way of life'. The 'political tension' of the plays stems from a 'tug-of-war between radical ideals . . . and a deeply-felt conservatism that is never fully resolved in the plays'. This duality which, 'sadly, history has shown resolves itself to the right', is seen by Marranca as embodying 'all that is good and bad in the conscience of the American people'. It is also 'the mark of Shepard's provincialism and his essential Americanness'.[12]

One problem with these generally perceptive criticisms is the assumption of the 'progressive' nature of the 1960s influence on Shepard (remember Marranca expressed surprise at Shepard's view of women, given his youth), which ignores the radical side of what is seen as the Western and conservative pole in the plays, conceding those themes to Reagan. However, if we stay with the problematic representation of women, many of the oppressive features in Shepard's work can be traced back to the 1960s and 1970s, the counter-culture and the rock culture rather than the myth of the West. In a short piece from *Hawk Moon*, 'WIPE OUT (To be read while listening to "Wild Horses")', Cobra Moonstar falls on his Les Paul Gibson. Having collapsed on his guitar he wishes he had a woman 'to make a coke run or massage his back or give him some head or just talk about something like early Yardbirds'. In the absence of a woman he ends up raping his guitar: 'The guitar seemed to dig it too. The harder he pumped the more she screamed.'[13] Admittedly this slight piece can be read as mocking the shallow macho fantasies of rock but similar fantasies occur elsewhere in Shepard's work, his description of *Operation Sidewinder*'s Honey, for example: '*a very sexy chick with long blonde hair and tight pants, high heels, etc.*'[14] This 1968 play resolves its confused politics (black students at Yale demanded its withdrawal from production) by a retreat into Indian myth, which exemplifies the casual appropriation of other cultures, typical of 1960s culture. The aspects of Shepard's early work which draw parallels between theatre and ritual, a parallel built partly on drug references, look remarkably shallow now. Jack Gelber's famous description of Shepard as shaman, 'a New World shaman', demonstrates the need to construct an alternative American identity. 'There are no witches on broomsticks within these pages. That's the Old World. Sam is as American as peyote, magic mushrooms, Rock and Roll, and medicine bundles.'[15] But this alternative to Mom, baseball, and apple pie also demonstrates the poverty of the counter-culture's imagination.

Shepard's writing is more interesting when playing (with) cowboys rather than playing (at) Indians. Critical references to his 'Americanness' or to masculinity in his work tend to overlook the complexity and contradictions of these notions. Certain speeches are often quoted in discussions of Shepard ('I was made in America. Born, bred and raised. I have American blood. I dream American dreams', from *Operation Sidewinder* or the Whitman references in *Action*), which tend to close off arguments and elide irony or contradiction. Falk's argument, cited above, leads us to a more interesting notion of masculinity in Shepard's work:

> To succeed, Shepard's males play at being *Men*, his females at being *Women*; that is, both sexes act out not necessarily what men and women *are* but how they imagine Men and Women *behave*. Their depictions, imagistically indebted to the mass media, are exaggerated, simplified, and codified, since advertising transmits to the culture the commercial, idealized representations of Men and Women that actual men and women rely on to define themselves.[16]

Shepard can be seen not as endorsing simplified images of masculinity but as investigating their production within the cultural imagination: 'Shepard's characters have been seduced and enslaved by manufactured images that designate "male" and "female," "hero" and "heroine," or even "mom," "dad," and "family."'[17] He *does* present a theatre of masculinity but with attention to the roles and masks involved rather than using naturalized cultural notions of masculinity and femininity. Masculinity becomes the object of an impossible quest, rather than being seen as the given fact of gender or the naturalized social notions and cultural images. In *The Tooth of Crime*, Hoss says to Crow: 'Now show me how to be a man.' Crow's answer points to the cultural substitution of images of masculinity for the missing fact: 'A man's too hard, Leathers. Too many doors to that room. A Gypsy's easy.'[18]

As opposed to the facile collage of images (cowboys, rock stars, pirates, outlaws, Mae West, Marlene, etc.) that makes up *Mad Dog Blues*, *The Tooth of Crime* investigates the circulation of the image in modern popular culture. In the central contest of styles between Hoss and Crow, a mixture of Western gun fight and the musical combat (the 'battle of the bands', reggae DJs, hip-hop's rappers) Hoss's sense of musical and cultural history is pitted against Crow's pure simulation of styles (an opposition picked up later in this book, with the discussion in Chapter 6 of music and tradition). At stake is success and power – 'turf' – but behind these the real contest appears to concern masculinity and the ability to mime its cultural images. At one point, Hoss wonders if there is still an 'outside' to his world's mix of science fiction, Westerns, crime, and music. The alternative is the terrain of populist rather than popular culture.

HOSS: What about the country then. Ain't there any farmers left, ranchers, cowboys, open space? Nobody just livin' their life.
BECKY: You ain't playin' with a full deck, Hoss. All that's gone. That's old time boogie. The only way to be an individual is in the game. You're it. You're on top. You're free.[19]

Like Hoss, Shepard is also 'in the game', working in a world of images as both writer and performer, but looking back to the promise of America's landscape. We have seen that the way he has been discussed, in both journalism and criticism, identifies him with this promise. So it is not just his work that is seen to be representing masculinity, it is also himself, combining in critics' views the positive and negative features of America's masculine myths and traditions. Although his work plays with the theme of the artist's escape – the Sam Peckinpah-style rescue of Cody in *Geography of a Horse Dreamer*, the mention of B. Traven and his escape to Mexico in *Curse of the Starving Class* – those escapes can never be as real for him as for writers who are not so involved with performance. Even his distance from publicity suggests not the mysterious silence of a Thomas Pynchon or J. D. Salinger but the taciturn cowboy mouth of Clint Eastwood. Even if there is no 'outside' to this world of images and representations, Hoss's question – 'What about the country?' – is central to Shepard's writing and the theme of the land will now be considered.

'What's happened to the lemon orchards?'

The above question is screamed by Wheeler, a Hollywood executive, as he looks out of the window at Los Angeles. The answer is that 'Those were plowed under to make room for the new lots.'[20] And that kind of juxtaposition of the natural or traditional with modernity is fairly typical of *Angel City*. The play's flaw seems to be its inability to decide whether Rabbit, who arrives in Hollywood with his medicine bundles, having travelled down by buckboard and 'a team a' horses', stopping off at all the missions, represents an alternative magic to that of the frenzied machinery of Hollywood. Is the shaman corrupted by the sham or is he complicit with its dreams of disaster? The discontinuity in landscape, from lemons to lots, suggests in a rather simplified way the themes of the country versus the city, the traditional versus the modern. Elsewhere, in Shepard's work as an actor, one can find a powerful, but ultimately rather reactionary, image of a *continuity*. In Philip Kaufman's film of Tom Wolfe's *The Right Stuff*, Sam Shepard plays the test pilot, Chuck Yeager. One resonant image occurs when Yeager is out riding in the desert, and stops to look down at the orange plane in which he will break the sound barrier. It's an image that confirms Shepard/Yeager as having the *real* right stuff; the cowboy loner as opposed to the team spirit of the astronauts, having personal integrity rather than their fame which is manipulated by politicians and NASA. At the level of rhetoric, the horse, desert, and plane fuse old and new frontiers, past and present pioneers; and the setting, the Mojave desert and what is now Edwards Air Force Base, is peculiarly apt as a setting for Shepard, being referred to frequently in many of his plays.

If both these images, one of discontinuity, the other of a continuous spirit, offer too simplified a picture of the connotations of the Western landscape, the plays provide more complex scenes. Although I have criticized above the somewhat empty nature of some of Shepard's collage-like works (*Mad Dog Blues*, for instance), part of his interest lies in his use of overlapping genres. The characters in *Curse of the Starving Class* were brilliantly described by Stanley Kauffmann: 'They are something like John Steinbeck's Okies seen by Donald Barthelme.'[21] His remark points to the gap between populist themes and their modern treatment. The play, which will be discussed later, not only fuses country and city worlds, farming and crime, but also plays with formal disruptions, its country themes visually interrupting its rather traditional form as a family melodrama, with a lamb in a pen on the stage's kitchen set: 'GET THAT SON-OF-A-BITCHING SHEEP OUT OF MY KITCHEN!!'[22] The settings often play with such overlapped worlds, as when Cody's two brothers break into the London hotel room in *Geography of a Horse Dreamer*, wearing Wyoming cowboy gear, covered in dust and carrying shotguns: '*Their costumes should be well used and authentic without looking like dime-store cowboys.*'[23] Cody works, under duress, for gangsters, dreaming of the winners of horse races. Instead of dreaming of horses, he now dreams of the Great Plains and complains that he cannot work (dream) unless he knows which country he is in. He's in need of landmarks: 'I'm dreaming American horses and we're probably in Morocco somewhere.' He pleads that he just wants to 'go back to Wyoming and raise sheep. . . . I'm from the Great Plains not the city. He's poisoned my dreams with these cities.'[24] But this obviously populist statement is contradicted by the rest of the play which generates its effects from the confusion or juxtaposition of places, just as Cody's skills return to him, together with an Irish accent, when he starts dreaming of dog races. It is significant that the record that Cody claims inspires him, turns out to be zydeco, the culturally mixed (cajun and black) music from Louisiana, suggesting against Cody's regionalist sentiments that the best inspiration comes from the blending of forms, histories, and cultures. The kind of bricolage recommended by Patti Smith's Cavale in *Cowboy Mouth*, which sets Shepard and Smith not in New York's Chelsea Hotel but in 'some border town, some El Paso town', and which mixes America and Europe, rock and roll and French literature, Johnny Ace, Mick Jagger, Villon, Nerval, Baudelaire, and Genet. The scene centres on a *'fucked-up bed'* surrounded by *'miscellaneous debris'*: a dead crow, hubcaps, an old tyre, a pink telephone. The walls are covered with *'Seedy wallpaper with pictures of cowboys peeling off the wall. Photographs of Hank Williams and Jimmie Rodgers. Stuffed dolls, crucifixes. License plates from Southern states nailed to the wall. Travel poster of Panama.'* There's also a set of drums, an electric guitar and amplifier, bottles of drink, and a Sears catalogue.[25] This kind of cultural detritus marks Shepard's fusion of tradition and the throwaway, populist themes and rock culture props – the kind of fusion suggested in a description of the stage toward the end of *True West: 'the effect should be like a desert junkyard at high noon'.*[26]

True West suggests a contest between old and new versions of the West: Lee is staying with his brother Austin in their mother's house in a suburb about forty miles east of Los Angeles. Lee's time in the Mojave desert and his criminal experience contrast with Austin's Hollywood contacts and his suburban comfort. When their mother returns at the end of the play, the brothers are locked in a violent struggle and her house is devastated. But the old versus new West theme, or the suggestion made by a critic that their mother is infected 'with what Shepard considers the most serious new-western sickness – alienation from the land', are undermined by the play.[27] I have already quoted the description of the debris in the living-room looking like a desert junkyard, and the play closes with the noise of a single coyote as the brothers stare at each other in the fading light, appearing *'to be caught in a vast desert-like landscape'.*[28] The coyotes are heard throughout the play, growing in frenzy as the action progresses. It is specified that they should not sound like Hollywood's stereotyped howls, and Lee comments on the difference between them and desert coyotes. They do give a sense of the wilderness still there in the suburbs, as they kill household pets among the affluence. The reversal of the brothers' trades (Austin goes out and burgles houses while Lee tries to write) or the turnaround when Austin begs to be taken to the desert, shows the oppositions being deconstructed. Beneath the comfort of the Californian suburb there is the violence and emptiness of the desert. The struggle between the brothers crystallizes around Lee's idea for a 'Contemporary Western. Based on a true story.' Austin mocks the scene that he types up – two men chasing each other through the Panhandle, both are in trucks with horse trailers and the chase scene continues on horseback. Austin's attitude changes when Saul, the Hollywood producer, is interested in the outline and cancels Austin's own project. When Austin says that the story is phoney, Saul replies that it 'has the ring of truth'. It is about 'the real West'. 'Why?', asks Austin, 'Because it's got horses? Because it's got grown men acting like little boys?' Saul says it has 'Something about the land', but Austin questions the relevance of this; he is the one who drives on the freeway, swallows the smog, watches television, and shops at the Safeway. That is the reality: 'There's no such thing as the West anymore! It's a dead issue!'[29]

The play suggests that the truth of the West is the metaphorical desert and real violence within the family rather than in the truth of any particular location, the Mojave or the suburbs. Instead of concentrating on fixed oppositions the play reveals internal divisions. The play suggests other works by Shepard. Its absent father, the alcoholic Old Man, resembles the fathers in *Curse of the Starving Class* or *Buried Child*. It has been suggested that *True West* can be read autobiographically: the two brothers seen as two sides of Shepard's life, Austin being the writer and Lee being Shepard's image, the desert drifter, the outlaw.[30] Whatever the autobiographical echoes, the family that appears across Shepard's work is a precarious and potentially explosive unit. Florence Falk comments on *Curse of the Starving Class*:

> The nuclear family unit is a war zone where blood (heredity) begets blood (homicide). *Curse of the Starving Class* is dominated by blood imagery; lambs and humans alike are sacrificial victims for the 'steak house,' Western style, that Ella wants to erect on the site of Weston and Ella's home.[31]

The traditional plot of inheritance (Shepard's *Buried Child*, for example, sets a narrative of inheritance on a Midwestern farm) is given a twist by being displaced from land or money to character traits or destinies – Wesley in *Curse* puts on his father's clothes and assumes his drifting identity, giving up on the land at the moment when his father has regained his faith in that economic and symbolic centre of populism. *Curse* does for farming what *True West* did for the Western landscape; by turning it into the terrain for the collapse of the family the play disentangles two themes which are generally inseparable in populist thought, the land and the family. In other words, Shepard's work performs the opposite of the films discussed in the previous chapter, which were able to revitalize the concept and unit of the family through the theme of farming and work.

Wesley's speech, early in the play, refers to avocados, coyotes, and stock cars: the agricultural, the natural, and the mechanical symbols of small-town escapism. It is a lyrical monologue that suggests both the promise of the land and the precariousness of the family. His mother, Ella, sees the land's promise in a different light; she has been talking to someone about selling the house and land, an action that shifts the value of land from agriculture to real estate, from avocado growing to property development. The populist theme of the land as a way of life is challenged by the idea of the land as an investment. Note Ella's stress on 'ordinary people' as a bridge from populism to people's capitalism:

> Thousands are being spent every day by ordinary people just on this very thing. Banks are loaning money right and left. Small family loans. People are building. Everyone wants a piece of land. It's the only sure investment. It can never depreciate like a car or a washing machine. Land will double its value in ten years. In less than that. Land is going up every day.[32]

There's a strange faith in the land as something you can profit on but without risk. It is as if the populist faith in the land has turned into this exemption of land from the market, seen in the assumption that land prices cannot fall. Taylor, the man behind her proposed deal, speaks of the land as 'full of potential'. 'Of course', he says, 'it's a shame to see agriculture being slowly pushed into the background in deference to low-cost housing' (p. 74).

Wesley tells his sister, Emma, that Taylor works for a land development agency, a fact which prompts him to populist rhetoric: 'it means more than losing a home. It means losing a country.' The rhetoric slides from populist distaste for the city lawyer/developer figure to science fiction: 'It's a zombie invasion. Taylor is the head zombie. He's the scout for the other zombies. He's only a sign that more zombies are on their way.' It's almost a sign that Shepard can't challenge Taylor's world convincingly through traditional populist rhetoric; an understandable problem but one that the zombie rhetoric does not solve as it seems to refer to a sort of counter-cultural contempt for 'straight' society.

Ella defends Taylor to her son and it is significant that the word 'speculator', one of the key terms in populist demonology, has become professionalized and respected: 'He's a speculator. That's his job. It's very important in this day and age to have someone who can accurately assess the value of land. To see its potential for the future.' Thus, in her eyes, leaving the land is not the tragic end to a way of life that we saw expressed in the last chapter's populist films. Instead, it's an occasion to be celebrated:

> It just needs one last little signature from me and its finished. Everything. The beat-up cars, the rusted out tractor, the moldy avocados, the insane

horse, the demented sheep, the chickens, the whole entire shooting match. The whole collection. Over. (p. 92)

Wesley has already warned his father of Ella and Taylor's plans, trying to convince him to work the land properly, to stop drifting and drinking and to join the California Avocado Association. Weston tells him, however, that it is too late and that he owes so much money that he has been thinking of selling as well. In a typical reversal, Weston, later in the play, rediscovers his faith in the farm, his pride in his property, and his ability to believe in a new start. Wesley then switches to a fatalistic point of view, arguing that it's too late for a change and that Weston is actually in danger from the men he owes money to. He suggests that the best thing Weston could do is to take the Packard and run to Mexico. Weston feels that he can't run as the land still holds a residual appeal: ''CAUSE THIS IS WHERE I SETTLED DOWN! THIS IS WHERE THE LINE ENDED! RIGHT HERE! I MIGRATED TO THIS SPOT! I GOT NOWHERE TO GO TO! THIS IS IT!' (p. 111).

Weston's explanation for how he ended up in this situation puts the blame on a credit culture. He was always borrowing and banking on the future being better. Although this seems akin to a more common populist plot of the debt-ridden farmer, it dissolves into a more general complaint about the pressure to participate in a society based around consumption. Another populist theme appears in Weston's speech, the difference between 'real' and 'paper' or 'plastic' financial values.

> The whole thing's geared to invisible money. You never hear the sound of change any more. It's all plastic shuffling back and forth. It's all in everybody's heads. So I figured if that's the case, why not take advantage of it? Why not go in debt for a few grand if all it is is numbers? If it's all an idea and nothing's really there, why not take advantage? So I just went along with it, that's all. I just played ball. (p. 112)

In the 1890s populist rhetoric the 'real'/'paper' or 'plastic' distinction rests on the priority of agriculture; the land is simply seen as 'more real' than city finance or law, although one must point out that populist arguments were directed more against 'middlemen' and speculators rather than against a credit economy. The point here is that Weston has all but forgotten the material basis for his rhetoric, as he describes deserting the farm for the world of plastic and debt, his grievance is with the need to play ball with a consumer culture. His discourse has already left the land; the sale of the family farm either to Taylor's corporate interests or for Ella's steak house is by now almost an afterthought. But although Weston has given up farming, his deals take us to a different landscape.

Weston has informed Wesley earlier in the play that he owns one-and-a-half acres of land in the desert. He bought it from a door-to-door salesman, who told him it was 'an investment for the future. All kinds of things were going to be developed. Golf courses, shopping centers, banks, sauna baths. All that kinda' stuff. So I bought it.' He borrowed money to put down the deposit, but then discovered the land to be 'A real piece of shit. Just a bunch of strings on sticks, with the lizards blowing across it.' There is nothing around it: 'Just desert. No way to even get water to the goddam place. No way to even set a trailer on it' (p. 79). Faith in the land has been displaced from agriculture to investment, and Wesley guesses that Taylor, the man who wants to buy their land, is also the salesman of the useless desert plot. Even after he has discovered how worthless the land is, Weston can still believe in it as a means to get rich. He thinks of financing the recovery of his avocado business through selling the desert acre.

> I'll resell that piece a' land out there! That'll give us somethin' to get us started! Somebody somewhere's gonna' want a good piece a' desert land! It's prime location even if it isn't being developed! Only a three-hour drive from Palm Springs, and you know what that's like! You know the kinda' people who frequent that place! One of 'em's bound to have some extra cash! (p. 105)

The renewal of Weston's faith in his property and in agriculture is built on his reproduction of the salesman's pitch about the desert investment.

Weston's desert land highlights a connection between land and the salesman rather than the farmer. This is an important corrective to the Jeffersonian tradition which sees agrarian independence as the heart of America's way of life. Commerce replaces cultivation and the salesman's spiel is seen as more important than the farming narrative. This is a theme with echoes throughout American writing, from the earliest Elizabethan accounts of the New World's bounty which, as Harold Beaver points out, sometimes resemble 'estate agents' brochures' in their lists of praiseworthy features and in their desire to 'sell' America to England, to promote trade and emigration to the New World.[33] Turning from Shepard to another modern playwright, David Mamet, we see, as it were, the reverse of Weston's story, the salesman's point of view. Mamet, who will be discussed in greater detail in a later chapter, spent 1969 working for ' "a fly-by-night operation which sold tracts of undeveloped land in Arizona and Florida to gullible Chicagoans" '. This experience of selling ' "worthless land to elderly people who couldn't afford it" ' was turned into the play, *Glengarry, Glen Ross*. Christopher Bigsby has usefully suggested parallels for the play, earlier examples of works which make swindles over land a central theme of their critiques of commercial corruption. He refers to Dickens' 'Eden' in *Martin Chuzzlewit* and 'the Tennessee lands' in Mark Twain's *The Gilded Age*, seeing Twain's land as 'the focus of financial speculation and an image of uncontrolled greed'. In an interview with Bigsby, Mamet argues that the frontier ethic was an idea to a great extent generated by the railroads and storekeepers, another instance of land being seen not as the source of stable values but as a way of getting something for nothing.[34] Mamet is interested in uncovering the commercial considerations beneath the cry of 'Go West!', but in both his view of the frontier and his play about selling land as a supposed investment, he is also concerned with the buyers' complicity, their willingness to project fantasies of instant wealth on to undeveloped and unseen land. He refers to W. C. Fields to explain how these fantasies link buyer and salesman: 'you can't cheat an honest man.' It's a line that certainly applies to Shepard's Weston.

Shepard, however, is not just concerned with this mirage of profit. Arid land in his work is also linked to more personal fantasies. A short piece from *Motel Chronicles*, part anecdote, part poetry, begins with a theft and ends with a memory.

He tried to boost an absolutely worthless print of a Cottonwood tree stranded in a dry desert basin from the
Chateau Marmont Hotel on Sunset Boulevard.

He is caught loading the picture into his pickup, and when asked why he was taking it he explains that he has this vision of himself in the landscape of the picture, lying under the cottonwood. He recognizes the tree from an old dream, and thinks that the tree in the dream was based on a childhood memory. He can remember voices through the leaves but not what they were saying nor who they were:

He told them he was hoping the picture would bring the
whole thing back.[35]

Instead of an immediate relation to the landscape (the landscape of phoney real-estate deals but also the definitive Western landscape, the terrain of Shepard's cowboy image), there's a relation of dream and memory refracted through an image. The image itself is significantly 'worthless' and also stolen from Hollywood, the Chateau Marmont on Sunset Boulevard. That location suggests another set of lost dreams and the piece suggests the central theme in Shepard's work – the transformation of the values of the West through the images of popular culture. Perhaps the anecdote also implies in miniature Shepard's method, trying to wrest personal meanings from the images of mass reproduction. A much more complex image of the West is at work here than the ones seen already: the West as the quintessentially masculine and American terrain of Shepard's work or the space created by fantasies of commercial greed. The desert image is now involved with a troubled quest into the past, as it is in the film Wim Wenders directed from Sam Shepard's script, *Paris, Texas*.

The title of Wenders' film is explained in an exchange between Travis (Harry Dean Stanton) and his brother Walt (Dean Stockwell), while they are driving through Texas. Travis produces his photo of Paris; Walt looks at the picture of bare ground and says, 'This is Paris? It looks just like Texas to me.' Of course, it's Paris, Texas, but the confusion continues when Travis says that he owns it and Walt at first thinks he means the photo not the land. Walt can't see why he bought it, 'There's nothing on it.' Why would he want a vacant lot in Texas? Travis cannot remember. He takes over the driving and Walt finds himself waking up to that classic Shepard landscape, the desert junkyard. As Travis begins remembering we find that his desert property is connected to the divisions within the family, the topic of the next section. This link between Travis' vacant lot and a personal quest, ties undeveloped land to a crisis within family relations and within heterosexuality. In Wenders' film and in the examples from Shepard's work discussed above, what confronts us is the *empty plot*: the unfulfilled promise of the American landscape and the collapsed verities of the heterosexual narrative. The populist truths of working the land and a construction of masculinity and femininity around the nuclear family are both simultaneously sought and denied.

Deserted families: *Fool for Love* and *Paris, Texas*

Shepard was asked in an interview why he thought country and western songs were always so sad. 'Because, more than any other art form I know of in America, country music speaks of the true relationship between the American male and the American female.' What, the interviewer asked, was that? 'Terrible and impossible.'[36] It is typical of Shepard to refer to a form which, at least to many theatregoers, conjures up images of 'Americanness' and conventional gender roles – one of the most parodied country songs must be 'Stand by your Man' – to make a point about a crisis within American heterosexuality. It demonstrates what is most interesting about his work and perhaps also suggests why that is so rarely discussed. For what Shepard's recent work does is to explore divisions within sexual and family relations within a frame of Americanness, and what criticism often seems to miss is the relation between frame and subject.

The critics quoted in the first section of this chapter (all writing before the works discussed in this section were created) saw the Western elements in Shepard's work as the most unquestioning about America and masculinity, but argued that features stemming from the 1960s acted as a radical critique. I have suggested that the reverse is a truer picture, and would argue that the strength of Shepard's work comes from the tension between our expectations about, say, cowboys, rodeos, country music, deserts, and what is actually performed by those figures or in that setting. One problem is that criticism so often stays with the setting, perpetuating or condemning the lone, male cowboy image, rather than discussing the work done on that image. An example from outside Shepard's work may clarify the point: Donna Deitch's recent film *Desert Hearts*, based on Jane Rule's novel *Desert of the Heart*, exploits the tension between a setting that seems to assume or denote American heterosexuality (the Nevada desert, the Reno casinos, the Western dress, even the period, 1959 and its early rock 'n roll) and a narrative of a lesbian love affair and conflict and passion between women. A similar tension seems to be characteristic of Shepard's work but it is not often discussed as such.

The publicity poster for Robert Altman's film of *Fool for Love*, carried the phrase 'Desire beyond the edge of passion' which, together with the picture, suggested a story of *amour fou* in a cowboy hat. The stage play, first performed in 1983, is however a narrative of family collapse and of the 'Imaginary' and imprisoning roles of masculinity and femininity. Shepard has talked of his desire to write differently, to scrape away mythic elements in order to find a starker form. He was asked if this meant trying realism: 'Well, it could be called realism, but not the kind of realism where husbands and wives squabble and that kind of stuff.'[37] *Fool for Love* is precisely an oblique reworking both of heterosexual arguments and of realism. Indeed the play's Old Man, a typical Shepard father figure, provides a curious definition of realism linked to love and marriage. He says he wants to show Eddie 'Somethin' real, okay? Somethin' actual.' Pointing to an imaginary picture on the wall, he tells Eddie that it's Barbara Mandrell and that he is married to her. 'That's realism. I am actually married to Barbara Mandrell in my mind.'[38] He ends the play pointing into space: 'Ya' see that picture over there? Ya' see that? Ya' know who that is? That's the woman of my dreams. That's who that is. And she's mine. She's all mine. Forever' (p. 77). He sits in the rocking chair staring at the imaginary picture while the lights slowly fade and Merle Haggard's 'I'm the One Who Loves You' plays. The Old Man's relation to his imaginary picture has echoes throughout the play. He himself is not seen by any of the characters except Eddie and May, and Shepard's stage directions tell us that he only exists in their minds, although they talk directly to him and acknowledge his presence. He is a kind of residual image of the father. May talks of her jealousy of Eddie and the Countess in terms of seeing a picture of them; a 'made-up picture' that 'invades my head', and this picture 'stings even more than if I'd actually seen you with her' (p. 28). The way that roles persist through these made-up pictures of fathers and lovers is one of Shepard's main concerns in the two works discussed in this section – the refracting and shaping of love by structure and images.

Fool for Love is 'to be performed relentlessly without a break', its set being a *'Stark, low-rent motel room on the edge of the Mojave desert'* (p. 13). The setting suggests the tension between claustrophobia and agoraphobia, the room and the desert, the classic setting of a play – realism glimpsed through an invisible fourth wall – on the edge of a classic American landscape. The two spaces also suggest a division around gender, the desert and its connotations of lone male action, the motel room and its connotations of the (often illicit) heterosexual couple. The play is structured around the overlapping dichotomies, male/female, outside/inside, past/present. The arrival of Eddie brings signs of 'authentic' American maleness, all linked to the outside world of action (broken down cowboy boots, jeans that smell of horse sweat, a pair of spurs – Shepard stresses not cartoon 'cowboy' spurs – hanging from his belt, his bucking glove for rodeo riding, a ten-gauge shotgun and a bottle of tequila, two steer ropes, one of which is turned into a lariat which Eddie ropes the bedposts with). Throughout the play the implosion of the family indoors is juxtaposed with sporadic explosions of violence outside: headlights rake the stage, shots are fired, there's the sound of tyres burning rubber, Eddie's horse trailer explodes, and horses are heard screaming. The play begins with Eddie telling May that he has just driven 2,480 miles to see her, crying as he drove. Her reaction is to the space of that love, its probable setting: 'I'm not going back to that idiot trailer if that's what you think.' Eddie says he is moving it, 'I got a piece of ground up in Wyoming.' But again May rejects this idea of land, ridiculing its masculine associations: 'Wyoming? Are you crazy? I'm not moving to Wyoming. What's up there? Marlboro Men?' (pp. 22–3). The conversation continues through a door, May having shut herself in the bathroom, with Eddie unfolding a pastoral vision of the trailer on his land, a corral for the horses, a vegetable garden, chickens. May shouts from behind the door:

I hate chickens! I hate horses! I hate all that shit! You know that. You got me confused with somebody else. You keep comin' up here with this lame country dream life with chickens and vegetables and I can't stand any of it.

Eddie's love is proved through movement, driving 2,000 miles, but works towards stability, the trailer finally anchored on a piece of ground. May reappears and gives a truer picture of this pastoral domesticity – with her stranded in the trailer, 'with the wind ripping through it', waiting for the Butane to arrive, or 'Hiking down to the laundromat in the rain' (pp. 23, 25). Later they argue about the man who is coming to see May, with Eddie saying he's 'gotta' be a twerp'. May's reply is, 'Anybody who doesn't half kill themselves falling off horses or jumping on steers is a twerp in your book' (p. 32).

Even with this critique of masculinity, it might be suggested that we are still within a conventional spatializing of gender, albeit one where May rejects the male world of action rather than complementing it. But the play introduces more radical divisions, and instead of constructing May and Eddie around difference (male /female) it focuses on their more disturbing similarity (brother/sister). The Old Man links the two of them but finds that his paternal role is unreadable: 'I don't recognize myself in either one a' you. Never did. 'Course your mothers both put their stamp on ya' that's plain to see. But my whole side a' the issue is absent, in my opinion' (p. 49). His 'whole side a' the issue', the phrase suggests not only paternity and birth but also an argument with sides and issues, and the possible incest narrative ('possible' because there are several versions of events), renders the heterosexual argument problematic. Eddie tells Martin (May's friend) that May is his (half-) sister, and explains their relationship: 'our Daddy fell in love twice. That's basically how it happened. Once with my mother and once with her mother.' The Old Man adds that 'It was the same love. Just got split in two that's all.' Martin wonders why Eddie and May didn't meet until high school. Eddie explains that their father 'had two separate lives. That's how come. Two completely separate lives. He'd live with me and my mother for a while and then he'd disappear and go live with her and her mother for a while' (p. 63). There is a structure of symmetry and alternation, a symmetry broken after years when Eddie's father started staying in the house all the time. Then the Old Man began going for long walks, one of which is remembered by Eddie in a long monologue about walking across the fields with him in the dark, seeing the screen for the drive-in movie in the distance with Spencer Tracy silently moving his mouth. He watches his father through the glass door of a liquor store as he buys a bottle, then they walk to the far side of the town and stop at a small, white house. There's a 'hot, desert breeze and the air smelled like new cut alfalfa'; a woman comes to the door and while his father embraces her, Eddie sees behind them, inside the house, May. As he continues with the story, May opens the bathroom door and appears behind Eddie and Martin, and listens to the end of the narrative:

> She just appears. She's just standing there, staring at me and I'm staring back at her and we can't take our eyes off each other. It was like we knew each other from somewhere but we couldn't place where. But the second we saw each other, that very second, we knew we'd never stop being in love. (pp. 64–7)

May challenges the story, calling it fiction, but she continues to say that she knows the whole story and will finish it. (This prompts an exchange between the Old Man and Eddie, with the Old Man worried by what May might know.)

May reverses the narrative, as a woman takes over the telling so a woman takes over the quest, and she talks of her mother's search for the Old Man:

> he kept trying to keep her at a distance because the closer these two separate lives drew together, these two separate women, these two separate kids, the more nervous he got. The more filled with terror that the two lives would find out about each other and devour him whole.

She tells them of her mother's excitement and nervousness as they walked through a small town, convinced that they had found the right place: 'she knew she was trespassing. She knew she was crossing this forbidden zone but she couldn't help herself.' All day they peer through the windows of houses until they finally find the Old Man's house, where they stand outside watching through the window as Eddie, his mother, and the Old Man eat their supper. At this point the Old Man interrupts her story to say to Eddie that May is 'off the wall' with her narrative – 'You gotta' do somethin' about this' (pp. 71–2). May carries on, telling Martin that the Old Man disappeared after her mother had found him, and speaking also of her love for Eddie, their inability to be apart. Her mother became so anxious about this love that she went to see Eddie's mother, a visit which led to the latter's suicide. This leads to another challenge from the Old Man, another aside to Eddie: 'You're not gonna' let her off the hook with that one are ya'? That's the dumbest version I ever heard in my whole life.' He introduces the idea of *versions*, denying the suicide and returning to the notion of *sides*, saying to Eddie: 'I wanna' hear the male side a' this thing. You gotta' represent me now. Speak on my behalf. There's no one to speak for me now! Stand up!' He demands that Eddie correct May but Eddie tells him that the suicide really happened (pp. 72–3).

The Old Man gives a final explanation for this double love, asking how could he have rejected May's mother's love – 'We were completely whole.' But as he talks of wholeness, Eddie and May stare at each other. The Old Man again demands that Eddie act against May, act as his son, represent masculinity: 'Speak to her. Bring her around to our side. You gotta' make her see this thing in a clear light.' But Eddie and May move toward each other, ignoring the paternal command:

> Stay away from her! What the hell are you doin'! Keep away from her! You two can't come together! You gotta' hold up my end a' this deal. I got nobody now! Nobody! You can't betray me! You gotta' represent me now! You're my son. (p. 74)

As the two embrace an explosion is heard from outside and fire lights the window, the Countess has returned and set light to Eddie's horse trailer.

Robert Altman's film of *Fool for Love* opens up a gap between sound and image in its visualization of the monologues quoted above, the images seen contradicting the memories heard. This has the effect of weakening the play's claustrophobic intensity while also replacing the idea of sides and versions of the family narrative with a more abstract question of truth. The play's monologues give a sense of space and movement (the quest across fields or through towns) that gains importance through the motel room setting. The film's flashbacks and varied settings lose this tension between inside and outside, and there is an attempt to replace this through a series of shots which underline the importance of doors and windows in order to introduce themes of voyeurism and exclusion. In the play, doors are emphasized in terms of the inside/outside opposition, not so much in terms of exclusion as division, with people talking through a door, for example. Shepard's oblique relation to realism and to conventional theatre can be heard as well as seen with the play's slamming doors; a gesture that has dramatic echoes, some critics suggesting Ibsen's *A Doll's House*, but that also carries associations of the clichés of conventional theatre. In Shepard's case, the doors are amplified by microphones and a bass drum placed in the frame, so the cliché of bourgeois drama's heterosexual squabbles booms with American violence, as loud as the Countess's Magnum. The point is to reveal the violence that is implied on this border between the outside and inside, with the implications that has in a play about jealousy and incest. This can return us to Eddie and May's monologues and the Old Man's anxious promptings.

One notices how symmetrical the memories are, mirror-images reversed around gender: Eddie and his father walk at night, May and her mother by day; they both walk through the town, Eddie's father in search of May's mother, May's mother in search of the Old Man; both quests end at points where the inside and outside meet, the porch of May's house, the window of Eddie's; both feature images worryingly deprived of sound – Spencer Tracy's mouth moving on the distant drive-in movie screen, Eddie and his mother talking without May and her mother being able to hear, and with the Old Man silent. But the accounts concern a challenge to division and the disruption of symmetry, for if the Old Man characterizes his love with May's mother as wholeness, and if he informs us that his love for two women was the same love, just split in two, this combination of division and wholeness is not a resolution but a threat. May tells us how, as the two separate lives came closer together, the Old Man felt devoured. If his fear there is of his two lovers discovering each other, his worry at the end of the play is of that most extreme denial of the inside/outside structure – incest – as he shouts 'You two can't come together!' The two fears are linked in the play to violence as the only exit from the heterosexual argument; the boom of the door both in the Countess's shots and arson (the vengeance of the 'other woman') and in the revelation that Eddie's mother shot herself. Love is triangular (the picture in May's head of Eddie and the Countess, the Old Man's split love), or an incestuous, implosive wholeness (May and Eddie with the still visible, still audible but absent parental presence, the only two characters aware of the Old Man), or 'realistic' as the Old Man terms his imaginary marriage to Barbara Mandrell. American heterosexuality is revealed as terrible and impossible, to return to Shepard's comment on country music.

Shepard's operation here is, quite strictly, one of deconstruction: the set of binary opposites that structure the play (male/female, inside/outside, and so on) are unravelled by incestuous desire and slamming doors, and divisions within terms undermine differences between them. The Old Man insists on these differences and wants Eddie to take sides within the heterosexual argument, asking him as the male side to challenge May's version and deny Eddie's mother's death. Love is divided but also constructed through images, and the positions of masculinity and femininity, that seem at first so assured, are seen to be founded on division, on the split love of a present-but-absent father. This knot of problems is revisited in *Paris, Texas*, another work which sets a crisis of masculinity in the American desert, opening with a problem of identity that concerns borders and the family.[39]

In *Scenes In America Deserta*, Reyner Banham writes:

I have not done what one has been supposed to do in deserts ever since the time of Moses – I have not 'found myself.' If anything I have lost myself, in the sense that I now feel that I understand myself less than I did before.[40]

When Harry Dean Stanton's Travis walks out of the desert at the beginning of Wenders' film, it seems that for him too the desert is a place of loss, loss of identity and of language. Other parallels can be drawn out from the film and from Banham's book. Although *Paris, Texas* has various settings (Los Angeles, Houston) a comparison suggests that its themes are centred on its opening desert landscape. Banham discusses the religious associations of the land, connecting American deserts to the Protestant conscience. One could think of Channel Four's publicity for the televising of this film '*Paris, Texas*, a Story of Redemption' – or remember the sermon in the film when Travis is walking over a bridge and the viewer first hears and then sees the apocalyptic preacher shouting to the cars below that the whole godforsaken valley is doomed, right out to the goddamn Mojave desert. Banham's suggested links between science fiction and the Mojave, with the desert echoing and generating science fiction imagery, together with the desert's connection to space (its own open spaces, the vision of it as being like a lunar landscape, and the more practical links around the space programme, air-bases, test-sites, etc.) find their counterparts in Hunter's obsession with space. Hunter, Travis' son, played by Hunter Carson, talks abut spaceships, tells Travis about the big bang theory of creation, and reacts to the news that his mother, Jane, is now living in Houston by saying that's where the Space Center is. Desert images, of course, are most obviously present in popular culture in Westerns, and both Banham and the film refer to this familiar iconography, the film through ironic modern echoes of the West (the make of Travis' pickup, a Ranchero, the name of a motel, the Plainsman), and through Wenders' continued interest in John Ford's *The Searchers* and its theme of the family quest. Some of the most interesting parts of Banham's book are his interrogation of his aesthetic response, his surprise at what seems to be a 'natural' reaction to 'natural beauty', and his tentative explorations of the possible connections between his love of deserts and his knowledge of abstract art. A similar theme occurs in *Paris, Texas* where the resonant but empty landscape of the opening seems to enable Wenders to do without self-conscious references to other films while still interrogating the mystery of cinema, but in a barer, starker form than, say, the film-within-a-film device of *The State of Things*. In the film's concluding exchanges between Jane (Natassja Kinski) and Travis, the booth suggests the institution of the cinema, as she is watched through a two-way mirror, looking at Travis, and thus at the camera and the film's viewer. With her room lit and Travis and the cinema audience sitting in darkness, she says, 'You realize I can't see you even though you can see me?'[41] The space of the booth is the space of cinema, and of a related commodification of women, as well as being, as I'll argue later, a setting that is reminiscent of the psychoanalytical situation. Yet what is enacted in these exchanges is Shepard's very American narrative of violence, passion, and crisis, fools for love in a burning trailer. The isolation and intensity of Travis and Jane's dialogue, and the directness of Wenders' self-reference, seem to be prepared by the blank landscape of the opening. And the themes generated by the desert echo across the other settings, Los Angeles suburbia and Houston's high-rise hotels.

I will return to these concluding scenes but it is first necessary to say something about the film's portrayal of the family. Like *Fool for Love, Paris, Texas* revolves around images of the family. When, in Los Angeles, Travis, Walt, Anne, and Hunter sit and watch a home movie of a visit made five years before by Walt and Anne to Travis, Jane, and Hunter, the film's image of the family and the connotations of a home movie are contradicted by the present situation, the absent mother and the doubled or divided father. After watching it, Hunter says 'goodnight dad' first to Walt and then to Travis. This problem of the father is introduced when Walt telephones Hunter from Texas, opening the conversation with 'Hi Hunter, it's daddy' and then telling him that he's in Texas to visit his father. Later, Walt reminds Hunter that Travis is his real father, but Hunter's attempt to explain Travis' presence to a schoolfriend reveals a more complex relation: 'He's my father's brother. No, they're both brothers. No, they're both fathers.' The day after the screening of the home movie, the Mexican maid finds Travis with a pile of magazines and asks him what he is looking for. 'I'm looking for *the* father.' She asks if he means his own father and he replies, 'No, just a father, any father. What does a father look like?' She tells him that there are many different kinds of father but he says, 'I just need one.' 'You think you're going to find him in there?' 'Well, I don't know where else to look.' She realizes then that he is searching for an image that he can use himself, and the scene continues with Travis in front of a mirror, being coached by her in the costume and deportment of masculinity. She asks if he wants to be a rich father or a poor one and she rejects his wish to look 'in between', a category that does not exist for fathers. She tells him that he must look up at the sky in order to be a rich father, and to have the appropriate dignity she advises, 'you must walk stiff, senor Travis'.

Many elements combine in the scene: the film's comic but poignant use of the, as it were, 'Martian' perspective of Travis having to be resocialized; the significant fact that this cultural training in how to look like a father comes not from the obvious source of ideology and image, the magazines, nor from Walt and Anne's understanding, but from the hispanic maid, demonstrating Travis' ease with Mexican culture and also suggesting the role played by hispanic cultures in the construction of models of American masculinity, a role witnessed by the very word *machismo*. This invention of an ideal father coupled with the role of the mirror suggests the psychoanalytical theories of Jacques Lacan, specifically his notions of the symbolic and the imaginary. The mirror stage as formative in the development of the child's subjectivity is the central event of Lacan's imaginary, with the child recognizing itself in the image and aspiring to the image's fictional wholeness, and thus developing a sense of self. Lacan's influence was felt in the 1970s across the field of cultural analysis, perhaps especially in film theory where the mirror stage was taken up, sometimes simplistically, as an illuminating analogy for the audience's relation to the screen. The spectator/screen relationship cannot be simply identified with the child/mirror because of the role of the symbolic (language, gender position) in adult subjectivity; here that means the search for the father, the images in the magazines, the hispanic/American relationship, Travis' combination of adult status and childlike naïvety, the emphasis on the rich father, and so on. The imaginary and the symbolic – and the ideological – are seen to interconnect.[42] The film picks up the mirror theme in the concluding booth scenes, but also in a whole series of 'mirrorings', instances which stress family love and division, often family love *as* division.

At the family meal in Los Angeles the camera picks out a kind of visual rhyme or mirroring when we see both Walt and Hunter's feet tapping under the table, establishing a bond between them and excluding Travis. Then there are the series of meetings between Travis and Hunter at the school, where Hunter begins by rejecting the embarrassment of walking home with his returned father, rather than driving like everybody else. The first meeting is shot with them looking at each other across a road which other children are crossing; Hunter whispers to a school friend and gets a lift home. The second time, after Travis' lessons in image in front of the mirror, Hunter walks but stays on the other side of the road. However, the dividing road leads to them becoming more comically self-conscious about the mirroring effect, and when Travis stumbles into a dustbin Hunter mimes tripping on the other side of the road. The reason for Travis' stumble in any case is his look across, and finally he crosses the road as they near the house. The third meeting at school is actually during school hours. Travis has just bought his pickup and without getting out of the truck, he talks to Hunter across the road and through the chainlink fence that Hunter holds on to. The theme of mirroring and division is extended by the introduction of language and the film's stress on the ways that communication is mediated.

To return to Travis with his magazines, mirror, and the maid's advice on the image of the father, another theme suggests itself: the relation between image and reality around the family or images of heterosexual love. The photo that provides the title is also a heavily mediated primal scene; Paris, Texas was where Travis' parents first made love, so he buys the vacant lot as a vague search into his origins: 'So I figured that's where I began . . . I started out there.' He mentions to Walt, after the exchange about the photo, their father's joke about their mother being the girl he met in Paris. Later that memory takes on a more serious note when Travis tells the story to Hunter. Travis talks about his mother to Hunter – she was 'not a fancy woman', but Travis' father repeated the Paris joke until he came to believe it. Travis says that his father 'looked at her but he didn't see her'. Instead he saw a mirror image, in other words the reversal of those images through the mirror/window in Houston where Travis looks at Jane but she can't see him. The joke about Paris turns into a belief; the image is taken for reality, just as Walt originally misunderstood Travis' photo and thought that he had bought the photo, the image of Paris, Texas, and not the land. Following Travis' reminder of their father's joke about Paris, Walt tells Travis about his business, making billboards for advertising. Travis' response is 'So *you're* the one who makes them . . . I love them.' And Walt has to point out that he's not the only one. This discourse about images is taken up in a conversation between Walt and Anne. Anne expresses her anxiety about Walt's encouragement of a bond between Travis and Hunter, her worry about losing Hunter: 'You keep promoting this father and son business between them.' This prompts the reply, 'It's not business. Travis is his father and Hunter is his son.' Walt continues: 'What's this promoting bullshit? Do you want us to keep on pretending that we're the parents of my brother's son? How long do you expect Hunter to buy that?' During the scene, in another instance of how language and the family are mediated, physically divided, we see Hunter listening to the conversation through the wall. What I want to stress here is the language of advertising and commerce – 'promoting . . . business . . . buy'. The family that seems 'normal', and seems precisely to be like an advertisement for a/the family, Walt, Anne, and Hunter, discusses itself exactly in terms of credibility and commerce. The 'real' family, however, is not a site of authenticity but of violence, loss, and absence. Any critique of the Californian 'norm' is itself undercut by the divisions of the real family, and by the obvious reality of Walt and Anne's love for Hunter. The memories of Travis and

Jane's marriage tell of love turning into obsession and violence. Travis remembers his desire to get away and Jane's attempts to escape, his wish for a place with no landmarks and his extreme brutality to her. Finally, he wakes up to find the trailer on fire and Jane and Hunter gone. He talks of running through the flames, and then carrying on for five days 'until every sign of man had disappeared'. The desert is the place outside signs and language, where Travis refuses to speak, a period of his life which is blank, which was like 'a gap'. Although both Shepard and Wenders are fascinated by the relation between signs and the desert, signs (for motels and so on) on the edge of the desert, they seem to suggest an outside to culture, which is however not an alternative but a silence, an absence.

It's important to underline that there is no positive alternative due to the theme of mediated communication, which in other hands might suggest a critique of the modern or the technological but here functions to suggest unavoidable divisions between parents and children, men and women. When Hunter and Travis set off to find Jane, there's a scene when Hunter, sitting in the back of the pickup, separated from him by glass and talking over a walkie-talkie, tells his father about the speed of light. These portable radios are used when they stake out the bank where they know that they will see Jane, as if it is a male trap for female criminality. The scenes in the booth, the obvious centre of this theme, are themselves framed by scenes of mediated vision or language. When Travis arrives at the place where Jane works we see a missed exchange of glances, the audience watching Jane's back until John Lurie asks Travis to leave, and as he turns we see Jane turning in the mirrors behind the bar, looking over her shoulder at Travis' retreating back. Before he goes back for his second visit to Jane, Travis tapes a message for Hunter, telling him via technology that 'I was hoping to show you that I was your father. You showed me that I was.' He tells him that as he tore Jane and Hunter apart, he must bring them back together. We next see Hunter listening to the tape sitting by the hotel television, next to the room's enormous windows. And the film ends, after the final scene in the booth, with Travis down on the street looking up at the hotel windows while in the room, next to this expanse of glass, Hunter and Jane embrace. The separation within the scene prevents a simple ideological endorsement of the family. Apart from the home movie we see, there is never a point where the three of them are together or where Jane and Travis actually have an unmediated conversation or exchange of looks.

When Travis first enters one of the booths, he describes the woman he wants to see, but instead of Jane another blonde woman in a nurse's uniform appears. He asks what the woman can see, and she says she can see the same as he can. What to him is a window is a mirror for the woman, so the peepshow builds in its own excuse; women become commodified images (the nurse's uniform as male fantasy) but they are presented as if they are looking at themselves, disguising male voyeurism as female narcissism. When he first sees Jane, her explanation of her job makes it sound less a part of the sex industry and more a parallel to psychoanalysis. Early psychoanalysis focuses on the woman, on the 'talking cure' which is a question of listening to the hysteric. Here, men are constructed as the problem – what do men want? – as Jane says, 'I just don't know exactly what it is you want.' She describes her job as just talking or just listening, literally unable to see the customers in the booth, she is not allowed to 'see' them after work. When Travis returns the second time, denying having ever visited before, he turns his back on the two-way mirror and begins to tell the story of their marriage. The sound cuts from him speaking into the phone to the sound Jane hears over the speaker. This image of separation by glass and communication over a phone carries a specific visual parallel, the prison scene where visitor and prisoner are divided by glass and only able to speak via a phone. *Paris, Texas* therefore suggests that Travis and Jane are prisoners of gender, locked in roles of masculinity and femininity which make genuine contact impossible. Jane finally says his name and moves right up to the dividing screen; Travis turns to face her and as she is so close the camera picks up a reflection where his face is superimposed on hers, framed by her hair and thus possibly suggesting their son, male but fair haired, Hunter. She turns the light off on her side, destroying the cinematic space of light and darkness, and enabling them to see each other dimly through the screen. He tells her where Hunter is. She turns her back to him, so he is now looking over her shoulder and both are now facing the audience/the camera. She talks about how she used to invent speeches to say to him but both now find conversation difficult. Her final phrase is a chilling implication of the failure of love, the crisis of heterosexuality: 'Now I'm working here, I hear your voice all the time. Every man has your voice.'

The film also constructs division around nationality. Its first line is spoken by the doctor to the collapsed and mute Travis, delivered in a German accent: 'You know which side of the border you're on?' The idea of the border is taken up by Travis' Mexican experience (Mexico often functioning in Shepard's plays as the place of escape and refuge), his Spanish song, his talk with the maid, and so on. But this cultural or national division is linked to questions of sexual difference, as the scene with the maid suggests, and also with the discussion of Travis and Walt's mother. Travis asks Walt, after they have been talking about Paris, Texas, what their mother's maiden name was. It was Spanish he remembers, and Walt says 'well, her father was'. As Stephen Heath wrote about Orson Welles' *Touch of Evil*: 'The film uses the border, the play between American and Mexican, the passage from country to country' as a way of mapping differences on to each other, national and gender.[43] In Wenders' film the play is also between American and European, from the doctor's accent to Anne's French origins and, especially, within the title itself. Cultural exchanges and misunderstandings are linked to the impossible communications within the family or between lovers. Some critics tried to arrest these oppositions within the film, setting up a strict dichotomy between European art and American narrative, with some seeing Shepard's work as being emasculated by Wenders' European self-consciousness, and others seeing the film as undermined by Shepard's American sentimentalization of the family. This seems to miss the point of the film's play with borders.

Wenders had approached Shepard for the title part in his Zoetrope film *Hammett*, but when this collaboration never happened, he suggested a film built loosely on the short pieces in Shepard's *Motel Chronicles*. From this idea *Paris, Texas*, emerged. Wenders has said that he feels their partnership is no coincidence. After all, they are both believers in an imaginary America, a true West:

> Maybe Sam is looking for something similar in America to what I was looking for out of Europe and that I saw in America, and Sam sees in the West. That of being a kind of hope, or a place where there was still some sort of change taking place. I don't know. Or at least the West for him – at least in the plays of his, there is still this mythical place that for me America is.[44]

Wenders' long-running love affair with American music and film culture, and his astonishing sensitivity to certain American landscapes, runs through his work from *Kings of the Road* (containing the line 'The Americans have colonized our unconscious'), to *Alice in the Cities, The American Friend, Hammett,* and *The State of Things*. The production and financing of *Paris, Texas* demonstrates the practical nature of international exchanges: Wenders' company has the symptomatic name, Road Movies, Berlin, and the money was raised in England, France, and Germany. From this international co-operation we can pick out some final mirrorings between Wenders and Shepard, Europe and America.

If Europeans invented America, before and during its exploration and settlement, as a space for religious freedom, a second chance for fallen man, and an Edenic world of natural abundance, then modern American policies and attitudes have, as it were, invented Europe, through postwar aid, through support for the end of European empires, and through the creation of markets, power blocs, and strategic areas. Wenders has found this on a personal level, saying that as a deracinated German, America gives him a sense of European identity.

> If you're in America, a funny thing happens – you start calling yourself a European, which they never do here. People ask you where you come from, and you say 'Europe', because it sometimes seems unnecessary to make the distinction, and in a way I like that a lot.[45]

Similarly Shepard has discussed the period when he lived in London. He says about *The Tooth of Crime*: 'It's an interesting thing that happened with that play, because I wrote it in London – it's been called an American play, right, but it was written in the middle of Shepherds Bush.'[46] As a more general point, there is his comment on a necessary distance:

> I mean it wasn't until I came to England that I found out what it means to be an American. Nothing really makes sense when you're there [in California], but the more distant you are from it, the more the implications of what you grew up with start to emerge.[47]

These exchanges, looking from Europe to America, looking West within America, looking from America back to Europe, allow a network of cultural relations to emerge on the terrain of an imaginary America.

So Shepard's work, which as we have seen is so often discussed in terms of an unproblematic 'Americanness' and masculinity, develops, in an American and European collaboration, a moving and complex study of the imprisoning nature of masculinity and femininity. 1970s American cinema gave us a haunting image of urban alienation, Travis (Robert De Niro) in his cab in Scorsese's *Taxi Driver*, his social contact mediated by the glass that separates him from the world, even his passengers divided from him, glimpsed in the rearview mirror. Wenders and Shepard in the 1980s create another Travis, at first locked into silence, and when Walt opens the front passenger door for him climbing instead into the back. Travis whose desert experiences testify not to the virtues of American male independence, but to a crisis within heterosexual love and the family. Here populist themes collapse into an empty plot: both a hollowed-out narrative and an arid desert development.

4 'Things fall apart':
loss in recent American fiction

Robert Dallek, in his study of Reagan's symbolic politics, quotes the presidential reaction to criticisms of his economic policy and welfare cuts; meeting congressional leaders in April 1982 he dismissed the Democrats' argument that his policies were hurting those on a low or middle income. It was all newspaper propaganda: ' "I read that crap about my program." But "we haven't thrown anybody out in the snow to die," he said.' Dallek also cites Reagan's outburst in March of that year, against television news, an example of the post-Gutenburg president falling out with his chosen medium.

Reagan attacked the TV coverage for slowing down the nation's economic recovery. 'In a time of recession like this,' he said, 'there's a great element of psychology in economics. And you can't turn on the evening news without seeing that they're going to interview someone else who has lost his job or they're outside the factory gate that has laid off workers – the constant down-beat that can contribute psychologically to slowing down a new recovery that is in the offing. Is it news,' Reagan asked, 'that some fellow out in South Succotash someplace has just been laid off . . . or someone's complaint that the budget cuts are going to hurt their present program?'

He wondered, seemingly without irony or awareness of how his presidency has been built around image and use of the media, whether the networks ' "aren't more concerned with entertainment than they are with delivering the news. . . . They're looking for what's eye-catching and spectacular." '[1]

We recognize the language and the theory that a glorious economic recovery would appear if only the 'moaning minnies', to use Thatcher's phrase, would stop talking about unemployment, poverty, or the low pay and lack of job security for many of those who do have jobs in the 1980s. If we stop looking at the recession's effects, it will simply go away. Reagan asked if it was news that somebody in South Succotash someplace has been laid off; the question asked in this chapter is, is it fiction? The short stories and novels that will be considered seem to provide a fiction for the 1980s, partly by being so aware of the previous decades. The ambivalent politics or the ambivalence towards politics displayed by this fiction, together with its choice of characters and settings, make it central to any discussion of contemporary populism. It revisits the terrain of populism mapped out in the earlier chapters (the West, the South, the Midwest, the small town), often with the cynicism about politics which will be discussed in the next chapter, and with an awareness of popular culture which will be treated more fully in Chapter 6.

It is always problematic, if tempting, to unify writers, creating schools and movements by overlooking differences and diversity, or to relate fiction directly to its economic or political context – here's a recession, here's the renewal of the American short story. There is a connection but it is not one clarified by simplistic notions of economic determinism nor by journalistic ideas of an '80s zeitgeist. Some of the fiction considered here was written before Reaganomics and much of it is set in the recent past, and we have the further problem of the timelag between American and British publication. It would also be a mistake to see this writing as simply a reaction to the harshening of the economic climate. Characters reach for drinks, slam doors, throw plates, lose lovers or jobs but the point of this fiction is how people cope with these events and how they experience them as private rather than representative. The challenge of this writing is perhaps not so much to find these characters representative of 'Reagan's America' but rather of our own feelings of not having control over our lives, and of our own difficulty in seeing our jealousies and anxieties socially rather than privately.

Instead of conflating these writers into a unified movement, I will trace across the different styles and wide social range of the characters certain recurring motifs and assumptions. However varied these styles are they still mark a shift away from the ludic texts of postwar American fiction (the games with truth and the self-reflexivity of writing associated with the encyclopaedic, allusion-laden novels of Pynchon, the postmodernist deadpan fragments of Donald Barthelme, the playful metafiction of Barth). Instead of asking what a text is, this fiction seems to have simpler questions, but as these are asked with a bewildering absence of landmarks they are as challenging to commonsense views of the world and language as postmodernist texts. Instead of the vertiginous autonomy of language these narratives centre on the absence of discourses adequate to the characters' feelings. Realism here neither reassures nor naturalizes and it is permanently undermined by a kind of surrealism of the everyday. There are many traditions which could help place this fiction: traces of Hemingway in the laconic prose, hints of Southern Gothic in the enjoyment of the eccentric, parallels with the regionalist women writers of the late nineteenth century, the local colourists like Sarah Orne Jewett, for example. The short story form also reminds us, possibly against the grain of our European expectations, that alongside the tradition of novels that seem to reflect the vast scope of America through their own bulk and sheer density of allusions, there has always been a tradition of the concise, the short stories of Poe and Hawthorne rather than the epic of Melville's *Moby Dick*, the city sketch rather than the naturalist panorama, the vignette as opposed to the Great American Novel. It almost seems with new American fiction as if this tradition of economy in style and narrative is particularly suited to capture hardship within the American economy. A parallel from music suggests itself, as Springsteen's songs have moved from a celebration of the street to an acknowledgement of a bleaker world 'where lately there ain't been much work on account of the economy' ('The River'), so his style has become more economical, a craft learned from films and fiction, and his 'rock poetry' of romanticized streets and gypsy angels has given way to compressed blue-collar narratives. To begin to investigate this sparse new fiction, we can turn to characters who are literally, and often metaphorically, directionless or lost.

Where are we?

'Where are we?', these characters ask, underlining the aimlessness of their travel or their shaky grip on directions. The first-person narrator of Jayne Anne Phillips' 'Fast Lanes' with her dress smelling of rum and disturbing memories of her previous night in New Orleans:

> 'Where are we?' I asked.
> 'Somewhere in east Georgia.'[2]

Or Anne Tyler's Charlotte, taken hostage by an incompetent bank robber, out on the road in a stolen car:

> From the little I could see, I guessed we were traveling through farm country. Once we passed a barn, and then a shed with the sleepy clucking of hens inside it. 'Where on earth *are* we?' I asked.
> 'How would I know? Virginia, somewhere?'[3]

Charlotte, with her lucky charm, a badge from a cereal packet saying 'Keep on truckin'' and her hundred-dollar traveller's cheque, has been preparing to cut herself off from husband and home for a long time. Being taken hostage merely precipitates her move. They spend so much time in their stolen car that she feels that 'it was like a second skin', and in a similar way, the narrator of 'Fast Lanes' feels that her reality has been reduced to the road and the radio and the continuous movie unrolling outside: 'The truck is what there really was: him and me and the radio.'[4] The title, 'Fast Lanes', testifies to driving-as-metaphor but if this entanglement of cars and lifestyles suggests Kerouac's *On the Road*, Phillips' characters aren't the Beat Generation but the beaten generation of the 1970s.

There has always been an ambiguity at the core of the myth of the American road: travelling as freedom or travelling as a necessary escape, something imposed not chosen. Mark Twain's great achieve-ment in *Huckleberry Finn* is precisely that he combined both; the journey down the river is an adolescent drifting from the rules of society given urgency by Jim's flight from slavery. In fact Huck wants to escape *from* precisely the things that Jim wants to escape *to* – families, relatives, jobs, money, in short what oppresses the adolescent but is denied to the slave, citizenship. If modern American popular culture has been persistently autocentric, celebrating the freedom of the road, it has also recognized a darker side to travel, those forced on to Route 66 like Steinbeck's 'Okies' driving to California, having been driven off the land. The characters in Phillips' fiction drift through a mixture of choice and circumstance, the woman in 'Fast Lanes' is getting a ride home through Texas and Louisiana in Thur-man's Datsun. Thurman has lived in Berkeley, Austin, Jackson, Eugene, Denver – 'all the western floater's towns'.[5] We are one stage on from drifting, floating shows even fewer ties to solidity. Their journey is set in 1975. In her 'Rayme – a Memoir of the Seventies' Jayne Anne Phillips writes of communal houses in West Virginia in 1974, focusing on Rayme's crack-up but placing it in a context of a floating community of people 'consulting a series of maps bearing no relation to any physical geography'. Their eventual diaspora leads to a suicide in the mountains, to Belize, to Oakland, to Nicaragua, with some staying 'in West Virginia to continue the same story in even more fragmented fashion'.[6] For the best story in her collection *Black Tickets*, 'El Paso', she takes us back to Texas in 1965 but again the mobility of characters both before and after the time of the narrative is emphasized. One is glimpsed a couple of years later in Toledo racing junk cars, or there's the blonde dancer who comes from Maine but has lived everywhere, or people taking off in a truck with thirty pounds of Mexican grass to meet a connection in Detroit or heading north for Ottawa.[7] In 'Country' Billy and the narrator drive down from Youngstown when the mills close, rolling into 'no-man's-land West Virginia': 'This ain't the South, Billy muttered, his head in his arms on the steering wheel, This is the goddamn past.'[8] Phillips investigates the question 'where are we?' by looking at where we were, by delving and driving into the past.

A personal investigation of the past is found in Raymond Carver's very moving 'Where he was: Memories of my Father'. Carver takes us back not only to his father's personal struggles but also to the struggles of the period, discussed earlier in this book, when he tells us that his father walked, hitched, and rode in box cars to get from Arkansas to Washington State in 1934, looking for work. 'I don't know whether or not he was pursuing a dream when he went out to Washington. I doubt it. I don't think he dreamed much. I believe he was simply looking for steady work at decent pay. Steady work was meaningful work.' After picking apples, he worked building the Grand Coulee Dam. When he had saved some money, he bought a car and went back to Arkansas, 'to help his folks, my grandparents, pack up for the move west. He said later that they were about to starve down there; and this wasn't meant as a figure of speech.' It was then he met his future wife, and 'this big tall country girl and an ex-farm hand turned construction worker' were married by a Justice of the Peace when they were about to leave for Washington. 'My mother spent her wedding night with my dad and his folks, all of them camped beside the road in Arkansas.' He heard Franklin D. Roosevelt dedicate the dam and said that he didn't mention those who died building it. Then he got a job at a sawmill in Oregon, then he moved to Yakima, Washington, later still he went to northern California.[9]

Carver continues to trace his father's other struggles but the point I want to extract is this interweaving of family and history. The Depression and the New Deal drive Carver's father to take to the road, not 'pursuing a dream' but following the basic American populist demand, 'steady work at decent pay . . . meaningful work'. What is also stressed is the experience of work and the overlooked casualties of history, not the Grand Coulee Dam as dedicated by Roosevelt but the friends who died building it. We can move from family history back to fiction; the couple in 'Fast Lanes' are drifting but drifting back in history. They argue about the recent past and the present situation: Thurman is more optimistic, nostalgic for the fun of the previous years just after the draft ended, a period, in his male view, of laughter, sexual freedom, banjos, and flutes. He also tells the narrator that as she's from West Virginia she should be back there mobilizing against the stripmining; he sees himself as a 'good hippie carpenter' and argues for the radical potential of the working class while the narrator feels that the present mood is one of detachment. They are also driving back towards their families. The road spatializes history; 'where are we?' suggests the present loss of direction and the journey traces where that loss originated from, in terms of the family and of recent history.[10]

Given this linking of mobility and history, of drifting as *determined* – as in chosen or as in shaped and produced by historical forces – it is interesting to note the number of accidents in this new fiction. Anne Tyler's Charlotte wakes up to find that their car has gone off the road. Jake says, 'I was just driving along not thinking a thing and next I know I'm in a wheat field.' Falling asleep at the wheel is an extreme symptom of his lack of control over events and ending up in a field an extreme form of being lost. In another Jayne Anne Phillips story a woman returns to visit her separated parents. She leaves on a long drive to see her lover; setting off after her father has hosed down the car, she hits a deer. The story ends with her reaction to the accident, summoning up memories of her family before it was divided. Luke, in Elizabeth Tallent's 'Keats', drives into the back of a Cadillac on the way to Cheyenne – 'It was like running into a fucking black dinosaur.... His Greenpeace bumper sticker was all smashed up.' In Bobbie Ann Mason's 'Still Life with Watermelon', Louise Milsap's life seems ruled by the arbitrary: her husband leaves his business, buys a cowboy hat from Sam's Surplus and heads off to Texas in a T-shirt that says 'You better get in line now 'cause I get better-looking every day' to be a 'born-again cowboy'. Louise loses her job at a supermarket and begins painting pictures of watermelons as she's heard that a rich collector will buy any painting of melons, but at the end of the story the collector is in hospital, no pictures are sold, and her husband returns having totalled his pickup north of Amarillo. The unexplained accident in this empty landscape, like the rich collector's stroke, underlines the seemingly motiveless disruptions of this world where unemployment, problems within marriages, illness, and a wrecked pickup are blurred together. Another story from the 'Dirty Realism' collection, Richard Ford's 'Rock Springs', is about Earl, Edna, and Cheryl driving down to Tampa-St Pete, heading for good times in Florida and away from bad cheques in Montana. They are driving in a cranberry Mercedes that Earl stole from an ophthalmologist's lot in Montana, but the oil light flashes on half way through Wyoming and they are stranded near Rock Springs. The malfunctioning car literally and symbolically undermines the idea of the freedom of the road and the promise of mobility as another chance in life. In the 'More Dirt' collection, cars and trucks tend to have something wrong with them, testifying to a slipping economic position: the convertible leaking oil in 'Fishing with Wussy'; the truck with the buckled frame and a hole in the radiator in 'The Contas Girl'; the rusted convertible with a hole in the floor in 'Escapes'.[11]

The accidents that punctuate this fiction bring together the economic, the social, and the personal, all seen as the intrusion of the arbitrary. Characters believe in the linked terms of luck, chance, accident; things happen to them, a passivity that covers crashed cars, broken relationships, lost jobs. The accident challenges a stable world of meaning – one can explain how it happened but the personal reaction is still 'why me?' The characters avoid taking on their own responsibilities and also avoid allocating blame, so the domestic, the economic, and the social blur into the arbitrary: 'My marriage had just fallen apart. I couldn't find a job. I had another girl. But she wasn't in town. So I was at a bar having a glass of beer, and two women were sitting a few stools down, and one of them began to talk to me.'[12] The flatness of the first-person narration and the accumulation of problems makes the reader of a Raymond Carver story wary, as the narration captures that mixture of hardship and self-deception that characterizes the hard-luck story. Stories without a first-person narrator also mix domestic and economic problems under a rubric of 'bad luck'. Al in 'Jerry and Molly and Sam' feels 'Nothing was going right lately.' There is talk of cutting back at work ('They were laying off at Aerojet when they should be hiring'); his wife has just talked him into renting a more expensive house; he is involved with Jill ('Now he was having an *affair*, for Christ's sake, and he didn't know what to do about it' – note the way he seems more surprised by the word 'affair' than by the fact of his relationship). 'Al was drifting, and he knew he was drifting, and where it was all going to end he could not guess at. But he was beginning to feel he was losing control over everything. Everything. . . . What was he going to do with his life? he wanted to know.' Then his wife's younger sister has given them a dog, one more problem and the one he decides to start with. 'This was Al.'[13] Al is fairly typical as a Carver character. 'Mr Coffee and Mr Fixit' begins with 'I've seen some things', such as his sixty-five-year-old mother kissing a stranger:

> Things are better now. But back in those days, when my mother was putting out, I was out of work. My kids were crazy, and my wife was crazy. She was putting out too. The guy that was getting it was an unemployed aerospace engineer she'd met at AA. He was also crazy.
>
> His name was Ross and he had six kids. He walked with a limp from a gunshot wound his first wife gave him.[14]

'Crazy' stands in for causality; the problems aren't made intelligible but just laid out for us. 'This was Al'; that was Ross.

The literary theorist Todorov once suggested that short stories were not as popular as novels because readers cannot lose themselves in them; the brief duration of the narrative does not allow the reader to forget that it is literature not life. Alternatively, one could say that short stories are enjoyed precisely as 'slices of life', their compressed anecdotal nature convincing the reader of their verisimilitude in a way denied to the longer, more obviously written or plotted narrative. This combination of an effect of reality and one of the literary is a contradiction at the heart of this new fiction's concerns. And one notices how easily chapters of novels could be (have been) printed separately as short stories or how, for example, Frederick Barthelme has recycled stories from his collection *Moon Deluxe* into chapters of his first novel, *Second Marriage*. The significance of this lies with assumptions about causality and conclusion. The theme of much of this fiction, the passive way that people experience their life as something happening to them, rather limits ideas of resolution. Having established the characters' lack of control over their lives, the writer surrenders the chance for neatly rounded conclusions. It is this absence of control over their destinies, the subject of the fiction, rather than any convention of the open-ended narrative that leaves so much of this fiction unresolved. This is also connected to the theme that runs through much of the work considered in this book, that life goes on, where what might seem to be a reassuring cliché gains a harder edge through life being seen so consistently in terms of work and struggle. Martin Scorsese has talked about the confusion over the ending of his film *Mean Streets*, when Johnny (Robert De Niro) and Charlie (Harvey Keitel) are shot:

> people say they're both dead at the end. They're not. They're not. Or they say that Johnny Boy's dead, and Charlie's just wounded. They're not. They're not dead. The fact is they have to go on. That's the worst part. That's the whole thing. Going on.[15]

However much the characters of this fiction try for defined conclusions, leaving homes, making new starts, the whole thing here is also 'going on'.

The short story as both obviously literary and a slice of realistic anecdotal life is also a remarkably appropriate form for capturing the relation between emotions and culture that is central to much of this fiction. Love, jealousy, self-pity, grief: all of these place us uncomfortably on the border of the personally unique and the culturally coded, the real and the artificial. Raymond Carver's fiction concentrates on areas where either language seems inadequate and the appropriate phrase or discourse is missing, or on emotions where language comes easily but with too much cultural baggage, capturing the problem that just as one feels most authentic and individual (being in love, for example) one is most ensnared in already existing scripts. A man obsessed with the idea that his wife may once have been unfaithful to him, ends up, uncharacteristically, in a bar. 'Were there other men, he wondered drunkenly, who could look at one event in their lives and perceive in it the tiny makings of the catastrophe that thereafter set their lives on a different course?' Carver's prose is distanced from the character in order to show his own distance from his life; the drunken but slightly pedantic language combines truth and self-dramatization in almost equal measure. On returning home he finds his wife asleep, and again he is torn between his confused reaction and the weight of cultural stereotypes of masculine behaviour. Again, the point is about 'going on':

> What, after all, should he do? Take his things and leave? Go to a hotel? Make certain arrangements? How should a man act, given these circumstances? He understood things had been done. He did not understand what things now were to be done. The house was very quiet.
>
> In the kitchen he let his head down onto his arms as he sat at the table. He did not know what to do. Not just now, he thought, not just in this, not just about this, today and tomorrow, but every day on earth.[16]

Grief is another emotion where intensely personal feelings find only the secondhand language of culture. Ann in 'A small good thing' reacts to her son's death in hospital:

> 'No, no,' she said. 'I can't leave him here, no.' She heard herself say that and thought how unfair it was that the only words that came out were the sort of words used on TV shows where people were stunned by violent or sudden deaths.[17]

In 'The compartment', Carver links the absence of a domestic language, a way for Myers to talk to his son, with a more obvious absence of language as Myers travels through France unable to understand train announcements or surrounding conversations. The story begins with the break-up of his marriage and the memory of a violent quarrel with his wife which ended in a fight between him and his son. After years of silence the boy writes to Myers and closes his letter with the word 'love', which puzzles Myers and finally brings him to Europe. His travels are a series of lonely misunderstandings of European culture. On the train to meet his son, he decides not to go through with the reunion and finds that someone has stolen his watch and that his luggage is lost. The foreign setting merely highlights a puzzled relation to the world and its language which exists in the broken-up home as much as in the bewilderment of the tourist.[18]

In 'Feathers', Carver captures the tension between emptiness and a surprising richness at the heart of an improvised culture. A work friend asks Jack and his wife over for a meal to meet his wife and child. The friend's name is Bud, emphasizing a male world of friendship and work, but the story's focus is on the anxiety and insecurity felt outside of the world of male buddies. At the opening of the story Jack remembers the birth of Bud's son and the scripted response to this event. Bud comes to work with a box of Dutch Masters cigars, each with a wrapper saying 'IT'S A BOY!' 'I didn't smoke cigars, but I took one anyway. "Take a couple," Bud said. He shook the box. "I don't like cigars either. This is her idea." He was talking about his wife. Olla.' Carver looks at the power of these ideas of how to behave and the anxiety that they both create and cover over. Jack once rang Bud's house but 'blanked' when Olla answered as he couldn't remember her name. This kind of social blankness, and the models of behaviour that are imported to fill it, are the story's subject. Jack and Fran discuss the supper invitation, wondering whether they are supposed to take something to the meal, and the tension between that uncertainty and its relation to media models comes out in Fran's sarcastic suggestion that Jack takes the cigars. '"Take them. Then you and him can go off to the parlor after supper and smoke cigars and drink port wine, or whatever those people in movies drink."' The drive to Bud and Olla's takes them through the country, 'we saw pastures, rail fences, milk cows moving slowly toward old barns'. When Jack admires the house which has corn growing on either side of the drive, Fran just says, 'It's the sticks out here."' In the garden they can see but not name, 'green things the size of baseballs hanging from the vines'. However, the story never juxtaposes rustic simplicity to urban fragmentation nor sophistication to the sticks. The meal and the meeting appear to provide an occasion for satirizing a form of cultural awkwardness, but the story's details – a peacock, the extraordinary ugliness of Bud and Olla's baby – create something stranger and more unexpected. The evening is finally frozen as a turning-point: Fran looks back at it as the moment when things changed for her and Jack, but Jack remembers it as special, a moment of communality before things started to fall apart. The change came later, 'and when it came, it was like something that happened to other people, not something that could have happened to us'.[19]

In a way, 'Feathers' provides a compressed history of earlier debates about the nature of American society and fiction. The nineteenth century saw a stream of complaints from writers that America lacked history, that a novelist could not generate romance from a landscape so bare of Gothic props (ruined abbeys, ancient castles, and so on), that the realist novelist needed the European codes of class, caste, and manners that gave the European novelist the resonant background for his or her narratives of property, paternity, and marriage. Against this idea of the blankness of America, there was the belief in the country's natural and social abundance; Whitman's rhythmic lists of the diversity and heterogeneity of American life rather than Henry James's exiled Americans pursuing culture in Europe. Carver's synthesis of emptiness and mystery, the ordinary and the menacing, is a peculiarly American one. Without falling into a mystique of the road, these stories hold out both the promise and the threat of mobility. The themes of this fiction, especially its clash between residual traditions or beliefs and a modern context, can be related back to the works discussed in the previous chapters, the transformed agrarian landscapes of Chapters 1 and 2, Shepard's staging of a collision between populist themes and popular culture. But rather than the fields and deserts of the works considered earlier, this fiction takes place in a space between the city and the country, not a landscape of authenticity but a space of transition filled with both traditional and contemporary elements: religion and feminism, regional identity and popular 'mass' culture, families and broken relationships. The next section will examine some of the typical settings and themes of this fiction.

There it is

It has been suggested above that much new American writing differs from that of an earlier group of writers whose fiction explored the self-referentiality of language and narrative. A model of fiction as play gives way to a model of fiction as craft, as work, and this is possibly one reason why this writing often concentrates on work, on unemployment, or on the unwaged work of women. This stress on work is connected to populist themes of work as productive of meaning and value, but it has a more immediate context. That is, in Ted Solotaroff's words 'the one genuinely revolutionary development in American letters during the second half of the century: the rise of the creative writing programs'.[20] Writers support themselves through teaching writing as a craft on University courses and in workshops. It is perhaps tempting to see this as linked to the number of short stories and novels about 'roots', reflecting that perennial advice to write from experience and one's own background.

The new fiction overlaps with the writing discussed in Chapter 2 and has been reviewed in these terms. Diane Johnson's review of Bobbie Ann Mason's *In Country* and of Ann Tyler's *The Accidental Tourist* was signalled on the cover of the *New York Review of Books* by the phrase 'hick chic', and Johnson refers to Ann Hulbert's 'Rural chic' article, which I discussed in Chapter 2. Johnson begins her review with a passage from each novel, followed by a passage which is her description of a Norman Rockwell painting. She suggests similarities between the new fiction with its 'fashionable settings in the rural or small-town America among lower-middle-class people' and Norman Rockwell's folksy version of the heartland. This devalues the fiction's achievement and prepares the reader for her conclusion that Mason's and Tyler's novels 'are in a sense Reaganesque dream novels, where the poor are deserving and spunkiness will win'. Tyler's version of Baltimore and Mason's small town suggest 'all of small, middle, rural America'. They share not only a type of setting but also a way of writing, in which meticulous description, a hint of caricature, and a narrative distance combine to place both author and reader as detached spectators. 'Everyone', Johnson writes, 'has remarked the popularity of such settings in recent fiction' but with different interpretations of this popularity. Is it a reaction against the artistic hegemony of the city or a return to '*Tobacco Road*-style realism'? Perhaps the city's metaphoric resonances have been overexploited, hence the shift to the small town, although, as Johnson says, it is difficult to generalize about such a diverse range of writers. She suggests that *In Country* 'seems less a work of fearless realism than one of romantic pastoral charm in a long tradition which includes, among other books, *Little Women*'; whereas Unger's *Leaving the Land* is more in the tradition of Steinbeck or Caldwell. 'After all, two views of rural life have always existed in literature as in painting, formal opposites, like Boucher and Breughel.' To an extent I agree with this distinction, which is why Unger's novel was discussed earlier rather than in this chapter, but the reading of Mason's novel as 'romantic pastoral' seems to misrecognize both its setting and its argument.

Johnson sees their effect of narrative distance as the new feature of these novels. Both novelist and reader, she argues, know more about the characters than they do themselves. The reader becomes 'vaguely patronizing' in his or her superiority to characters who just 'experience a mute feeling usually of disappointment'. But is this not a fairly general experience of reading? The reader 'knows', for example, that Jane Austen's Elizabeth and Darcy are in love and will marry, well before the characters themselves do, and, as that example suggests, this kind of knowledge generates suspense from the tension between our expectations of the conclusion and the narrative obstructions to that conclusion. More relevantly to the fiction in question, the reader knows more about Emma Bovary than she herself does, but Flaubert challenges that knowledge and the novel is, indeed, *about* the gap between Emma's romantic desires and the culture of the author and reader. Flaubert is relevant here, partly because of his influence on earlier women regionalists (Sarah Orne Jewett, Willa Cather, Kate Chopin) but also because Emma Bovary introduces the question of popular culture, which Diane Johnson's review avoids.

For as soon as one notices that Bobbie Ann Mason's characters have Talking Heads tapes on their Walkmans or Springsteen on the car radio, an image of rural charm will no longer serve to characterize the novel. Johnson pursues a parallel with painting beyond the Rockwell comparison and into more interesting areas. The characters are seen as 'flat', in the sense that they seem to have been rendered with a painter's eye, 'carefully, in full color, in a keen-eyed way'. She suggests that writers are moving away from confrontation with their combination of an 'almost photorealistic surface with a strongly ameliorative point of view'. Another substantial misrepresentation of *In Country* is Johnson's point that the Vietnam war is in the past of the novel, while 'in the present . . . nothing bad can happen'. I will return to *In Country* to suggest that its achievement is almost exactly the opposite, but the view that the book is a 'Reaganesque dream novel' must first be challenged. Johnson denies the realism of Tyler and Mason, saying in a resigned way that perhaps it is 'tiresome in the reader to insist upon reality. After all we don't require it in our president.' 'Confrontation,' she concludes, 'is not the national mood, and these are books of our times.'[21] As the opening to this chapter suggests, I also think these books are of our times, but in Mason's case I would argue that the work also directly challenges the 'Reaganesque dream': in subject, taking on the war described by Reagan as 'noble' and also criticizing the government's treatment of veterans; and also, importantly, in terms of setting, for Mason's small town is far from being a rural retreat from modernity or a place of traditional values and the populism of the right-wing 'silent majority'.

As a generalization, it seems true to say that this new fiction resists the temptation to create pastoral arcadias. It may often concern those retreating into nature, whether they are hunting ducks or joining a commune but there is none of the belief in essential agrarian values that we saw in Chapter 1. The characteristic landscape of this fiction is neither the city nor the field but a blurred space between: the fishing trip that commences in the suburb, the wheatfields glimpsed from the car or the Greyhound bus window, the trailer park and the whole *inter*urban landscape of roadside diners, billboards, barns, and buildings seen in the distance. In Carver's 'How about this?', Harry and Emily drive down a country dirt road, 'an astonishing trail of dust rising behind them'. They are in 'flight from the city', supposedly making a new start by roughing it in the country. But Harry's optimism vanishes: 'Now, the rolling pasture land, the cows, the isolated farmhouses of western Washington seemed to hold out nothing for him, nothing he really wanted. He had expected something different. He drove on and on with a rising sense of hopelessness and outrage.' When they arrive at her father's old house,

Emily says, 'There it is', and Harry says, 'Well, we're here.'[22] The past holds out no solution, nor does the pastoral. Bobbie Ann Mason's rural world is not one of, in Johnson's words, 'romantic pastoral charm'. It is seen by the seventeen-year-old Sam as alien with that vision put in the language available, not Jeffersonian visions of past certainties but science fiction.

> Irene turned on her headlights, and they glided on, twisting on the back roads, past old farms with remodeled houses. All the houses were near the road, and the barns were leaning, and the silhouetted farm equipment was standing silent and still, looking like outwitted dinosaurs caught dead in their tracks by some asteroids.[23]

It is a world of broken machinery rather than lost values. Sam looks around her grandparents' farm taking stock of the world that her father knew before he was killed in Vietnam.

> She thought she could comprehend it. Everything he knew was small and predictable: Jesus bugs, blue mold, hound dogs, fence posts. He didn't know about the new consolidated county high school, rock video, M.A.S.H. He didn't know her.[24]

It is important that the world of new American writing is not seen as confined to the rural and that its democratic inclusiveness is recognized. The need for journalism to divide and pigeonhole could separate recent fiction into 'yuppies' and 'hicks'. The fast-lane, cocaine novels of the city, like Bret Easton Ellis' *Less than Zero* or Jay McInerney's *Bright Lights, Big City* versus *Leaving the Land* or *In Country*. But things fall apart in both sets of novels, and the world of Porsches is connected to the world of pickups by the constant threat of the unstable. In a way that is reminiscent of William Dean Howells in the nineteenth century, Carver unites various new writers by his encouragement and recommendation of, for example, both McInerney and Unger. There is also the ease with which writers like Elizabeth Tallent or Tobias Wolff can move from representing cowboy bars to faculty meetings, from car salesmen to architectural engineers. Reading this fiction in Britain where novelists seem to have carved out small territories of specialization (High Church society or middle-aged women academics in North Oxford or disillusioned journalists in Islington, and so on), this mobility is one of the most refreshing features of the writing. The academics in this fiction, as opposed to the work of either Malcolm Bradbury or David Lodge, are not confined to the Humanities. They dissect swans; they study space through telescopes the length of a Greyhound bus and joke about Carl Sagan; they are experts on tropical birds.[25]
A passage that Frederick Barthelme uses in his short story, 'The

Browns' and, slightly revised, in his first novel, *Second Marriage* gives the tone of much of this new fiction in its wry, self-aware, rather than Whitmanesque, appreciation of the everyday.

> I told her I was ready for anything. I thought that sounded pretty good – wry and romantic, something from a modern movie full of wood-sided station wagons and blue-green pools, the kind of movie Hollywood started making in numbers about five or six years ago, in which ordinary life is made fun of and made mysterious and beautiful at the same time. Those are my favorite movies now, which is why I thought my line was pretty good. It didn't thrill Allison.[26]

Barthelme's world is one of baffled heterosexuality. It is as if the adults in this fiction are still locked in the awkwardness of adolescence, or as if the rules of heterosexual relationships have been changed, as indeed they have by the theory and practice of the women's movement, but nobody quite knows what the new rules and goals are. Henry, in *Second Marriage*, is faced with his wife's friendship with his ex-wife, Clare. Clare talks of moving in with Henry, Theo, and Theo's daughter, Rachel. 'We'll be a domestic-unit-of-the-eighties', Henry says.[27] In the short story, 'Monster Deal', Barthelme satirizes men's response to the transformations between men and women. The story's role reversal – Jerry hoovering, Tina setting up deals, going out and getting drunk with Karen – is not due to 'liberal' intentions. It just seems to be happening. Jerry talks about the 'awkward stuff' that is happening to him: 'I bump into doorframes, hit my head on cabinet doors, trip on the legs of the bed – one morning last week I fell down trying to put the orange juice back into the refrigerator.' Tina is at least six feet tall, and Ruth, at work, used to be a college wrestler. The reversal of stereotypes is not only physical, but is also happening at work. Jerry and Larry talk about how all the newspaper deliveries are now made by women.

> '... I don't think I've missed a paper in a year. The phone installers and the cable people are women too. And the UPS people. I've got this one UPS girl who always brings stuff to the house, you know? All decked out in that brown – she looks great. And my exterminator is a woman, a teen-ager. She hates it when I'm there alone and she has to spray. I make a lot of jokes, but that doesn't seem to help.'[28]

Barthelme mingles satire and sympathy in order to render these bemused relations, a mixture of residual stereotypes and attempts at new improvised ways of living. Elizabeth Tallent captures the contemporary situation in a startling and witty image in her story 'Natural Law'. The narrator sells cars at Isaac's Scientific-Upkeep Used Car Lot, and as a publicity stunt he is on stilts inside an iguanodon suit. His wife, Mia, has left him to try to be a dancer in New York.

> Now I wear the cotton T-shirt that Mia left, the one that says 'Sisterhood Is Powerful'. It seems safe to wear within the papier-mâché dimensions of the iguanodon. His eyes may be shadowy and somewhat pensive, and there is a skewed slant to the corners of his mouth, but he is undoubtedly male.[29]

The combination of the T-shirt's slogan and the resonances of the male dinosaur suggest his own inability to know what is expected of him, either by Mia or by contemporary codes of sexuality. Mia says, on the telephone from New York, that he has shown no sign of coming after her:

> 'Is that what I'm supposed to do, come after you? Isn't that a little archaic?'
> 'Christ,' she said. 'I thought if I could have counted on anyone to be archaic, it would have been you.'[30]

Surprising, often surreal images, like a man in a dinosaur suit on a New Mexico car lot, are not uncommon in this fiction. A woman in Tallent's 'Asteroids' talks about her husband, who used to listen to faith healers on the Mexican radio stations as he drove all night to Texas to hunt antelope. He rings her from a taxidermist to ask for a divorce, and tells her that he has been seeing a woman in Texas who was once Miss Indian America but now teaches est.[31] In Richard Ford's 'Empire', Sims and Marge are crossing Montana by train to see Marge's sister, who is in a mental health unit in Minot having tried to kill herself. She used to teach in Seattle but had been living with a Sioux Indian who made metal sculptures from car parts on a reservation, until his recent arrest by the police. In addition she is a Scientologist.[32] Such combinations are, I believe, influenced by three areas: the experiments with alternative lifestyles of the 1960s and 1970s; the influence of photography; Vietnam. The attempts to forge alternative ways of living, from the counter-culture to the ecology movement, are the most obvious cause for an odd (to a British reader) combination like this one in Richard Ford. The influence of photography is perhaps less obvious.

Diane Johnson was quoted above on the photorealistic surface of the new prose. The parallel is useful as much of this work also gains its effects from splitting the descriptive work of realism from its ideological promise of creating a knowable, meaningful world. Christopher Bigsby's comment on David Mamet can be productively applied to this fiction. Mamet, he says, has something of the artist's eye for creating painterly tableaux where realism is subtly deformed, as it is in art by the photorealists whose own portraits of urban vacuity combined realist aesthetics with self-conscious techniques that destabilize the reality they seemed to embrace.[33]

But beside this parallel with an art movement there is a more general point about photography itself. Photography, as Susan Sontag has argued, is peculiarly fitted to represent America, combining a Whitmanesque embrace of the everyday with a mixture of realist images and a casual surrealism. The case made by Sontag for photography's surrealist sensibility (its love of extremes, its eye for the grotesque, its ability to highlight banal but startling juxtapositions of modern life, its love for the free-floating signs of American architecture), illuminates this fiction's ability to mix realistic description with the surreal and the unexpected.[34] Vietnam's surrealist influence is perhaps most associated with the images of films like *Apocalypse Now* or books like Michael Herr's *Dispatches* and their interpretation of the war as a rock 'n' roll conflict. The point I would like to make here, though, concerns the way that Vietnam resists conventional narrative, having no clear beginning, middle, or end. 'For most Americans in Vietnam ... nothing in the war, it seemed, ever really began for any particular reason, and nothing in the war ever really ended, at least as it concerned those still living and unwounded.'[35] Beidler's study of the writing to come out of the war discusses its odd mixture of the literary and deadpan reportage, ways to make the war signify, or even ways to remember it. 'As they used to say in Vietnam "There it is." It was the only possible comment at the time, and it perhaps still comprehends much of what one can say even in retrospect.'[36] The war and the writing it produced can be seen as an influential model for the new fiction's ability to combine the flatly descriptive and the surprising image.

Back in the world

Back in the world: a phrase taken from the Vietnam war, also the title of Tobias Wolff's collection of short stories, and meaning the return home after a year 'in country', a tour of duty in Vietnam. The war echoes in small ways through much of this fiction. If elsewhere the Viet vet stalks the film and television screens, dramatized as a potential explosion of returned violence, here the war is a constant reference, quite often a false reference as characters make out that they were in the war which, in fact, they were lucky enough to escape.[37] But Wolff's title suggests, as the book is not 'about' Vietnam, a continuity between veterans of the war and veterans of the 1960s and 1970s. Like Lawrence Kasdan's film, *The Big Chill*, the vet and the ex-radical are faced with similar adjustments to contemporary reality: 'Where are we?', 'There it is,' 'Back in the world.' Two women writers will now be discussed who do not discuss the war as being the property of one generation, but frame it instead in a perspective of family and communal history.

One of the first things such writing displaces is the idea that Vietnam 'invented' veterans and related notions of the war as a loss of small-town innocence or as America's Fall. Jayne Ann Phillips weaves memories of other wars into her writing; in 'South Carolina' we find the sentence, 'The town slept and remembered wars.'[38] And in *Machine Dreams*, she traces a continuity of war and loss through a family's history: Mitch's World War Two, intervening worries about Korea and 'Civil defense', then Billy going MIA (Missing In Action) in Vietnam. This continuity is then framed by other events, other family history, the two realms (male and female) blurring as when Mitch meets Jean at a VFW (Veterans of Foreign Wars) dance. Danner describes, in 1972, her mother's continual passing on of advice, her preparations for loss: 'Her admonishments are low-key and continuous, as though a war is coming, rationing, proud impoverishment, or a death: something requiring fortitude.' Throughout the novel fragments of language drift in and out of Danner's memories: snatches of pop songs from the radio or her mother's voice, 'one continuous sound weaving through the days and nights. *Pretty is as pretty does, seen and not heard, my only darling, don't ever talk back to your mother . . .*'. America in the novel must be reduced to be affirmed; and the big country shrinks to a chopper crew ('These guys are the only country I know of and they're what I'm defending – I'm not stupid enough to think my country is over here') or to the family, divided by divorce, with children dispersed to Vietnam and California. As Danner says, 'my parents are my country, my divided country. By going to California, I'd made it to the far frontiers, but I'd never leave my country. I never will.'[39]

Mason's achievement with *In Country* is to bring so many histories together: family history with the death of Sam's father in the war, her uncle Emmett's post-Vietnam problems, her mother's remarriage, her grandparents' farm; the historical trajectory that leads from the fall of Saigon to the invasion of Grenada, the latter supported by 90 per cent of Sam's history class; finally the history of popular culture as Sam, in a town that has no mall but does have a Burger Boy and a McDonald's, watches MTV, listens to Springsteen, talks about Boy George, but also wants to find out about the 1960s not just the war but the Beatles, the Doors, Grace Slick being played in Vietnam.

Characters talk about *Ghostbusters*, Joan Rivers, *The Invasion of the Bodysnatchers*, and Mason's subject is the way worlds collide, rural and video cultures, Vietnam and M.A.S.H., and Sam's attempts to make sense out of this mix in a town where they don't want to hear about the war just as they didn't want to hear about hippies and war-protesters, just as a sleeveless T-shirt is considered 'too punk' in Hopewell. It's a novel about culture as much as it's about the war. If the war continues in its psychological effects and in its physical fall-out (Sam is very worried that Emmett was exposed to Agent Orange), it also continues in songs and films. Sam tries to find out more through a mixture of diaries, histories, and popular representations.

The large number of black soldiers in Vietnam has been pointed out and Sam's mother makes a similar point about the class make-up of the dead and the veterans.

> 'It was country boys. When you get to that memorial, you look at the names. You'll see all those country boy names, I bet you anything. Bobby Gene and Freddie Ray and Jimmy Bob Calhoun.... You look at those names and tell me if they're not mostly country boy names. Boys who didn't know their ass from their elbow.'

'In Country' – the title phrase fuses Vietnam and the American country, looking at the transformations of rural America as well as at the war. Sam goes into a mall in Maryland, en route to the Washington monument, and looks at the *Born in the U.S.A.* album. The following passage blends a pervasive consumer culture with Vietnam and rural Kentucky, the image for this mental collage being taken from MTV.

> The mall is split by a median strip of tropical plants, thriving under skylights. The palm trees are tall, and the vines – familiar houseplants – are climbing them. Sam stands transformed by the trees and the thick foliage. They become the jungle plants of Southeast Asia. And then they change to cypress trees at Cawood's Pond, and the murky swamp water, infested with snakes, swirls around her. All of these scenes travel through her mind like a rock-video sequence. She wishes she knew the song that goes with it.[40]

Bobbie Ann Mason has spoken about her difficulty when starting to write, taking years of living in the North before she could turn to her background in Mayfield, Kentucky. She felt like 'an exile of sorts' and talks about her 'culture-shock', but it was realizing that 'many of those people back home were going through culture-shock too' that gave her her subject. She admires, and has written on, Nabokov, and has said: 'In some ways, comparing myself to him is like comparing Willy (*sic*) Nelson to an opera singer, but I felt connected to him because he had the sensibility of an exile, was working with two opposing cultures which made him peculiar, the same way I felt myself.'[41] What is important is that this exile from Main Street, from the world of small-town populism, is not seen as a personal loss of roots but as a more general cultural process.

British writing often seems obsessed with a kind of national decay, a faded grandeur and shabby gentility located in peeling boarding-houses, once grand seaside hotels, crumbling country houses; a peculiarly English breakdown recurs in fiction and drama, quiet schizophrenia, senility, sherry sipped furtively behind lace curtains. New American fiction seems to capture, in a more convincing manner, the *mess* of modern life: the flickering televisions, the broken relationships, the bounced cheques and unpaid bills. Writing that, as Jayne Anne Phillips has said about Carver's work, deals with 'how things fall apart and what is left when they do'.[42] Writers like Pynchon have explored the parallels between fiction-making and the larger plots of modern history; this fiction deals with lower-case history, the compromises of everyday working and domestic relationships. The reason why a sparse tale of a car thief in Wyoming speaks to a non-American audience is partly because we all, Europeans and Americans, live like these characters on the border between various traditions (domestic, familial, communal, regional, class) and the ubiquity of modern popular culture.

This fiction challenges critiques of popular culture as manipulative and the related theories that make it over-important: socialist, feminist, and conservative arguments that see the media as the most powerful causal force; discourses such as rock journalism or the sociology of subcultures that overlook other determinants. Instead people here are seen as also constructed elsewhere within families, schools, regions, and the larger divisions of class and gender. The characters dream and struggle to make sense of their lives on the contemporary frontier that marks the meeting of cable television and community, MTV and home. The anxiety many of them feel rarely crystallizes into politics, but both the tiresome self-analysis of the 'Me generation' and the desire to return to a simpler and mystified past are avoided. Instead, there is the nagging feeling that things have gone wrong: 'a distracted, restless feeling like the feeling you have forgotten something when you are too far from home to go back for it'.[43] The feeling that it shouldn't happen to us, but somehow it has.

5 American crime: 'Debts no honest man could pay'

Crime is a disease. Meet the cure.[1]

The important distinction here is not between political and non-political offenders, but between the profitable illegalities perpetrated with impunity by those who use the law, and the simple illegalities that the penal system uses to create a standing army of criminals.[2]

Familiar American pieties are always linked to criminality. That's why they're familiar American pieties.[3]

Milk, honey, and the beekeeping franchises

In David Mamet's 1975 play, *American Buffalo*, the inept and unstable petty criminal Teach bursts into a definition of that American cornerstone, free enterprise. It's the freedom 'Of the *Individual* ... To Embark on Any Fucking Course that he sees fit. ... In order to secure his honest chance to make a profit.' He asks if he's out of line or if this statement makes him a Commie. He reminds Don, the owner of the junk shop that gives the play its setting, that the 'country's *founded* on this'. Without it they are 'just savage shitheads in the wilderness .... Sitting around some vicious campfire.'[4] The free enterprise he has in mind is breaking and entering. As Christopher Bigsby has pointed out in his study of Mamet, the speech parodies the principles of the American revolution but the audience is forced to see the underlying parallel. Teach sees free enterprise as separating American individualism from Native American co-operation – the Indians as savage shitheads sitting around vicious campfires. But the play's title refers to a coin; the symbol of the West, the buffalo, has been reduced to money.

To introduce one of the themes of this chapter we can take a closer look at one of Teach's founding fathers, as seen by a historian and by a politician in a George Higgins' novel. Garry Wills centres his study of the intellectual and historical context of the Declaration of Independence, *Inventing America*, on Jefferson, but he sees Samuel Adams as the most influential figure at the first two Congresses, the 'truest Cromwellian' fusing 'the highest religious zeal with the lowest political tricks'. Even in Massachusetts people were not sure of his precise involvement in, for example, the Boston Tea Party or the first shots at Lexington. Wills talks of his 'grand vision', his embodiment of the 'Commonwealth tradition' but also of his

> curiously modern arsenal of weapons – street theater, surgical rioting, leaked documents, staged trials, managed news. He even had his own 'wire service' – the committees of correspondence, serviced by Paul Revere. The greatest gift of Adams, however, was for that distinctive American contribution to politics: the caucus.[5]

In *A Choice of Enemies*, George V. Higgins has his drunken Speaker of the Massachusetts State House, Bernie Morgan, talk of the public's disillusion with politics. They expect the House to be like Kennedy, Plato's *Republic*, and America's founding fathers, all combined. Bernie's career is based on deals not ideals, on the granting and calling in of favours. He complains that he's never heard 'a single word from Plato about this year's budget deficit for human services. It's almost like he isn't interested.' Bernie Morgan gives another view of Samuel Adams, concentrating on a continuity rather than on Wills' combination of Protestant principles and modern techniques. If the public feel that there's a gap between America's revolution and its day-to-day politics, he closes the gap by claiming that politics has always been about trade-offs, deals, and corruption:

> 'I bet old Sam Adams there when he was raising hell about the king, I bet he had a little dodge going on there one way or other, if the Revolution didn't work out he was gonna be a tax collector or some idiotic cousin of his was right in line to get some nifty job.'[6]

Or as Leo Rosen, a young journalist in the novel, says:

> 'The first thing anybody taught me when I got here was that when somebody tells he's got something he wants to do that'll wind up making everything between Albany and the ocean into a land of milk and honey, find out if his family's got the beekeeping franchises locked up.'[7]

Higgins' novel about the mood of withdrawal from politics as Watergate was breaking, *A City on a Hill*, again juxtaposes American myths about politics with the murky reality. The novel gets its title from the two quotations which preface it: John Winthrop, the designated governor of the Massachusetts Bay Colony, giving a shipboard sermon en route to Boston in 1630, saying 'wee shall be as a Citty upon a hill. The eies of all people are uppon Us', a phrase used by Kennedy addressing the Massachusetts legislature while awaiting inauguration as President in 1961, that appears as the novel's second epigraph. However, the novel casts politics as a game or a business, a professional rather than idealistic matter.[8] In novels such as *Missionary Stew*, *The Mordida Man*, and *The Porkchoppers*, Ross Thomas maps out a region where law, academia, journalism, and politics meet, generally secretively. *The Porkchoppers* concerns a dirty campaign for president in a large union. It is prefaced by a definition of a porkchopper as a corrupt union official and by the pointed statement that 'The events and characters in this book are fiction and if any of them ever happened to the American labour movement, it is not only sheer coincidence, but also something of a pity.' The novel's fixers and experts come from various backgrounds, ranging from journalism to the FBI to politics and the professional election fixing of Indigo Boone, whose claim to fame is that he stole Chicago for Kennedy in 1960, and a campaign manager whose MA thesis on 'The Use and Misuse of the Pension Fund of the International Brotherhood of Teamsters, Chauffeurs, Warehousemen and Helpers of America' won him job offers from two large unions.[9] Part of the appeal of these novels is the idea of being an insider, penetrating through political rhetoric and journalists' reports to the real (and hence *dirty*) story underneath. Eleanor Rhodes in *The Mordida Man* wrote her doctoral dissertation on 'Parameters of Deception in the Second Nixon Administration' and she goes to work for Bingo McKay, a behind-the-scenes political and economic expert, who promises 'I can't guarantee you anything except money and the fact that you're gonna be close to the nut-cuttin', if that's the kinda stuff you're interested in.'[10] She's not the only one who wants to be close to the 'nut-cuttin'' – readers of thrillers also want this, partly to confirm their cynicism about politics and their populist discontent with the official face of government.

A traditional figure for converting this cynicism into an ethical code is the private eye, Hammett's operatives or Chandler's Marlowe confronting the widespread corruption of law and government. This figure lives on in Robert Parker's Boston private detective, Spenser. In *The Widening Gyre* he is hired to protect a fundamentalist Congressman, Meade Alexander, who is running for Senator. When approached for the job he is asked if he has any trouble with Alexander's politics and replies, 'I have trouble with everybody's politics.' Although sceptical about Alexander's appeals to tradition, Spenser also opposes the contemporary political scene with a reference to an old-fashioned code. When he goes to see Alexander's opponent, a Congressman with criminal connections, Washington politics becomes the target for his jaundiced wit: 'The corridor was full of young preppy-looking women, congressional staff, bustling about, tending to the nation's needs. A pork barrel to be shared, a log to be rolled, in quest of more perfect union.' As Barry, the Congressman's aide, exits briskly Spenser thinks: 'Nobody in D.C. was spinning his wheels. There was probably a boon to be doggled and Barry was anxious to get to it.'[11]

The discourse of populist discontent with politics is not confined to the private eye's traditionally epigrammatic wit. Elmore Leonard's Joe LaBrava worked for a period scanning threatening letters to the President:

> Letters addressed to 'Peanut Head Carter, the Mushmouth Motherfucker from Georgia.' Or that ever-popular salutation, 'To the Nigger-loving President of the Jewnited States.' ... There was a suggestion, LaBrava said, the President ought to be 'pierced with the prophet's sword of righteousness for being a goddamn hypocrite.' Fiery, but not as practical as the one that suggested, 'They ought to tie you to one of those MX missiles you dig so much and lose your war-lovin ass.'[12]

Hate-mail, of course, exists in other countries but this populist distrust of politicians is not confined to such letters, as evidenced by the 'gonzo journalism' of Hunter S. Thompson, whose fear and loathing of politicians can only be paralleled in the British press by cartoonists (Thompson, of course, has often worked with Ralph Steadman). A Thompson line like 'Hubert Humphrey is a treacherous, gutless old ward-heeler who should be put in a goddamn bottle and sent out with the Japanese Current' is close to the inventive, violent language of this chapter's crime fiction. Interestingly, the politicians (temporarily) liked by Thompson tend to be placed in a populist tradition. A relevant example for this chapter is Thompson's extravagant praise for Jimmy Carter's speech, while still Governor of Georgia, criticizing the system of criminal justice in 'the voice of an angry agrarian populist'.[13]

Themes discussed in previous chapters will reappear here transformed by their urban setting and their crime genre embodiment: the kind of populist cynicism that I have just sketched out and its identification of business with criminality, blurring the divisions between legal and illegal economies; a self-conscious use of an *unofficial* language, a tough, rhythmic celebration of the street's demotic styles which, as suggested above, is a way of talking back to politics; the problematic masculinity constructed in this style and in notions of crime and policing that are anchored in a concern for *work* rather than morality. The last chapter looked at loss in recent American fiction and there is a certain continuity from the baffled men and women of that fiction, with their lost jobs and broken relationships, their domestic violence, their drinking and petty crimes. My title phrase 'debts no honest man could pay' suggests an extreme version of that loser's trajectory, as well as having a more obvious relevance for this book as it comes from Springsteen's 'Johnny 99', the song from *Nebraska* that he played in response to Reagan's use of his name in a campaign speech. Explanations of crime as caused by 'bad luck' or environment, both suggested in the song, link various images of American crime, from the old Warner Brothers gangster movies to liberal criminology. The album *Nebraska* constantly refers both to films and to crime, calling on the various figures of American criminal myth: the outlaw, the fugitive, the serial killer of Malick's film *Badlands* and Springsteen's song 'Nebraska', or the brothers in love with the same woman, one becoming a law officer, the other moving outside the law ('Highway Patrolman'), or the small-time criminal gambling on one big success, familiar from songs (think of the numerous hustlers and drifters in Tom Waits' songs), in writing (the lowlife genre, 'Runyon', and so on), and films. This figure appears on *Nebraska* in 'Atlantic City' (which takes its title from Louis Malle's film *Atlantic City*) where Springsteen repeats the line about debts no honest man could pay.

Malle's *Atlantic City* portrays a city being brutally modernized. The demolition of old buildings sets the scene for the film's ironic nostalgia, as Burt Lancaster looks back to the stylish and individualistic days of gangsterdom. Its plot pits the old and the young, retired petty criminals and hippy hustlers, against the more organized, more corporate world of large-scale drug dealing. Here we can see a connection with populist critiques of corporate America: from the 'robber barons' to the world of the trusts, from gangsters to the world of organized crime. A similarity can be observed across these worlds. Upton Sinclair, a socialist writing early this century about anti-monopolistic feeling, stated:

> This power of concentrated wealth which rules America is known by many names. It is 'Wall Street', it is 'Big Business', it is 'The Trusts'. It is 'The System' of Lincoln Steffens, the 'Invisible Government' of Woodrow Wilson, the 'Empire of Business' of Andrew Carnegie, the 'Plutocracy' of the populists.[14]

This is echoed in Richard Stark's *Point Blank*, in which his brutal hero Parker takes on organized crime: 'The funnies call it the Syndicate. The goons and hustlers call it the Outfit. You call it the Organization.'[15] In both cases individuals – the outlaw, the private eye, the investigative journalist, the lone policeman – take on the world of covert power. Further parallels between crime and business will be considered in the next section.

Business and crime: the Street and the street

> It's like this. . . . There are some people who are in business, who move
> in the realm of profit and loss pure and simple . . . and who just naturally
> pick up that pistol when trying to locate capital. Then there are these
> low-IQ trigger-pullers who just like to play very very rough, especially
> with themselves. They think dying by the gun is noisy enough that it
> must make sense and they figure it just can't hurt that much, something
> that noisy. . . . Some are in it for profit, Jamie, and others are in it for
> loss.[16]

Kyle McLaren in Elmore Leonard's *Stick* gives advice about investments for a living but, as she tells her stockbroker father, she is no
longer satisfied: 'I want to *do* something, see tangible results.' When
young she studied sociology and dated sociology majors, but

> textbook conversations ran out of gas and when they took the Orange
> Line to Dudley Station and prowled through Roxbury she found she
> could not study 'real people' statistically: they were in a life that made
> hers seem innocent make-believe. Still, she was drawn to the street,
> fascinated, feeling a rapport she didn't understand.

When she tried to tell her father this his reply was, 'there was the
Street and there was the street. One was neither more real nor unreal
than the other.' But the Street, the world of Wall Street, seems to
her to be 'concocted, invented in the name of commerce; while the
other was concerned with existence, degrees of survival'. She still
believes in this distinction, and when she compares 'her Street with
the ghetto street – or with rural, suburban or industrial streets, for
that matter – she felt insulated, left out of life'. She only deals 'in
paper, in notes, contracts, certificates, coupons, with a self-conscious
feeling of irrelevance'. And she tells her father that she wants to 'get
into manufacturing, make something'.[17] Kyle conflates two oppositions into the single dichotomy between real and unreal. One of
these oppositions has been discussed earlier in this book as one of the
central themes of late-nineteenth-century populism: finance capitalism versus manufacturing, paper ('notes, contracts, certificates,
coupons') versus production, *making* something. What is interesting
about her relationship with Stick is that while she has a nagging
feeling of being insulated from reality, he notices the similarities that
undermine the other opposition between the Street and the street.

Stick's employer Barry feeds off Kyle's financial expertise and also
deliberately hires Stick and Cornell, both ex-convicts, in order to mix
the Street with the street and project himself as one who knows both
realms and is able to speak as easily to ex-car thieves as to his broker.

Stick learns from Barry and, especially, from Kyle and he says to Cornell: 'I was just thinking ... that making a phone call to your broker in the back seat of a Cadillac doing sixty miles an hour with the air conditioning on is an awful lot easier than going in someplace with a gun, isn't it?'[18] Kyle thinks about the possibility of helping Stick get started: 'from armed robber to investment counselor. Forget the gun, Stickley, there's an easier way to make it.'[19] What bridges the two worlds, making Barry's attempts at street styles and Stick's interest in investments possible, is that earlier populist opposition. Both armed robbery and playing the market are seen as opposed to making something, a matter of style, nerve, and knowledge rather than production. I'll return to ways in which crime is, however, seen as work but this parallel between the Street and the street can be followed up in the plays of David Mamet.

Mamet has concentrated his criticisms of the American success ethic on the kinship between crime and business. Talking about his work he looks back to Veblen, whose work at the turn of the century demystified the leisure class and looked to engineering and production as opposed to finance capitalism. Mamet draws on Veblen to give a context for the smalltime criminals of *American Buffalo*:

> As Thorstein Veblen says, the behaviour on this level, in the lumpenproletariat, the delinquent class, and the behaviour on the highest levels of society, in the most rarefied atmosphere of the board room and the most rarefied atmosphere of the leisure class, is exactly identical. The people who create nothing, the people who do nothing, the people who have all sorts of myths at their disposal to justify themselves ... they steal from us.[20]

This view that there's no difference 'between the *lumpenproletariat* and stockbrokers or corporate lawyers' acknowledges that 'part of the American myth is that a difference exists, that at a certain point vicious behaviour becomes laudable'.[21] (One could think here of the John Landis film *Trading Places* and the way that Dan Ackroyd and Eddie Murphy end up as partners. Commodity broking and hustling in the streets are seen as quite compatible.) At the core of Mamet's critique is the American ability 'to suspend an ethical sense and adopt instead a popular, accepted mythology and use that to assuage your conscience like everyone else is doing'.[22] So inept criminals planning a burglary in *American Buffalo* can be seen as engaged in the 'same thing that goes on in board rooms all over this country. It's the same thing that goes on in advertising agencies.... How can we get the American people to bend over.'[23]

Given Mamet's populist distaste for the non-producer ('people who create nothing. The people who do nothing') it's interesting to note that one way that his criminals cope with this suspension of ethics is, as we shall see, to adopt an image of professionalism, a code of work. The other cultural alibis that unite business and crime substitute central American myths for ethics. Success, whether for Mamet's criminals in *American Buffalo* or his salesmen in *Glengarry, Glen Ross*, is linked to the persistence of the frontier ethic and its mythology of masculinity. Mamet has pointed out that the cry of 'go West and make your fortune' originated from storekeepers and the railroads (and, one could add, the state) playing on people's greed rather than their ideals. He cites W. C. Fields who pointed out that you can't cheat an honest man.[24] This line is obviously relevant to Mamet's real estate salesmen in *Glengarry, Glen Ross*, who can sell worthless land because of the assumptions shared by themselves and the buyers. Mamet's note prefacing the play talks about his own experience in a Chicago real-estate office and explains some of the salesmen's terms. The appointment arranged between a salesman and one of the 'gullible Chicagoans' is called a *lead*, 'in the same way that a clue in a criminal case is called a *lead* – i.e. it may lead to the suspect, the suspect in this case being a *prospect*'.[25] The salesmen are driven by competition and the play builds to a break-in at the office and the theft of the leads. Bigsby comments that 'criminality is not merely a result of competition; it is an essential element of the business'. He cites the note about the term *lead*, saying that 'The confusion of realms is clearly deliberate, so that the actual crime involved in robbing the real-estate office is merely an objectification of the crimes daily perpetrated in the name of business.'[26] But this overlooks the further confusion of realms in that the word 'lead' links selling to policing, not stressing the salesmen's criminality but their similarity to detectives closing in on a suspect. Like a 'friendly' policeman in an interrogation, the salesmen re-enact the near-criminal nature of the potential buyer's American dreams. Shelly 'the Machine' Levine goes through a deal that he thinks he's just closed: 'I tell them. "This is now. This is that *thing* that you've been dreaming of, you're going to find that suitcase on the train, the guy that comes through the door, the bag that's full of money." '[27] To talk them through a deal is to enact the perfect crime, to catch that criminality, the bag full of money, and if they don't take the chance they are found guilty of being both unmanly and un-American.

Bigsby brings out the way that criticism of Mamet, especially in reviews of *American Buffalo* which concentrated on the characters' lowlife criminal status and frequently obscene dialogue, works to distance the audience from the characters and make the play into a naturalistic study of a subclass. He shows how this overlooks the poetic quality of the language and he also quotes Mamet on what might be at stake in these reactions. Mamet says that the play was about American business ethics:

> I felt angry about business when I wrote the play. Businessmen left it muttering vehemently about its inadequacies and pointlessness. But they weren't really mad because the play was pointless – no one can be forced to sit through an hour-and-a-half of meaningless dialogue – they were angry because the play was about them.[28]

But he's also said that the play wasn't about other people; telling Bigsby in an interview that he and the actors felt that they were doing a play about themselves.[29] The play can be about writers, businessmen, and burglars if the characters are granted representative status. Mamet says that critics refused to consider Teach and the others as metaphors, although in other drama the wealthy or those dying from cancer had been seen as metaphors for a larger social condition.[30] Another artist who has been seen as realistic in a similarly reductive way, closing off references and resonances, is Martin Scorsese. There is a similar concentration on obscenity and violence in his work at the expense of any idea that Scorsese's films might have something to say about, for example, masculinity in general rather than just representing boxers, petty criminals, and small-time Mafia figures.

Mamet and Scorsese share a similar approach to their characters, with Mamet once telling the director of a production of *American Buffalo* that his thieves were all trying to be excellent men but 'society hasn't offered them any context to be excellent in'.[31] That suggests Springsteen's 'debts no honest man could pay', sharing a notion of the inevitability of failure or crime (or failure in crime). It is also an apt line for the characters of Scorsese's films, such as *Mean Streets*, *Taxi Driver*, and *Raging Bull*. Charlie (Harvey Keitel) in *Mean Streets* has to negotiate the entangled codes and contradictions of New York's Little Italy – Catholicism, masculinity, the organized crime of the Mafia, the disorganized life of friends like Johnny Boy (De Niro) – to the extent that he has to be reminded that there are contradictions between his life and beliefs, and is told 'You know, Saint Francis was not a numbers runner.' Scorsese's *Taxi Driver* and Mamet's *Edmond* have strong similarities; the main characters in both are unsettling combinations of victims and aggressors, moving through a world of pimps and pornography until a familiar American identification of violence and redemption proves impossible to resist. *Edmond*, like *Taxi Driver*, portrays New York with a combination of realism and almost dreamlike stylization.

If *Glengarry, Glen Ross* blurs together the realms of selling and stealing, *American Buffalo* uses the words 'business' and 'friendship' to cover shifting and unstable partnerships.[32] The words are used almost as fetishes to disavow the solitude and powerlessness of each of the characters. Bigsby notes that Teach is described as a 'friend and associate' of Don's, a phrase also used to introduce Bernie Littko in Mamet's *Sexual Perversity in Chicago*.[33] Private and public worlds, friendship and business, are inextricably linked. In a world of arbitrarily changing criminal alliances this entanglement leads to contradiction and violence. Teach tells Don: 'I don't fuck with my friends, Don. I don't fuck with my business associates. I am a businessman, I am here to do business, I am here to face facts.'[34] The play uncovers the emptiness under each of these terms: friends, business, especially facts. The repetition of 'business' in the play is part of the substitution of a professional code for morality. Although this professional code is undermined by the incompetence of their planned burglary, it is one of the ways in which Mamet sees crime as a metaphor for business ethics. Teach persuades Don not to rely on Bob as his partner, 'a guy can be too loyal, Don. Don't be dense on this. What are we saying here? Business.'

'I mean the guy's got you're taking his high-speed blender and a Magnavox, you send the kid in. You're talking about a real *job* ... they don't come in right away and know they been *had*...

You're talking maybe a safe, certainly a good lock or two, and you need a guy's looking for valuable shit, he's not going to mess with the stainless steel silverware, huh, or some digital clock.'[35]

Teach puts himself forward as a professional, dividing criminals into those who know what they're doing, businessmen like himself, and amateurs like Bob. This professional code can be seen as the reverse point to the populist view of the criminal being like the stockbroker the non-producer *par excellence*. It's a way of reinserting work into crime and a way of introducing *rules* into what might seem an anarchic realm. Examples of this could include Frank Ryan's very funny 'ten rules for success and happiness' in armed robbery in Elmore Leonard's *Swag*. Ryan enters his career with Stick, having been a car salesman, and some of his rules parody the American selling philosophy – '1. ALWAYS BE POLITE ON THE JOB. SAY PLEASE AND THANK YOU.'[36] Or the professionalism of Cadillac Teddy in *Kennedy for the Defense* by George Higgins. One of Kennedy's clients, Teddy Franklin is a car thief, but a specialized one: '"Your Porsche, your Corvette," Teddy said, "your Jaguar, your Mercedes? I can get you them. But I'm not used to them, you know?"'[37] The point lies in the specialization which turns breaking the law into making a living; hence rules like not being greedy, only stealing three Cadillacs a week, for example. In the world of crime fiction the most rule-governed figures, precisely because they operate outside the official law, are the private eyes with their private codes: Hammett's Sam Spade, Chandler's Marlowe, Macdonald's Archer. In a different way, some recent crime fiction stresses the shared knowledge that links lawyers, criminals, and detectives in a world where crime, its detection, and its prosecution are not seen morally but as work. This work is obviously in conflict (stealing cars, catching car thieves, defending or prosecuting them) but shared experience and knowledge leads to wry grins of recognition across this conflict; admiration of how well someone is doing a job, humour at how badly others are performing. Certain uses of language and ideas of masculinity bind this world together and, as we have seen, connect it to the business world.

Writers can establish a continuity for their work and a density for their realism through using the same main characters and settings – Chandler's Marlowe and Los Angeles, Ed McBain's 87th Precinct. The self-consciousness of realism in Leonard, Higgins, and others will be discussed later, for the moment I want to stress that realism is not just a literary choice but also a position on this world and on the relays that link politics, law, policing, and crime. K. C. Constantine's *Always a Body to Trade* is a classic example of realism as an attitude and educational process, as the novel deals with police chief Mario Balzic's attempts to inform a new major, who made 'law and order' an issue in his campaign, of the realities of crime and policing. Crime, he points out, cannot be prevented or eradicated only regulated:

> 'Mr. Mayor, if I was unemployed through no fault of my own and I had run out of options to find honest work, I would soon find dishonest work. The fact is that unless you are born rich it takes money to live in this society, and you have to get it one way or another – I don't care what the WCTU thinks of how you do it, or the PTA or the DAR or the AMA or the ABA. You got to have tickets to ride, and not too many people care how you get the tickets. Just so you get them.'[38]

He underlines his argument about the impossibility of preventing crime by referring to prisons:

> 'there is no more controlled society anywhere. There is absolute gun control, for example. There's prohibition not only of alcohol but of every other controlled substance. There are frequent searches of residences and of bodies. There is no Bill of Rights to protect anybody from anything, from illegal search and seizure to cruel and unusual punishment.' (p. 30)

But crimes still happen in prisons, lots of them.

Later in the novel he undermines the mayor's belief in detection: 'I don't know where you get your ideas about how police "solve" murders, but I'm gonna give you a real fast course in reality.' The

145

police 'live on informers. We uphold the law on them, we "solve" cases on them. They're our blood, Mr. Mayor' (pp. 50–1). The notion of corruption is the next to go: Balzic says 'Mr. Mayor, bad guys don't corrupt good guys. Good guys see bad guys making it and they go tell the bad guys if they want to keep on making it, they're going to have to set a little something aside for the good guy fund' (p. 110). Mayor Strohn calls this cynical and the atmosphere certainly resembles the novels discussed in the first section where politics was seen to be a matter of deals and trade-offs. Balzic asks the mayor to listen to a conversation he is having with Leroy, a black fugitive wanted on drug charges who possesses photographic evidence of the corruption of an agent of the Bureau of Drug Enforcement. Again it's part of the mayor's education – 'you're about to see how most crimes get solved' (p. 184). Feinstein, a deputy US attorney, arrives to sort out the deal with Leroy and takes over Balzic's educational function. Shocked by the bargaining the mayor talks of a travesty of justice. Feinstein tells him, 'You are confusing some sort of morality – God only knows which brand yours is – with the successful prosecution of serious felons.' For Feinstein, Leroy, a habitual felon with information, is treasure and he explodes: 'For God's sake, man, what the hell do you think the law is all about? It's trade, it's bargain, it's compromise, it's negotiate, it's deal, deal, deal!' Mayor Strohn is still amazed: 'There is no thought of justice here. There is no thought of order here. Or law. Neither one of you is talking about creating a better place to live' (pp. 196–8). Instead, he says, all they are talking about is specifics. But it's not just the specifics he objects to, although Constantine's point is this gulf between rhetoric about crime and its messy reality, it's also the *style*. It's not just that Leroy is not going to be punished but also that he is sitting with the chief of police eating fried chicken and potato salad and drinking rum and coke; and that there's a rapport between Leroy and Balzic – before the mayor arrives there are some wonderful pages where the two discuss fried chicken, kolbassi, braciole, and the need to cut the 'may-o-naise with yo-gurt'; and finally that he, the mayor, is being called a 'jive motherfucker' by a black habitual criminal with drug problems. This issue of language and the rapport between policeman and criminal will be the subject of the next section. But the politics of these lessons in the reality of policing needs clarification.

It is important to stress that these novels are not, by and large, to be classified with the ubiquitous rogue cop of films and television. The rogue cop (like Eastwood's *Dirty Harry*) is trying to fight both crime *and* the law. His crusade is against the red tape (in other words, protection of people's civil liberties) that hamper his pursuit of crime. There are occasions in Elmore Leonard novels where the policeman hero bends rules or acts outside the law (*Glitz, Split Images, City Primeval*), but this stems from a combination of personal reasons and established practices (again the idea of policing as work) rather than being a moral crusade. A comparison of George Higgins and Michel Foucault may illuminate the distinction.

In *The Patriot Game* Pete Riordan goes to a meeting with prison superintendent Ken Walker to try to convince him to block any pardon for one of his prisoners. Walker and Riordan are old friends but the meeting also involves Fred Mayes and Oscar Dietz. Riordan mocks their notions of reform and rehabilitation and Mayes' language, drawn from psychology and sociology and full of phrases like 'foreshortened parameters', 'conceptual grasp', 'the structural dynamic of the rehabilitative environment'. The stage is set for a familiar conflict: liberal, obstructive administrators more concerned for the criminal than the victim, versus the tough law agent who restates in blunt language the 'commonsense' view of crime and punishment, in other words the most reactionary and most common form of populism in the crime genre. But the picture gets more complicated: Walker enjoys Riordan's mockery of reform and jargon but later confides that the old punitive way didn't work either, for tough measures failed to prevent riots, rackets, and fights. Maybe, he says, Mayes' reforms and rehabilitation schemes can get them through the summer without having to call in the National Guard. 'Maybe he can't. Maybe this thing, maybe nobody can run it. Maybe it just can't be done.'[39] Instead of the expected reactionary position, we are left with the impossibility of prisons, and that, of course, is where Michel Foucault comes in.

In his very influential study of 'The birth of the prison', *Discipline and Punish*, Foucault challenges what might seem self-evident by pointing out that the movement for prison reform is not recent: 'It does not even seem to have originated in a recognition of failure. Prison "reform" is virtually contemporary with the prison itself: it constitutes, as it were, its programme.' And the accompanying discourses and mechanisms which are supposed to correct the prison appear to 'form part of its very functioning, so closely have they been bound up with its existence throughout its long history'. The history of the prison does not follow the expected chronology – establishment, failure, reform. 'For the prison, in its reality and visible effects, was denounced at once as the great failure of penal justice.' So Foucault revises and reverses the problem and asks what is served by this history of failure. He suggests that prisons are not intended to eliminate offences but 'to distinguish them, to distribute them, to use them'.

Penality would then appear to be a way of handling illegalities, of laying down the limits of tolerance, of giving free rein to some, of putting pressure on others, of excluding a particular section, of making another useful, of neutralizing certain individuals and of profiting from others. In short, penality does not simply 'check' illegalities; it 'differentiates' them, it provides them with a general 'economy'.[40]

Is not this precisely what Balzic tries to teach the mayor? What emerges is the question of *dealing with crime*, not just dealing with in the Clint Eastwood/Sylvester Stallone way of the vigilante cop, but also *dealing* with, in other words, being part of a process of tolerating some crimes, allowing plea-bargaining to get a conviction or encourage informers, and so on. A complicated machinery of crime, policing, and law which does not eliminate so much as regulate. Or as the prosecutor in *The Judgment of Deke Hunter* says: 'When I came in here ... I thought I was going into law enforcement. And now I know, what I'm really doing's law adjustment.'[41]

Language, the body, masculinity

Joan: Men.
Deborah: Yup.
Joan: They're all after only one thing.
Deborah: Yes. I know. (*Pause.*)
Joan: But it's never the *same* thing.[42]

Bernie: Equal Rights Amendment? Equal Rights Amendment? I'll give you the fucking Equal Rights Amendment. Nobody ever wrote *me* no fucking amendments. Special *interest* groups, *okay* ... but who's kidding who here, huh? (*Pause.*) We got baby seals dying in Alaska and we're writing amendments for *broads*? I mean, I'm a big fan of *society* ... but this bites the big one. I'm sorry.[43]

a line's got to scan. I'm very concerned with the metric scansion of everything I write, including the rhythmic emphasis of the word 'fucking'. In rehearsal I've been known to be caught counting the beats on my fingers.[44]

Conventional comments on the language of American crime fiction stress the laconic style of the hard-boiled school or the witty one-liners of the post-Chandler private eye. What is striking about George Higgins or Elmore Leonard is the generosity of their writing rather than its economy. Some of Leonard's minor characters seem almost unnecessarily well-drawn – the extraordinary Judge Guy in *City*

Primeval or Jill Wilkinson, the supervisor of the Crisis Center in *LaBrava*, who only appears for a few pages but who is somehow realized for the reader.[45] In Higgins one notices irrelevant conversations, often foul-mouthed monologues which are often gratuitous in plot terms, characters who are loquacious rather than clipped.[46] These points are among the most enjoyable in the novels, and are characteristic features showing just how well both Higgins and Leonard can write, but what do they actually serve? This excess of language over and above narrative is obviously connected to realism: the irrelevant detail confirms that the fiction is lifelike; the dialogue creates an important atmosphere of male rapport and humour; and, finally, this realism, as suggested in the discussion of Constantine above, gives an *unofficial* view of crime and its detection, moving away from moral views and political rhetoric to what actually happens. The language reflects this move, as we will see later, in its relentlessly unofficial, frequently obscene vernacular. There is also the sense that for the cops, criminals, lawyers, politicians, and businessmen of this world style is as important as information. One notices the role of circumlocution in Higgins' dialogue, needlessly indirect and very enjoyable. Here is a character talking about a fugitive, 'the word was that he had every sidearm Colt Firearms ever made and one or two extra from Remington Arms that you could put up against your shoulder for a little extra range'; or, as an expanded way to say 'drugs': 'folks ... coming down off of stuff guys fly into cornfields in light planes in the middle of the night'.[47] This establishes a masculine world of anecdotes but it may partly stem from a professional unwillingness to name things directly, serving not only the novels' humour but also implying their world of secrecy.

Higgins' career in the law (he was a lawyer in the Massachusetts Attorney General's Office, an assistant DA, and then ran his own law office) also suggests language's role as rhetoric; realism in writing a novel stems from the research and then persuasive delivery of making a case. Generally, this world is one where language *performs*; whether you are asking a jury to find the defendant not guilty or demanding that a shopkeeper hands over the contents of his till, or shouting 'drop the gun', language is working not describing. We are in the area of speech act theory identified with the work of Austin's *How to Do Things With Words* (1962), the world of crime is one of 'illocutionary' speech acts, where something is done in the saying, as in 'you are sentenced to five years', and of 'perlocutionary' acts where discourse has an effect (you drop the gun, you hand over the money, you find the defendant not guilty). Austin finally saw that all language was performative, for informing or affirming can also be seen as actions.[48] Perhaps because their language is so openly performative, performance is a way of life for the characters I have considered. In Bigsby's words, Mamet's characters, 'tell stories, perform roles and stage dramas as they seek to win the women, close the deal or simply deny the banality of their experience'. This is most obvious in *Glengarry, Glen Ross,* for the salesman is 'the creator of myth whose stories must be compelling if he is to survive. He is Scheherazade.' Mamet's salesmen are 'forced to treat as real the fictions they promulgate. They live on their wits and are, indeed, brilliant performers.'[49] I quoted earlier one of the salesmen, Shelly 'the Machine' Levine going through his spiel, reliving it with a colleague. After their first successful armed robbery Leonard's Stick and Frank Ryan repeat the lines they used in a kind of post-performance congratulation.[50] In *Stick,* Kyle tells him he's an actor; in *Glitz* Nancy thinks Victor could be an actor, though in fact he's a cop.[51] Leonard's own self-consciousness about the genre leads to the marvellous comic set-piece in *Stick* where a Hollywood producer tries to persuade people to invest in a film about drug dealing in Miami, talking about the 'vermin' on the streets, unaware that two of his potential investors are in fact dealers.[52] It also informs his best novel, *LaBrava.*

LaBrava compresses different representations of crime: *film noir* provides a character, the retired actress Jean, and the plot; the procedural school is drawn on with views of the Miami police at work; the important theme of redneck machismo gives us the violent Nobles; the surreal and scuzzy landscape of South Miami Beach's art deco hotels, Cubans, and retired Jewish women provides a contemporary setting; and this mixture is captured by the photographer-hero LaBrava as well as by Leonard. This photography gives the novel an interesting awareness of histories of representation. The novel starts with Maurice and a gallery owner discussing LaBrava's work. He is compared to Diane Arbus (thus commenting on the novel's own theme of the surrealism of the streets) and to Walker Evans, suggesting a modern documentation of a contemporary Depression (see Chapter 2 for my discussion of Evans and Agee). Indeed, it turns out that Maurice worked as a photographer for the Farm Security Administration, 'documenting the face of America during the Depression'.[53] There is a strong link between photography, the city, and crime, for example Weegee's *The Naked City.* LaBrava's photos capture the reality of street life through its many poses and performances: 'people ... showed him their essence ... behind all kinds of poses' (p. 19). LaBrava wonders about his possible book – *South Beach*: 'It seemed strange though – ask thirty or forty dollars for a book full of pictures of people who'd never see it, never be able to afford it.' Talking about the language of art criticism, overheard comments such as 'His work is a compendium of humanity's defeat at the hands of venture capital', he retreats to a populist idea of work and making a living, 'I thought I was just taking pictures' (p. 101). The novel dramatizes, with a great deal of humour, some potential dangers of writing and reading crime fiction – voyeurism and sentimentality, for example. Maurice, who documented the Depression, who speaks with 'a soft-urban-south accent that had wise-guy overtones, decades of street-corner styles blended and delivered, right or wrong, with casual authority', implies a reference back to the history of realism and naturalism, for his surname is *Zola* (p. 8). As with Constantine's Balzic, (whose name is a mere vowel away from Balzac and who overlooks the human comedy of corruption in Rocksburg, PA), realism is not just a literary style, it is part of the novel's subject.

It is the small details that create the realism of these novels and the reader's pleasure in that realism. In Leonard's and Higgins' novels, it is not so much that the same protagonist occasionally reappears across different works, but that minor characters are repeated, slipping across novels and consolidating a world. Thus Higgins gives his lawyer, Jerry Kennedy, two novels as the main character but he also introduces him as a minor figure in *Imposters*. And with a comic intertextuality, Jerry Kennedy talks about a Boston investigator called Spenser, a playful reference to Robert Parker's private eye hero (*Kennedy for the Defense*). This sort of repetition of characters is more akin to a realist panoramic tradition (Balzac, for example) than to the idea of a series of novels built around the same hero (Parker's Spenser, Chandler's Marlowe, etc.). But the feature of realism in this work that I will concentrate on is the demotic energy and rhythm of the novelists' language, which is similar to that found in Scorsese and Mamet. The way characters talk links realism as a style ('this is what the streets sound like') to realism as an attitude.

Mickey, the suburbanite tennis mom in Leonard's *The Switch*, finds being kidnapped a lesson in values, discovering the truth about her businessman husband's morals, becoming attracted to one of the kidnappers, and also learning how to swear. In an early conversation with her son, she means to say 'let's cut out the bullshit' but substitutes 'baloney' instead. Later, telling a story to Louis, one of her kidnappers, she says that she used 'Oh, bullshit' to a shop assistant; '"You said that?" Louis said ... "Well, it's a start."'[54] It is worth comparing Eddie Murphy in *Beverly Hills Cop*, where the sure sign that the besuited and rule-bound Beverly Hills police have decided to back Murphy's streetwise unorthodoxies is that one after another says 'shit'. Both Higgins and Leonard get some comedy from their foul-mouthed characters. The casino manager in *Glitz*, proud of all his friends in showbiz, is bet a hundred dollars that he cannot last a flight down to Puerto Rico 'without saying "fuck" in one form or another at least once. . . . He could barely speak. He'd start to say something and there'd be a long pause, like he was learning a foreign language. Finally he said, "Fuck it," and handed me a hundred-dollar bill and said he was going to do it on his own.'[55]

And in a long and bravura passage, which deserves to be quoted in full for its comic effect, Higgins presents a wonderful exchange between Costello, a political fixer, and Mahoney, a small-time building contractor who is waiting for Bernie Morgan, Speaker of the Massachusetts State House.

'I think you've got some kind of disease,' Costello said thoughtfully.
'The fuck you talkin' about,' Mahoney said. 'I ain't fuckin' sick'.
'There's some kind of a disease people get,' Costello said. 'Some kind of sickness that makes them swear all the time. They can't help themselves. I think you've got it. It's the only explanation for your vocabulary.'
'My what?' Mahoney said.
'Excuse me,' Costello said, 'I should've thought. You probably can't understand anything else, either. The only fuckin' explanation for your fuckin' vocabulary.'
'What fuckin' vocabulary?' Mahoney said.
'Tourette's Syndrome,' Costello said. 'It's a fuckin' sickness fuckin' makes you fuckin' swear all the fuckin' time.'
'Bullshit,' Mahoney said. 'All I said was where the fuck is he? He's the fuckin' Pope or somethin', comes in any time he wants? I haven't had no fuckin' dinner, you realize that? I get up, I have to get up inna fuckin' morning. I been up since fuckin' five thirty, right? I had my lunch and that is fuckin' it. All I had to fuckin' eat since fuckin' noon. I'm fuckin' hungry. That mean I got somethin' fuckin' wrong with me, for Christ's sake?'[56]

A gap opens up between rhetoric about crime and the real language of policing. In *Split Images* a homicide detective, Bryan Hurd, is being cross-examined about an incident in which another policeman, Kouza, shot a black youth called Darius during a Detroit campaign named STRESS, Stop the Robberies, Enjoy Safe Streets. The snappy acronym and populist slogan are undermined during this story of an unnecessary shooting. Hurd says that Kouza called for Darius to remain where he was. Asked the exact words used, Hurd remembers: 'He said, "Freeze, motherfucker. Don't move."'[57] In Leonard's masterly *City Primeval* the language used by police and criminals refuses dominant 'liberal' ideas of talking. For example, when a woman journalist asks Cruz why he never talked about his work with his ex-wife, the Detroit detective tells her an extraordinarily brutal story of a rape and murder solved that day. The implication seems to be, how do you talk about this reality except with colleagues and in its own tough, masculine language? When Cruz sees a marriage counsellor who asks if he has ever had a homosexual experience, he replies with a story about when he was working for the Vice Squad, engaged in entrapment of gays. When his masculinity is challenged he answers with a street anecdote rather than in the psychological, confessional mode of dominant American assumptions about speech.[58] This point can return us to Scorsese's films, punctuated as they are with music and four-letter words.

Scorsese has been criticized for the violence, crude language and, above all, for the sexism of his films. As with Mamet's plays a masculine world is both criticized and celebrated and language is central to this doubleness, suggesting the characters' brutalization but also their bizarre eloquence. These are voices not heard elsewhere, which raise important questions about repression, the body, and language. In *Taxi Driver*, De Niro links a blocked language to a blocked sexuality. His taxi brings home physically the gaps between people speaking, and in the scene in which he talks to the political candidate, Palatine, about cleaning up the streets, one sees and hears the gap between the raw material of populist campaigns about crime and the way that that language of the street is recycled into an official populism, the issue of 'law and order'. In Chapter 3 a crisis within heterosexual relations was investigated around the long scene in *Paris, Texas* where husband and wife are separated by glass. In *Taxi Driver* the most famous scene is probably De Niro talking to himself, actually threatening himself, in the mirror – the 'are you talking to me?' scene. He is divided from himself, let alone others, and speaking to himself he can only threaten violence. It is as if some responses to Scorsese's work wish to disavow this language; as if, in Judith Williamson's words, 'liberating films have to show liberated people'. She uses Scorsese to criticize a desire to see the world and, especially, masculinity as it ought to be, not as it is – a point like the one I have examined in crime fiction. She says:

> what seems to be demanded more nowadays by those with ideals of liberation is a cinema of the superego: as if to make a 'sensitive' or 'progressive' film now, you have to show people *being* sensitive and progressive.... But it is also *repressive*, this desire for cleaned-up images of oneself and the world. Change certainly doesn't come through denial. ... Cleaning up the screen doesn't necessarily help anyone clean up their act: it's precisely repression, a refusal to face things, that produces violence.[59]

It's also repression that produces the obscenities that stutter rhythmically through Scorsese's work, a masculine language that is in crisis. Bigsby characterizes the language of Mamet's plays as a 'sexually charged language drained of its sexual content'; a description that recalls Pauline Kael's review of *Taxi Driver*: 'There is practically no sex in it but no sex can be as disturbing as sex. And that's what it's about; the absence of sex – bottled-up, impacted energy and emotion, with a blood-splattering release.'[60] Scorsese's films focus on this explosion of the male body and masculine language. The boxer Jake La Motta played by De Niro in *Raging Bull* turns on others in his disturbed masculinity, undermined by repression and jealousy, and finally turns on himself, De Niro showing the destruction of his body through a massive gain in weight. And in an extraordinary scene, conceived by Schrader as a masturbation scene, De Niro takes his frustration out on himself, smashing himself into the walls of his prison cell. Ian Penman wrote: 'When he no longer has any strength (faith) left in his prick, he literally goes to seed. He becomes a real prick. He beats himself against a wall.'[61] Obscenity is the place where the somatic meets the semiotic, it's the body in language, a question of putting your body where your mouth is. Don's line in *American Buffalo* – 'Action talks and bullshit walks' – has action talking, language walking, a strange entanglement of discourse and violence.[62]

The body is always threatened in crime fiction, obviously by violence but also by the private eye or the cop's self-inflicted wounds, all that endless bourbon, coffee, and smoking. Robert Parker qualifies this tradition with his private eye hero, Spenser. He gets hurt but keeps himself fit – working out, running – he drinks but he also, in a parallel with his private ethical code, turns food into a ritual. Two policemen come to see him after a shooting and he makes breakfast: 'French Roast' coffee, 'whole wheat cinnamon and raisin bagels . . . some all natural cream cheese'.[63] This precision is obviously intended to qualify toughness and make his masculinity more complex. Parker's stress on fitness is fairly modish but there are other voices bemused by all this running. Hunter S. Thompson covering the 1980 Honolulu Marathon wonders why people enter, 'we may be looking at the Last Refuge of the Liberal Mind'.[64] And the writers I have discussed seem deliberately to refuse the last two decades' ideas about the body, the new centrality of health, of diet, of exercise in discourses addressed both to women and men. Constantine's Balzic is horrified when he finds that the mayor expects the police to go out jogging; Bryan Hurd in *Split Images* tries jogging once, runs a mile and goes home and vomits – 'It's not only boring, it makes you sick.'[65] In Higgins' *Imposters*, Constance Gates is woken up by the swimmers, tennis players, golfers, and joggers outside her condo unit. It's six-thirty and while outside people sit down to decaffeinated coffee and croissants, she has a hangover, the taste of Mexican food in her mouth, and the local police chief in her bed, smelling of body odour, Old Spice, and two packs of unfiltered Luckies a day.[66] The juxtaposition of health outside and the unhealthy scene within does, at the level of the body and contemporary discourses about health, what obscenity does at the linguistic level.

This masculine language and values is seen as anachronistic, a residual survival which looks back to the world of Westerns. In *Glengarry, Glen Ross* the salesmen define their masculinity against John who runs the office and has the power but not the experience, and thus is feminized, 'you're a *secretary*, John'. Roma turns on him, 'Whoever told you you could work with *men*?'; he is hired to help '*men* who are going *out* there to try to earn a *living*. You *fairy*.' He doesn't understand the code of the partner because he only knows offices, not the streets. Roma complains that it's 'not a world of men. ... We are the members of a dying breed.'[67] The language mixes notions of police partners with the elegiac mood – dying breed – of a Peckinpah Western; yet the point is that this is so obviously a fantasy of masculinity stemming from impotence and anxiety about jobs and money rather than from simple sexism. The frontier persists in Leonard's 'High Noon in Detroit', *City Primeval*, a study of the bond between cop and criminal. We have already seen how Cruz uses masculine anecdotes against challenges about his sexuality. The woman journalist accuses him of being indifferent to women; 'They don't fit into your male world'. She also thinks he is trying to 'look like young Wyatt Earp. ... The no-bullshit Old West lawman.' She sees him as playing a role, 'Like John Wayne or somebody. Clint Eastwood.' He admits that he thinks that 'movie detectives looked like cowboys'.[68] His rapport with the killer Clement Mansell excludes Carolyn Wilder, Clement's lawyer. When he talks to Mansell, Clement suggests that their situation has nothing to do with breaking or upholding the law, they are both just making a living and playing a game. It is a different world which ordinary people only enter as victims or witnesses. Raymond points out that in the past they would have settled things personally. Cruz feels that it's like 'a little kids' game except it was real' (pp. 86, 101–2, 104). Carolyn criticizes the attitude: 'Mano a mano. No – more like High Noon. Gunfight at the OK Corral. You have to go back a hundred years and out west to find an analogy' (p. 139). Her view of Clement is 'The Oklahoma Wildman. Born somewhere between fifty and a hundred years too late' (p. 199). She feels that neither of them have grown up; Clement feels that he and Cruz are alike (pp. 248, 273). Leonard manages to analyse this foregrounded masculinity and its anachronistic models, to criticize it, to link it to work, and to actually make it sympathetic in the person of Raymond Cruz. Behind this excellent novel one might see the working history of the genre novelist, as Leonard started by writing Westerns.

Linked to *City Primeval*'s replaying of *High Noon* in Detroit is Leonard's fondness for choosing characters from the South or West to play his most unpleasant characters. It is a way of criticizing models of American masculinity while retaining traditional male heroes (although Leonard's women are certainly well-created). Some of his sympathetic characters are also from the South, both Stick and Frank Ryan in *Swag*, for example, and Stick still has a fondness for country music. But *Stick* contains the unstable Chuck, the violent Moke, and the drunken Cecil, 'that hardbone back-country type.... You did not talk to the Cecils of the world drunk; you threw a net over them if you had one.'[69] There's Roland Crowe in *Gold Coast*, the 'prehistoric creature from the swamp'; 'the backcountry gangster, the Miami Beach hotdog, the good-ol' boy with his cowboy boots on the coffee table'.[70] Or Richard Nobles in *LaBrava*, 'Homegrown jock' with a 'back-country drawl'; 'A swamp creature on the loose'; with a 'confident, all-American boyish face. Hometown hero – the hair, the toothpick, the hint of swagger in the set of silver-clad shoulders'; a man who, in an amusing echo of Johnny Cash, once shot an eagle just to see it die.[71] In a novel so self-conscious about representation, this all-American, redneck machismo seems a deliberate comment on television and film populism, a comment on the supposedly lovable good old boys of *The Dukes of Hazzard* or the kind of role that Burt Reynolds played in films like *White Lightning* (1973) or *W. W. and the Dixie Dance Kings* (1974). In the latter he played an affable Southern outlaw, and recently he has directed himself, by all accounts unsuccessfully, as Stick. It is certainly possible for him to play a Leonard hero but it would be more interesting, and more in keeping with Leonard's criticisms of American masculinity, for him to have played one of the vicious rednecks in the Leonard canon.

In this chapter I have tried to open up the contradictions in populist views of crime, exploring the gap between the rhetoric and the messier reality revealed in this fiction. Where these novels, plays, and films end up politically is hard to say: possibly either in a cynical withdrawal from politics or in a slightly sentimental statement of basic needs, for example, in Higgins' *Imposters*, where love and work seem to offer a way out of an otherwise pervasive corruption, or in Mamet's statement: 'We need to be loved; we need to be secure; we need to help each other; we need to work.'[72]

6 'Are you ready for the country?': tradition and American music

> She turned the radio on, hoping to hear Bruce Springsteen. Somehow there was a secret knowledge in his songs, as though he knew exactly what she was feeling. Some dumb song by the Thompson Twins was playing.[1]

Over the last couple of years, diverse bands and singers have been seen as heralding the return of American rock or as offering a contemporary country music functioning beyond the stereotypes of rhinestones and rednecks. This chapter is not intended as a critical or subjective account of this music, but perhaps a personal memory can introduce the issues at stake. A few years ago, when the Thompson Twins' career was at its height, I heard one of the band being interviewed on the radio, talking about a recent tour of America. They had been amazed when playing in Austin, Texas, to find that their image and music had penetrated what they obviously thought of as the sticks. Fans turned up, knowing the words to their songs, and dressed and styled in imitation of them. Praising MTV and acknowledging the power of video, they totally overlooked the traditions of music associated with Austin. The interview seemed to me to be proof of what was happening with the British pop invasion of America – haircuts were replacing history. Come 1984 and Springsteen's *Born in the U.S.A.*, and the host of American bands that started to appear, the situation seemed reversed. The guitar had re-emerged, along with phrases like the 'trad-rock renaissance' or the 'New Authenticity' or 'New Sincerity' music. But instead of talking about invasions, musical rather than military images give a better picture of the *exchanges* between Britain and America. This chapter concerns the call and response of British pop and American rock or country, or, to take an image from the black music tradition, still current in rap, it sees the two countries as the protagonists of answer songs, each reply being closely bound up with what came before.[2]

Michel Foucault has suggested that when studying the discourses of science or the social sciences, one can uncover a regime of truth, where the true is not the opposite of the false but a construction of discourses and institutions. People do not speak 'the truth', they speak 'within the truth' (*dans le vrai*), obeying the rules that shape what can be recognized as true at that historical and discursive moment. Something similar happens within rock journalism, especially in interviews; it could be called speaking 'within the hip', referring to influences and musical genres that will be recognized as fashionable, as the right thing to listen to at this moment. Hence all the lines in interviews: 'We've always loved soca/blues/jazz/film scores/African music/funk/hip-hop, it's just never really come out in our music before.' The choice of music revealed as an influence or a pleasure generally signals a shift in style on behalf of those interviewed, as well as the shifting nature of hip reference-points. Recently, it is noticeable that country music is often the revelation: 'We've always really loved George Jones or Patsy Cline', and so on.

In 'The grain of the voice', Roland Barthes argues that music criticism inevitably turns to the adjective. 'Music, by natural bent, is that which at once receives an adjective.'[3] The following adjectives recur through reviews of the new American music: rootsy, rural, corn-fed, rustic, hickory-smoked, massive, mystical, soaring, chiming, jangling, Byrds-like, organic, celestial, folky; also, to give the other side of the critical coin, mediocre, regressive, reactionary, uninspired. What these choices demonstrate is how much talking about music is involved with versions of an imaginary America. Perhaps visions might be more accurate than versions, as so much of this music and the discussion of it relates to cinema. Music, landscape, and films are knotted together and some of these versions will be untangled in the next section.

The landscape of music

> I wanted to get this American, earthy sort of expansiveness. That emotion you feel when you look out over a plain and see the sun set, y' know? ... Yeah – when you hear the hog feeders rattling sort of thing and a buzzard crowin' in the back ... I wanted that sort of feeling in this band but I wanted it to be kind of *wild* at the same time. To have that sort of sincerity, that sensitivity, but also to have that kind of preacher-who's-been-drinkin'-four-bottles-of-Jack-Daniels-feeling. I wanted those to combine.[4]

Reyner Banham, without doubt one of the best commentators on European perspectives on the United States, argues, in his essay 'Mediated environments *or: You can't build that here*', that the influence of American architecture cannot be gauged through normal influence studies. Instead one must look at the effect of certain American scenes and environments as they work through the popular media. The effects he's talking about cluster around suburban lawns, the Manhattan skyline, the Los Angeles freeways and Las Vegas. The point that is useful here is his argument that the influence of American environments 'performs less *in* the media than *around* them'. American architecture is seen as 'the building blocks out of which are assembled the environments in which the action of Pop takes place, a kind of continuous back-projection'; pop signifies here not just music but a whole culture of films, fashion, advertising, and television.[5] This suggestive comment highlights the role this 'back-projection' plays when listening to American music or attempting to describe it. American music is heard with visual images in mind, and not just when it is actually attached to visual images (film, advertising, videos). Our memories of films, television, photography are brought into play, mediating music through ideas of the American city or country.

The back-projection image implies an identification of popular culture and America, and it seems true that almost all the diverse music produced in Britain in the 1980s is somehow related to an imaginary America. Reggae would appear to be the exception, looking to Jamaica rather than the United States, but its own history is shaped by exchanges with black American soul music. And the music that does make a point of walking out of this continuous American film to construct an alternative, is marked precisely by this need for an alternative. Its 'Europeanness' only makes sense when juxtaposed by the America that frames its choice of, say, German art traditions and the avant-garde. The starting-point of its cultural politics is America. I will discuss Paul Weller's uneasy mixture of Orwell and the Isley Brothers, Parisian or Italian chic and the Labour Party, in the conclusion to this book, where the discourse of anti-Americanism is considered. There are certainly musicians who make a point of their 'Englishness' but this is constructed in an American frame. It is like the 'English breakfast' offered to tourists in Spain, not the breakfast actually eaten at home, but bacon and eggs and tea as signifiers of 'home', making sense because of the surrounding foreign scenes and phrases. The pastoral charm of Virginia Astley's music, for example, works in the same way. A comparison that takes us to a central point is the way that 'naturalness' is constructed in advertising, with real ale or brown bread given their values not by being prior to the artificial but by being surrounded by it. This is significant on two counts: it points to the way that the American renaissance is seen as 'real' as opposed to the artifice of pop, and it also suggests that this 'real' is constructed in the same way as the artificial, which gives the notion of tradition an interesting twist. John Cougar Mellencamp is a good example. By his central involvement in Farm Aid and through *Scarecrow*, a record which looks at the effect of the farm crisis and the loss of family farms in the Midwest, he has gained some critical respect as well as popular success. The paradox is that even though he is from Indiana and still lives there, his populist image is complicated by his previous media history, attempts to turn him into first Bowie and then Springsteen. His 'natural' image, the image of him as natural and probably the image he feels natural in, is produced by the same apparatus of video and photography as another star's glam artifice. So although the opposition might appear to be a rural American real versus the shallow world of British pop, both must operate within an Anglo-American world of the mass production, distribution, and consumption of images.

A chain of oppositions is linked to the American rock invasion versus the British pop invasion: adult/child, tradition/fashion, film/video, playing live/expensive production, guitars/synthesizers, sense of place/international travel, work/leisure, narrative/image. The populist theme of work is reflected in the almost mythically long shows given by Springsteen. The American conservative columnist, George F. Will, wrote that 'If all Americans ... made their products with as much energy and confidence as Springsteen and his merry band, there would be no need for Congress to be thinking about protectionism.'[6] But against this kind of offensive opportunism, there is the appearance with Springsteen and many of these bands that playing is almost a utopian form of work, as it goes beyond the work/leisure opposition by being both fun and labour. If we want the opposite image to the sweating bar band playing live, it is the seamless, sweatless production of modern pop, and even more it is the world of pop videos. If American music is resonant with films, then the pop of the British pop invasion was associated with videos, where image replaces narrative and selling replaces telling. For videos take both their visual style and their reason for existence from adverts; they are after all promos for a product as well as being a product themselves. Videos by the likes of Spandau Ballet, Duran Duran, and Wham foregrounded images of travel: exotic settings, beaches and cocktails, and the unimaginative sexism of models in bikinis. Groups would claim that these were parodic, a pastiche of a consumer's paradise, but parody and pastiche are the lifeblood of adverts. When videos referred to films the effect (remembering, say, an Ultravox video) was of an advert's parodic reference without its humour. The promise of travel without any idea of a journey; an exoticism which was banally familiar; the spectacle of money and consumption rather than production. The objection is not a moralizing one, it is an aesthetic complaint about the poverty of imagination deployed in the most expensive settings. For all the talk of style, the dressing up did not seem expressive but more like a children's game: let's play pirates, Indians, fighter pilots. It seemed to underline the point that the assumed pop consumer was now seen as younger than ever before. One of the points I will return to is the way that tradition in American music suggests music across generations, not in the sense that a whole family would know who Boy George is, but in its awareness of history and in its confrontation with adult emotions.

Against videos and their tourist notions of travels, American bands hold out the idea of both size and specificity in their sense of place. If the image of American mainstream rock had been one of identically bland groups playing in identically massive stadia, and if the desire of the British pop groups was to crack the charts, break into the American market, then the effect of this music has been to break America up, to stress regional differences and diversity. Instead of a homogenized monolithic culture, there is the Mexican music of East Los Angeles' Chicanos Los Lobos, or Jason and the Scorchers' statement: 'what we are is just an American rock and roll band who come from a Southern, Middle American approach rather than with an East or West Coast approach.'[7] Behind many of these bands one can trace the influence of the Band – not necessarily a musical influence, more a question of an attitude to America and its music. The Band, despite their Canadian origins (Levon Helm from Arkansas was the exception) or, perhaps, because of the distance that Canada gave them, celebrated America 'by letting the country speak for itself, in as many voices as can be crammed onto a twelve-inch disc'.[8] Greil Marcus, in his discussion of their music, wrote that it 'gave us a sure sense that the country was richer than we had guessed' through their 'determination to find plurality and drama in an America we had met too often as a monolith'.[9] Against a view of the United States as capitalist Amerika, they offered *Music from Big Pink*, generous music from a specific place.

> Against a cult of youth they felt for a continuity of generations; against the instant America of the Sixties they looked for the traditions that made new things not only possible, but valuable; against a flight from roots they set a sense of place. Against the pop scene, all flux and novelty, they set themselves: a band with years behind it, and meant to last.[10]

Their love for the diversity of American music (blues, jazz, gospel, country, rock and roll) led them to combine elements to produce a music that was never fussy about authenticity but always seemed 'as if it would sound as right to a gang of beaver trappers as it does to us'.[11] Marcus praises their sense of the land, their fine awareness of the metaphoric resonance of a name, and of the literal fact, of a place like 'The Great Divide'. Their songs, he writes, are meant 'to cross the great divide between men and women; between the past and the present; between the country and the city; between the North and the South'.[12] The wager was, and still is, to unify America without eliding its divisions.

The point to be stressed is the combination of a sense of place and tradition with an ability to mix styles, forge new connections, and address contemporary realities while keeping a sense of history. Recent black music, for example, has combined a sense of a local scene (New York hip-hop culture, Washington's Go-Go music, Chicago and house music) with an openness to other influences, from Kraftwerk to heavy metal, and a constant awareness of the history of funk and soul music, as well as a reference to the surrounding world of consumer and media culture, from brand names to cop shows. Some of the most potent developments of the 1980s have been deliberate blurrings of black and white music, Prince's encyclopaedic whirl through musical styles and images, or rap's bravura appropriation of that most unfashionable of things, the hard rock guitar solo. Their antecedents have been hybrids as well, the drug-soaked funk or blues of Sly Stone or Hendrix. Similarly, reference points for new American bands (REM, Jason and the Scorchers, Los Lobos, the Long Ryders, Rank and File, Blood on the Saddle, Lone Justice) have tended to be figures or bands who worked on the borderlines of musical genres and traditions (the Byrds, the Band, Creedence Clearwater Revival, Gram Parsons, Neil Young). The terms cow-punk, country pop, country rock, testify however inadequately to a tradition of fused genres and hybrids. The point is, and I will return to this later, that talk of a return to roots, whether that is seen as a refreshing blast of authenticity or a regressive retreat from the challenges of today's music, misses the fact that the tradition has always involved these marriages of old and new. When the Long Ryders talked of Gram Parsons and the Sex Pistols as musical influences, they may have been making a rather calculated appeal to the British rock press, but the tradition they were trying to place themselves in implied just that kind of hybrid.

Other combinations appeared. After playing for over a decade Z Z Top gained commercial success by adapting their Texas boogie to the 1980s pop radio and dance floor. Tom Waits, whose work had always blended American musical and writing styles (R & B, blues, jazz, Tin Pan Alley), reached new heights of achievement and critical acclaim with *Swordfishtrombones* and *Rain Dogs*, works which collaged the avant-garde and the traditional, the small town and an international landscape. Waits' work has always had a sensitivity to junk and an awareness of discarded Americana, that makes songs like 'Soldier's Things' (from *Swordfishtrombones*) or 'Broken Bicycles' (off *One from the Heart*) recall the pathos of waste in the work of Thomas Pynchon. Waits' work invites critics to cross-reference forms and genres: Edward Hopper has proved a favourite critical reference (as he has with reviews of Raymond Carver's fiction, discussed in Chapter 4) – Kerouac, Bukowski, Chandler, and Kurt Weil are often mentioned. His characters have ranged from the low-life petty criminals of *Small Change* to the almost John Updike world suggested by 'Foreign Affairs'. One of the issues constantly raised across discussions of American culture is that of masculinity. American writing from Hemingway to rap has often been criticized for its macho concerns. Where British song-writers might tend to *comment* on such issues, their American counterparts are more inclined to *dramatize*, locating characters' ideas through point of view and compressed narrative rather than condemning them. Waits' songs display a range of masculine positions, from songs of sentimental domesticity to hard male boasting, from a poignant love song like 'Blue Valentines' to the commodified sex of the street, from marital rowing to the B-movie *amour fou* of his drifters, straight out of a James Cain novel or a Nicholas Ray film. These forms of address are indexed to musical genres – R & B, musicals, country, or jazz ballads – and although it could be objected that it is women who have to run the gamut of this male desire, the point is this desire and masculinity are revealed as culturally constructed and as contradictory. The difference in styles and in their connotations produces enjoyably dislocating effects, as if James Brown suddenly turned into Cary Grant.

The consistent cinematic aura of Tom Waits' musical world has led him to an appropriately closer involvement with films, with parts in *Wolfen* and *Paradise Alley*, and a productive association with Francis Coppola, writing the soundtrack for *One from the Heart* and playing roles in *The Outsiders, Rumble Fish*, and *The Cotton Club*, even meeting his wife through her job as a Zoetrope scriptreader. As he furthers the theatrical side of his work, brought out in his musical *Frank's Wild Years*, and gains parts beyond cameo-length as in Jim Jarmusch's *Down by Law*, Waits demonstrates an ability to write and perform across genres and forms. I have suggested above that reference to films is part of American music's resonance, whether that is through associations with an American landscape or direct allusion (the Long Ryders' name, for example is a double reference to the Byrds and to Walter Hill's Western), or actual involvement (the Blasters' appearance in Walter Hill's rock and roll fantasy, *Streets of Fire*). Ry Cooder neatly compresses my argument about cinema and tradition through his combination of superb film scores and an almost archaeological interest in America's musical heritage. A further link between American song-writing and films lies in what might be called the economy of genre, in other words what is gained from revisiting similar characters, settings, and themes through their accumulated connotations. Kate Lynch has suggested that at the time of Springsteen's *Darkness on the Edge of Town*, with the encouragement of Jon Landau, 'Bruce came to see himself as a genre artist in the manner of a Sergio Leone, a John Ford or a Flannery O'Connor, whose characters and situations are perpetually re-explored.'[13] It is certainly the case that *Nebraska*, arguably his finest work, shows the influence of films as a great gain in economy and suggestiveness.

Another important cluster of associations concern the South. Images of the South can be introduced through four linked songs: Neil Young's 'Southern Man' and 'Alabama' where liberal concern for the South's bigotry is evoked in images in slavery, miscegenation, lynching, and the Klan; Lynyrd Skynyrd's answer song 'Sweet Home Alabama', where the South rejects the Northerner's advice, staying with its self-image of just folks and good old boys; finally Warren Zevon's 'Play It All Night Long' which refers to 'Sweet Home Alabama' but rejects both liberal concern and redneck bonhomie for an American Gothic world of incest, crazed Vietnam veterans, drunkenness, and madness. It was Randy Newman's great achievement to combine all these versions of the South on *Good Old Boys*, a populist masterpiece which even includes a song by Huey Long. To come up to date, one can see reactions to a New South in songs like Springsteen's 'Darlington County', where two buddies drive south in search of work or in the 'New Country' sophistication of a singer like Rosanne Cash. As factories have moved to the relatively non-unionized Southern states, and capital and middle-class Northern immigrants have arrived in the transformed Southern cities, some images of the South reflect these economic shifts. But old versions live on, and the South rises again in new American rock music with some traditional images of stars and bars, swamps and sharecroppers, harvest moons and hot nights in Georgia.

Elsewhere in this book discussions of representations of rural America, of Shepard's deserts of division, of recent fiction's portrayal of the culture shock caused by the meeting of the small town and popular culture, and of Elmore Leonard's downhome criminals, have revisited the terrain – literal and symbolic – of populism, charting its transformations. A work studied earlier, Agee and Evans' *Let Us Now Praise Famous Men* felt its mission to be to resist the stereotypes and discourses that had accumulated around the figure of the sharecropper. But images of rural labour are still so strong that they continue to resonate in songs like 'Still Tied' by Jason and the

Scorchers or Lone Justice's 'After the Flood' with its evocation of life going on in the face of natural disaster. Some of the musicians have backed up these themes through involvement in Farm Aid and with attempts to inform rock audiences of the economic hardship of rural America, as discussed in Chapter 1. Some critics have challenged musicians' rights to rural subjects, suggesting that Los Angeles bands are just playing at sectionalism, drought, and rock 'n' roll, sushi-eaters pretending to be shitkickers. But although some songs gain from the personal experience behind their writing, there seems no point in replaying arguments about authenticity along the lines of can whites play the blues? It is also arguable that some of the bands who have discovered country as a way out of a post-punk cul de sac are as relevant and enjoyable as those who profess to be keeping traditions alive. The question of how to represent the South, and rural America in general, is raised in an Ellen Gilchrist short story, when her fourteen-year-old heroine, in the process of discovering Dorothy Parker and cigarettes, is driven through 'God's Country' by her father. She thinks that her mother would see the locals as 'white trash' while her father sees them as 'the salt of the earth'.[14] Between the dismissive and the mythicizing, both built on notions of work, the Southern poor as either idle and shiftless or as given grace through their proximity to the soil, there lies the weird. The archetypal Eastern intellectual group, Talking Heads, dismissed America's Norman Rockwellish interior in 'The Big Country' on their second LP, but singer David Byrne then started to use the voices and gestures of Southern Baptist sects, a part of his much-criticized but very productive strategy of borrowing from the world's cultures and musics. With the film, book, and music of *True Stories*, Byrne now seems to be interested in taking America's populist pulse by dramatizing the hopes, fantasies, eccentricities, and conspiracy theories of the heartland, still viewing them ironically but adding affection for the local.

The South seems to offer both extreme Gothic marginality and central American authenticity, both incest and farmers. The contradictory representations of the region can be seen clustered around recent appropriations of Elvis. In a short prose piece from *Hawk Moon*, 'The Curse of the Raven's Black Feather', Sam Shepard mixes the mystique of the road with thoughts of the Rolling Stones. Driving and thinking of Keith Richards, the narrator also muses on Kerouac, on the famous car wrecks that litter America's mythic landscape. Then, in an image which fuses Keith Richards' hair, Edgar Allan Poe's poem, and Roger Corman's film, he takes a feather from a raven that has crashed into his car. The feather speaks, demanding that he drive south and even when he tries to escape by heading north, the signs still read 'South'. The raven's voice commands him to take the feather to a junkyard in Noir, Louisiana, and leave it in the glove compartment of an old black 1936 Pontiac. He surrenders to the journey:

> I've always been pulled toward darkness. Toward black. Toward death. Toward the South. Good. Now I'm heading the right direction. Away from the quaint North. Away from lobsters and white churches and Civil War graveyards and cracker-barrel bazaars. Toward the swamps, the Bayou, the Cajuns, the cotton mouth, the Mardis Gras, the crocodile.[15]

The South as the nexus for darkness, death, and portents of disaster has become the favoured lyrical and musical terrain of Nick Cave, who patrols a mythic landscape of decadence and haunted drifting (Tennessee Williams and Hank Williams), a region saturated with religion, resonant of sin and redemption. In 'Tupelo' the birth of Elvis Presley, and all that that implies in terms of the 'birth' of rock 'n' roll, is seen in terms of a visitation on a community, the singer urging his listeners to 'looka yonder' and read the mysterious portents of Elvis' birth and his twin brother Aaron's death. The emergence of rock 'n' roll's first star is surrounded with all the Second Coming symbolism of a backwoods the-end-is-nigh congregation. If, as Greil Marcus suggests, the uncontrollable mystery of the Sun sessions was the escape of hillbilly hedonism from the fear and quietism of country music, and the pain and sin of the blues; if the idea behind early rock 'n' roll was Saturday night without the concept of sin, good times without a price to pay, then what Cave re-introduces is precisely those themes of guilt, pain, and anxiety, setting against the release of potential in this music his own almost caricatured blues knowledge of the price that will be exacted. Marcus writes about Presley creating out of a hillbilly culture something that would transform 'not only his own culture, but America's'. He analyses that extraordinary achievement, turning a belief in a good time into a way of life: 'that one young man like Elvis could break through a world as hard as Hank Williams', and invent a new one to replace it, seems obvious only because we have inherited Elvis's world and live in it.'[16]

The economic facts that constrained Southern hedonism are traced by Marcus through Vernon Presley's move from Tupelo to Memphis, and through music that has charted that shift and its cost in terms of loss of the land and the new reality of the city.

> The earliest picture of Elvis shows a farmer, his wife, and their baby; the faces of the parents are vacant, they are set, as if they cannot afford an unearned smile. Somehow, their faces say, they will be made to pay even for that.[17]

He argues that although that is not heard as such in Elvis's music, it's an absence that structures that music. A sense of how much he must have wanted success is given through the contrasting resignation of the surrounding country music, and through the fact of Vernon Presley being a failed sharecropper. In Jason and the Scorchers' 'Broken Whiskey Glass', there's a sense of both worlds, the hurt of country and the assertion of rock 'n' roll. And the song's verses are a scathing putdown of attempts to visit the ways of life underpinning this music, to play at it rather than live it, to be a blues tourist or to read Elvis books and pop some pills as a short cut to the music's meaning. The song suggests the experience necessary to produce 'white soul heroes' rather than the posthumous myths, 'legend's trashy dreams'. But a popular imaginary America in Britain is precisely a meeting of trashy dreams and rockabilly, merging stages of Presley's journey from Tupelo to Memphis to Hollywood and Vegas, mixing 'white trash' with the trash aesthetic.

The OED's entry for 'tacky' shows that the word started as a noun for a 'degenerate "weedy" horse' and through transference and class assumptions, became 'A poor white of the Southern States from Virginia to Georgia', taking on a career as an adjective meaning 'Dowdy, shabby' in a quotation from 1893. Etymology is destiny: in the trajectory of this word one can see the move from sharecropper's son to bad films and Vegas; casting light on how the signifiers of class have moved from obvious poverty – 'shabby' – to the contemporary meaning of 'tacky' as 'bad taste', which is pertinent in considering why dominant British attitudes to country music have revolved around an idea of kitsch; it also helps explain why the Cramps can so successfully combine rockabilly and low-budget horror, both versions of 'tacky'. If the Cramps' journey has been from New York to East Hollywood, rather than from Tupelo to Memphis, their music still comes out of the South as well as out of the drive-in gore double-bill. Their landscape is shaped not only by teenage werewolves but also by versions of the South, its music and its associations such as religion, ironically echoed by the band in their title, *Songs The Lord Taught Us*. *A Date With Elvis* suggests a wry look at the two-way culture shock of rock 'n' roll's explosion and its containment through Hollywood. 'Aloha from Hell' wittily compresses both sin and family viewing. As well as the traditional swamp menace of songs like John Fogerty's 'The Old Man Down the Road' off *Centerfield*, there have been many post-punk hybrids of rockabilly, country, the blues (all styles generally associated with authenticity, specific regions, specific histories) with a trash or punk sensibility, as in the Cramps or as in the Gun Club's fusions of blues and punk, past and present styles of despair. In fact the Gun Club's *Miami* through its very title suggests layers of contemporary culture built over swamps; Mailer's image for the city was that it was like sellotape stuck on pubic hair. A conclusion about tradition can extend this idea of a clash or fusion of past and present.

Tradition: 'File Under Water'

With the new pervasive presence of pop videos, the massive coverage that the new pop stars (Duran Duran, Wham, Boy George) got in the Fleet Street press rather than in the rock press, the 1980s seemed to promise music without either the unifying factors of punk or much promise of diversity, a homogenized pop of laundered black styles. The search for an alternative often returned to black music, but for certain rock journalists and audiences America's other traditions held out the antidote. Rock had been dismissed by, successively, punk, disco, pop, each of which tended to present rock as an embarrassing conservative survival. Its return was, to some extent, due to the fact that it had never really gone away, but also because some sense of history appeared to be needed. Even the American music that just pre-dated punk avoided the 'year zero' rhetoric of its British counterpart. People such as Patti Smith, Tom Verlaine, or Richard Hell were more open about influences or their own pleasure in past music than British punk's pose of amnesia and a clean break with history. America's heterogeneity offered space for a recovery of traditions, which embraced regional and musical diversity. It provided a necessary pluralism to set against the world of the new pop. Uses of the past differed: post-punk hybrids, careful archaeological excavations of traditional and ethnic music, cross-generational fusions. The latter seems significant in that British pop seemed to aim for a younger and younger audience while British rock (Dire Straits, for example) provided good taste and in-car listening for an older audience. Against this one could set Springsteen's return not only to his childhood or teenage experience but to his parents' working and domestic life as well: 'there ain't a note I play on stage that can't be traced directly back to my mother and father.'[18] One of the features of the cover photograph of Jason and the Scorchers' *Fervor* was a poster adver-tising a Hank Williams' concert from 1953, and the back cover went further back into the past with a sepia photograph from Jason's grandparents' wedding.

Uniting a recovery of past Mexican styles of music and thus recovering a previous generation's experience within a more political sense of community, Los Lobos have produced a Chicano music, from East Los Angeles, appealing across audiences and generations.

Listening to *How Will the Wolf Survive?* I recalled *The Autobiography of a Brown Buffalo* by Oscar Acosta, perhaps better known as Hunter Thompson's crazed Samoan lawyer in *Fear and Loathing in Las Vegas*. One of the themes that runs through his autobiography is how his confused identity was linked to repressed musical traditions. 'Fuck,' he thinks, in an imaginary conversation with his analyst, 'I haven't heard a song in Spanish since I was a kid.' He jokingly tries out other ethnic identities: 'There is something about my bearing that cries out for history. I've been mistaken for American Indian, Spanish, Filipino, Hawaiian, Samoan and Arabian. No one has ever asked me if I'm a spic or a greaser.' He remembers listening to the radio when a child, 'During the commercials my mother would sing beautiful Mexican songs, which I then thought were corny'; she tells him that he will like them when he grows up but in 1967, 'as a buffalo on the run, I still thought Mexican music was corny'. He travels to Juarez and remembers the way that speaking Spanish had been discouraged at his Californian school. He enjoys the beauty of the language and its songs. A meeting with two Mexican prostitutes brings home his anomalous position, he is '*mexicano* and yet I couldn't even offer her a drink in our language!' At the border, crossing back into the United States, he is asked if he is '*americano*' and told: 'Next time I suggest you have some I.D. on you. You don't look like an American, you know?' In a cheap hotel he wonders about these encounters: 'One sonofabitch tells me I'm not a Mexican and the other one says I'm not an American. I got no roots anywhere.'[19] The book ends with his idea of joining Chicano community politics, and inventing an identity out of his rootless mix of traditions. The parallel is suggestive not because one should now expect Los Lobos to become overtly political, but because Acosta emphasizes the politics implied in the recovery of traditions, questions of cultural identity that are answered not by polemic but by accordions.

What some American music suggests, both in itself and in the campaigns that musicians have been involved with (Farm Aid, Springsteen, and Southside Johnny's publicizing of the Food Bank system) is the theme I have investigated elsewhere: the populist power of countering economic conservatism from culturally conservative positions. In this way reclaiming traditions can be seen as radical – literally, a return to the roots – setting history against capitalism's attempts to deny continuity and against pop's timeless present of consumption. There is also a sense as I have suggested that the tradition is not just vitalized through fusions with contemporary styles and sensibilities, it is in itself a tradition of just such fusions, of hearing the old through the new and placing the present through the past. The concept of roots is perhaps too static to capture the economic shifts that shape American culture. Traditions are always on the move, and country music, for example, has often been shaped in both form and content by these displacements: moves from the country to the city or cross-country quests for work. Dwight Yoakam opposes Nashville's synthetic country with his own return to the honky-tonk, but the history that he refers to is one of travelling traditions rather than fixed origins. Born in Kentucky, brought up in Ohio, and now based in Los Angeles, Yoakam can look back to Merle Haggard's Bakersfield, California, upbringing and his songs of Okies migrating to California, for an example of how tradition is as much to do with people on the move as with fixed values. The cars and trains of blues and country music testify to the links between tradition and enforced mobility. The 'purity' of Yoakam's music is transformed anyway by the fact of playing to rock audiences, forging an alternative route for country music by supporting the likes of X, Los Lobos, Lone Justice.

In an interview, Rank and File introduced American political traditions into the context of musical traditions. Their own music has moved from their time as the Dils, a San Francisco political punk band, to country; a move symbolized by their literal relocation in Austin, Texas. They suggested that American radicals such as Emma Goldman or Big Bill Haywood were shaped by American experiences that made them considerably different to European Marxists. Comparing Big Bill Haywood to Wild Bill Hickock, they suggested an American tradition of immediate confrontation rather than theoretical work, 'Burn, baby, burn' rather than *Das Kapital*, linking this to the continuing hold on American thought exerted by the frontier experience. It's why, they said, America had Big Bill Haywood and then added, that it was also why they had Presley.[20] However, the differences between America and Britain must not become too fixed. There is a two-way flow of influence and pleasure, with American musicians revealing obsessive knowledge of rare English pop songs, or with British musicians over the last twenty years re-introducing America to its own traditions (R & B, blues, soul, country). Elvis Costello through his *King of America* and his excellent collaboration with T-Bone Burnett, as the Coward Brothers, has demonstrated the potential for productive exchanges. And his work producing the Pogues can act as a reminder of the links between Irish and American musical traditions, the Irish origin of some rural American country music, the popularity of country in Ireland now, Peter Case's cover version of the Pogues' 'Pair of Brown Eyes'.

Questions about the use of the past or the choice of styles in cultural production are always broadly political. Even the language of working within versus opposing outside (parliamentary roads to socialism, *Top of the Pops* as a means to an audience), reform versus revolution, use of the past versus an absolute break, all suggest a parallel. In Marxist theory these questions have been raised most productively in the arguments between Brecht, Benjamin, Adorno, and Bloch, and with Lukács' defence of tradition and realism against modernism. For Lukács,

> the tradition handed down to the present by the 'progressive' epochs of the past was a set of compelling norms, a mortmain that literary legatees must honour on pain of disinheritance. For Bloch, on the other hand, this history was the *Erbe*, a reservoir in which nothing was ever simply or definitively 'past', less a system of precepts than a sum of possibilities.[21]

Lukács criticized Bloch and the modernists: 'They regard the history of the people as a great jumble sale'; something to be used or stolen from. In Bloch's eyes, Lukács wrote, the cultural heritage was 'a heap of lifeless objects in which one can rummage around at will, picking out whatever one happens to need at the moment. It is something to be taken apart and stuck together again in accordance with the exigencies of the moment.'[22] He suggested that the modernists saw only rupture and that they formed an anarchistic mirror-reversal of the evolutionary ideas of reformism, rather than a correctly dialectical analysis of continuity and discontinuity. The language seems, at points, surprisingly close to arguments within music journalism: the past-as-jumble-sale, the cultural heritage as something to be taken apart and stuck together in new combinations. This tends to have been the way that pop's magpie-like borrowings have been deplored or have been theorized as a post-modernist strategy. American traditions, however, can include both poles; being as much about retrieval and reassembly as they are about continuity. Thus, traditions that have always been shaped by displacement and fusion meet a situation where the most authentic keeper of the flame still has to produce that authenticity through a recording and image apparatus that transforms that authenticity, and markets it precisely as 'real' or 'pure'. This seems to have moved beyond any opposition between a strategy of retrieval and a great tradition.

Recent American music has reaffirmed the possibilities of conventional musical formats (voice, bass, guitar, drums) and also reaffirmed the 'openness' of America. A return to tradition does not show an exhausted imagination in this case, but a demonstration of diversity and difference where the fashion had been to see both America and rock music as monolithic. It has also proved successful at crossing generations, styles, and forms, and drawing on films and fiction for its resonance. Kate Lynch discusses Springsteen's song 'The River', linking it to other songs by him and also suggesting

Flannery O'Connor's short story 'The River' and Hank Williams' 'Long Gone Lonesome Blues' as possible references.[23] Rivers provide a suggestive image to conclude with, allowing a range of reference from the contemporary (REM's recent 'Cuyahoga') to the historical (the documentary film, *The River*, which followed the Mississippi from Minnesota to New Orleans and was made by Pare Lorentz for the Farm Security Administration). This watery image implies a fluid relation to the past while also summoning up cultural allusions as well as the American landscape. More pertinently, there is the original title for REM's *Reckoning*, 'File Under Water', implying the difficulty of pinning down American music.

When it was suggested that contemporary writers were distanced from earlier writers because they knew more, T. S. Eliot pointed out that the earlier writers were precisely what the contemporary ones knew. It's a point that T-Bone Burnett cited to stress the contemporary importance of figures like Hank Williams and Muddy Waters. He continued, in order to stress the diversity within this tradition:

> You know ... there's this place where a river runs into an ocean and the fresh water and the salt water all get mixed in together. And that's what America is about, and that's what American music is about, and that's what rock and roll is about. It actually wasn't *invented* by anybody, and it's not just black and white, either. It's Mexican and Appalachian and Gaelic and everything that's come floating down that river.[24]

Eliot, writing on Mark Twain, argued that the river subverts linear narratives, beginnings and ends. The quotation suggests a way to approach American traditions, concentrating on diversity and drifting.

> Like Huckleberry Finn, the River itself has no beginning or end. In its beginning, it is not yet the River; in its end, it is no longer the River. What we call its headwaters is only a selection from among the innumerable sources which flow together to compose it. At what point in its course does the Mississippi become what the Mississippi *means*? It is both one and many; it is the Mississippi of this book only after its union with the Big Muddy – the Missouri; it derives some of its character from the Ohio, the Tennessee and other confluents. And at the end it merely disappears among its deltas: it is no longer there, but it is still where it was, hundreds of miles to the North. The River cannot tolerate any design, to a story which is its story, that might interfere with its dominance. Things must merely happen, here and there, to the people who live along its shores or who commit themselves to its current. And it is as impossible for Huck as for the River to have a beginning or end – a *career*.[25]

Huck can take us back to another beginning that cannot really be pinned down to a single source. Marcus sees rock 'n' roll beginning where Huck Finn ends; with the music's dream of a permanent Saturday night: 'Why not make an escape from a way of life – the question trails off the page of *Huckleberry Finn* – into a way of life?' Huck even appears at the Sun sessions as Marcus writes that if 'That's All Right' 'was a threat, it was also another ride on the raft'.[26] Black and white music taking to the river.

The river provides an image for the role of tradition in American music, but another tradition exists which does not celebrate the diverse voices and cultures feeding into American music. To see this tradition we must return to a British context, the subject of the next chapter and the conclusion. From the early days of jazz to today's range of musics there has been a continual reaction, an occasionally racist ('jungle drums') defence of a threatened British culture from an invasion of 'American trash'. Music has not been the only form that has been opposed, popular fiction and cinema and, especially, television have all been prime targets for the tradition of 'Americanization'. The history of this reaction provides a better understanding of contemporary debates about popular culture and populist politics.

7 The long reaction: 'Americanization' and cultural criticism

In May 1986, *New Socialist* appeared redesigned by Neville Brody, with Michele Barrett and Rosalind Coward as new associate editors, and with a central debate called 'Style Wars'. In this Robert Elms argued for the radical value of 'style' and David Edgar defended the heritage of the 1960s. Both the debate itself and the contributors' pieces were unfortunately predictable, but Elms' argument for 'Ditching the Drabbies' provides a useful starting-point for understanding a crucial dovetailing of debates about populism and popular culture. Elms confuses an important argument against a puritanism of the left with his own irrelevant and incoherent praise of style. The article often refers to a lost closeness to the people, a golden age when socialism was not only popular but also, of course, well dressed, and blames the middle-class new left of the 1960s for the loss of this popularity. Elms rummages through history for stylish moments – Russian Constructivists and miners' galas, Basque berets and union banners – but when he wants to translate style into political effect he reaches for *populism*. In the mysterious golden age of the left, 'we had the glamour of populism'; socialism 'had the oratory and the art to move the masses with the power of its always populist message'; the new left's crime in the 1960s was 'to strip socialism of its stylistic clout and rob it of its vital populism'; Neil Kinnock has made clumsy, 'ill-informed stabs at populism' but Ken Livingstone's defence of the GLC was 'sharp, intelligent, populist, humorous'; finally, the left's goal must be 'to become a credible, modern, populist mass movement'.[1]

Elms' stress on populism and style is intended to oppose a puritanism of the left which manifests itself in a patronizing critique of popular culture and consumption (a desire for a video recorder or a holiday being seen as signs of embourgeoisement). Despite Elms' caricature of the 1960s and his muddled history, this is a valuable argument, for socialism that speaks so often of needs, hopes, and aspirations must also come to terms with pleasures and desires. This is one important strand of my discussion of the British reaction to

American culture. This chapter will consider the history of this reaction, tracing the fear of 'Americanization' from the nineteenth century to today's debates about *Dallas*, providing a framework for the analysis in the Conclusion of the cultural and political issues at stake in recent debates about Anglo-American relations. The themes and topics of earlier chapters will reappear, transformed by the shift from American culture to British consumption. First, having seen the rather vague but central role that 'populism' played in Elms' article, it is necessary to sketch out some of the arguments surrounding populism in the 1980s.

Pessimism and populism

Populism has become a key term in British politics in the 1980s, as a part of analyses of the ideological appeal of Thatcherism and as a central issue in debates about strategies of opposition and realignment on the left. Descriptions of Thatcher's appeal inevitably focus on her populism, her radical mobilization of 'the people' against the postwar social democratic consensus. Stuart Hall, for example, has repeatedly analysed the politics of Thatcherism as an authoritarian populism exploiting the feelings raised by issues like law and order, the nation, and race, and putting those feelings into a language of everyday 'common-sense' domesticity. The populist rhetoric of petit-bourgeois 'good sense', reminiscent of French Poujadism, helped to persuade voters that monetarist toughness and an onslaught on trade union power would solve Britain's economic problems. Nationalism and the foreign policy image of the Iron Lady were aided by the Falklands War and gave the populist rhetoric a boost at a crucial moment. The potential conflict between Thatcher's social and economic anti-statism based on a belief in the free play of the market, and the idea of a strong state enshrined in her nationalism and idea of law, rocked the Tory government during the Westland crisis, costing her Cabinet Michael Heseltine and Leon Brittan. The argument over the 'rescue' of Westland helicopters opened up questions of Britain's future and, temporarily, divided the Conservatives. Whether Westland should be part of an American or European industry raised the issue of whether Britain should continue to look to the special relationship with the United States or should, through European co-operation, aim to become part of a more independent and united Europe. A more successful protest was over the proposed sale of Leyland's truck division to General Motors. The symbol of the English countryside, the Landrover, proved a more powerful rallying point for Tory backbenchers than the idea of European co-operation. Labour may

175

have seized the rhetorical advantage at these moments of government weakness but this has often involved a problematic appropriation of nationalism. Since this patriotism is widely perceived to be the preserve of the Conservatives, Labour's advantage has been quickly snatched back. This tricky knot of the left, the patriotic, and Britain's relation to Europe or America will be examined in greater detail in my Conclusion where the protest over the US raids on Libya will be discussed.

Other ways in which a Conservative vision has presented itself as a populist one include Nigel Lawson's dream of 'popular capitalism' and a shareowning democracy; and Norman Tebbit's diatribe against 'postwar funk' (possibly the closest parallel to the themes of the American new right), a critique of the pernicious effects of 1960s thought, the breakdown of moral standards and parental responsibility, the consequent law and order problem, and so on. Lost standards are to be restored by mobilizing workers against unions, parents against teachers, viewers against broadcasters, the people against liberalism. Labour has tried to challenge the Conservatives on this terrain, Neil Kinnock, especially, portraying Thatcherism as a foreign deviation from British decency, and Labour as the genuine voice of 'the moral majority'. This similarity of rhetoric has generated an unease about left populism, a feeling that one effect of the success of Thatcherism has been a retreat from socialism, disguised under a rubric of realism, reassessment, or realignment. Since the late 1970s there have been a series of splits or debates within the Labour Party, the Communist Party, the feminist movement, and within the analysis of popular culture. These disputes are related, and understandably conflated, but not identical. It is also important to remember that a positive or negative response to these changes does not necessarily reflect an opposition between, say, the right and left wings of the Labour Party. Labour's right and their 'hard' left can agree, for example, that the working class is being wrongly eclipsed by 'trendy' issues of gender and race. What some see as a retreat from class politics into a populist pursuit of alliances has also been seen by various writers and political figures, across a range of positions, as a necessary questioning of basic beliefs in the light of a transformed society and economy, and as a productive and belated awareness of the new social movements and single issue campaigns.

It has been argued that a pessimistic overestimation of Thatcher's success has resulted in a wholesale discarding of principles, which will not guarantee a recovery for socialism, but lead to defeat as it fails to offer a genuine alternative vision. In all these debates one notices suspicions that populism is a slippery slope: opposition to the sale of council houses is rethought, nationalization becomes social ownership, full employment is no longer considered possible; class struggle gives way to designer Marxism and tactical voting; feminism moves from a critique of the family and heterosexuality to a cele-bration of Madonna; advertising, soap operas, romances, game shows, are all found to have positive features. Elizabeth Wilson, participating in debates about feminism's relation to the class struggle and trade union politics, expressed her unease: 'there are dangers in becoming too populist – one minute the family's all right, and the next minute Christianity's all right, and the next minute any old thing is all right. That's a caricature, of course, but the ambivalences of populism do make it dangerous.'[2] Wilson's warning is echoed in debates about the analysis of popular culture.

Judith Williamson complains in 'The problems of being popular' that the words 'reactionary' and 'revolutionary' have faded from the left's vocabulary. Contemporary 'glossy left magazines' and left-wing academics are busy 'picking out strands of "subversion" in every piece of pop culture from Street Style to Soap Opera'. So feminists retrieve romances discovering their power to resist patriarchy, a resistance found 'by feminist intellectuals in almost every part of feminine culture'. *Marxism Today* argues that Fergie can be seen as progressive; Jane Root's *Open the Box* presents, in Williamson's view, an uncritical perspective on television, whereby if people enjoy soap operas the latter cannot be criticized without being patronizing. Williamson asks why the left has become so uncritical, embracing the popular rather than promoting radical alternatives to it. Her answer is linked to the context sketched out above: 'the left's post-'79 awareness of the right's successful populism, known to many as "Thatcherism"'. Her 'charitable' interpretation of this 'obsession with selling council houses and wearing designer clothes is that the left is trying to "get in there" where so far only the right has colonised popular pleasures'. Her more critical view portrays the left as pol-itically demoralized, and socialist intellectuals as not only pessimistic but bored, their rediscovery of pleasure in popular culture being thus both a desperate political strategy and also a personal compensation. She compares this middle-class approach to working-class pleasures with the 'Mass Observation' of the 1930s. The left is finding out what most people already knew, but its failure to encourage or develop radical alternatives to popular culture is the core of Williamson's complaint. Rather oddly, she suggests that we are all tired now, relaxing with *Dynasty* rather than reading Brecht, although quite what Brecht would have made of this rigid division between serious work and popular culture is another matter. Rather than seeing the pleasures found in popular culture as 'good' in themselves, Williamson argues that different, more radical ways must be found to fulfil those pleasures.[3]

Instead of Williamson's opposition between criticizing and celebrating popular culture, it is necessary to see that in some of the work she attacks, and indeed in her own writing elsewhere, there is an alternative which neither condemns nor embraces popular culture but actually looks at it, how it works, how it is used and consumed. Her critique of the 'yuppie left' confuses several different discourses and movements: the left's new stress on style and presentation, in part a search for an easy answer to the appeal of the right, but also part of a very necessary updating and professionalizing of campaigning machinery; a Marxist and feminist tradition of interpreting works from both 'high' and popular culture as 'subversive'; post-structuralist and postmodernist theories of subjectivity and pleasure; finally, recent work on popular culture and consumption which has moved from a model based on interpretation to one looking at pleasure and use, mapping out a *space of enjoyment* where the material and social constraints of reading or viewing (class, gender, family structure, the relations between work and leisure) meet fantasy (for example, Jane Root's *Open the Box* and the Channel 4 series based on it, Kathy Myers' book on consumption, *Understains: The Sense and Seduction of Advertising*, David Morley's *Family Television: Cultural Power and Domestic Leisure*).

Williamson's argument simplifies popular culture in a way that seems to stem from a tradition of worries about 'mass culture' and 'Americanization'. Cora Kaplan's response suggested that 'Williamson's model of popular culture and the forms of its reception are dangerously oversimplified.' The article does not distinguish between 'the different national origins and different genres of mass popular culture', as if all its examples belonged to 'the same ideological continuum'. Williamson also fails to differentiate between the social and gender positions of those who consume popular culture. Instead, as Kaplan says, the audience is simply split 'between us and them'; a 'clued-up intelligentsia' who ought to be reading Brecht but are slumming it in front of the television, and the passive 'politically ignorant rest', who 'have no critical purchase on the cultural commodities they are offered'. But the reception of popular culture is both active and heterogeneous. Kaplan talks of her own surprise at finding British socialists interested in John Ford's Westerns:

> In a sixties American left constellation, westerns and thrillers were seen as generically as well as ideologically right-wing. And so they were for the American audience. But in Britain the genres and narratives of American popular culture acted as a kind of wedge, forcing into the open,

through contrast and a wild dissonance, the class-bound complacency of the Great Tradition of British Culture.

In a way Kaplan seems to have just relocated Williamson's simplifications – 'And so they were for *the* American audience' – but the stress on transatlantic changes is valuable, and the idea of the potential radical charge of American culture as consumed here is central to my own argument. The popular works of one country which seem 'most in tune with dominant, conservative values, can oddly enough, act in another social and political context as a lens through which the conservative order is ridiculed'. The enjoyment of watching *Dallas* or *Dynasty* here may well be not so much that they recruit our fantasies as that they also allow us to take a certain comic distance from them. This does not mean that American serials are radical, rather that they do not have a fixed ideological message and that they are received differently by different audiences. Kaplan's useful argument opens up something more complex and confusing than a simple labelling of cultural products as 'progressive' or 'reactionary'. For 'one nation's, one generation's, one gender's mainstream (and mostly conservative) cultural products become part of the radical cultural agenda of another society, era or sex'.[4] It is important to realize that this insight goes against the grain of a long and influential tradition which sees American popular culture as homogeneous and as something which 'invades' or 'colonizes' British culture. Where Kaplan sees the radical potential of American popular culture in a British context, others have seen, for over a hundred years, the threat of 'Americanization'.

Culture and shiny barbarism: the long reaction

Christopher Bigsby has argued that 'Americanization' is a term belonging to a world 'for whom the modern experience is coeval with the American experience'. The emergence of a popular culture based on mass reproduction, and the experiences of urbanization, industrialization, and consumerism, are confused with the country with which they are most identified. Thus 'opposition to popular culture and complaints about Americanisation have often amounted to little more than laments over a changing world'. The United States being seen as having a causal rather than an emblematic link to change means that America is identified 'as the source of the problem rather than the place where that problem first surfaced on a considerable scale'. Bigsby suggests that 'Americanisation frequently means little more than the incidence of change'; and change, especially perhaps new cultural forms, provokes established patterns of reaction. The new is 'characterised as brash, crude, unsubtle, mindless and, as Matthew Arnold insisted, destructive of taste and tradition'.[5] America is mobilized as the paradigm of the traditionless, the land of the material not the cultural. Arnold's *Culture and Anarchy* sees it as 'that chosen home of newspapers and politics . . . in the things of the mind, and in culture and totality, America, instead of surpassing us all, falls short'.[6] The important opposition though is not between culture and anarchy but between tradition and democracy. There is a crucial conflation of complaints about popular fiction or mass circulation newspapers with resistance to the hard-won nineteenth-century extensions of education, literacy, and the franchise.

Both of the Leavises quote a passage by Edmund Gosse, written at the end of the 1880s and published in *Questions at Issue* in 1893. Gosse picks up Arnold's rhetoric of anarchy and American materialism, and he warns of 'the spread of the democratic sentiment' reaching the realm of culture with 'the traditions of literary taste, the canons of literature, being reversed with success by a popular vote'. Until now, he writes, the uneducated or semi-educated mass might not 'appreciate the classics of their race', but they have acknowledged the 'traditional supremacy' of the established canon. However, this deference may now be at an end:

> Of late there have seemed to me to be certain signs, especially in America, of a revolt of the mob against our literary masters. . . . If literature is to be judged by a plebiscite and if the plebs recognize its power, it will certainly by degrees cease to support reputations which give it no pleasure and which it cannot comprehend. The revolution against taste, once begun, will land us in irreparable chaos.[7]

Gosse's use of America as a warning (America's present will be Britain's future), becomes a standard trope in the rhetoric of Americanization, but the language of the piece displays a displacement of terms and anxieties from the political sphere to the cultural. The 'democratic sentiment', 'a popular vote', 'the mob', 'a plebiscite', 'the plebs', 'the revolution against taste': the danger is supposedly bad taste but the terms are blatantly political. Instead of the barricades, we have the canon and the literary tradition overseen by the 'literary masters'. Fears of riot or of organized protest – trade unions rather than Philistines – underpin this blurring of extended literacy and the spectre of the mob.

The Leavises see Arnold and Gosse's fears as reality and therefore the necessity is not to give warnings but to organize resistance. F. R. Leavis' *Mass Civilisation and Minority Culture* (1930) announced that while it 'is a commonplace that we are being Americanised', it is a commonplace 'that seems, as a rule, to carry little understanding with it.... For those who are most defiant of America do not propose to reverse the processes consequent upon the machine.' Forty-two years later the critique is the same, as Leavis denounces in *Nor Shall My Sword* (1972) 'American conditions': 'the rootlessness, the vacuity, the inhuman scale, the failure of organic cultural life, the anti-human reductivism that favours the American neo-imperialism of the computer.'[8] What one notices in Q. D. Leavis's *Fiction and the Reading Public* (1932) is the distrust of pleasure, with popular fiction being repeatedly compared to a drug. Replacing a Protestant tradition of reading as self-improvement, she found a fallen world of easy stimuli and passive pleasure. 'The temptation to accept the cheap and easy pleasures offered by the cinema, the circulating library, the magazine, the newspaper, the dance-hall, and the loud-speaker is too much for almost everyone.'[9] This echoes Victorian anxieties about sexuality and its regulation, Leavis continues to worry about the need for self-discipline, but it also seems oddly like the passage from Judith Williamson quoted earlier. Where Williamson worried that we were watching *Dallas* rather than reading Brecht, Leavis is concerned that Milton is being replaced by the bestseller. There are obvious differences, of course. At times Leavis sounds so alarmed by 'mass culture' she almost seems nostalgic for mass illiteracy. But the comparison is worth making in order to stress the link between the 'culture and society' tradition outlined by Raymond Williams and socialist work on popular culture and ideology. The link is overdetermined by other influences, for example, the work of the Frankfurt School, but these other sources also reinforce cultural pessimism. The recent responses of Marxist critics to postmodernist theory and practice have shown that cultural pessimism, élitism, and distance from popular culture is still a common position.

The Leavises' campaign against the 'mass' and the 'Americanized' suggests several points of resistance where minority culture might take its stand. The pastoral is mobilized against the popular, the organic community against mass society:

> From Burke's musings on the great trees of England to Leavis's on *The Wheelwright's Shop* the same communitarian image endures. There is always a Village Green under siege from crass, irreverent materialism of some kind; the life of significant soil must be saved before it is too late.[10]

This makes an interesting comparison with the American agrarian traditions I discussed in earlier chapters. English rusticity is raised in a gesture combining nostalgia and criticism but, unlike the American traditions, it is detached from politics, a refuge rather than a site of opposition. There is inadvertent humour in a rare example of resistance given by Q. D. Leavis. She writes that she is informed that we have in British Honduras, 'a community which in deliberately setting out to resist American influence is actually preserving a traditional way of life'.[11] Chris Baldick entertainingly demolishes this assertion by looking at the country's economy, dominated by the USA, and social structure. He concludes:

> If it is a minority culture one is looking for, a small colony of former slaves ruled and owned by a handful of whites and plagued by poverty and illiteracy is of course a fairly safe place to start looking, and to this extent Leavis was quite consistent in pointing to such an unlikely-sounding source of hope.[12]

The Leavises' real resistance revolves around *Scrutiny*, with its considerable influence (on universities, on the training of teachers, on the teaching of English in schools, and so on), and with a more complex attitude to America. *Scrutiny*'s writers broaden and problematize the debate: for example, Denys Thompson wrote that if 'England is less Americanized than America, it is in the discreditable sense that less resistance to the advance of civilization has been developed: no English university has yet produced a *Middletown*.' The reference is to the Lynds' 1929 study, an 'anthropological' critique of the industrialized culture of a Midwestern town, also drawn on by Q. D. Leavis. America provided *Scrutiny* with a comparison that could advance their project of building a critical, professional intelligentsia. Thus one of the most powerful uses of American writing was Q. D. Leavis' use of Veblen in her critique of English literary and academic circles. Writing in 1939, she argued that literary criticism in England was deformed by its amateur disregard for values and by its class basis which she found typified in Cyril Connolly's *Enemies of Promise*. She compares the educational and social background seen in the book with that of the United States: 'the advantages Americans enjoy in having no Public School system, no ancient universities and no tradition of a closed literary society run on Civil Service lines, can hardly be exaggerated.' As Francis Mulhern has commented, there is an interesting doubleness: 'For *Scrutiny*, the USA was both the homeland of modern "machine civilization" and the advance post of opposition to it.'[13]

In Dick Hebdige's 'Towards a cartography of taste', debates about popular culture are seen to revolve, from the 1930s to the 1960s, 'around two key terms: "Americanisation" and the "levelling down process"', with fundamental national values threatened by the *'spectre of Americanisation'*. Hebdige delineates a 'negative consensus' of cultural 'if not political conservatism' which links such diverse writers as Waugh, Orwell, Eliot, Leavis, and Hoggart. 'Though there was never any agreement as to what exactly should be preserved from the pre-War world, there was never any doubt amongst these writers that clearly *something* should.' For Eliot and Leavis it was minority culture, for Orwell and Hoggart it was the working-class community which needed protection against the affluence and inauthenticity of mass culture.[14]

This negative consensus solidifies around Americanization:

> References to the pernicious influence of American popular culture began to appear whenever the 'levelling down' process was discussed and the concept of 'Americanisation' was swiftly and effortlessly absorbed into the existing vocabulary of the 'Culture and Society' debate.

If there were fears of Soviet expansion, given the Cold War frame, 'American *cultural* imperialism demanded a more immediate interpretative response.'

> Whenever anything remotely 'American' was sighted, it tended to be read at least by those working in the context of education or professional cultural criticism as the beginning of the end.

The United States was seen as the prime 'homogenizing agent' and the scale of both its production and consumption 'began to serve as the image of industrial barbarism':

> a country with no past and therefore no real culture, a country ruled by competition, profit and the desire to acquire. It was soon used as a paradigm for the future threatening every advanced industrial democracy in the Western world.

As I have outlined above this is not in itself new. America-as-threat goes back to the mid-nineteenth century and the reason that Americanization is 'absorbed' into the Culture and Society tradition is because that is where the term came from. Hebdige, however, sees these representations as different in that they operated in 'the arena of public, explicitly *populist* discourse and were circulated in a wider number of printed and broadcast contexts', during the war and its aftermath. 'Americanization' was no longer applied *to* newspapers, it was a term *in* newspapers. 'This wider "official" resistance to American influence' stemmed from 'the American military presence in Britain from the early 1940s onwards and Britain's increasing dependence on American economic and military aid.' The GIs provided a startling and direct experience of American popular culture, and Hebdige concentrates on the ambivalence of these first British reactions.[15]

If there had been 'covert hostility' to the GIs' affluence, this hardened into a more generalized anti-Americanism after the war due to a public resentment of the transformed power relations seen in Britain's loss of Empire and decline as a world power and America's increasingly dominant international role. And specifically, 'the War Debt and the continuing reliance on the American military presence in Europe provided a dual focus for popular resentment'. This 'popular' response was matched by the way that American culture, especially popular music, was policed by institutions such as the BBC. Hebdige seems to suggest that given postwar austerity and a climate of demand for change, America could be blamed for the imposition of rationing or resented for its affluence, but also that its potentially subversive music was itself rationed in order to prevent it increasing discontent. Americanization became more and more common as a kind of short-hand: 'By the early 50s, the very mention of the word "America" could summon up a cluster of negative associations.' As an adjective, 'Americanized' could 'contaminate' whatever it was placed next to, leading to a 'fixing of a chain of associations (between youth, the future, America, and crime) which has since become thoroughly sedimented in British common sense'. In journalism and cultural criticism, youth culture is caught in a grid of equations, 'between America and mass culture, between Americanisation and hom-ogenisation, between America's present and Britain's future'.[16]

New commodities and increased affluence were seen, in a left variant, as undermining the working-class community, deradicalizing a workforce through increasing doses of leisure. The other new consumer who featured in the 1950s debates was the teenager, a specific example of working-class hedonism and Americanized youth. Another debate revisited by Hebdige is the 'streamlining' one. He argues that a combination 'of *accessibility* and *reproducibility* (a million streamlined Chevrolets, a million streamlined radios)' produced the sense of threat felt by the cultural critics. The threat is to a traditional intellectual sector valuing 'the "authentic", the "unique" or at the very least the "honest" and the "functional"'. The key to under-standing this is Walter Benjamin's classic essay on the transformation of art by a context of mass reproduction, 'The work of art in the age of mechanical reproduction'. Hebdige also cites Gramsci's critique of the Italian intellectual reaction to the emergence of 'Americanism'. Gramsci predicted that the introduction of American-style mass production – 'Fordism' – into Italy would intensify economic exploi-tation and extend the realm of the state across private and public life. 'But he refused to deplore the changes in the *phenomenal* forms which inevitably accompanied such structural adaptations.' Hebdige quotes Gramsci's analysis of the site of, and the reason for, resistance to American cultural influence: 'In Europe it is the passive residues that resist Americanism (they represent "quality") because they have the instinctive feeling that the new forms of production and work would sweep them away implacably.'[17] English cultural conservatives, 'irrespective of their overt political affiliations', saw in 'the image of a streamlined car, in the snatch of "hot" jazz or "ersatz" rock 'n' roll blaring from a streamlined speaker cabinet', what Benjamin predicted as mass reproduction's effect on the cultural heritage. 'They were right to perceive that what was at stake was a future – their future.'

Against this conservative reaction, Hebdige concludes with 'alternative definitions of America and American influence which were circulating at the time'. He points out that our present context contradicts the fears that Americanization would flatten society and eradicate differences. The 'sheer plethora of youth cultural options currently available . . . most of which are refracted however indirectly through a "mythical America"' suggests that these fears 'about the homogenising influence of American culture were unfounded'. Instead of the homogeneity of the same, youth culture finds the diversity of difference.

American popular culture – Hollywood films, advertising images, packaging, clothes and music – offers a rich iconography, a set of symbols, objects and artefacts which can be assembled and re-assembled by different groups in a literally limitless number of combinations. And the meaning of each selection is transformed as individual objects – jeans, rock records, Tony Curtis hairstyles, bobby socks etc. – are taken out of their original historical and cultural contexts and juxtaposed against other signs from other sources.[18]

In other words, consumption here is not a passive surrender but also an active appropriation, imposing meanings and attempting to determine images rather than be determined. In addition, one can also see that something new is created in the meeting of national cultural groupings and what Bigsby calls a 'Superculture'. For as American popular culture is exported, it is also transformed; 'at each cultural interface, it becomes in effect, a Superculture, a reservoir of shifting values and images splashed like primary colours across the consciousness of the late twentieth century.'[19]

Hebdige argues that if 'positive images of America did persist throughout the period', they operated, as it were, out of sight of the discourse of Americanization, being 'constructed and sustained underneath and in spite of the "official" authorised discourses of school and State'.[20] Richard Hoggart found 'the most striking feature in working-class attitudes to America' to be neither suspicion nor resentment, 'but a large readiness to accept' and the idea that Britain could learn about being 'up to date' from America. Hoggart saw advertisements as building on this, glorifying the new and the young, and using 'a growing minor mythology imported from America, but modified for British tastes'. The energy of the teenage gang, of popular music and style, 'the reverse of everything dusty and drab', Hoggart sums up the appeal as a 'kind of shiny barbarism'.[21] Hoggart's barbarism and the continuing romance of the States described by Hebdige, found their stronghold in marginalized genres such as crime fiction and comics.

Crime in a candy-floss world

Hoggart considers a range of cultural products from bestsellers to 'the American or American-type serial-books of comics, where for page after page big-thighed and big-bosomed girls from Mars step out of their space-machines and gangsters' molls scream away in high-powered sedans'. In comics, magazines, and novels a fantasy genre of American crime flourishes, the chosen fiction of British working-class youth, 'the reading of juke-box boys' who spend their evenings 'in horribly lighted milk-bars'. The milk-bar passage is justly famous: the place testifies to 'an aesthetic breakdown', the customers are male teenagers 'with drape-suits, picture ties, and an American slouch'. They cannot afford endless milk-shakes so they make a cup of tea last an hour while playing the echo-loaded American music on the jukebox. 'The young men waggle one shoulder or stare, as desperately as Humphrey Bogart, across the tubular chairs.' It is one of the classic scenes of Americanization: 'Many of the customers – their clothes, their hair-styles, their facial expressions all indicate – are living to a large extent in a myth-world compounded of a few simple elements which they take to be those of American life.'[22] An important element in this 'myth-world' is their reading, the crime and science fiction paperbacks which Hoggart sees as a form of pseudo-pornography. He compares the gangster fiction with the 'spicy' reading that circulated in his youth, Edwardian visions of naughtiness on ottomans. Hoggart thinks that these novels have been replaced since the mid-1930s by a 'new style in sex-novels spreading from America', possibly inspired by James Cain's *The Postman Always Rings Twice* and similar to the work of Mickey Spillane. Their titles are terse, and their authors 'are usually American or pseudo-American, after the manner of the American shirt-shops on the Charing Cross Road'. The cover-girls are brutalized pin-ups, promising a sadistic, violent view of sex, and the 'style is debased Hemingway'. The endings are often sentimental; the tough-guy hero and the floozie 'both climb aboard the car, and head for the next state'.[23]

Hoggart connects the worrying portents he finds to a loss of community and to a relation between powerlessness and a compensating fiction of sadism and violence. But it is important to note that Hoggart's approach is a complex and qualified one. He admits that the crime genre 'undoubtedly has in parts a kind of life', and a certain enjoyment seems to come through in his parodies of pulp fiction. He sees Americanized crime fiction as 'realer' than much sensationalist writing, growing out of a modern, urban experience. He denies that the reading is linked to delinquency. What worries him is the fantasies the genre encourages rather than any idea of a simple effect.[24] In other words, Hoggart gives us criticism not just moralism, which is noteworthy in the light of some of his successors. *The Uses of Literacy* concludes with a warning not to take viewing or reading out of context, and not to overestimate the role of popular culture: 'People are not living lives which are imaginatively as poor as a mere reading of their literature would suggest.' Hence, his attempt to give a larger view of the texture of working-class life, and the residual traditions and solidarities which shape it. 'Most contemporary popular entertainment encourages an effete attitude to life, but still much of life has little direct connexion with it.'[25] 'Effete' introduces an important element in the rhetoric of Americanization, for cultural criticism often sees popular culture as somehow emasculating viewers/readers. The working-class male consumer is feminized through his loss of an active relation to entertainment; popular culture, especially television, being seen as producing passive fantasizing which is culturally coded as feminine.

George Orwell also contributed to this concern about American crime, both real and fictional. In 'The decline of the English murder', Orwell opens with the Golden Age of English murders, roughly 1850–1925; crimes best savoured on a prewar Sunday afternoon, the *News of the World* providing the perfect post-Sunday lunch crime. The classic murder requires a professional middle-class setting, its motivation mixing a tension between adultery and respectability possibly involving small amounts of money as well, the ideal weapon being poison.[26] All this has changed and Orwell turns to the most infamous crime of the war years, the Cleft Chin Murder. 'The background was not domesticity, but the anonymous life of the dance halls and the false values of the American film.' An eighteen-year-old waitress and an American army deserter went on a six-day spree of random, senseless murders. She described herself as a strip-tease artist, he referred to his past as a Chicago gangster, both claims being false. The chance killings had the German rocket bombs as their backdrop. 'Indeed, the whole meaningless story, with its atmosphere of dance-halls, movie palaces, cheap perfume, false names and stolen cars, belongs essentially to a war period.' Its other context is

Americanization, the cause of the murder's decline from the suburbs to the senseless.

> Perhaps it is significant that the most talked-of English murder of recent years should have been committed by an American and an English girl who had become partly americanised. But it is difficult to believe that this case will be so long remembered as the old domestic poisoning dramas, product of a stable society where the all-prevailing hypocrisy did at least ensure that crimes as serious as murder should have strong emotions behind them.[27]

Orwell ends with the possible benefit of hypocrisy, and in an earlier piece on American crime, 'Raffles and Miss Blandish' (1944), he suggests the possible values of snobbery.

This article juxtaposes *Raffles*, the 1900 version of 'glamorized crime', with its 1939 counterpart, James Hadley Chase's *No Orchids For Miss Blandish*, which Orwell introduces with the phrase, 'Now for a header into the cesspool.' He looks at 'the immense difference in moral atmosphere' between the two books, and the implications of that difference for popular attitudes to crime and the law.[28] Orwell, like Hoggart, not only disapproves of popular crime fiction, he also recognizes its power. Chase's novel 'is not, as one might expect, the product of an illiterate hack, but a brilliant piece of writing, with hardly a wasted word or a jarring note anywhere'. What is most notable about the novel is that all of it, '*récit* as well as dialogue, is written in the American language; the author, an Englishman who has (I believe) never been in the United States, seems to have made a complete mental transference to the American underworld.' Orwell discusses the characters' corruption and the sadism that replaces 'normal sexuality'. In this world might is right, a mood which Orwell links to the novel's popularity in the Blitz of 1940. One explanation for its success is that readers who are passive victims in real life enjoy the chance to be vicariously masterful. But there is also the context of Americanization: 'it is necessary to refer again to the curious fact of *No Orchids* being written – with technical errors perhaps, but certainly with considerable skill – in the American language.' Orwell turns from the war to the American crime genre, not just books but 'pulp magazines', some of which Orwell sees as sado-masochistic pornography, sold before the war as 'Yank Mags'. English imitations had not been so convincing, and English crime films had not been so brutal: 'And yet the career of Mr Chase shows how deep the American influence has already gone. Not only is he himself living a continuous fantasy-life in the Chicago underworld', but he can also count on a mass audience able to recognize this world and its slang. 'Evidently there are great numbers of English people who are partly Americanised in language and, one ought to add, in moral outlook. For there was no popular protest against *No Orchids*.' Although Chase's books did later run into trouble with the authorities, they obviously struck a chord within the popular imagination.[29]

Orwell returns to the widely-held assumption that the book was American, and he detects American influence behind the moral equation between the police and the criminals and, more generally, in the glamorization of the criminal which he sees as running from the mythology of the Western outlaw up to the fascination with Al Capone and the Chicago underworld. Orwell views Chase as a kind of mass culture Carlyle, a prophet of power. Orwell calls the ideology behind this power-worship 'realism' – 'the doctrine that might is right' – and he links Chase's 'realism' to George Bernard Shaw's admiration for dictators, to English intellectuals' devotion to Stalin, and to a general trend in popular fiction to side with the powerful rather than the underdog. What alarms Orwell is an extension of moral ambivalence from the 'serious novel' to 'lowbrow fiction'; intellectuals may have long discarded sharp distinctions between right and wrong but these have generally survived in popular fiction. 'But the popularity of *No Orchids* and the American books and magazines to which it is akin shows how rapidly the doctrine of "realism" is gaining ground.' Chase's novel is a fantasy of power appropriate 'to a totalitarian age'. Orwell thinks that it is possible that Chase's success might be an isolated event, stemming from the war's tedium and brutality, but if similar books 'should definitely acclimatise themselves in England, instead of being merely a half-understood import from America, there would be good grounds for dismay'. He chose *Raffles* for his comparison because it is also morally ambivalent, but it is still structured by codes of conduct and taboos: 'In Mr Chase's books there are no gentlemen and no taboos. Emancipation is complete, Freud and Machiavelli have reached the outer suburbs.'[30]

Orwell uses 'realism' not as a literary term but as a description of a moral atmosphere and a cult of power. In my chapter on American crime fiction I also argued that 'realism' was more than a stylistic matter in recent crime novels, arguing that it was a challenge to 'law and order' rhetoric, replacing a world of moral absolutes with a world of work. But Orwell needs to be challenged on his own terrain by different views of realism in the crime writing of the 1930s and 1940s. Raymond Chandler saw the writers connected to the American crime magazine *Black Mask*, most notably Hammett, as taking murder away from country house libraries and vicarages and placing it back in its real social landscape, the urban mean streets, a move from an English model to the American city and vernacular. This can be seen as a questioning of power rather than a fantasy of it, as Hammett and

Chandler reveal the complicity between the wealthy and the legal system, between business and the police, between crime and civic corruption. Ken Worpole's *Dockers and Detectives* states the case for this realism:

> it was in American fiction that many British working-class readers, including political militants, found a realism about city life, an acknowledgement of big business corruption, and an unpatronizing portrayal of working-class experience and speech which wasn't to be found in British popular fiction of the period, least of all in the crime novel obsessed as it was with the corpse in the library, the Colonel's shares on the stock market and thwarted passion on the Nile.[31]

Worpole's research reconstructs the 'popular reading' of the 1930s, supplying a British context that contradicts the pessimistic discourse of Americanization. Interviewing retired trade unionists and political activists about their youthful reading, Worpole found that many mentioned American writers, the naturalists such as Dreiser and Upton Sinclair and later novelists such as Dos Passos. He also discovered the popularity of American detective fiction, which he argues was an important influence on the development of British working-class fiction, providing a model of an urban vernacular, 'masculine style'. He discusses the problematic elision of women's experience in this gender-specific writing, but what I want to extract from his research is the experience of readers glad to find the absence of snobbery, gentlemen, or middle-class adulteries, the very features whose absence Orwell mourned in Americanized crime fiction. William Keal, a retired trade unionist and labour movement activist, told Worpole about his early reading, stressing the democratic and demotic pleasures of American writing, the kind of pleasures that I suggested to be the strength of George Higgins and Elmore Leonard.

> I read H. G. Wells, Arnold Bennett, all those people, but they weren't my kind of people. You always had the edge of class; and what intrigued me about the American writers – of course they had a class system as well – but they were talking the way we talked.... What came through with the Americans was really a brutal and realistic attitude in language.
>
> Hemingway was the first because it was his idea that it was in the dialogue that you could do everything, rather than building up descriptive passages.... The clarity of the phrase; he was using the vernacular which I liked.[32]

Looking back to Hoggart's and Orwell's fears about the Americanization of the crime genre, their predictions about its hold on the popular imagination seem justified. The American crime genre now appears as a powerful and ubiquitous 'imaginary America' spread across fiction, television, films, and music, and as one of the dominant routes into American culture for Europeans. Those streets and car chases, the precinct rooms full of weary cops drinking coffee, the seedy offices of surprisingly honourable private eyes, the lovers on the run heading for the state line: we know these as a veritable cartography of crime. But Orwell's own example of James Hadley Chase does not have to be seen under the rubric of Americanization. For images of American crime have always been a co-production with Europe, Chase's contribution to the mythical American underworld is not an extreme case of the Americanized imagination but part of a lengthy tradition of responses and contributions to the crime genre. Instead of the 'invasion' or 'infection' model of the discourse of Americanization, there is a complex series of exchanges between Europe and the United States which produce this neon-lit terrain of crime. Landmarks here would include the European directors who went to Hollywood, Lang or Hitchcock, for example; the influence of Marcel Duhamel's *Serie Noire* crime novels (Duhamel asked Chester Himes to write his first novel) and, more generally, the response of French intellectuals to the American hardboiled novel; the genre of *film noir* and the role played by German Expressionism and French criticism in the shaping of its style and status.[33] These examples suggest that representations of American crime should not be seen as an invading force but as part of a more complex relation of influence crossing between Europe and the United States. They also imply that productive comparisons could be made between the responses of different nations' intellectuals to the threat or promise of American culture. If the response of many British intellectuals has been a defensive warning of the dangers of being overrun by American culture, the rhetoric of Americanization has not been confined to this role of prophesying cultural doom; it has also organized campaigns which concentrate on certain scapegoated cultural forms or genres. This is, as it were, the cutting edge of Americanization, the point where certain cultural products and their consumption become criminalized. To discuss this, we must turn from crime fiction to horror.

Consuming fears

Martin Barker's 'Strange History of the British Horror Comics Campaign' investigates the 1949–55 campaign which led to the Children and Young Persons (Harmful Publications) Act being passed in 1955. The campaign against 1950s horror comics prefigures the 1980s campaign against horror videos. On both occasions people joined in a rhetoric 'in many cases without looking at the objects of their wrath at all, let alone looking at them with any clear or consistent method of analysis'. I will discuss the 1980s video campaign later, but the comics campaign is a crucial episode to examine as Barker's argument demonstrates the link between Americanization and an ideology of Britishness. The campaign changed its emphasis from the comics' national origin to their genre: until 1953 the comics were referred to as 'American' or 'American-style' comics, but the Act and the discussion leading up to it avoided these terms, the chosen names being 'horror comics' or occasionally 'crime and horror' comics. Behind that change of nomenclature lies a significant political episode, for while the debate included a Tory government and involved teaching unions in their role as professional guardians of children's welfare, it originated from a more surprising source. Barker's research uncovered the role of the Communist Party in turning horror comics into an issue.[34]

Barker turns to the Communists' 1951 Cultural Conference, quoting from a special issue of the party journal *Arena*, 'The USA Threat to British Culture'.

> This entire issue of *Arena* is devoted to the American threat to British culture, to all that is good and vital in our national tradition. Needless to say, as will be clear from the contributions, the threat comes from the reactionary elements in USA society, and there is no question of an attack on American culture as such.

In practice, this attempt to distinguish the 'good and vital' in British culture and the 'reactionary elements' in American culture collapsed. Barker argues that as far as the United States was concerned, 'apart from a narrow band of "good guys", *all* American culture got condemned', matched by a 'completely homogeneous view of British culture'. Sam Aaronvitch spoke to the conference about American penetration of the British film industry, book trade, music business, and academic life: 'Every possible bad facet of American life was being exported – including, of course, McCarthyism.' The party strategy was to organize around the theme of Americanization, and Barker cites the assistant general secretary, George Matthew's comments in 1950: 'Relate any question affecting the masses to the issue of national independence.' Barker traces a shift from a political discourse to ideas of American culture as 'debased'. Some members were wary of 'the dangerous nationalism implicit in this approach', and tried to distinguish ' "jingo patriotism" from the patriotism that was now organising resistance to American domination', but the difference did not survive in the comics campaign. This is a problem that we will come across elsewhere, a problem of the left and the patriotic, which, I will argue in my conclusion, stems from an unnecessary linking of political opposition to American policies with the discourse of Americanization. Barker sees the CP of the 1950s as in need of a popular broadbased campaign, hence they played down overtly oppositional rhetoric about American imperialism and foregrounded the threat to British culture. Amongst the talk of American crime, American comics, American publishers, British publishers were not mentioned, for 'this anti-Cocacolization' needed to see the comics as an alien threat to British values, traditions, and children.[35]

Barker argues that 'while the problem is political (American imperialism), the solution is totally apolitical (national decency and higher values)'. A question of world politics and power relations is translated into a cultural crusade. The call was for a coalition of parents, teachers, churches, trade unions, women's institutes, to mobilize against American comics and in defence of Britain's cultural heritage. A consensus did form around this line as the parliamentary debate in August 1952 demonstrated. Throughout the debate comics were referred to as 'American-style comics', and Dr Horace King explained, 'We want to keep our English ways. What we get from America is not the best of American life . . . but all that is worst in America.' The Conservative spokesman, Sir Hugh Lucas-Tooth, agreed, calling the comics a 'crude and alien' idiom. As we have seen from Hebdige's article and from Hoggart and Orwell, a certain anti-American feeling existed in the country at large, often provoked by the figure of the GI. It was these ' "gum-chewing, pasty-faced" young working-class Americans who brought the comics over, and part of the reaction was just plain English snobbery'. Barker interviewed Joe Benjamin, a CP member at the time of the campaign, and asked him if there had been anti-American feeling involved in the campaign. Benjamin's answer shows a familiar identification of the modern with the American, with Englishness seen as essentially pastoral.

> JB: No, categorically, no: there was no anti-Americanism in the campaign. . . . We wanted to get back to some kind of English tranquillity. It was a very romantic notion, of countryside, Merrie England, Elgar's music. . . . And anything that was American was material, and brash, and vulgar, and that included their comics, their motorcars.
> MB: You don't count that as anti-American?
> JB: We saw that not as anti-Americanism, but as very pro-British.[36]

The shift in this response from anti-Americanism to pro-Britishness provides in miniature an idea of the transformation within the campaign's rhetoric and strategy. Overt, political anti-Americanism was dropped as was the idea of the comics having direct effects (copycat crimes, for example). They are replaced by 'a moralized, depoliticized' argument revolving around children, horror, and degradation or corruption. Barker sees this as a move from a claim that is potentially testable to an unempirical moralism: 'a change from "these comics are doing the following calculable damage" to "these comics are morally objectionable and *horrible*" '. Comics no longer generate delinquents, they seduce the innocent. Hence their change of name, from 'crime' or 'American-style', to 'horror'. Barker sees this changed name as revealing more about the campaign than about its object; what it reveals is '*a search for the lowest common denominator* which would bind together all supporters'. The campaign's longevity and its success 'depended on a rhetorical commonsense, a *refusal to theorise*'. The campaigners narrowed their conceptual base to an apolitical moralism, narrowing their target as well, snipping horror out of the chain of associations surrounding Americanization (pulp fiction, films, jazz, etc.), in order to avoid having to argue their position. The moral stance assumed harm by keeping the effects vague and untestable but the source specific. As the campaign built up to legislation it had to be narrow and specific in order to draft and pass a bill. 'But within its limits, there was only emotion and rhetoric ... the result of the narrowing was less *precision*, not more.' The comics were still seen as 'evil', but rather than criminalizing their readers they now corrupt. What do they corrupt? Barker's answer is 'the "mind", the "atmosphere", "values" and "proper development": the words signify nothing testable, but rest entirely on a tacit agreement about the meaning of these things.' Unlike the parallel campaign in America, there was no opposition to this consensus although attempts to extend the campaign to other popular forms were challenged. The comics, like today's horror videos, were unfamiliar to many and their actual audience was scattered, voiceless, and disorganized, mostly young working-class men and women rather than children. The audience was neither vocal nor consulted, and the British publishers were not so committed to the form as Bill Gaines, the US publisher of EC comics, who put up a spirited challenge to the American campaign.[37] With no real opposition a consensus of activists, politicians, moral campaigners, and teachers crystallized into an unchallenged common sense.

Barker deconstructs the arguments proffered by the theoreticians of the comics' evil effects, opening up the differences between their positions. He finds that the leading English critic, George Pumphrey, differed greatly from the Americans. Unlike the critics in the United States, Pumphrey avoided both effects and politics. Rather than arguing a case his judgements are characterized by a tone of 'obviousness', suggesting that the comics are self-evidently 'horrid'. In this, Barker argues, Pumphrey was the perfect publicist for the British campaign, constructing in his work not a theory of effects but 'an

English utopia, in which children are naturally and instinctively good, love good literature, hate bad grammar'. Barker outlines the assumptions:

To-all-good-parents-and-teachers-and-true, there is an obviousness about the moral issues that makes politics, analysis and argument quite redundant. He speaks as one who knows that his listeners will instantly recognise their shared upbringing, their shared values. 'Everyone knows' what is harmful to our children. Who needs a theory (even an implicit one) about effects? Ordinary people know just by virtue of being ordinary.

This 'ordinariness' is a national characteristic: overt anti-Americanism was no longer necessary to this English common sense, for the alien does not need to be named, it will instantly be recognized.

A heritage was at stake: Englishness, good manners, proper English language, fine literature. People who have these things know instinctively that anything else is harmful. In the name of traditional values they defend traditions for reasons that do not need saying – for to say them, to make them a matter of truth or falsity, would destroy their very status as the obvious traditions that make us what we are: English.[38]

From this we can extract the important point that the discourse of Americanization is shadowed and generated by an unquestioned ideology of Englishness. The comics campaign demonstrates this link very clearly by the way that anti-Americanism was so swiftly eclipsed by the defence of national traditions.

Barker's analysis of the comics themselves offers many insights into the nature of horror as a genre. It also provides an example of the benefit of Barker's stress on the specificity of genre and on the *activity* of consumption. He discusses the self-consciousness of both the genre and of its consumers, seeing horror as tending towards parody. The campaigners against the comics argued, as do their modern counterparts campaigning against horror videos, that increased exposure to these forms would lead to greater harm or, at best, to desensitization. In this they see consumption as a passive surrender to images, but Barker argues for an active notion of reading (or viewing in the videos argument), for the more readers know a genre, the more aware they are of conventions. Readers or viewers become more conscious, more comparative, as they become able to draw on more references and examples. Barker argues that the comics produce doubt rather than degradation; their narrative twists and shocks generate scepticism not brutalization. And, ironically, he points out that the subtler a strip was, 'the more likely it was to be the object of vilification' by the campaign.[39]

A campaign that started as a deliberate political strategy ended by being seen as a spontaneous and apolitical movement fighting for decency. The CP were complicit with this depoliticizing as they tried 'to make a virtue out of the very tendencies which were creating a climate against politics': 'defence of the British heritage; concern from a standpoint of humane values at violence and brutality; and defence of those values as embodied in our children'. A party obviously opposed to McCarthy's anti-Communist crusade 'ended up using notions not at all alien to McCarthyism ("tradition", "heritage" and "defence of childhood") to attack and help silence a powerful piece of anti-McCarthyism'. Barker is referring to 'You, Murderer', a comic strip that was an explicit attack on anti-Communist hysteria but that was singled out for criticism by the *Daily Worker* which obscured the strip's purpose by printing frames out of context. As McCarthyism grew out of the notion of the un-American, so the British comics campaign broadened its appeal by dropping rational argument in favour of a specific variant of nationalism: 'The British were distinctive, not racially, but in terms of their cultural level.' Britain might become 'Great' again by the export of 'our' culture: 'Then the world darkened, and started carrying its culture to the British.' The traditions of 'Britishness' were besieged by Americanization. The comics were not the real object of the campaign: 'the time had spawned a shapeless sense of threat to those feelings of idealism and Britishness. The comics became their outlet, their scapegoat.' The ideology of Britishness excluded certain discourses from the comics debate. The terms of the campaign 'set it above politics. It was concerned with "heritage", "traditions", "all our future".' These notions excluded the overtly political, supposedly transcending class politics in the name of national and cultural unity. In order to 'preserve something cultural, to safeguard an essential Englishness against outside corruption', English methods were necessary. Thus the campaign organized around an unquestioned heritage, and necessarily rejected scientific investigation which would have denied 'the instinctive knowledge ordinary people must have as British citizens'. For 'The comics were cultural artefacts, and the British were cultured in the best sense of the word.' Therefore the campaigners could assume that the comics were self-evidently harmful, and any challenge to that idea of self-evidence would also challenge the ideology of Britishness.[40]

Barker concludes by arguing that the comics should not have been banned; they were not the cause of national anxiety but a displacement of it. Themes from the campaign are politically relevant today and the 1980s, as already suggested, provide a parallel with the campaign against horror videos. Barker suggests that both campaigns are characterized by a refusal to theorize and by a reliance on the self-evidence of their claims. In both cases this acts to prop up an ideology of English 'ordinariness', an unquestioned idea of national traditions. The involvement of the CP in the 1950s and of feminists in the 1980s campaigns is seen by Barker to be a dangerous alliance with a national moralism that has been a key element in the new Toryism of the Thatcher years.[41] This 1980s context raises issues that are central to any understanding of populist politics today.

Populism and pleasure

Alan Wolfe, in an article in *New Left Review*, discusses the American right and the contradictions in their thought, between individualism and conformity, discipline and freedom, etc. His conclusion provides a useful starting point: 'The American right cannot make up its mind whether it is the party of the id or the party of the superego.'[42] That indecision is mirrored by Thatcherism's oscillation between control and liberation from restriction, a potential contradiction that shapes cultural policies. The most recent attempt to introduce a bill extending the 1959 Obscene Publications Act to cover television and radio was introduced in 1987 by Tory MP Gerald Howarth, and testified to the Thatcherite contradiction – a belief in economic deregulation combined with strict moral regulation. Richard Sparks has suggested that this is not a sign of logical weakness but of 'multiple strategies', seeing Thatcherism as able to speak to Mrs Whitehouse and her supporters 'in the language of law and order, patriotism and solid English commonsense', while energetically advocating the deregulation of the media, criticizing Public Service Broadcasting, and entrusting the future of new cultural technologies to the market. These different strands strengthen each other; 'the deregulation of the cultural markets stimulates the very sense of disorder which simultaneously guarantees the law and order vote.' Although Sparks casts Mrs Whitehouse in a rather sympathetic, even tragic, light, minimizing the effects of her agenda-setting campaigns, he captures precisely the contradiction of today's Thatcherite consumer-citizens: 'dutifully hedonistic producers and consumers by day, baying surrogate vigilantes by night'.[43]

The climate of concern about broadcasting, about the effects of 'sex and violence' on television, film, and video can be gauged by looking at some of the legislation proposed in the 1980s. There has been the Bright Bill (the Video Recordings Bill, 1984), Winston Churchill's proposed extension of the Obscene Publications Act to broadcasting which failed in 1986, and Gerald Howarth's reworking of that proposal in 1987. In a different politicization of the issue, explicitly informed by feminism, Labour's Clare Short proposed a ban on tabloid pin-ups (the 'Page Three Girls'). Party politics may shape the tone and target of these interventions but there is an alarming degree of consensus across the parties. As Simon Watney pointed out with the Winston Churchill amendment: 'A mere 31 Labour MPs voted against the measure yet had it got through it would have guaranteed a complete criminalisation of all images of homosexuality within British culture.'[44] Outside Westminster one finds such strange alliances as feminists and Mary Whitehouse agreeing on the disturbing effects of horror videos, putting aside their vast differences over sexuality, the family, 'traditional values'. As with the comics campaign discussed above, the debate assumed that the videos were self-evidently 'harmful' and displayed an ignorance of the object of discussion. Thus MPs watch a video of clips taken out of context from a wide range of television drama and films, or a collection of the most violent scenes from horror films, and on this basis pontificate about standards, values, obscenity, and corruption.

The term 'video nasty' gives a good impression of the role of the self-evident; there may be arguments about terms like 'obscene' but 'everyone' can agree on what is 'nasty'. So much of the opposition to the Bright Bill, and to the assumptions of the 'video nasty' debate, involved an insistence on complexity: criticizing the research methods that had 'proved' that a large percentage of children had seen video nasties; insisting on both aesthetic and political grounds that there was a need to distinguish between horror films rather than ignoring the differences between and within genres; pointing out the history of 'moral panics' about new or popular cultural forms.[45] As the popular press, the moral campaigners, the MPs, and some feminists saw only what they wanted to see, and rarely analysed the films themselves, it was necessary to insist on specificity. Most of the films referred to in the debate, as Martin Barker pointed out, came from a branch of the Italian film industry or from the United States, the American films being made for a 'drive-in' audience, often made by young film-makers for a young audience. Other better known American horror films were also included in the debate, partly because of a feminist analysis that argued that much of the genre, and not just the low-budget video nasties, invited the viewer to identify with male assaults on women, but mostly because the arguments ignored the need for criticism, analysis, and differentiation between films.

There is a long history of the fears provoked by new cultural forms, with novels, plays, melodramas, music hall, newspapers, films, comics, rock/pop songs, and videos, all in turn being seen to encourage crime or disorder or, at least, declining moral and social standards. From the late nineteenth century to the present these worries about popular culture have been linked by cultural criticism to Americanization. In the case of horror videos the differences between the spaces and contexts of consumption which arise when American film becomes British video, link this specific debate with more general anxieties about cultural consumption. There are important relocations in the shift from film to video: from public, social space (the cinema) to domestic, private space (the home); from a collective, almost ritualized viewing (a cinema audience laughing or screaming or sharing a tense silence) to the campaigners' alarming scenarios of obsession/initiation (the solitary male viewer able to stop the video, to replay scenes, to watch compulsively and increase identification, or the group of children who would be refused entrance to a cinema but who can watch entranced at home, hypnotized by the televised horror in the corner of the living-room); from American teenagers to British children. While I do not accept these terms as accurate descriptions of viewing, they do provide an insight into a powerful image in the discourse of Americanization. The horror movie comes off the American screen and enters the British home, threatening children; in this image the consumption of horror dovetails into the horror of consumption. For television has been seen as one of the crucial beachheads for American culture's invasion, 'American trash' replacing and undermining British domesticity and culture. Here the rhetoric itself resembles a horror movie: viewers become zombies, hypnotized, taken over, drugged, rendered passive, turned violent, in this Invasion of the Heritage-Snatchers.[46]

Although the rhetoric outlined above suggests horror movies it is applied, in the discourse of Americanization, to mainstream television as well as 'video nasties'. As Ien Ang says: 'In many European countries nowadays there is an official aversion to American television series: they are regarded as a threat to one's own national culture and as an undermining of high-principled cultural values in general.'[47] Ang's study, *Watching Dallas*, sees the saga of the Ewing family as 'the symbol of a new television age', surrounded by American pride in its glossy values, with a fascinated European press adding to its myth, but also attended by concern. This centres on 'the steadily growing influence of American consumer capitalism on popular culture', with *Dallas* seen as 'more evidence of the threat posed by American-style commercial culture against "authentic" national cultures and identities'. So *Dallas* became both a source of jokes and media gossip and a symbol of 'cultural imperialism'. The fear is that existing American cultural hegemony in the field of film and television will be increased by new technologies such as cable and satellite broadcasting. Left to the market more American series will be screened until domestic cultures will be flooded. Ang adds a note of caution: 'the mere idea of a threatened "cultural identity" contains elements which do more to conceal than to clarify the nature of the phenomenon and the problems described.' Rather than promoting genuine alternatives, countries can fall back on quotas in a 'misguided form of protectionism', and European television companies will produce cheaper copies of American formula-programmes. What is more, 'a stubborn fixation on the threat of "American cultural imperialism" ' blinds critics to the fact that 'since the 1950s the mass consumption of American popular culture has been integrated to a greater or lesser degree into the national "cultural identity" itself, especially in Western Europe'. Ang also raises the question of who finds this a problem; who are the 'guardians of the "national culture" '? 'In the millions of living rooms where the TV set is switched on to *Dallas*, the issue is rather one of pleasure.'[48]

Ang argues that there is no single key to *Dallas* – its popularity crosses different nations, contexts, ways of viewing. Her book is based on responses to an advertisement asking people to write to her, telling her why they watched *Dallas*, what they liked or disliked, and what others thought of their viewing. Her stress on pleasure is introduced with an interesting comment on *Dallas*'s production values, suggesting that for European viewers American images do not just *give pleasure*, they *signify pleasure*.

> The hegemony of American television (and film) has habituated the world public to American production values and American *mises-en-scène*, such as the vast prairie or the big cities, the huge houses with expensive interiors, luxurious and fast cars and, last but not least, the healthy- and good-looking men and women, white, not too young, not too old. Such images have become signs which no longer merely indicate something like 'Americanness' but visual pleasure as such.

With familiarity, the audience recognizes these scenes and images as pleasurable, implying a narrative promise of excitement and suspense. Ang quotes Simon Frith, from *Sound Effects*: 'America, as experienced in films and music, has itself become the object of consumption, a symbol of pleasure.'[49]

Ang sees her correspondents as trying to negotiate a path between their pleasure and the disapproval of what she calls 'the ideology of mass culture' (by this she means not the ideology produced by mass culture but the official discourse that disapproves of mass culture). Her study uses *Dallas* to chart how people combine an awareness of the critique of mass culture with their enjoyment of the series. She finds viewers who watch through a kind of filter of irony, turning melodrama into comedy (a point that translates well from Ang's Dutch context to a British one, as people watch American series through the jokes of Clive James or, above all, Terry Wogan). Ang's viewers show that they have internalized the critique of mass culture ('*Dallas* is bad') but have also found ways of legitimating their enjoyment: liking *Dallas* because it's so bad it's funny; affirming their pleasure but saying they are aware of its 'dangers' (sentimentality, escapism, materialism, sexism); finding messages in it that the official discourse might approve of, the evils of greed, for example.[50] These negotiations also depend on the contexts of viewing; watching *Dallas* alone a viewer admits to identifying with the characters, watching with friends introduces the social pleasure of a distanced, ironic viewing. This stress on the context of viewing also characterizes David Morley's *Family Television*, which investigates the way television is used and controlled within the context of family power relations. His research suggests the role that gender plays in a household's differentiated relation to viewing. Ang's argument that the critique of mass culture causes people to feel defensive about their pleasure in viewing is reinforced here by women's feelings of guilt at time spent watching their favourite programmes. One woman interviewed by Morley cannot affirm her pleasure without simultaneously down-grading it, as she says 'Typical American trash really. I love it!'[51] Guilt about Americanized pleasures is intensified by the low critical value given by both society and the family context to the woman's choice of programmes.

If the above discussion suggests the power of the critique of mass culture over viewers, Ang stresses that there are other ways of watching and enjoying, especially what she terms 'the ideology of populism'. This is the opposite to her idea of 'the ideology of mass culture', and is characterized by her as 'first and foremost, an anti-ideology': 'it supplies a subject position from which any attempt to pass judgement on people's aesthetic preferences is *a priori* and by definition rejected, because it is regarded as an unjustified attack on freedom.' She sees this populist discourse as anti-intellectual, sedimented in phrases like 'There's no accounting for taste', and forming a common sense that functions at a practical rather than a theoretical level. These ideas, Ang says, are 'assumed almost "spon-taneously" and unconsciously in people's daily lives', suggesting that this is why they hardly appear in the letters sent to her. But Ang argues that if 'the ideology of mass culture' (the critique of mass culture, the discourse of Americanization, etc.) has a hold over the way people *talk* about watching television, it does not necessarily 'prescribe people's cultural *practices*'. The 'normative discourses' of 'the ideology of mass culture' expressed in institutions such as education, and discourses such as cultural criticism may be *counter-productive*. People may reject these prescriptions 'not through ignorance or lack of knowledge, but out of self-respect', and 'the ideology of populism' justifies such a rejection by refusing 'any paternalistic distinction between "good" and "bad"', thus replacing guilt with pleasure. 'The stricter the standards of the ideology of mass culture are, the more they will be felt as oppressive and the more attractive the populist position will become.' The culture industry itself endorses this 'cultural eclecticism', suggesting that aesthetic judgements are impossible or irrelevant in the face of personal tastes and pleasures. In other words, 'the ideology of populism' can operate in the blind spot of 'the ideology of mass culture', ignoring prescription and stressing pleasure. For pleasure is *the* category that is ignored in the ideology of mass culture. In its discourses pleasure seems to be non-existent.' It's a point that Ang makes specifically when she talks of the left's problems with theorizing pleasure and feminism's past disregard for women's pleasure in viewing/reading, feminism uniting with 'the ideology of mass culture' to discount the pleasures of soaps, romances, and melodramas.[52]

Ang's account seems mistaken in its strict division of the ideological field (theoretical/practical, organized, institutionalized/spontaneous, etc.), which overlooks the way that 'the ideology of populism' is not just personal and 'spontaneous' but has social sites and chosen targets. Instead of, as Ang suggests, refusing to criticize, the populist position is as dismissive of modern art, for example, as the critique of mass culture is of *Dallas*. Modern art is inevitably seen by the popular press as a con trick ('bricks at the Tate!') or greeted with baffled derision at the 'pseud' and pretentious art world. More importantly, Ang's argument is heavily qualified by the popular press, at least in an English context, organizing a populist discourse around television. This is not a spontaneous response by the viewer, nor an untheorized resistance to the prescriptive paternalism of 'the ideology of mass culture', but a deliberate appeal to those feelings, organizing them, pinning them down to certain images and narratives, and to a certain politics. The left deplores, for obvious reasons, this configuration of sexism, soaps, and Thatcherism, but it is rare for socialists or feminists to actually look at how this works, how this configuration is constructed. An excellent exception is Patricia Holland's analysis of the *Sun*'s 'Page Three girls', questioning the paper's address to women readers.

Holland begins with the paper's sense of 'fun', an organization of pleasure and emotion which addresses the reader, inviting him or her to join in. Holland finds she is not invited, 'To put it bluntly, I know the *Sun* does not want me.' Her criticism of the *Sun*'s sexism is pre-empted and placed by the paper's construction of such objections: 'The *Sun* does not want spoilsports, killjoys, those who are not prepared to join in the high jinks, the sauciness, to allow a flirty encounter to brighten their day.' This is how the *Sun* speaks to women, inviting them to join in this vision of heterosexuality as saucy fun. Its news which is 'news of sex, is backed up by sexualisation of public events'. Pop stars, soap opera actors/actresses, the royal family, Page Three pin-ups, a world of fun and human interest, where Joan Collins rubs padded shoulders with Margaret Thatcher, where questionnaires about sexy lingerie are juxtaposed with racist editorials. Holland's article focuses on Page Three as a narrative and the way the *Sun* addresses women. There are contradictions in the paper's project: it assumes heterosexual monogamy while suggesting more risqué alternatives.[53] It also, I would add, provides another example of the contradiction noted earlier between consumption as liberating and as needing to be rigorously policed. So the *Sun* at times seems to agree with the radical feminist argument that 'pornography is the theory, rape is the practice', printing stories of rapists inspired by 'sick videos'. Yet the paper denies that its own softcore images have any effects, the ubiquitous breasts of Samantha Fox are merely harmless fun. The 'law and order' editorial goes alongside the sexist images, a juxtaposition that means, as I will argue, that one must distinguish between two populisms.

Holland rejects the *Sun* while noting that millions of women do read it, but her most productive insight is in seeing that her rejection is anticipated and pre-empted by the *Sun*. It is itself rejected rather than ignored.

> What the *Sun* is rejecting is moralism of any sort, bureaucratic power disguised as moral and cultural values, the whole range of attempts to put something over on you, to push you around, re-expressed in terms of elevation, education, propriety. The *Sun* rejects all that in the name of a working class whose rise to prosperity is still a live memory.

Work disappears from the paper's conception of the working class, as it addresses a class 'defined by its modes of consumption rather than its place in production'. Readers are unified around 'their forms of entertainment, by cultural attitudes rather than by class solidarity'. 'Traditions of working-class discipline and organisation are rejected along with the middle-class bureaucrats, social workers and cultural moralists.' The argument is clearly demonstrated by the gap between the way the paper addresses its working-class readers and its treatment of its own printers. The paper organizes against its own workers by portraying them as a source of disorder, to be placed alongside immigrants, muggers, striking miners, social security 'scroungers', and other enemies within.

The *Sun*'s call for a particular kind of sexual liberation fits into this pattern. Sex is fun, a leisure activity, one of the rights of the consumer. Thus the organisation of gender roles takes place in terms of class identification. It is the moralists, the educators, the social workers who are the spoilsports, condemning Page Three as sexist and degrading.[54]

Socialists and feminists are lined up in a regulatory, killjoy alliance: the 'loony left', 'barmy bureaucrats' in the EEC, the 'Whitehall wallies' of Britain's own bureaucracy, all want to interfere unnecessarily, to police fun, to regulate pleasure. It's a position that is specifically populist rather than libertarian. The *Sun* stands for a double populism. Firstly there is a 'law and order' populism that backs up its racism and its opposition to unions, and which enters the arena of culture with topics such as 'video nasties', controversial television drama, and other cultural products which the paper will campaign against. However, it also mobilizes what Ang would call 'the ideology of populism' against 'the ideology of mass culture', denying the right of cultural criticism to look down on what is seen as harmless fun. It is the combination of these populisms which enables the paper to attack some cultural works as dangerous pornography, while insisting that its sexist imagery is innocent amusement. Another effect of this combination is to suggest that socialism and pleasure are mutually exclusive.

Consumption is linked to pleasure in such a way as to appropriate the latter, and popular culture, for the right. For Thatcherism to be linked to fun may seem extraordinary but it may be explained in part as the identification of pleasure with *private* rather than *social* experience, and consumption with property (precisely the right to buy). Both Thatcherism and the *Sun* mobilize a populism of 'law and order' and strong policing – of culture as well as of the inner city – alongside this populism of freedom from interference. The two can reinforce each other (property as space of pleasure and property as security) or contradict each other (economic liberation of the media and moral regulation of cultural products), although as we have seen these contradictions can work in Thatcherism's favour. In my Conclusion I will discuss the possible historical origin of this link between pleasure and the right, but it is important here to consider why the left should challenge this link and why that presents problems. The left's difficulties with consumption and pleasure prevent this space from being successfully contested. A suspicion of consumption runs through Trevor Blackwell and Jeremy Seabrook's study of the 'Reconstruction of the Post-War Working Class'. They try to avoid arguing that the British working class were corrupted by 1950s affluence, but while they see the gains in the quality of life they also retain a notion of prosperity and popular culture as weakening the solidarity and identity of the working class. They see some goods as lightening people's lives but they ask, 'what other function, other than their ostensible purpose, they serve?'[55] The idea of the washing machine as conservatism's Trojan horse displays a certain nostalgia for ideas of Americanization and embourgeoisement.

This kind of continuation of Hoggart and Orwell now competes with other analyses of consumption, including attempts by the left to see consumption as 'progressive' or 'subversive'. That context was glimpsed at the opening of this chapter with a survey of fears about a drift into populism, where Judith Williamson was quoted on the perils of being popular. She returns to this question in 'The Politics of Consumption' where she suggests that people, having little sense of choice or control in the world of work, find both individual and social meanings and identities in consumption. She argues that Thatcherism has captured certain popular needs, but that it cannot fulfil these needs. People get something from consumerism so the left's task is to think of different ways to answer these needs. Instead of following the right-wing initiative on the sale of council houses, and dropping their opposition to the policy, socialists should develop other ways to give council tenants a feeling of security, and challenge the current view that ownership is the only legitimate form of control.[56] This valuable argument runs into difficulties as it moves from housing and privatization to personal consumption. Videos and personal stereos are seen as symptoms of a privatization of entertainment. Williamson suggests that such products may not be radical in themselves but they do stem from 'potentially radical' needs, 'needs both sharpened and denied by the economic system that makes them'. Thus powerlessness in the economic sphere is partially answered by consumerism and fashion, and the 'rather demoralized generation of the '60s left', turn to 'style' after their previous distrust of fashion. Consumerism offers a chimera of autonomy, power over one's life rather than power in the political and economic spheres: 'the realm of the "superstructure" is, for consumers and Marxists alike, a much more fun place to be.'[57] There is something rather simplistic about this equation: you want to change the world, instead you change your haircut. Williamson sees theories of consumption as either overly academic or as populist slumming, ignoring the importance of consumerism as a terrain of political struggles over the meanings and uses of culture, an importance testified to by Williamson's own work. Translating her analysis from wishful thinking (unspecified new ways to meet needs and desires) into practice has mainly ended up with sermonizing (Trotsky plus Tamla Motown), or the development of largely disappointing sub-genres (the socialist or feminist private eye novel).

The relation between the social and subjectivity is problematic, leading to a confusion of needs, pleasures, and desires, and a temptation for socialists to reduce questions of subjectivity to the economic, to avoid a language of pleasure and desire for a rhetoric of need and aspiration. It is difficult to assign products to discrete spheres of need or luxury and attempts by cultural criticism to police that distinction (a fridge is a gain in the quality of life, a video recorder is a false answer to real problems), may well be counter-productive in the ways described above by Ang and Holland. Terry Lovell has pointed out the obvious fact that is often forgotten in debates about consumption: 'people do not read novels and go to the movies *in order to* consume (bourgeois) ideology and thereby meet the ideological requirements of capitalism.' Things are bought and consumed for their use-value to the individual consumer, and Lovell argues that there are no reasons to assume that the use-values of cultural products and the pleasures they offer their consumers, are identical with the ideological needs of capitalism. 'What is required here, and what Marx's writing nowhere supplies, is a marxist theory of capitalist consumption. Within any such theory, use-value would have to be a central concept.'[58]

Lovell's argument suggests that the politics of consumption are more open than Williamson or Seabrook suggest. Williamson argues that video recorders or personal stereos are not in themselves 'radical' but they do express radical needs. It may well be more productive to reverse her point – there are no reasons why such products should be seen as in themselves 'reactionary'. The point is how the pleasures of consumption are articulated, and the associations of these pleasures can be changed by highlighting the connections between social policies and private enjoyment. The social nature of pleasure should be stressed rather than commentators just bemoaning its current forms. For example, the connections between culture and transport policies could be communicated (youth culture being probably more dependent on the availability of late-night transport than on, say, style commentators). The city is the ideal site of this social re-articulation of pleasure, and some of the policies pursued by Labour before the GLC was abolished demonstrate how this could be put into action. I have suggested above that two populisms address cultural questions, using the *Sun* as a way of clarifying this. One populism links culture to 'law and order' in campaigns against horror videos or demands for a stricter regulation of cultural products, and this has been seen to have links with fears of 'Americanization'; the other populism rejects such fears and sees consumption as simply personal taste and harmless fun. In fact, this combination polices popular culture, stigmatizing individual artists or works or even whole genres and placing them outside the arena of approved pleasures. It is possible that some current ideas on culture and on crime proposed as Labour policies could challenge this right-wing populism, and I will end this chapter with a brief examination of these.

On both sides of the Atlantic crime has played an important part in populist politics. 'Law and order' campaigns by the right have worked to criminalize protest and have often acted as a disguised appeal to racism as well as drawing on more general moral themes of declining national values with promises of a restoration of past virtues and certainties. Recent suggestions from the left have challenged the Conservative notion that 'law and order' issues are their natural territory. During Mrs Thatcher's years of office crime rates have risen and clear-up rates have dropped, the prison system has been in almost permanent crisis, and riots have erupted, the summer of 1981 seeing the first mainland use of CS gas. Answers from the right have been predictable: more money and more powers for the police, tougher sentences, more prisons, and the usual demands for a return to capital punishment. The left has moved from earlier, critical criminology with its focus on the media's creation of panics about crime, from nostalgia for idealized working-class communities of the past, and from the ultra-leftist variant, the glamorization of the criminal as a quasi-revolutionary figure. There has been an increasing recognition that crime is a real problem rather than simply the creation of the media, and that it hits working-class communities harder than the affluent suburbs. These real fears about crime have contributed to the populist appeal of Thatcher for working-class voters, intensified by the portrayal of Labour as the 'anti-police' party. Labour's attempt to break with this pattern was seen in their proposals for realistic, preventative measures put forward in the 1987 general election. While the Conservatives increasingly emphasize order rather than law, focusing on policing strikes and demonstrations, and continuing a worrying erosion of civil liberties, Labour has begun to rewrite the agenda with a programme of assistance for people to improve the security of their homes, and a stress on the accountability of policing priorities to local communities, as well as a recognition of the specific demands of women for safer streets. The gap which exists between community policing needs and actual policing strategies offers a chance for a populism of the left to democratize these priorities and prevent the worsening of relations between the police and inner city communities, while refusing the Conservative policy of criminalizing whole sections of society.[59]

Labour's recent thinking about the arts, as evidenced again in their election proposals in 1987, shows signs of tackling the other strand of populism by recognizing the centrality of culture, both economically and in terms of people's experience. However, one major problem here running through British oppositional thinking, has to do with America. The persistence of the Americanization argument and the increasingly harsh anti-Americanism shown by the left are stumbling blocks for any attempt to analyse popular culture. They also act to prevent debate about the British identity, and this is one of the main strands of my Conclusion.

CONCLUSION:
President Rambo's poodle

From special relationship to 51st state

> All right you Limey has-been I'm going to say it country simple. You
> have been taken over like a Banana Republic. Your royal family is nothing
> but a holograph picture projected by the CIA.[1]

Across a range of discourses and forms (journalism, books, political
rhetoric, music), phrases build up into an image of Britain as a US
colony or client state: banana republic, Airstrip One, the unsinkable
aircraft carrier, the 51st state of the USA, among others. A number
of issues get fused and confused in these uses, thus actually making
it easier for the right to paint specific criticisms of the United States
as kneejerk anti-Americanism: American policies in the Middle East
and Central America, the relation of Britain to the United States, and
American 'cultural imperialism'.

The special relationship between Britain and America has been
challenged, critics suggesting that the relations between the two
countries resemble colonization rather than partnership. Thatcherism
is seen as complicit in the Americanization of Britain, and the left's
rhetoric about American encroachment on British sovereignty is
partly motivated by a desire to challenge Thatcher's patriotic Iron
Lady image by focusing on her subservience to American interests.
A number of issues have generated this concern but these specific
political questions are expressed in such a way that they are obscured
by the history of anxieties about America outlined in the previous
chapter. The 1980s have seen several points of conflict between
British and American interests: Reagan's invasion of Grenada, and
American policy in the Middle East and Central America. The American nuclear and military presence in Britain linked anti-nuclear
protest to questions of sovereignty around images such as the Americans being seen as an 'occupying army', through worries about 'dual
key' and the extent to which the British government would be
consulted in any nuclear confrontation. Nuclear anti-Americanism

managed to cross some political divisions, with opinion polls revealing a certain Gaullist streak in the British public, a British deterrent proving more popular than Cruise missiles. The opposition has also pointed out the tendency for the Conservative government to suggest that Britain can learn from American models of health care, welfare, arts funding, and other areas. The crucial mediating role here has been played by right-wing think tanks, acting as a bridge between the American new right and Thatcherism. Britain's industrial independence has been undermined, according to the opposition, by the Conservatives' willingness to see companies taken over or sold off to American competitors (the Westland helicopters affair and the proposed sale of part of British Leyland which provoked Tory rebellion as well as opposition criticism). American interests are also accused of overriding British scientific and technological development, with the implications of 'Star Wars' research for British scientists, and with the extension of US licensing regulations to British high-tech companies.

I am not arguing that these issues are unimportant but that the way they have entered political debate introduces a nationalism that blunts their critical power, and an anti-Americanism that obscures the specificity of the questions raised. A related issue concerns the problems of critiques of the influence of American culture. There are two main problems: the links between American culture and British popular culture, and the difficulty of separating a radical critique from the traditions of conservative cultural criticism. Paul Weller's career which has taken him from the Jam to the combination of style, soul, and socialism that marks his recent work with the Style Council and Red Wedge, provides examples of this difficulty. As his politics have become more focused and more overt, Weller's attention has turned to the pernicious effects of American influence on Britain. In 1985, Weller told an interviewer that the Style Council song 'Come to Milton Keynes', was 'bound up in Americanization'. He expanded on his theory of American influence on postwar England: 'we have got some of the things like clothes and records and aesthetic things, but you can't take one without having the other' – the other being 'mass consumerism'.[2] The relation between personal consumption ('clothes and records and aesthetic things') and 'mass consumerism' is untheorized. The implication would seem to be that there is a distinction between one's own choices and other people's seduction by commodities – 'I buy things I like, you are trapped in mass consumerism.' The logic of Weller's comment also leads to an identification of the pleasure offered by aspects of American culture with an endorsement of the society and system that produced them. It is important to stress against this that the pleasure of the consumer is not exhausted in his or her contribution to, say, record company profits. Popular culture, especially youth culture, should not be seen as either essentially rebellious or alternatively as simply passively compliant. Notions of pleasure, use, and subjectivity may help to explain how it can be both. Weller's attachment to notions of 'Englishness' and his love of black American music comes into contradiction. He admires 1960s Tamla Motown but as he can only hear 'politics' in overt political statements he has trouble thinking of the music as political, and if we followed his argument above, ownership of Motown records would also be an endorsement not just of the philosophy of the artists but also of the working practices of the label's founder, Berry Gordy, and ultimately of American capitalism *per se*. These problems partly stem from not seeing the use-value of cultural products (a problem touched on at the end of the previous chapter), partly from not being able to think of pleasure politically, but mainly from an identification of enjoyment of American cultural products with capitulation to the official ideologies of America.

The publicity for the Style Council's short 1987 film, *Jerusalem*, emphasized the letters 'usa' in the title, either by capitalizing them or by picking them out in stars and stripes. However ironically this 'eruption' of America into the title was done, it still suggested a Blakean vision of the children of Albion selling out their birthright, not for anything as traditional as a mess of pottage but for a pair of jeans and an order of french fries. This is linked to the political context outlined above but its cultural sources are also important, as is Weller's attempt to suggest an alternative to Americanization. Although the break-up of the Jam and the formation of the Style Council was seen as a rupture, continuity can be traced around the ideas of mod: a sense of working-class style, especially notions of European style, combined with a backdrop of American black music. Weller's politics seem to stem in part from George Orwell, and an Orwellian sense of 'decency' and 'Englishness' can be detected beneath his concern about Americanization. The Style Council's attempt to find an alternative to American cultural hegemony maintained mod's chosen soul music but played up mod's Europeanism, stressing a visual style drawn from Italy or France. Even here, Europe was reduced to commodities rather than a genuine sense of European cultural reality, Weller producing a shopping list and a cluster of tourist images – Italian shoes, Parisian cafés, and so on. Ironically, it often looked as if the notion of Italian style was filtered through American images; Weller's suit and haircut echoing Al Pacino rather than a deeper sense of Europeanism. The idea of café society suggested the world of Colin MacInnes' *Absolute Beginners* and its mythicized portrait of Soho, that European pocket in London where MacInnes' characters go to hear American jazz. Since MacInnes, along with Orwell, is one of the few writers referred to by Weller it is interesting to see how the novel approached anti-Americanism in the late 1950s.

The narrator of *Absolute Beginners* tells a friend that 'It's a sure sign of total defeat to be anti-Yank.' He may disapprove of American influence, but that is not the same as anti-Americanism:

> Because I want English kids to be English kids, not West Ken Yanks and bogus imitation Americans, that doesn't mean I'm anti the whole US thing. On the contrary, I'm starting up an anti-anti-American movement, because I just despise the hatred and jealousy of Yanks there is around, and think it's a sure sign of defeat and weakness.

Instead one should support 'the local product', for America may have 'launched the teenage movement' and Sinatra may have been 'in his way, the very first teenager', but Britain must 'produce our own variety', a local youth culture not an imitative one. The ideal is to balance national pride with a critical thrust: 'It's because I'm a patriot, that I can't bear our country.'[3] The passage sees anti-Americanism as not just envy but a 'sure sign of defeat and weakness', symptomatic of a Britain reacting to the loss of empire. The novel's Jewish poet, Mannie, says that the 'price of riches is that you export reality to where it is you get your money from', and as Britain starts to lose its overseas power and markets, 'reality comes home again to roost'.[4] Part of this uneasy return of reality is the shift from imperial power to multi-cultural society, and MacInnes suggests a link between anti-Americanism and the novel's other sign of hatred, jealousy, and weakness – racism. MacInnes' optimism about British youth culture seems to rest on the opportunity of appropriating American forms for British subjects, rather than rejecting American culture. An example of such an appropriation in the 1980s might be not Weller's earnest contradictions but the clever mobilization of Englishness shown by Morrissey of the Smiths, who mixes references to literary traditions with camp allusions to music hall, a blurring of gender in the songs' scenarios with a precise sense of English settings, who places Oscar Wilde alongside James Dean, and 1960s British films of northern working-class life alongside Andy Warhol's 'stars'. These juxtapositions are underpinned by the tension between Morrissey's voice and lyrics and Johnny Marr's guitar and general ease within rock's mid-Atlantic traditions.

MacInnes' pessimism about British culture links racism and anti-Americanism, seeing them as symptomatic of a post-imperial power declining into nostalgia and xenophobia. Those symptoms still persist and are expressed most vehemently in the field of popular culture by

Julie Burchill. Burchill has spent a decade moving from punk journalist to more general commentator, writing for *NME*, *The Face*, *Time
Out*, the *Sunday Times*, and the *Mail on Sunday*, and her provocative
contributions have always had a populist edge to their iconoclasm
(for example, her assault on the middle-class left and her desire to
bring back hanging). A reading of her collected journalism reveals an
increasing obsession with the United States, condensing many of this
conclusion's themes. Appropriately for such a combative writer, war
provides the stage for her most blatant populism. In a piece called
'Falklands: No Island is an Island', Burchill tries to transform the
Sun's Argie-bashing into emotional anti-fascism, and popular jingoism into an assault on Thatcherism, demonstrating the dangers of
populist efforts to recapture patriotism from the right. She crows
over the blows to national pride given to the Americans by Vietnam
and Iran, suggesting that the United States has 'nothing to teach
Britain about the art of war' and that they should try sending their
boys to Sandhurst. She displays her political incoherence through an
extraordinary comparison of Britain and Israel as countries willing to
act outside American influence.[5] She accuses Mrs Thatcher of not
living up to her tough image, saying that she had to call up her 'Sugar
Daddy' – Reagan – first. Here we start to see what is at stake,
an unwillingness to let the Thatcher government appropriate the
patriotic: 'Thatcherism is not patriotism; it is a bid to become the
latest State of the USA.' The many people on the left who recognize
their own feelings in this phrase might start worrying at the slippage
from reclaimed patriotism to imperial nostalgia. For Burchill worries
about Thatcher wanting to hand over our 'Colonies' – Gibraltar,
Ulster, the Falklands – in order to appease the Americans, 'so that
we can get on with the business, pure and simple, of being an
American colony'. Burchill produces an amusing variant on the right's
familiar line of 'Why don't you go and live in Russia then?', seeing
Mrs Thatcher as 'not a politician but a groupie; she should buy a
one-way Pan Am ticket, a rah-rah skirt and a pompom and go and
cheer Ronnie from the sideline for the rest of her days' (pp. 112, 113).
It is not that all discussion of Americanization will follow Burchill's
lines, nor that her coupling of support for anti-imperialist movements
in, say, Vietnam, with nostalgia for 'our' empire is typical. But
Burchill's deliberately provocative style and well-honed populist
instincts reveal the unspoken 'little Englander' assumptions that anti-
Americanism is intimately bound up with. Many people on the left
would appear to agree with Burchill's notion of Britain's need for an
independent role, 'not just to be America's bomb site. The Americans
are the vandals of the world and want to make a trash heap of the
world, like their own country is' (pp. 114, 115). But this demonstrates

contempt for America and Americans rather than political opposition to the Reagan administration.

The link between patriotism, nostalgia for empire, and what is seen as Thatcher's personal and ideological, and nationally humiliating, admiration for the United States, introduces questions of gender, via a rhetoric of masculinity and femininity, into the discourse of Americanization. Ronnie and Maggie are caricatured as a kind of nuclear romance, and Thatcher herself has unconsciously echoed Burchill's cheerleader joke when she described herself as Reagan's 'greatest fan'. In a piece called 'A Christmas wish: the end of America', Burchill sees the special relationship as 'the most malignant threat to postwar British sovereignty – *castrated* by a compliment!' (p. 118, emphasis added). Sovereignty's metaphor is gender: the greatness of Great Britain is threatened, emasculated, feminized. This metaphor also functions, as we have seen in the previous chapter, in discussions of Americanization and consumerism, with the passive, feminized spectator, and it will be discussed later in sections on masculinity as spectacle, and on the Libyan bombing raids. It condenses different strains of anxiety about America, worries about popular culture and about Britain's role as a world power, while, ironically, being a feature of Americanization *itself*. For the practice of psychohistory, the analysis of foreign policy in terms of phallic power and so on, is a crude psychologization of politics more associated with American academics than with British socialists. At some point however, precisely because it is so overdetermined, it proves almost irresistible.

Burchill's attempt at an oppositional patriotism brings out all that is ambivalent about populism. If much of what she says about American colonization could find a home in the speeches of Tony Benn, we have also seen that her idea of Airstrip One, of Britain as the latest state of the USA, is linked to nostalgia for an empire and worry about Mrs Thatcher's stewardship of our remaining 'colonies'. It is therefore not too surprising that her Christmas wish piece has as its opening a quotation from Enoch Powell rather than a politician of the left. Powell's 1983 speech on the American need to overestimate the Russian threat is cited by a woman whose public initiation into politics was through punk, the Anti-Nazi League, and Rock Against Racism. Burchill argues that America is 'now well into its third bout of post-war insanity' but we could wonder if the use of Powell, the 'prophet' and opportunist of racism, the guardian of Ulster, does not point to a derangement closer to home (p. 118). But that question, the issue of British decline and homegrown tensions, is precisely what the discourse of Americanization silences: Britain's problem is that we have been 'castrated' by a special relationship.

We *are*, in the eyes of the world, nothing more than another island protectorate of the USA, a cooler Hawaii, a richer Puerto Rico, populated by people who talk differently from Massah and have more colourful costumes but never deviate politically from the mainland and have no opinions of their own whatsoever.

Since Britain did not refuse the 'insult' of Cruise missiles, and here Burchill conveniently overlooks the role European leaders played in the missiles' deployment, then we no longer deserve independence – 'here's your red, white and blue grass skirt, *catch!*' (p. 119). The feeling that lies behind this is crucial: Britain once an empire is now a colony, once a country that *made* things, now less a country than a theme park, a display of colourful costumes and customs for American tourists, with the skirt adding the theme of feminization. The linked metaphors of this anti-Americanism are colonization, feminization, and 'ethnicization', the latter meaning the feeling that instead of the British ruling 'natives' they have become 'natives'. It's worth pausing to wonder who actually has this feeling of colonization. Public opinion polls in 1986/7 have shown that people in Britain were beginning to feel threatened rather than protected by the special relationship, and that they felt Reagan to be more of a threat to world peace than Gorbachev. However, there is a kind of histrionic self-pity in comparing our own deindustrialization and decline as a world power to the debt-ridden Third World. Where people do feel 'colonized' in Britain is by the British state in Northern Ireland, Scotland, or Wales, and where they feel humiliatingly dependent seems more likely to be in Housing Benefit Offices, in DHSS queues, on hospital waiting lists, on Youth Training Schemes, in the cracks of a declining and undemocratic Welfare State rather than in a queue at McDonald's or Kentucky Fried Chicken. 'Americanization' is systematically blind to these crises within the British state, for that is precisely its effect, to displace analysis from British decline on to threats to sovereignty and culture.

Burchill criticizes the demonology shaping US foreign policy: 'A "Communist" country is now any which wants a little more from life than to be an American missile base/brothel/tourist trap' (p. 120). But she denies the possibility for any critical thinking or dissent within the United States, and the country is portrayed as totally 'Other', first as mad and then as unreal, 'not a REAL country but a phony state'. She concludes with a ferocious passage where the idea of the Ugly American is no longer a rhetorical flourish adding polemical power to an analysis of capitalism or imperialism, but instead is the central, practically the only, element of the analysis. American adventurism is madness/jealousy/vulgarity. Uncle Sam has become Charlie Manson:

> America is one big Manson Family, misfits stuffed to bursting point with ignorance, hate and resentment, holed up in their huge ranch against the rest of the world, making the occasional marauding raid into the homes of the beautiful (from S. Tate to states of grace such as North Vietnam and Nicaragua) and killing them for the beauty and ease the thug outsider knows it can never have.

The United States is a cross 'between a playpen and a mental asylum, full of huge unhinged children with a craving for sweet things and the capability to destroy the world'. She mourns the fact that we cannot 'disinvent' America, 'any more than we can disinvent herpes, or the Bomb, or snuff films, or any of the other remarkable gifts America has blessed us with' (pp. 121–2). That final list is a classic ploy of the Americanization argument, one found elsewhere in Burchill's prose. In 'Greeneland revisited', she talks of America exporting its moral fundamentalism, its Cold War hysteria, along with 'their missiles, their herpes and their sick video films, all the other things that America gives to countries better than it so it won't look like such a conspicuous pile of garbage any more'. The previous chapter has traced the Americanization argument from Matthew Arnold to the 'video nasty' debate, and it is interesting that Burchill throws 'snuff films' and 'sick video films' into her list of grievances. The paradox is that her stand against American fundamentalism and 'moral incontinence' ends up appealing to homegrown, nationalistic 'moral panics' (p. 142).

From colony to theme park: the idea of colonization may stem, as we have seen, from an imperialist nostalgia, but the related theme park image is generated not by the loss of colonies but by the loss of industries. In another Burchill collection, *Damaged Gods*, she attacks a new ideology of leisure. Old industries, 'expendable little things like coal and steel', wind down 'in favour of "leisure technology"'. Again, Americanization haunts the argument.

> Leisure, entertainment, fame: in the Eighties they became our liberty, equality and fraternity. Britain, as the favoured offshore island of the USA, was commissioned not to produce lowly bananas or orphans but ENTERTAINMENT; Tom Wolfe wrote of the day Britain would be one big theme park, and all its citizens 'Viddies' – characters in videos made for American consumption. When it was suggested in 1985 that Battersea Power Station be made into a leisure park, it begged a bitter pun. Great Britain, 1985: all leisure and no power.[6]

From power to leisure, the shift is into what is uneasily termed the 'post-industrial society'. The term generates unease because it seems to promise both a high-tech utopia and a world of permanent mass unemployment, and it is worth pointing out that both right and left have been divided over whether to fear or celebrate this future. Similarly, there are odd mirrorings across the ideological divide. There has been a strange parallel between the prophets of the service industries and the celebrants of style; while the *Face* seemed to suggest that British youth spent (or should spend) their time sipping cappuccino and listening to jazz, Lord Young repeatedly announced from the Tory Cabinet that British youth should be manning the espresso machines. Manufacturing disappears.

As Burchill reminds us this 'post-industrial' future raises specific British anxieties. One of these is the idea of Britain's heritage becoming more marketable than its industrial products. The past is *not* a foreign country, it seems that we live in it. As the passage suggests, however, the exportable English image is not only the Royal Family, country houses, and Shakespeare, it is also youth, pop, 'viddies'. There is a pattern of fears: what happens in America today will happen in Britain tomorrow (the recent example of this is the media panic about the expected arrival of 'crack', a more potent form of cocaine); if America provides our future we provide their past, Britain's history is packaged for the tourist gaze or even exported abroad, as is the British contemporary scene (pop, fashion, style). A recent reversal of this pattern is illuminating: Richard Gephardt in April 1987, as part of his campaign for the Democratic presidential nomination and as part of his fight for protectionism, warned an Iowa audience of the threat that Japan and Taiwan pose to the US economy: 'unless we change ... America could become a modern day Great Britain.' For Britain to be America's future, the subject must be economic decline.

Someone who played an important role in winning Burchill access to wider audiences is Peter York, who as commentator on youth culture, as Style Editor of *Harpers and Queen*, and as business consultant, has carved out a niche in the contiguous but antagonistic worlds of music journalism, fashion magazines, and market research, a position whose interest has been obscured by the success of his 'Sloane Rangers' piece. Peter York repeated many of the themes of Burchill's comments on leisure, and also cited Tom Wolfe's view of Britain's future, in his South Bank Lecture, 'The Englishness of English Design', broadcast on ITV on 12 April 1987. However, his argument problematized the idea of Americanization. He focused on Britain-as-theme-park, cleverly using postcards and products to suggest our international image, a twinning of heritage and youth culture (the Beefeater and the punk), with a gift for style and ideas which is seen internationally as fantasy rather than design, and with no corresponding commercial sense or manufacturing culture. This moves us from Americanization (something done *to* Britain) to a historical view of a British cultural and industrial failure, a failure to turn an early industrial revolution into the basis for an industrial, modern, bourgeois culture with its appropriate institutions and ideology (something Britain failed to do). The argument and its references (Martin Wiener's *English Culture and the Decline of the Industrial Spirit*, for example), link York's lecture to an important analysis of Britain by writers identified with the *New Left Review* in the 1960s. To turn to this analysis is to turn from Americanization to Britain's crisis.

British decline: the neutered lion

Perry Anderson and Tom Nairn analysed British history by suggesting that British development was marked by certain absences and peculiar alliances. They argued that a common interest had been forged between a governing landed class and an emergent bourgeoisie based on: the expansion of empire, the economic harmony through the nineteenth century between agriculture and industrialization, and 'the joint front formed by the landowners and the bourgeoisie against the proletariat which arose in the industrial revolution'. This last point is interpreted as the key to understanding the British state. For here Britain differs from the most common pattern of the emergence of modern states, an alliance between the new middle classes and the people against absolutism or feudalism or colonial rule, with the French Revolution being the classic model. It was argued that the English Civil War was not quite an equivalent historical upheaval; by being the 'first bourgeois revolution' it was also, in terms of this model, the weakest.[7] Thus the 'Origins of the present crisis', the postwar crisis of modern Britain, have a lengthy history, with resolutions continually demanded and deferred. Tom Nairn suggests that the 'governing elite and the liberal intelligentsia, and the dominant sector of the economic ruling class, all have an obvious vested interest in the state', while the 'industrial bourgeoisie and the working class do not', remaining, however, unable to modernize the state.[8]

This argument provides a context for York's pronouncements on the peculiarities of English design. Another writer with roots in this analysis helps put Burchill's militarism and imperial nostalgia in perspective. Anthony Barnett's writing forms a comprehensive indictment of the linked problems of the British crisis and attempts at resolution. His analysis of the Falklands war offers a persuasive explanation of the underlying historical currents leading to the conflict and its extraordinary rhetoric. Barnett details the strategies successive governments have adopted as ways to break with decline: Wilson's 'technological revolution', Heath's entry into the EEC, trade union 'reform', Thatcher's conviction politics and her assault on the postwar consensus, combining monetarism, anti-union legislation, and the need for managers to manage and governments to govern. And on the sidelines, there is the SDP, 'that lost tribe of British politics, a bourgeois political party', which with its real attachment to Europe and its commitment to electoral and constitutional reform, promises radicalism while remaining, for the most part, opportunistically conservative.[9] Barnett sees Britain's decline as having two aspects: the first is the transformation of the nation from a leading world power to a secondary one. This became inevitable during the Second World War as part of the emergence of a Europe overshadowed by the United States and the Soviet Union, with decolonization and the Suez crisis revealing the full extent of this change. 'The collapse of Britain from a position as a leading world power with a giant Empire was definitive and irreversible. It was not caused by internal failure so much as overwhelming external change.' The other aspect is the unnecessary side of the decline, which is that Britain became one of the least economically successful of the second-rank nations.

> That Britain would cease to be a global power was inevitable. But that it had to become an economic cripple was not. The rational task of modernization in Britain, then, is to make the UK a relatively thriving but nonetheless second-rank country. The reality of Britain's position in the world needs to be embraced politically, rather than denied or defied, for any significant turnaround that would allow its people to achieve, say, the standard of living in Holland.[10]

It is this denial of Britain's real position that Barnett traces through the Falklands war, especially in the continuing importance of what he terms Churchillism. The latter is revealed in Thatcher's statement that the war 'put the Great back into Britain'. While she has 'overseen an acceleration in the relative decline of the UK compared to other second level powers, she has asserted a Churchillian renaissance that has wonderfully transported the country back into becoming a world power once again'. But this is only an extreme form of a postwar illusion, and Barnett quotes Harold Wilson in 1964, 'we are a world power, and a world influence, or we are nothing'. Hence, for example, Britain's excessive military expenditure. 'To become merely a northern European country with a per capita income of others is too paltry an ambition. It might mean a doubling of the national product, but in terms of Britishness it is treason.'[11] This analysis places questions about Britain centre stage, hence its importance here, for the discourse of Americanization serves to displace or deny these issues, preventing 'the reality of Britain's place in the world' from being 'embraced politically'. Just as the American air bases and missiles provide the most understandable motivation for anti-Americanism and for a rhetoric of 'American madness', so the British 'independent' deterrent provides the most extreme material and rhetorical occasion for this British illusion. David Owen's stance on defence has been to try and sound simultaneously Atlanticist, European, and patriotic. The 1987 general election campaign inspired him to attack Labour by borrowing the fantasy of British potency from Thatcher's rhetoric, almost parodying Barnett's description of Churchillism. He warned that 'a great country that decides to behave like a second rate country can expect no favours and deserves none'. NATO and the special relationship would be damaged by Labour's policy:

> Uncle Sam is not about to go on bended knee to Mr Kinnock's Britain. If the British electorate vote him in, the Americans will withdraw, and quickly. They will shake their heads in amazement that we can voluntarily emasculate the British lion, but as good democrats they will accept the verdict and move out of Britain leaving us to look after ourselves as a toothless, shorn and neutered lion.

To remain great is to avoid offending the Americans, an odd paradox. While to wish to be a non-nuclear European country, to cast off the nuclear signifier of a 'great country' is *emasculating*, is to become 'a toothless, shorn and neutered lion'. Here is the mirror image of Burchill's 'castrated by a compliment'; attempts to think of Britain's power realistically are blocked by an imperial phallic nostalgia, whether that leads to Atlanticism or to anti-Americanism, it stems from national delusions of grandeur.

From producerism to consumerism

Tom Nairn's *The Break-Up of Britain* put forward the argument paraphrased above about the absences that mark British history, and he discusses the demands from the 1880s to the 1980s for a 'revolution from above', which would 're-establish the primacy of the productive sector over the City and finance-capital'.[12] This point provides something of a bridge between the themes of American populism as discussed earlier in the book and the topics of this conclusion. We have encountered elsewhere the important American opposition between producerism and finance capital, the populist

juxtaposition of the prairie farmer and the city speculator. My discussion of American crime also looked at the way crime and finance
have been linked by writers like David Mamet and Elmore Leonard.
These populist themes have been given a topical resonance by recent
events on both sides of the Atlantic. The fall of Ivan Boesky, the most
famous of the Wall Street arbitrageurs, and subsequent investigations
leading to arrests on the trading floor of the New York Stock
Exchange, have strengthened a populist criticism of financial ethics,
of unfettered mergers encouraged by the political climate of the
Reagan years, of insider dealing, all leading to demands for tighter
regulation. Significantly, the American investigatory body, the Secu-
rities and Exchange Commission, was founded in another period of
populist distrust of Wall Street, the 1930s. In London, the City threw
up cases of insider dealing and a major scandal stemming from
Guinness' 1985 takeover of Distillers. A poll taken by the Institute
of Directors revealed that 60 per cent of company chairmen thought
that the public image of the City had worsened since 'the Big Bang'
removed restrictions and opened up the City to a new age of international competition.

This deregulation and internationalization gave the City a higher
media visibility than before, so stories of insider dealing and Department of Trade and Industry investigations found an already established context of yuppies, extraordinarily high salaries, old school ties
being replaced by new high-tech, Porsches, cocaine, and serious
money. Interestingly, this has proved another occasion for the Americanization argument, the pressure for deregulation coming partly
from the American security houses. This has led to the City's most
risible defence where its financial ethics are said to have been undermined by national or class outsiders, by the Americans or by the
'barrow boys' now manning the VDUs. It has also produced demands
for effective regulation of the City and both general and specific
criticisms of the financial sector. Labour's Robin Cook, for example,
made the telling comparison of the government's attitude to fraud in
the City with its pursuit of fraud by social security claimants, suggesting that the fraud squads of the DHSS and the DTI might be
swapped. More generally, Labour has tried to build a consensus
between their proposed policies and the interests of the manufacturing
sector, a consensus in which the City is the enemy of industrialists
and socialists alike. Labour has thus questioned the benefits of takeover bids, seeing the City as speculating in the ownership of companies
rather than raising finance for them. Labour has also criticized the
City's 'short-termism' in this, its focus on immediate returns rather
than on a long-term industrial strategy, a focus which leads to a
weakening of British industry as capital leaves the country, companies

cut back on research and development and pursue immediate profits rather than planning.

This criticism of the City is linked to opposition to privatization and Mrs Thatcher's 'casino capitalism' as part of Labour's attempt in 1987 to mobilize a producerist rhetoric against the Conservatives' claims of economic success, the main condemnation being the millions excluded from work. Labour's rhetoric centres on crucial oppositions that parallel those of American populism: making things versus making money from money, in other words producing value rather than speculating on it; the reality of manufacturing decline versus an illusory consumer boom; and, mapped on to these in a way that is both geographical and mythical like the American landscapes of authenticity, the division between south and north. Labour's producerism can sound at times like nostalgia for a 'real' working class working in 'real' industries, and the Conservatives' successful answer to Labour's 1987 challenge was to paint socialism as somehow dated. But proposals for a national minimum wage and for genuine training schemes offer Labour a chance to reconsolidate the unemployed, low-paid, non-unionized, often part-time workers and those working in both the service and the manufacturing industries. The populist appeal to the connotations of work, of labour/Labour as the past ('The Country's Crying Out For Labour'), is revived in an attempt to come to terms with a changed present; the labour/Labour of the future needing to address a world of work no longer dominated by that figure who fuses masculinity, the collective power of the unions, and the power of both industry and those who work in it (the British version of the heroic worker in Soviet art). The nostalgic component has parallels with the themes of American populism but there is a specific national history behind this attempt at a new British producerism.

Tom Nairn's discussion of the division within British capitalism between 'the consistently declining productive sector and the highly successful City sector' has already been cited. The history of this division again provides links between American populism and British developments. The period of the American People's Party sees the United States and Germany take the lead in industry, and this late-nineteenth-century moment in Britain sees the joint rise of the financial sector and the new imperialism. In Nairn's words, 'one part of the capital of England was in effect converted into an "offshore island" of international capitalism, to a considerable degree independent of the nation's declining domestic capitalism'. J. A. Hobson's turn-of-the-century analysis, *Imperialism*, was mentioned in my Introduction as providing the flipside, as it were, to the populist critique of trusts and monopolies in the 1890s. Where the populists saw a worrying concentration of domestic power, Hobson saw a concentration, a blocking, of capital leading to the search for new markets and America's new role in the 1890s as an imperialist power. Nairn draws on Hobson's analysis to argue the connection between Britain's financial sector and empire, and also to comment on Hobson's picture of a parasitical southern Britain and a productive north. He looks at another piece by Hobson, his analysis of the 1910 general election, finding parallels between that election and Thatcher's 1979 victory. Hobson provides a more accurate description of division than Disraeli's 'Two Nations'. In 1910, he wrote that 'Two Englands' had emerged, 'a Producer's England and a Consumer's England', northern industry and southern cultural and financial hegemony.[13] As Nairn suggests, that division is recognizable today, but it is not only between the north and south, it is also mapped in various ways on to the relations between Britain and the United States. Anxiety about America is married to anxiety about consumerism, as we have seen in the previous chapter and with Paul Weller, for example. With those general worries in mind we can now turn to a specific product, one identified with both 'Americanness' and youth culture.

Heritage and the button fly

Jeans are simultaneously one of the basic units of international dress and a powerful symbol of America. They combine a symbolic appeal with being functional. And, like Coca Cola, jeans go beyond the discourse of Americanization by their self-evident international success combined with their connotations of an 'imaginary America', the romance of the cowboy for example. Just as Coca Cola fought the 'Coke wars' with Pepsi around notions of the original, the classic, 'the real thing', so the jeans manufacturers have to re-introduce notions of difference into their mass market, pushing different styles, targeting different sections of the market, preventing consumers from taking their product for granted. And their advertising campaigns condense many themes of this conclusion: tradition and mass production, consumption and work, the heritage of authenticity, masculinity.

Tim Lindsay of Bartle Bogle Hegarty talked of the problems this advertising agency had with their campaign for Levi 501s:

Quite apart from Libya, the US is always a pretty dangerous place. As over half of all jeans are sold to the 16–24 market, what we had to do was sell heritage without selling Ronald Reagan. The answer was to pick an almost mythical time and place that everyone in the market is familiar with, yet is sufficiently long enough ago for them not to know anything about.[14]

To 'sell heritage without selling Ronald Reagan' and to disentangle 501s from F-111s (Lindsay's reference to the US raid on Libya), the past is mobilized, an imaginary America is created. The 1986 ads featured Sam Cooke and Marvin Gaye songs, and Nick Kamen wearing his jeans in the bath and removing them in a launderette; the 1987 ones had Rachel Roberts as a GI's girlfriend trying on the jeans that were his parting present, to the sound of Percy Sledge singing 'When A Man Loves A Woman', and Eddie Kidd braving nightclub bouncers in his black 501s to the tune of Ben E. King's 'Stand By Me'. The adverts were extraordinarily successful: sales of the jeans increased by 800 per cent, Nick Kamen was launched on a singing career on the strength of his new fame, Carling Black Label advertised lager with a parody of the launderette ad. John Hart, the marketing director of Levi Strauss, declared at a conference devoted to 'consumer lifestyles', that the campaigns showed that 'heritage, authenticity, and integrity were back in fashion'. In the elided contradiction between heritage/authenticity/integrity, and fashion, different strands of populism are woven together.

If the match of images and music in the adverts had learned from the pop video, they also had a direct effect on the pop market with Ben E. King and Percy Sledge's songs going to numbers one and two in the singles chart in March 1987. What the adverts managed was a periodization of the timeless, a paradox glimpsed in the slight disjuncture between 1950s images and 1960s music, that familiar but not too precisely located past that Tim Lindsay spoke of. Two Golden Ages are grafted on to each other, the classic age of soul music and the 1950s birth of teenage culture, basically, in this myth, rock and roll and James Dean. The pop scene was already bowing to soul music through reissues and cover versions, and this heritage was then soundtracked on to images that might previously have suggested rock and roll. These moments of authenticity give Levi 501s the glamour of a double heritage. And a taken-for-granted commodity became once more a matter of names and styles, of manufacturers' competition and consumers' choice. Discussing Dick Hebdige earlier, Walter Benjamin's 'The work of art in the age of mechanical reproduction' was cited, Hebdige extending Benjamin's argument about the effect of mass reproduction on the unique aura of the work of art to the threat to tradition and traditional intellectuals posed by American design and popular culture. Benjamin saw that the culture industry reproduced the capitalist contradiction between the forces and relations of production found elsewhere. He argued that the film studios' response to 'the shriveling of the aura' was 'an artificial build-up of the "personality" outside the studio': 'The cult of the movie star, fostered by the money of the film industry, preserves not the unique aura of the person but the "spell of the personality", the phony spell of a commodity.'[15] This helps explain the 501s' construction of heritage as fashion, the authentic as current style. Fashion mediates between the aura and mass reproduction, the idea of designer clothes being a way of re-introducing the signature into the market-place, recovering the auratic name in an arena of mass production and consumption. Without the designer's name, Levi 501s overcome the distinction between tradition and mass production, by selling heritage as well as trousers. The current Wranglers' campaign, on the other hand, deliberately divorces production from style, suggesting that the latter is not bought by the consumer but created by him or her – 'The fit is Wrangler. The style is all your own.'

Marx referred to the commodity as 'congealed labour', and Marxist analyses see the commodity, be it a film or a toaster, as repressing the context of its production. 'Congealed labour' describes the visual representation of some jeans adverts as well as their commodity status. Consumption is invited and production elided by a display of work. Before the 501s campaign, the same advertising agency made the 1983 Levi's 'rivets' and 'stitching' adverts, which both referred to and displaced the actual production of the jeans, the work of their manufacture being invisible while its quality was metonymically demonstrated through a Hemingwayesque film of ocean fishing. These adverts show the first signs of a strategy that would lead Levi's to return to the 501s, a stress on heritage, history, and company image. Levi's jeans were patented as riveted trousers in 1873, as tough trousers for outdoor workers, cowboys, miners, farmhands. The company claims that the stitching on the back pockets is the oldest clothing trademark in the world. Also established in 1873 were the rivets and the button fly. The 'Two horse' patch was added in 1886 signifying the company's guarantee to replace any jeans that tore, and the now famous 'red tab' trademark was added as a new trademark in 1936.[16] The functionalism of the rivets and the stitching are now more a matter of company image and tradition than an appeal to people to buy Levi's as working clothes. The Lee Rough Riders campaign of 1986 consisted precisely of images of 'congealed labour', work frozen as history and tradition: the male models stand shirtless in a field holding a scythe, or clutch a hawser while watching a crane, or stand in front of an oil well, in jeans and vest, holding a large wrench. Underneath there is the slogan – 'The Jeans That Built America' – while in the corner one sees the Lee Rough Riders patch ('Founded Kansas 1889') and this information: 'Authentic Styling.

Heavyweight $15\frac{3}{4}$ oz. denim. Original leather patch. Stonewashed finish. Copper rivets. Brass buttons. Heavy duty fly. That's how we build the jeans that built America.' The production of the jeans and the images of labour are linked around words such as 'authentic' and 'original', and associations of strength and solidity: 'heavyweight' denim, copper rivets, brass buttons, 'heavy duty fly'. The adverts claim that we 'build' the jeans, not from the actual factory work of production, but out of those blocks of authenticity and originality, just as the jeans *built* America. The tense is significant as work is seen as history, as the past. The images indeed refer to industries that have been in trouble in the 1980s – oil and farming, for example – not to locate them in any present crisis but to associate them with a golden age of heroic labour. Another issue raised by these images, and by the shift from producerism and populism to consumerism and populism, is masculinity. The images suggest the link between masculinity and work but transform that into spectacle, a topic which will be discussed later.

Other ideas of heritage need to be considered which relate to previous discussions of American populism. The names and histories of the jeans manufacturers summon up that archetypal American male, the cowboy (Wranglers, Rough Riders, etc.), and adverts often build on this cowboy image, stressing the jeans' toughness. I discussed the role that the cowboy plays in Sam Shepard's work in an earlier chapter. In *Fool for Love* his stage directions emphasize that Eddie's clothes should not be an image of 'the real thing' but actually marked by labour: broken-down cowboy boots, dirty jeans that smell of horse sweat, a pair of spurs hanging from his belt, old and used ones, '*not cartoon "cowboy" spurs*'.[17] Horse sweat is of course banished from the airbrushed world of advertising images although it is ironic that, as we saw in Chapter 2, Shepard's emphasis on authenticity and work has been turned back on him by critics who see his role in *Country* as part of a fad for muscular rusticity. Another work considered in that earlier discussion of agrarian representations was James Agee and Walker Evans' *Let Us Now Praise Famous Men*. From Evans' photographs you notice that the tenant farmers wear denim overalls, what Agee calls 'the standard or classical garment at very least ... of the southern rural American working man: they are his uniform, the badge and proclamation of his peasantry'. He turns a painterly eye on these clothes. These overalls need no 'stonewashed finish' as they are worked in and thus worked on by age, use, weather, and the body: 'The structures sag, and take on the look, some of use; some, the pencil pockets, the pretty atrophies of what is never used.' Agee's observations risk pretension but, through their exactness and Agee's search for precise analogies, they find beauty. Thigh pockets are stretched and opened, 'fluted, like the gills of a fish'. The clothes are bought large and shrink until they fit:

> The whole shape, texture, color, finally substance, all are changed. The shape, particularly along the urgent frontage of the thighs, so that the whole structure of the knee and musculature of the thigh is sculptured there; each man's garment wearing the shape and beauty of the induplicable body.

Texture and colour are transformed 'by sweat, sun, laundering, between the steady pressures of its use and age', taken into 'realms of fine softness and marvel of draping and velvet plays of light which chamois and silk can only suggest not touch', suggesting the 'textures of old paper money', and capturing 'a region and scale of blues, subtle, delicious, and deft', seen elsewhere only in 'rare skies, the smoky light some days are filmed with, and some of the blues of Cézanne'. The overalls fascinate Agee, partly because of their achieved individuality, each with 'some world of exquisiteness of its own'. Here there is a different relation of the mass produced and the individual, not the consumer's choice or sense of style, but the individual's labour and his 'induplicable body'.[18]

Agee describes overalls and shirts, the meagre wardrobe of a tenant farmer, noticing the gradations caused by difference in age. The most recent are still dark, still have visible seams, bright buttons, and firm cloth: 'They have taken the shape of the leg, yet they are still the doing as much of machinery as of nature.'

> The middle-aged are fully soft and elegantly textured, and are lost out of all machinery into a full prime of nature. The mold of the body is fully taken, the seams are those of a living plant or animal, the cloth's grain is almost invisible, the buttons are rubbed and mild, the blue is at the full silent, greatly restrained strength of its range ... the garments are still wholly competent and at the fullness of comfort.

With the old, 'the cloth sleeps against all salients of the body in complete peace', and the way they hang below the knee breaks totally from the original form 'into foldings I believe no sculptor has ever touched'. The blue is now so faint it verges on silver, 'and is a color and cloth seeming ancient, veteran, composed, and patient to the sense of being, as too the sleepings and the drifts of form'.[19] Work here is a process not a static image, as the clothes bear witness to time, physical labour, and the weather. The overalls become part of the organic discipline of tenant farming, a part of nature rather than machinery. The comparisons to works of art are valid not just as description (Cézanne blues, sculptural folds) which would suggest an overly distant and aestheticized view of labour, but as another image of the body's work, individual labour rather than the overalls' original context of mass production, and the personalizing of the clothes through work. Interestingly, it has been possible since the 1970s to purchase this patina of age with jeans being sold as pre-faded or stonewashed. The artistic comparisons also suggest that the overalls are a truer record of agricultural labour than actual images such as Millet's peasants, the heroic workers of Socialist Realism, or the Rough Riders' model with his scythe.

The adverts may want to tell us that the jeans are tough, heavy duty, and so on, although this depends on make and model, but they speak of work as a guarantee of authenticity rather than as a process of labour. They wish to sell us heritage, but they also want to suggest pleasure not toil. We move from American populism's producerism to British consumption of American goods and images, and the different populism formed by this reception. Hence the choice for 501s of 1950s images and 1960s music, and the appearance of that figure who cropped up several times in Chapter 7, the GI, for partly what is staged in these adverts is not just first love but also the historical first encounters with American postwar popular culture. Here again we are invited to consume not just an American product but 'America' itself – with a relevance to that opposition between socialism and pleasure found in Chapter 7's discussion of the *Sun*. Opening her election campaign in May 1987, Mrs Thatcher described socialism as outdated, as having the air of the 1940s about it, a vision of shortages, rationing, and restrictions, and this seems connected to the well-worn scare tactic of claiming that a Labour government would make Britain resemble Eastern Europe. These two references are also linked by our subject, jeans and American popular culture.

Trevor Blackwell and Jeremy Seabrook describe Labour's crippled attempts at planning after their 1945 landslide victory. A war-torn economy was made even weaker by the Americans' 'unexpected insistence on the immediate repayment of loans', leading to austerities that were in some cases worse than the scarcity of the war years. As they point out, if the austerity was exacerbated by the United States, the prosperity of the 1950s was based on 'a developmental model inspired by that of the United States' and partly identified with American popular culture. But the rationing and regulations of the late 1940s provided a different identification based on memories of coupons for bread and other shortages of basic goods.

Milk was rationed until 1950, as were flour, eggs and soap. It is perhaps these images that are recalled by pictures of long queues in Prague and Warsaw in later decades and which are drawn on by those who would assimilate the post-war experience of labourism to the failures of the socialist regimes of Eastern Europe. In 1947, at the time of the dollar crisis, even the consolations of Hollywood were withdrawn.

Labour thus became identified with 'red tape, controls, scarcities and high moral purpose'; while the Conservatives promoted themselves 'in the historically unlikely role of the party of freedom, fun and the fat of the land'.[20] One can see how films constructed fun as an oasis threatened by the busybody, snooping state of the war and postwar years (in Ealing comedies such as *Whisky Galore* or *Passport to Pimlico*, for example), an alternative site for the community to rally around. Themes from this period echo in the Britain of the 1980s: the black market spiv offering luxuries unavailable from the rationed economy becomes the wide boy of Thatcherism's 'black economy' in many successful television comedies (*Minder, Only Fools and Horses*, for example), which comically link illegality to Conservative anti-statism rhetoric. Much of the humour of *Minder*'s Arthur Daley, for example, is his pose as struggling Thatcherite entrepreneur held back by the red tape of an interfering state.

Alan Bennett's *A Private Function* provided a 1980s view of the 1940s, with a community hypersensitive to class differences finally uniting around an illegal pig, 'sinking their differences to do down the Government Man, the snooper whose job it is to ensure that unlicensed pigs were found and licensed so that they could not be slaughtered and eaten privately, that is, in addition to the ration'. Dick Heckstall-Smith, writing in the *Guardian* in 1985, said that the fact that the film could be watched as a comedy was actually, historically, tragic. He compared the radical proposals of Labour's 1945 government with the Thatcherite present: the miners' strike, mass unemployment, the privatization of national assets. Classically, he blames Americanization; the reaction to Labour's proposals was 'massively and vociferously supported by the constant sweet stream of seductive Coca-Cola/McDonalds/Hollywood/Kill-A-Commie-For-Mommy propaganda'.[21] *A Private Function* splits private pleasures from public functionaries and government snoopers. If the 501s adverts display American culture as seen by the newly affluent 1950s, other images bring out this opposition between (American) pleasure and (socialist) bureaucracy. One jeans advert, for example, played on the notion of the Soviet and Eastern European hunger for jeans and western popular culture, which has become a cliché of reports from the Eastern bloc. The advert's hero returns to Russia under the suspicious and forbidding eyes of bureaucrats and secret policemen; back at his austere flat he rummages in his cheap suitcase and produces a book on James Dean and a pair of jeans. The British encounter with American popular culture in the 1950s finds a parallel with the representation of contemporary Soviet youth. This is not just western self-regard or propaganda, but also a distorted reflection of real struggles in Eastern Europe, as seen in the clampdown on the Czech 'Jazz Section'. In this context, American culture represents not capitalist seduction but an expression of the desire for some form of social and cultural autonomy.

Instead of asking 'how do these images represent pleasure?', one must also ask 'what pleasure do they represent in themselves?' I argued above that work becomes an image, a spectacle, in these adverts, and that has interesting implications for the representation of masculinity. For, if American populism gives masculinity a basis in work, these adverts display both work and masculinity as a spectacle, as visual pleasure. There are still simple identifications of denim and maleness (perhaps the crudest being the adverts for Denim Aftershave), but in other images masculinity has moved from being active, virile, and unquestioned, to being the object of vision. The eroticization of the male body in recent films and advertising, and the consequent reworking of the assumed perspective of visual pleasure (male viewer/female object), is linked to the fashion industry's response to the sexual politics of the 1970s and 1980s. Earlier gay styles parodied/reproduced certain mythicized forms of 'macho' masculinity, the cowboy or the biker, for example (the disco group Village People provided a comprehensive and witty collection of such images in the 1970s). Now advertisers seem to be promoting for heterosexual men features associated with gay men, in the 1980s emphasis on style and on working on (and working out) the body. Thus the 'New Man', supposedly a sign of men responding to feminism's critique of masculinity, has been appropriated by advertising as a new type of consumer, defined not by taking more of a role in parental and domestic labour but by buying boxer shorts.

The jeans adverts mix conventional images of masculinity with the homoerotic, and privilege certain parts of the male body. Judith Williamson, questioning the gender neutrality of unisex styles, argued in 1984 that masculinity was being represented as an ideal for women. The 'womanly' is marginalized and ridiculed (male comedians in drag, for instance), while 'the most fashionable, most valued shape for both sexes is "boyish"'. She discusses jeans advertising, which concentrates 'heavily on bottoms; with pictures of male and female bodies alike poured into skin-tight jeans that mould sexually indistinguishable small, tight bums'. Even when jeans are advertised as fitted for girls, 'they are specially fitted for girls to *have* that skin-tight, boyish-bum *look*'.[22] What interests me is the possible contradiction between these signifiers of fashion and the 'Americanness' that frames them in the adverts. A Wranglers' advert in 1986 started with a political speech, the young candidate standing in front of an enormous stars and stripes. As he reached the end of his list of beliefs, checking all the lowest common denominators of American political discourse (democracy, the American way, freedom of choice), the perspective moved from the point of view of his audience to a point behind him where it lingered on his jeans as he declared his final belief ... in Wrangler jeans. Some people seemed to see the advert as unironic, as if the speech gave away the truth that the bottom line of the American dream was not lofty ideals but selling commodities. In fact, I would argue that it was as far from jingoism as, say, Jimi Hendrix playing 'The Star Spangled Banner', being self-consciously aware of its almost caricatured Americanism, and undermining its speech through its final focus on the body. Similarly, British responses to Bruce Springsteen often seem to lack any sense that his relation to America contains irony and ambivalence. The cover of *Born in the USA*, 'emblazoned with a picture of his ass and the stripes of the American flag', is another combination of denim, the flag, and the uncertain significance of the body. The cover invites connections while also resisting them; like the jeans adverts it plays with 'Americanness' rather than simply endorsing it. Springsteen once told a journalist that 'when you're up against big business and politics, you gotta have some muscle'.[23] But alongside this politics of physique, a populist version of beefing up 'the little guy', there are a group of films which seem to promote a muscular jingoism. These have been connected to both the idea of masculinity as spectacle and to American military actions and rhetoric. They bridge the worlds of the jeans adverts and 'Operation El Dorado', the US raids on Libya.

President Rambo's poodle

Arnold Schwarzenegger, former Mr Universe, star of *Pumping Iron*, *Conan the Barbarian*, *The Terminator* and, most relevant to this discussion, *Commando*, said of the new muscular cinema:

> With *Rocky*, I think Stallone did a big service to my career because he opened up a whole new type of movie, where the body is accepted and people go to see the body. It's a youth audience at the cinema today and they want physical actors like me and Stallone.

Critics have suggested that what the audience sees as well as the body is a revisionist history and a belligerent right-wing politics. This does not apply so much to *Commando*, which has a certain camp knowingness about the fetishism of weaponry and the centrality of the male body, but is relevant to Chuck Norris's *Missing In Action* and *The Delta Force*, and, most famously, to Sylvester Stallone's *Rambo*. Along with the different glamorization of fighter pilots in *Top Gun*, starring Tom Cruise, these films offer fantasy violence as a solution to political and historical complexity. The vigilante of the 1970s (Charles Bronson in *Death Wish*, Clint Eastwood's rogue cop, *Dirty Harry*) moves on to an international stage. Instead of the mugger-infested city, there is the communist- and terrorist-infested world, the two genres bridged by racist representations of the enemies within and without, and by the necessity for the hero to take the law into his own hands. America as the world's gendarme is represented as a maverick cop, cleaning up the Middle East in *The Delta Force*, refighting the Vietnam war in *Missing in Action* and *Rambo*. The standard criticism of these successful films traces their revision of history and their foregrounded machismo back to two sources of anxiety: after Vietnam and the Iran hostages crisis America is seen to have become self-conscious about its 'powerlessness'; meanwhile conventional notions of gender had been challenged by the women's movement and by gay politics. These anxieties are then seen as being 'resolved' by Reagan's invasion of Grenada, and by US interventions in Central America and the Middle East, and by the macho retribution dramas of Stallone and Norris. Thus this physical cinema is not just seen as aggressively reactionary and nationalistic but also as constructing this politics around masculinity, centring on phallocentric firepower: 'On posters, the new hero is usually pictured clutching huge, protruding weaponry.'[24]

However, the fact of the centrality of the body, the foregrounding of masculinity, is not a simple assertion of male power. The display of masculinity undermines its unquestioned status, for while these muscular men of action may be the opposite of the more overtly eroticized images used to sell jeans, like them they are there to be looked at, to be viewed as a spectacle in a very different way to earlier heroes such as John Wayne. Barbara Creed, in an article on feminism and postmodernism, takes a refreshingly open view of 'the increasing tendency in contemporary texts to play with the notion of manhood'.

> Figures such as Sylvester Stallone and Arnold Schwarzenegger (once described by an Australian critic as 'a condom stuffed with walnuts') could only be described as 'performing the masculine'. Both actors often resemble an anthropomorphised phallus, a phallus with muscles, if you like. (Parodies of a lost ideal or menacing images of an android future?) They are simulacra of an exaggerated masculinity, the original completely lost to sight, a casualty of the failure of the paternal signifier and the current crisis in master narratives.[25]

This awareness of what one could call the masquerade of masculinity in these films is rare. Salman Rushdie provides a more typical example of the critical response, his comment appearing in a review of the collection of essays edited by Mary Kaldor and Paul Anderson, *Mad Dogs: The US Raids on Libya.*

> The figure of Mr Sylvester Stallone, he of the oiled pectorals and fear of bombs at Cannes (should we call him Nambo-Rambo?), looms over these events like an incarnation of what Mary Kaldor calls 'the American madness'.

It is true that *Rambo* proved an almost inescapable reference in commentary on the US raids, but it is a reference that needs to be interrogated rather than repeated. Rushdie continues to comment on 'the American madness': 'This madness is, it seems to me, rooted partly in the sexuality of the American male (Mr Stallone, in the Rambo posters, carries a metal phallus that makes Dirty Harry's old Magnum look positively weeny).'[26] What does it mean to say that the US raids took place in Stallone's shadow or to place them as part of an 'American madness' or to see them stemming from the sexuality of *the* American male? Is this category intended to include all American men, or the men who flew the mission, or the men who planned and authorized it, or the fifteen- to twenty-five-year olds cheering on Stallone on the cinema screen? Somehow reference to *Rambo* has become obligatory and almost unconscious in its assumed self-evidence.

While those who actually watched *Rambo* probably saw it in the context of genre ('action' films, war movies, etc.) or Stallone's other films (the *Rocky* series, *First Blood*), the muscle-bound hero had a further career in the phrases of journalists and politicians. Rambo became applicable to everything, functioning as an adjective or as a vague description – 'to do a Rambo' – as a pun (the *Sun's* cricketing joke 'Rambotham'), as a parallel (Springsteen as 'the Rambo of Rock'), cropping up everywhere from tabloid journalism, to jokes, to reggae songs. These uses helped to create and confirm *Rambo* as a phenomenon while reacting to the success of the film. Newspapers began using 'Rambo' as a political reference in both writing and cartoons, though no longer specifically connected to Vietnam. Stallone's character became a kind of metaphor either for tough action or for foolhardy interventions, a usage that rubbed off on political discourse. However, alongside these vague references there was, and is, a specific usage where left-liberal distaste for the values assumed to be embodied in *Rambo* is grafted on to opposition to United States foreign policy in Central America and the Middle East. Either *Rambo* is added to a speech or editorial as shorthand for unthinking belligerence or, as we have seen above, the film is seen as having a closer link to American military interventions, offering a parallel solution to American post-Vietnam anxieties. These uses run through the *Mad Dogs* collection, *Rambo* cropping up as a kind of rhetorical punctuation.

On Tuesday 15 April 1986, among talk of minimum 'collateral damage' but with reports of civilian casualties contradicting this claim, the world learned that the United States had bombed the Libyan cities of Tripoli and Benghazi, their F-111 bombers having flown from British bases. Amid the international condemnations and demonstrations, the *Mad Dogs* volume was an impressively detailed addition to opposition to these raids. Stemming from the *END* (European Nuclear Disarmament) *Journal* collective, the book was written in a week, the contributors performing the very valuable service of providing a series of contexts and histories to inform discussion of the United States' action (the history of US bases in Britain, the British political context, European responses, the apparent absence of American dissenting voices, transformations in Cold War politics, the role of NATO, Libyan history, the west's attitude to the Middle East, the role of 'terrorism' in international politics and political discourse). 'Rambo' gets a mention across these contexts, but these references also function *against* these contexts, blocking analysis, confusing different realms, and denying the admirable stress on specificity shown elsewhere in the articles.

Each reference comes with a cluster of associations and assumptions. Peter Pringle discusses the way that the raids became a spectacle for American television viewers. Two o'clock Libyan time coincided with NBC and CBS news at seven on the American east coast; whether this was coincidence or deliberate stage management Pringle sees it as enabling viewers to react to the bombing as instant entertainment, 'indeed, the stuff of Rambo'. Here the Libyan bombing is seen as a precise parallel to Stallone's movies, another fantasy restoration of American pride and patriotism but with real casualties. A significant feature of this parallel is that it recognizes the role of *mediation* – Rambo is compared with Operation El Dorado Canyon via the television screen. Robin Luckham's contribution concludes with an optimistic vision of the opportunities offered by the European response to the raids, hoping for the de-alignment of Europe from NATO and the dissolving of the Cold War blocs, as well as for the building of relations with the Third World 'that are not based upon the politics of Rambo and Operation El Dorado Canyon'. 'Rambo' is no longer a film or a fictitious character but a handy sign for military unilateralism. Later in the volume, Richard Falk describes Reagan 'as an aspiring Rambo of anti-terrorist militancy', suggesting not only simplistic and aggressive policies but also an element of playing to public opinion. Falk also suggests the role that popular culture has in shaping this public opinion:

> the moral climate for race war on a permanent basis is being subtly established behind the facade of proceeding against a single crazed leader is [sic] reinforced by a series of images currently active in the US popular culture, especially films like *Invasion USA*, *Red Dawn* and the *Rambo* series. In each, a complacent America is ill-prepared for the coming of the barbarians – Third World terrorists somehow managed from Moscow by psychopathic intermediaries.[27]

The assumptions here seem more problematic than earlier 'Rambo' references.

An obvious problem with the above argument is that Falk's description is simply mistaken, particularly in the inclusion of 'the *Rambo* series', by which I assume he means *First Blood* and *Rambo*. Neither film is about the invasion of 'a complacent America' by Third World terrorists. The Rambo character was introduced in *First Blood* as the returning Vietnam veteran harassed by small-town law officers, because he is misrecognized as part of the counter-culture rather than as the 'homecoming hero', and so the war's violence boomerangs back to the heartland. This violence is then sent back where it belongs, as it were, in *Rambo* as Stallone returns to Vietnam. Like other films in this genre of muscular revisionism, Chuck Norris's *Missing In Action* for example, Stallone's Vietnam concentrates on those figures who keep the question of the war open and current: the veteran, the POWs supposedly still in Vietnam, those missing in action, the bodies that never returned. The films work to resolve these for the right, especially for the argument that the war could have been won if the military had not been held back by the politicians at home. This is a widespread right-wing version of Vietnam, held especially by the military; a recent example being Oliver North's angry retort to his Congressional questioners in July 1987: 'We didn't lose the war in Vietnam, we lost the war right here' – in Washington. And journalists, of course, have often compared Oliver North to Rambo. The films then rewrite history, repeating it as entertainment, and possibly offering a bridge between a right-wing explanation of America's defeat in Vietnam and public opinion. Even this is more complex and mediated than Falk's account of images preparing a 'moral climate', for its effect is qualified partly by the age of the films' audiences. We can remember Schwarzenegger's comments, opening this section, about the young audience for this physical cinema. If *Rambo* achieved a resonance beyond these viewers it was largely because it became a discursive phenomenon, not seen as a film but cited as a parallel, joked about as a media landmark, referred to in newspapers and cartoons, and so on.

The most extreme left-liberal responses to Stallone's success seem to suggest that *Rambo* has actually influenced Reagan's policies, a suggestion partly stemming from Reagan once quipping that he had learned from the movie. It is clear that other voices (the military, the State Department, academics, right-wing think tanks) and their versions of America's post-Vietnam 'weakness' have more effect on policy formation. So why is Sylvester Stallone mentioned more often than, say, Norman Podhoretz, the influential neo-conservative editor of *Commentary* and author of *Why We Were in Vietnam*? It is not that the films are innocent of ideology; it is a question of audience and sphere of influence. Chuck Norris turning his firepower on 'Arab' terrorists in *The Delta Force* reaches a large, and generally young, audience but it does not have the agenda setting and policy forming power of the extensive apparatus discussed by Edward Said in his *Covering Islam*. There, Said uncovered the interlocking discourses of journalists, television commentators, academics, area specialists, and others, arguing that these produce a monolithic vision of 'Islam' as militant, fundamentalist, and both threatening and dehumanized in its otherness.[28] Hollywood's cartoon violence and casual racism is not as directly influential as this linking of knowledge and power, of discourse and Rapid Deployment Forces. I would argue that protest focuses on the films for a variety of reasons: liberal distaste for the popularity of the cinematic equivalent of a 'Nuke Iran' badge; ideas of the vulnerability of a young audience to the glamorization of violence; the creation of a common ground between conservative critiques of 'mass culture' and radical critiques of right-wing ideology; and, finally, because it is easier to deplore Hollywood's products rather than criticize established academics, respected newspapers, television news programmes, the State Department, and the Pentagon.

As socialists, consciously or unconsciously, appropriate liberal or conservative horror at American popular culture, political analysis suffers, and an 'imaginary America' is produced that mirrors the orientalist production of 'Islam'. Just as American academics, journalists, and other 'experts' reduce the complex reality of the Middle East to the simplified image of the fundamentalist and fanatic 'other', so United States foreign and military policies are reduced to the image of Rambo or the cowboy president. It is a parallel creation of 'otherness', concentrating on popular culture rather than religion, but with a stress on madness to underline the parallel. The Socialist Workers' Party produced posters with pictures of Reagan and Gaddafi, asking who the real madman was. Reagan's characterization of Gaddafi as 'flaky' and unbalanced is reversed, and we have already seen Salman Rushdie link the Libyan raids to Rambo, the sexuality of American

men, and 'the American madness'. The last term stems from Mary
Kaldor's contribution to *Mad Dogs*, a piece that begins with a very
useful analysis of the way that 'terrorism has come to replace communism as a way of legitimizing US military action'. The airstrike
was not, as the official American explanation had it, an act of retaliation
for a specific terrorist act, nor was it some sort of psychological
catharsis banishing feelings of 'impotence'. 'It was about the global
role of the US. It was about the exercise of military power, and the
reassertion of a dominant American position, especially *vis-à-vis* its
European allies and the Third World.' The raid was 'the culmination
of a series of developments in US foreign policy and military strategy
which are intended to increase the visibility and utility of the American arsenal'. These include the introduction of cruise missiles; new
'offensive nuclear and conventional war-fighting strategies'; the Star
Wars project; the new Deep Strike strategy. Kaldor adds:

> These strategic developments are not just the mad Rambo acts of Reagan
> and his friends; they are a logical consequence of the cosmology of the
> Cold War and deterrence within which the Reaganites were born and
> bred.[29]

Leaving aside the peculiar point which seems to reduce politics to
which cosmology one is born into, the quotation shows an interesting
ambivalence. Note the use of 'just' – not 'just the mad Rambo acts' –
signifying the reluctance to give up the Rambo reference, and to
put aside madness in order to discuss a logic. Rushdie, of course,
reintroduces Rambo in his commentary on Kaldor. That is surely a
sign of analytical and political *failure*; it is more politically urgent to
see the Libyan raids as belonging to a history and a logic of military
strategies and political decisions. These must be analysed in order to
be opposed, but Rushdie's use of Rambo is prepared for by Kaldor's
own turnaround, as she discards analysis for a rhetoric of madness
and unreality.

Kaldor comments on the way that those who inhabit the military
machine, from pilots to the scientists who develop the weaponry,
insulate themselves from the consequences of the weapons by a
narrow focus on the technology. As a sign of the 'unreal' nature of
this world Kaldor points out the raid's name – Operation El Dorado
Canyon. I suspect that this point rests on an unspoken Hollywood
reference; the codename underlines the unreality of the thinking
behind the event because it suggests Westerns, John Wayne, and John
Ford. But what Kaldor is commenting on is the often observed fact
of the euphemistic descriptions in modern warfare. No government
calls its military actions Operation Arbitrary Bombing of Unarmed
Civilians, but somehow it is felt El Dorado Canyon is further removed

from the effects of warfare than a codename drawn from, say, Greek mythology. By the end of the piece, we have moved from unreality to fully fledged madness, in other words we have moved beyond the domain of analysis. Describing the way that terrorism now justifies military action and how US public opinion appears to be blind to the reality of this action's effects, Kaldor says, 'It would, of course, be wrong to treat this as a thought-out strategy.' There is something surprising about the way that her earlier discussion of this as precisely 'a thought-out strategy' now appears to be wrong. 'There is a kind of unreality about Reagan and his colleagues'; they are 'prisoners of their cosmology, creations of the manipulators of public opinion, no longer able to distinguish fantasy from reality'. Hence the adoption of Star Wars: ' "The force is with us," says President Reagan. And that may be part of the prerequisite of power in modern America. To be president you may have to be mad or be an actor. Carter's sanity did not last long.'[30] Her conclusion is that Europe must reject this 'American madness' and seek more independent policies towards Eastern Europe and the Third World. It is not that I disagree with this objective but that to arrive there Kaldor has returned to seeing the raids as 'just mad Rambo acts', sacrificing analysis to rhetoric. The raids no longer belong to a history of America's emergence as a superpower, nor to a logic of military strategies and political objectives. Instead they are the act of an administration suffering from fantasy or madness. As Reagan characterizes Gaddafi as irrational, so Kaldor sees Reagan, with both rhetorical moves being concerned to produce an image of absolute otherness: the non-European, crazed cowboy or Rambo figure; the un-American 'flaky' Arab terrorist. Both cases work against understanding, blocking an analysis that could explain the Middle East's grievances against the United States and undermining a historical comprehension of American power and its exercise.

Kaldor has been singled out for the startlingly clear way in which her article suddenly discards its useful historical argument. Other pieces in *Mad Dogs* provide a context for her rhetoric of otherness, giving a sense of the Europeanness or Englishness that is the basis for this characterization. Jamie Dettmer's contribution, 'Europe or America: The British Political Context', sees the Libyan raid as another sign of Mrs Thatcher's surprising misjudgement of 'the nationalist sentiments of the British electorate'. The Prime Minister who had frequently identified herself with national pride, seemed to make a series of mistakes leading up to her April 1986 agreement to Reagan's use of F-111s stationed at British bases for the attack on Tripoli:

over the winter, the Westland affair and the rows over the proposed sale of parts of British Leyland to Ford and parts of Austin Rover to General Motors gave the opposition parties the chance to tug the Union Jack away from Mrs Thatcher.

These events raised opposition to American dominance and preference for European co-operation on defence and industrial strategies, with pro-European Conservatives joining opposition MPs in criticizing the government. The Libyan raids caused increased questioning of the special relationship and of Britain's consent to the operation. Opinion polls after the raid revealed that two-thirds of the electorate opposed the bombing and disapproved of Britain's role in the action. But Thatcher's weakness was shortlived and this seems to stem from the opposition's tactic; tugging the Union Jack away from the Conservatives leads to short-term gains but also to a difficulty of building on those gains. Dettmer discusses the parliamentary debate of 17 April in which Neil Kinnock characterized Mrs Thatcher as 'a compliant accomplice rather than a candid ally of the United States President'. Dettmer argues that the debate did not address the real topic of the relation of Britain to Europe and America, nor did it seriously analyse the Anglo-American alliance. It confined itself to terrorism: Labour MPs and others attacked the action as more likely to increase terrorism than defeat it, also suggesting that the raid itself with its civilian casualties was terrorist in nature, and arguing that military action could not stand in for a political solution to the Middle East's problems.[31]

What also appear in the debate are the twinned themes of British impotence and the crudity of American power. Sir Ian Gilmour, for example, warned Reagan that he could not be ' "a sheriff in the Middle East and a rustler in Central America". Other attacks represented Reagan as an unabashed, ignorant cowboy.' This returns us to the role of American popular culture in this debate, a point Dettmer touches on. The *Economist*'s unease is mentioned. Their pro-American line looked for support not from opinion polls but from everyday British life. The *Economist* 'cited increased travel to the United States and adoption of American fashion' to stress British links, but Dettmer disagrees; 'wearing jeans, listening to Tina Turner and watching *Dallas* do not amount to a durable basis for an alliance'. Both the Libyan raid and the Westland affair highlighted a double relation to American culture: 'The trappings of popular American culture in Britain mask a growing disparity in political interests between the two countries.'[32] However, the logic of this should be taken further, for if pleasure in American popular culture does not imply support for American foreign policy, then opposition to those policies should rethink its use of images from popular culture (Westerns, Rambo, etc.) within its critique. Watching the televised debate from the House of Lords concerning the Libyan airstrike, it was interesting that many speakers expressed their moral and political distance from the bombing by recourse to the ubiquitous Rambo reference, demonstrating their ignorance of popular culture as well as their disapproval of the action. It seems likely that part of Reagan's appeal to American youth has been precisely his ease with references to popular culture, his Hollywood background demonstrating not his artificiality but his proximity to lives which are mapped through popular media landmarks. This is not to suggest that Labour politicians should start to enthuse about Stallone's films, but that rhetoric built on references to films that the speakers have obviously never seen, and clearly would not dream of seeing, reinforces what many people feel about the world of politics being a distant and self-enclosed realm without much grip on the everyday.

The entanglement of cultural critique and political opposition is complex; the discourses of 'Americanization' and of criticism of US foreign policy are deeply entwined. 'Rambo' looms not just over the raids but over the opposition to them, and the result is that a critical response is to a worrying extent not political, not even moral, but *cultural* – a criticism of US crudity rather than of militarism. Here 'the American madness' finds its real partner in the special relationship – 'the British illusion'. The relation of the two centres on ideas of empire. Anthony Barnett asked, in a review article on Seymour Hersh's *Kissinger: The Price of Power*, why British journalists and politicians persisted in their adulation of Kissinger.

> Surely it is because Kissinger represents what many British experts in international affairs would love to be. In the well-worn phrase that so captures the British illusion, we should be Greece to America's Rome. Translated, this means that top British specialists in foreign affairs, whether writers or politicians, desire – more than anything – to be Kissingers to the American Nixon. Their collective dream is to grease and polish its brute power with all their European experience of Empire.[33]

It is this fantasy, in which Britain is Greece to America's Rome, providing finesse and intelligence to tame and direct America's force, which is shattered by US unilateral acts that implicate Britain (the F-111s, the British bases) as an impotent and barely consulted partner. This I think explains 'Rambo' as used in the rhetoric opposing the American raids, an anxious linking of strength to vulgarity, an uneasy placing of muscular power. The reference to empire is highlighted in these debates by the tempting parallel between the Libyan airstrike and Suez. It is a reference that runs problematically through E. P. Thompson's contributions.

Thompson's first response, a *Guardian* article on 18 April announcing that CND had called a demonstration for the next day, begins by satirizing western notions of the Third World. He caricatures these attitudes by dividing the Third World into three categories: '(1) deserving wogs; (2) loyal wogs; and (3) bad wogs'. The word 'wog' is used to suggest the racism that sees American deaths as much more tragic than the loss of 'wog blood'. But 'wog' has another resonance; it belongs to *British* racism rather than American, and America's action keeps prompting British parallels. Thompson writes:

> The Americans behave today as if they were awarded by God some unique privilege above all other nations, just as the British once did in high Palmerstonian days. To mention this self-evident fact results in everyone clucking their tongues and saying one is 'anti-American'.

But although Thompson repeats his wish for a Europe that has emerged from the shadows of the superpowers, his anger is directed more at Mrs Thatcher 'and her lot':

> I knew they were destroying Britain but I did not know that the loss of any sense of national honour had gone that far. After selling out British industry and high technology with a secret 'Memorandum of Understanding' to Star Wars, they now let the scraggy wog-hunting US eagle roost on our pastures and lime our fields.

Our fields and pastures have been betrayed in a version of the 'Americanization' of Britain. In the call for a demonstration, Thompson wonders 'whether the traditions of our people have crumbled away into nothing but cynicism and the hunt for money'. A parallel suggests itself: 'In 1956, when Eden went wog-hunting at Suez, protesting people packed into Trafalgar Square and (after a diplomatic pause) Eden retired ill.' But, as Thompson says, in 1956 the United States upheld the rule of international law. In 1986 both Britain and America embraced 'the arbitrary Rule of War' instead. Thompson suggests that Britain's role was the 'more shameful'. 'The American eagle flies off from our land, and returns, satiated and gorged with blood. We don't even get any blood; we just get bloodied with the guilt.'[34] '*We don't even get any blood*': it seems an extraordinary phrase for a senior member of CND and END to use, as if it would have been more honourable for Britain to have bombed Tripoli. But matters of 'national honour' and 'the traditions of our people' are at stake and help to explain the rhetoric.

Thompson contributes two pieces to the *Mad Dogs* collection. The first is a 'Letter to Americans'. 'Dear Americans,' Thompson begins,

'I will explain to you why I am, just now, what you call "anti-American".' He combines family history (the fact of being half-American) with national histories (referring to the British bombardment of Beirut in 1841). If his British half should congratulate the US on following Britain's example of gunboat diplomacy, his American half is outraged. He asks what 'has caused this strange national self-exaltation, this isolationism of the heart, these intrusions upon others' territories and cultures, these Rambo reflexes?' It is perhaps odd to view the bombing as such a surprise, as if America had no history of military interventions, but Thompson is using his American heritage to criticize the American consensus in favour of the bombing. And if his American half 'feels outrage against my motherland, my British (or European) half regards my fatherland with shame. Those F-111s were launched from the English countryside.' He tells Americans that Mrs Thatcher is seen as 'the betrayer of our national integrity and honour'. The bombing has turned 'my fatherland into the Diego Garcia of the North Atlantic, a launching-base for your state terrorism'. Thus his British and American halves join in defending *traditions*, British national honour and 'American traditions' of liberal thought. He suggests that instead of European nations leaving NATO, the United States could be asked to leave. Europe would become 'safer' and American tourists might return to the Mediterranean: 'Where all of you, except for President Rambo, will be heartily welcome.'[35]

The collection ends with Thompson's account of the CND demonstration, 'The view from Oxford Street'. We have moved from England's green fields betrayed by Mrs Thatcher and polluted by F-111s, to the heart of contemporary consumerism. We have also moved from national honour to Third World status. When the F-111s set off on their mission, 'this signalled that Britain had been relegated to the Third Division – a little oil-state in the north-eastern Atlantic, or a bomber platform much like Diego Garcia in the Indian Ocean or Guam in the Pacific'.

> The British had joined the wogs of the Third World, and would have to make up their minds whether they were of the deserving and loyal or the bad kind. It was not much consolation to know that Mrs Thatcher had been nominated for an Oscar by the White House as the Third World's Most Loyal Wog of the Year.

The pattern is recognizable from writers discussed earlier, Americanization seen as colonization, the imperial nation that is now a banana republic. Among the protesters Thompson, the historian of English radical traditions, finds signs of an authentic, protesting 'Englishness', guardians of that English rural landscape that has been seen as corrupted and betrayed by the Americans and Thatcher, the logic of his argument leading to an oppositional pastoral: 'an eel-fisherman from the River Wye', 'a friend – a Warwickshire farmer with a gammy leg'.[36] The point made unconsciously is that these figures could hardly be mistaken for 'wogs'. 'Americanization' again brings us to a problem of British identity, specifically in this rhetoric the continuing hold of empire. For there seems to be no image for Britain as a post-imperial power, a European country like others. There are memories of when Britain ruled both waves and 'wogs', and these are repeated in Thompson's polemic alongside a recognition that America now has that superpower rule. But it is as if we must be either imperial or colonized, with Britain as empire or as banana republic, bomber platform, 'wogs'. Thompson ends with an unconvincing idea of a radical, rural 'Englishness', but the detours of his rhetoric help to demonstrate why many Conservative MPs, newspapers, and voters were also angered by the bombing. 'Great' Britain had been shown to be powerless by an event that could not but remind people of Suez, possibly *the* occasion that marked the end of Britain's imperial role. Ironically, the United States intervened to undermine the enterprise in 1956 but both occasions lead to resentment of America, for both underline the fact that Britain has lost its major power status. Politicians of all parties still refuse to adjust to this loss, the right's nostalgia for empire being mirrored by the left's rhetoric of Britain as colonized. Neither of these positions faces up to the fact of Britain's post-imperial status, and both lead to a displacement of this problem of British identity on to fears of Americanization.

Lloyd De Mause, editor of the *Journal of Psychohistory*, contributed an article to the *Guardian* on 'The secret psyche of Ronald Reagan', which takes the assertions that we have already seen (Rambo, the American madness, phallic weaponry) to extremes. It is illustrated by a cartoon of Reagan as 'Bimbo', a Rambo joke where Reagan's machine-gun is bent back and aimed at his head (the cartoon is by Cummings and comes from the *Winnipeg Free Press*). By extracting words from Reagan's speeches, almost at random, and conflating them with such separate campaigns as the anti-abortion protesters and attempts to raise awareness of child abuse, De Mause argues that America is suffering from a shared fantasy of child sacrifice, stemming, he argues, from guilt at America's prosperity. From these dubious methods and questionable ideas of a general affluence, he suggests that America's youth have responded to this fantasy by preparing themselves with war toys, militaristic videos, watching Rambo, and supporting Reagan over Nicaragua and Libya. The prospect of a war against Nicaragua is seen to extend through American culture 'portrayed in images of mounting sexual excitement, from cartoons of Reagan as Rambo pursuing Daniel Ortega with a phallic missile launcher, to images of erect missiles aimed at Central America'. It is claimed that, as is 'true of all wars', this prospect 'was heavily laden with macho display and hidden homosexual imagery'. But with no overt war in Central America, 'American homosexual conflicts had to be acted out in other areas'. Hence the Libyan bombing which 'released a Rambo reflex in the majority of Americans, as a phallic defence against the "softness" and "femininity" of prosperity'. Reagan and his advisers then started to 'use Gadafy as a container into which they projected their own femininity'. De Mause comments on the American right's long involvement in anti-gay campaigns as well as the more widespread post-Aids homophobia, linking these to White House reports channelled through the *New York Post* that 'Gadafy was a homosexual' and irrational ('He's turned into a transvestite druggie'). The signs of otherness are multiplied. The next encounter with 'dreaded femininity' was prompted by Gorbachev and the Reykjavik meeting over arms reductions.[37]

Just when the most frequent headline was 'Is Reagan Going Soft?', and when articles were 'loaded with the words "soft" and "impotent"'. The entire nation suddenly became fascinated with the subject of the condition of the President's penis.' De Mause continues:

> the President decided to undergo a urological examination and TV showed drawings of his penis, demonstrating how the cystoscope would be inserted through his urethra. A nationwide campaign of urine tests for drugs was announced, and the President and his staff all agreed to urinate into test tubes, eliciting cartoons all across the country showing men urinating together.

'Homosexual imagery' is seen to have dominated the media's build-up to Reykjavik. 'Editorials attacked everything that wasn't blatantly phallic', the world being divided into the 'hard' and the 'wimps'. As with earlier attempts at disarmament, the meeting 'was seen as a homosexual encounter', with the possibility of arms reduction threatening to 'leave us naked', in Reagan's words, 'to reveal our homosexual wishes', in De Mause's interpretation. A television commentator described the Reykjavik meeting as 'a blind date'. Although this discussion of imagery is provocative the argument is undermined by its reductive nature. There is no questioning of its assumptions of prosperity and war-fever. Finally Reagan's involvement in the sale of arms to Iran is seen to stem from childhood traumas at the hands of his alcoholic father. Irangate is rewritten as psychodrama.[38] De Mause's article can serve as a warning of the mystifications involved in generalizing from Rambo to American masculinity and foreign policy.

However, the rhetorical link between national identity and masculine virility throws an interesting light on British responses to the Anglo-American alliance and to the Libyan bombing.

We have seen writer after writer link Rambo and Reagan, and I have already suggested problems stemming from the place of conservative cultural criticism in a radical political analysis. What is noticeable is the way that Anglo-American cultural relations and political/military/industrial relations act as metaphors for each other. Britain is *invaded* by both television and air bases, and notions of gender and national identity are involved in both invasions. American cultural products are often marketed around masculinity, and those models of masculinity are then used as images for American military power. Britain's relative 'impotence' provides the corresponding term, so 'Americanization' and the coming of 'mass culture' are felt to have rendered viewers (in some arguments specifically the working class) passive, emasculated, 'feminized'. Equally, the threats to British sovereignty or to 'national honour' are portrayed as emasculating, a representation that parallels and reinforces the images of Britain as a banana republic. Opposition attacks on Mrs Thatcher's acquiescence in the Libyan raids focused on the undermining of national pride and integrity, the feminization and colonization of Britain. So the Prime Minister was described as Reagan's poodle, the virile and imperial bulldog having been reduced to a symbol of the feminine or effeminate. To underline what I have suggested is problematic in this rhetoric, the left has proved that their attempts to appropriate the patriotic (at the beginning of the Falklands crisis, at the time of Westland, in response to the Libyan raids) are self-defeating. To appeal to nationalism against conservatism may produce temporary successes, but that terrain is still perceived as the property of the right. An oppositional rhetoric that displays contempt for and ignorance of popular culture, while suggesting at times a nostalgia for British imperial greatness, founds its critique of 'the American madness' on 'the British illusion'. And that illusion fuels conservative ideology: the British bulldog re-emerged as the symbol of the Conservatives' successful 1987 general election campaign.

Conclusion

I have argued that the link between critiques of popular culture and opposition to US foreign policy works to block effective political analysis. It is necessary to separate conservative worries about the national cultural heritage from political opposition to American policies. This is not to suggest that pleasure in American culture is outside politics, rather that those pleasures are currently captured to a large extent by a populism of the right, and must be re-articulated. To borrow Benjamin's formulation, there is a need to politicize aesthetics not to aestheticize politics, and that means actually looking at both Reagan and Rambo instead of confusing them.

Reyner Banham has been cited at various points of this book – his work on American deserts in Chapter 3, his discussion of American architecture as the backdrop for pop culture in Chapter 6 – and he provides an exemplary account of the oppositional uses of American culture to conclude with. American popular culture can be mobilized against an established English consensus in a variety of fields. I suggested in the previous chapter that American crime fiction provides an example of this. Banham's 'Detroit tin re-visited' gives a self-conscious account of the polemical value that American car styling had in British debates about design in the 1950s. He remembers specific arguments, stressing an idea of 'we', 'our side', 'us members of the Independent Group at the ICA' versus 'our elders and betters' and their assumptions about styling and design. The combative tone leads to a wistful moment, when Banham regrets that unfortunately nobody in England knew that Roland Barthes was talking in 1955 about cars being the modern equivalent of cathedrals: 'If we had known he had said that we would really have bashed Paul Reilly and the CoID over the head good and proper.' What would have really annoyed the Council of Industrial Design would have been Barthes' simile – from cathedral to Citroën – and Banham also reveals the provocative and polemical value of the simile.

If tail-fins blasphemed against functionalism, and if cars with air conditioning seemed a tactless luxury in Europe, Banham says that his side was arguing that people still needed to stop and actually look at American car design. There they would see 'detailing that was not only crafty and often as elegant as a drawing by Ingres', but that also might prove fruitful in the design of other products. From Ingres to Detroit ... the tactic of the provocative simile continues with Banham's amused recollection that the British design establishment actually used phrases like, 'does not even look like a motor-car'. 'It is a bit like earlier generations of English critics complaining that Picassos didn't look like paintings.' For, as Banham points out, if it's a question of the number of talents in one place, 'then Detroit was to cars in the fifties what Paris was to modern art, say in 1910'. He ends the piece by applying art history's periodization to Cadillacs: their 'High Renaissance' moment, Mannerist Cadillacs, and so on.[39]

Banham's article is not just an amusing memory of a chromium snub to 'good taste', it also makes the important point that prejudice prevented critics from seeing what was in front of them. Its idea of 'our lot' is not mere nostalgia for generational and theoretical conflict, it's also locating the weaknesses of a critical establishment that referred to jazz and meant Al Jolson or that alluded to science fiction because critics had read Kingsley Amis on SF. Whereas Banham's side in the debate 'knew about SF and Detroit'. As we have seen in the last chapter with campaigns against horror, that still has many parallels; there are still plenty of debates where American/popular culture is alluded to and argued against, but *not known*. The next question that suggests itself is how do these uses of America against domestic smugness relate to our other feelings about American capitalism or foreign policy? In a piece collected in *New Society*'s *Arts in Society*, a volume that is exemplary in taking popular culture seriously while not overlooking pleasure, Banham himself asks just this question.

Writing on Richard Hamilton, Banham says that Hamilton's wife, Terry, summed up 'one of the crises of our time':

> how to reconcile unavoidable admiration for the immense competence, resourcefulness and creative power of American commercial design with the equally unavoidable disgust at the system that was producing it?

He reminds us, against the grain of the Americanization argument, 'how salutary a corrective to the sloppy provincialism of most London art of ten years ago US design could be'.

> The gusto and professionalism of wide-screen movies or Detroit car-styling was a constant reproach to the Moore-ish yokelry of British sculpture or the affected Piperish gloom of British painting. To anyone with a scrap of sensibility or an eye for technique, the average Playtex or Maidenform ad in American *Vogue* was an instant deflater of the reputations of most artists then in Arts Council vogue.

How could this 'discriminating admiration' be kept up 'in the face of the conditioned-reflex atomic sabre-rattling of the Eisenhower regime'? Banham suggests that Richard Hamilton came close to resolving this with his brilliant 1963 portrait of *Hugh Gaitskell as a famous monster of filmland*, which used 'technique that Madison Avenue could have envied, as the servant of political disgust'.[40]

Are these not better questions, *and better answers*, than talk of banana republics and cultural imperialism? Perhaps it is to pop art, certainly to popular culture, that we should turn rather than to George Orwell. Irony, anger, knowledge ... here is a way of combining politics and pleasure, a lesson from the 1960s still urgent in the 1980s.

Notes

Introduction: Looka yonder!

1 Norman Mailer on the British General Election, *The Mail on Sunday*, 5 June 1983, p. 6.
2 Stanley Kauffmann, 'What price freedom?' in Bonnie Marranca (ed.), *American Dreams: The Imagination of Sam Shepard* (New York, Performing Arts Journal Publications, 1981), p. 105.
3 Bill Buford, Editorial, 'Dirty realism: new writing from America', *Granta* 8 (1983), pp. 4–5.
4 Kate Lynch, *Springsteen: No Surrender* (London, Proteus, 1984), pp. 118–19.
5 William Adams, 'Natural virtue: symbol and imagination in the American farm crisis', *The Georgia Review*, XXXIX, 4 (winter 1985), p. 711.
6 Mike Davis, 'The new right's road to power', *New Left Review*, 128 (July–August 1981), p. 28.
7 Norman Mailer, 'In the red light: a history of the Republican convention in 1964', *Cannibals and Christians* (London, Panther, 1979), pp. 28–9.
8 ibid., pp. 34, 36, 50.
9 ibid., pp. 61–2.
10 Norman Mailer, *Miami and the Siege of Chicago* (Harmondsworth, Penguin, 1969), pp. 35, 67.
11 Joan Didion, 'Some dreamers of the golden dream', *Slouching towards Bethlehem*, (Harmondsworth, Penguin, 1974), p. 19.
12 Robert Dallek, *Ronald Reagan: The Politics of Symbolism* (Cambridge, Mass., Harvard University Press, 1984), pp. 28, 33.
13 Mike Davis, op. cit., p. 36.
14 ibid., pp. 29, 44.
15 Alan Wolfe, 'Sociology, liberalism, and the radical right', *New Left Review*, 128 (July–August 1981), p. 26.
16 Gillian Peele, *Revival and Reaction: The Right in Contemporary America* (Oxford, Oxford University Press, 1984), p. 3.
17 Davis, op. cit., p. 39; see pp. 39–40 for an analysis of the industries and bases of the new right's backers.
18 See Peele, op. cit.
19 Davis, op. cit., pp. 31–2; see also Peele, op. cit., pp. 56–65.
20 Peele, op. cit., pp. 65, 67.
21 ibid., p. 192.
22 Davis, op. cit., pp. 38–9.

23 ibid., p. 45.
24 Dallek, op. cit., p. 3.
25 Davis, op. cit., pp. 46–7; see pp. 47–9 for an analysis of the contradictions of 'The post-Gutenberg presidency'.
26 Richard Hofstadter, *The Paranoid Style in American Politics and Other Essays* (London, Jonathan Cape, 1966), pp. 7–9.
27 ibid., pp. 43, 93–4, 121, 110.
28 Wolfe, op. cit., p. 23.
29 Dallek, op. cit., p. 84; see pp. 83–6 for an account of Watt's career.
30 Tom Nairn, *The Break-Up of Britain* (London, Verso, 1981), pp. 347–8, 340; Lenin is quoted in Andrzej Walicki, 'Russia', in Ghita Ionescu and Ernest Gellner (eds), *Populism: Its Meanings and National Characteristics* (London, Weidenfeld & Nicolson, 1969), p. 72.
31 Jeffrey Richards, *Visions of Yesterday* (London, Routledge & Kegan Paul, 1973), pp. 229–30.
32 Jack Temple Kirby, *Media-Made Dixie: The South in the American Imagination* (London and Baton Rouge, Louisiana State University Press, 1978), p. 62.
33 Willa Cather, 'El Dorado: a Kansas recessional' (1901), *Collected Short Fiction 1892–1912*, Introduction by Mildred R. Bennett (Lincoln, University of Nebraska Press, 1965), p. 301.
34 Frederick Jackson Turner, 'The Middle West' (1901), *The Frontier in American History* (London, Holt, Rhinehart & Winston, 1962), p. 155.
35 Lawrence Goodwyn, *The Populist Moment* (Oxford, Oxford University Press, 1980), p. 264.
36 ibid., p. 133; and Fred A. Shannon, *American Farmers' Movements* (Princeton, New Jersey, D. Van Nostrand, 1957), pp. 136–7.
37 Richard Hofstadter, 'North America', in Ionescu and Gellner (eds), op. cit., p. 12.
38 Peter Worsley, 'The concept of populism', in ibid., p. 224.
39 ibid., p. 225.
40 N. B. Ashby, 'The riddle of the Sphinx' (1890), in George Brown Tindall (ed.), *A Populist Reader* (New York, Harper & Row, 1966), pp. 34–5.
41 Goodwyn, op. cit., p. 211.
42 ibid., pp. 334–5.
43 ibid., pp. 20, 135.
44 ibid., pp. 9–20.
45 William Jennings Bryan, 'Cross of Gold' speech (1896) in Tindall (ed.), op. cit., pp. 211, 210, 205.
46 Goodwyn, op. cit., p. 39.
47 ibid., pp. 175, 101.
48 Tindall, op. cit., Introduction, p. xii.
49 W. Scott Morgan, *History of the Wheel and Alliance and the Impending Revolution* (1889), in Tindall, op. cit., p. 24.
50 National People's Party Platform, in ibid., p. 93.
51 Henry George is quoted and discussed in John L. Thomas, *Alternative America* (Cambridge, Mass. and London, Harvard University Press, 1983), pp. 114, 129.
52 See Frederick Jackson Turner, op. cit., pp. 32, 148, 238–40.
53 Thomas, op. cit., p. 229.
54 ibid., pp. 274–5.
55 ibid., p. 344.

56 Fiorello LaGuardia, *Congressional Record* (10 January 1933), in Howard Zinn (ed.), *New Deal Thought* (New York, Bobbs-Merrill Co., 1966), pp. 229–30.
57 Ignatius Donnelly, *Caesar's Column* (1891), in Tindall (ed.), op. cit., p. 114.
58 George Michael interviewed by Mat Snow, *NME*, 28 June 1986, p. 9.
59 Greil Marcus, *Mystery Train: Images of America in Rock 'n' Roll Music* (London, Omnibus Press, 1977), p. 4.
60 Henry James, 'The question of opportunities' (1898), *The American Essays*, ed by Leon Edel (New York, 1956), pp. 198–200.

1 Family fields: the farming narrative

1 Nat Hentoff interviewing Bob Dylan for *Playboy* (March 1966), in Craig McGregor (ed.), *Bob Dylan: A Retrospective* (London, Picador, 1975), p. 103.
2 See Jeffrey Richards' discussion of populist cinema, *Visions of Yesterday* (London, Routledge & Kegan Paul, 1973), p. 278.
3 Lawrence Goodwyn, *The Populist Moment* (Oxford, Oxford University Press, 1980), pp. 45–6, 129, 134.
4 Governor Lewelling speaking to a Populist meeting in July 1894, in George B. Tindall (ed.), *A Populist Reader* (New York, Harper & Row, 1966), pp. 148–9.
5 Fiorello LaGuardia, *Congressional Record* (10 January 1933), in Howard Zinn (ed.), *New Deal Thought* (New York, Bobbs-Merrill Co., 1966), p. 231.
6 John Steinbeck, *The Grapes of Wrath* (London, Pan, 1975), p. 369.
7 William Adams, 'Natural virtue: symbol and imagination in the American farm crisis', *The Georgia Review*, XXXIX, 4 (Winter 1985), pp. 695–6.
8 Ralph Waldo Emerson, 'Man the reformer' (1841), *Selected Essays*, ed. by Larzer Ziff (Harmondsworth, Penguin, 1982), pp. 137–8.
9 James Agee and Walker Evans, *Let Us Now Praise Famous Men* (Boston, Houghton Mifflin, 1960), p. 322.
10 This is obviously a compressed history but the accounts I have drawn on for this section on the family are Stuart Ewen, *Captains of Consciousness* (New York, 1976), especially pp. 114–20; and Michele Mattelart, *Women, Media and Crisis: Femininity and Disorder* (London, Comedia, 1986), especially pp. 7–8.
11 John Fekete, *The Critical Twilight* (London, Routledge & Kegan Paul, 1977), pp. 69–70, 238.
12 John Steinbeck, 'Dubious battle in California', *The Nation*, CXLIII (12 September 1936), in Zinn, op. cit., p. 246.
13 ibid., pp. 244–5.
14 Goodwyn, op. cit., pp. xv–xvi.
15 ibid., pp. 269, 316.
16 Albert E. Stone, Introduction, J. Hector St John de Crèvecoeur, *Letters from an American Farmer* (Harmondsworth, Penguin, 1981), p. 7.
17 ibid., pp. 49, 65.
18 ibid., p. 43.
19 Stephen Fender, *American Literature in Context I, 1620–1830* (London, Methuen, 1983), pp. 133, 135.
20 Crèvecoeur, op. cit., pp. 51, 54.
21 ibid., p. 91.
22 Garry Wills, *Inventing America: Jefferson's Declaration of Independence* (New York, Doubleday & Co., 1978), p. 366; see also Fender, op. cit., p. 130.

23 Adams, op. cit., p. 700; Leo Marx provides a useful discussion of the difference between seeing Jefferson's view as agrarian and seeing it as pastoral, *The Machine in the Garden* (Oxford, Oxford University Press, 1979), pp. 121–9. He points out that the literary ancestry of Jefferson and Crèvecoeur's husbandmen is 'obscured by the peculiar credibility imparted to the pastoral hope under American conditions', p. 129. Alongside Marx's book, the other classic study is Henry Nash Smith, *Virgin Land* (Cambridge, Mass., Harvard University Press, 1950).

24 Adams, op. cit., pp. 701–5.

25 Frederick Jackson Turner, *The Frontier in American History* (New York, London, Holt, Rinehart & Winston, 1962), pp. 148, 238, 239.

26 Fred A. Shannon, *American Farmers' Movements* (Princeton, New Jersey, D. Van Nostrand, 1957), pp. 50–3; Goodwyn, op. cit., p. 70.

27 Shannon, op. cit., p. 53; Goodwyn, op. cit., pp. 20–5.

28 Peter Worsley, 'The concept of Populism', in Ghita Ionescu and Ernest Gellner (eds), *Populism: Its Meanings and National Characteristics* (London, Weidenfeld & Nicolson, 1969), p. 221.

29 Goodwyn, op. cit., pp. xx–xxi, 206–9.

30 Turner, op. cit., p. 353; Howells on Garland written for the 1899 edition and quoted in Tindall, op. cit., p. 1.

31 These quotations and the biographical material are taken from Thomas A. Bledsoe's Introduction to Hamlin Garland, *Main-Travelled Roads* (New York, Holt, Rinehart & Winston, 1965), pp. xv, xiv.

32 'Up the Coulé', in ibid., pp. 56, 58, 62, 63.

33 ibid., pp. 66, 69, 70, 78, 90, 91, 92, 101.

34 Bledsoe, op. cit., p. ix.

35 Willa Cather, 'Neighbour Rosicky', *Obscure Destinies* (New York, Alfred A. Knopf, 1932), pp. 40, 54.

36 Willa Cather, 'My first novels (there were two)', *On Writing* (New York, 1949), pp. 93–4.

37 A. S. Byatt, 'Afterword' to Willa Cather, *O Pioneers!* (London, Virago, 1983), p. 311.

38 Robert Edson Lee, *From West to East* (Urbana and London, University of Illinois Press, 1966), pp. 134–5; a useful critique of Lee's simple opposition between Western truth and Eastern artifice can be found in Stephen Fender's *Plotting the Golden West* (Cambridge, Cambridge University Press, 1981).

39 See Willa Cather, *Collected Short Fiction 1892–1912*, Introduction by Mildred R. Bennett (Lincoln, University of Nebraska Press, 1965), p. 495.

40 Cather, *O Pioneers!*, pp. 15, 19.

41 Willa Cather, *My Antonia* (London, Virago, 1983), p. 3.

42 Cather, *O Pioneers!*, pp. 111–12.

43 ibid., p. 48.

44 Walt Whitman, 'The women of the West', *Complete Poetry and Collected Prose* (Cambridge, Viking Press, 1982), p. 868.

45 Turner, op. cit., pp. 23, 349.

46 See Oscar Cargill, 'Afterword' to Frank Norris, *The Octopus* (New York, New American Library, 1981), for the novel's background. Page references for quotations from *The Octopus* are given in the text.

2 Country images: from Steinbeck's Okies to Hollywood's heartland

1 Carolyn Chute, *The Beans of Egypt, Maine* (London, Chatto & Windus, 1985); Chute's comments are quoted by Ann Hulbert, 'Rural chic', *The New Republic*, vol. 193, 10 (2 September 1985), pp. 27–8.
2 Quoted in Sylvia Jenkins Cook, *From Tobacco Road to Route 66: The Southern Poor White in Fiction* (Chapel Hill, University of North Carolina Press, 1976), p. 118.
3 ibid., p. ix.
4 ibid., p. 3.
5 ibid., pp. 185, 188.
6 Jack Temple Kirby, *Media-Made Dixie: The South in the American Imagination* (London and Baton Rouge, Louisiana State University Press, 1978), p. 64.
7 ibid., p. 45, and Cook, op. cit., p. 18.
8 For a discussion of these novels see Kirby, op. cit., p. 46, and Cook, op. cit., pp. 18–28.
9 Quoted in Kirby, op. cit., p. 56 (see also pp. 52–5), and Cook, op. cit., chapter 3, 'Faulkner's celebration of the poor white paradox', and chapter 4, 'Caldwell's politics of the grotesque'.
10 Kirby, op. cit., p. 80 (see also p. 49), and Cook, op. cit., p. 34.
11 John Fekete, *The Critical Twilight* (London, Routledge & Kegan Paul, 1977), pp. 58–9, 68–72, also the notes on pp. 233–8.
12 Cook, op. cit., pp. 36–7, 87, and chapter 5, 'The Gastonia strike and proletarian possibilities', chapter 6, 'Poor whites, feminists, and Marxists'.
13 Kirby, op. cit., pp. 58–62; Cook, op. cit., pp. 144–5; and William Stott, *Documentary Expression and Thirties America* (Oxford, Oxford University Press, 1973).
14 James Agee and Walker Evans, *Let Us Now Praise Famous Men* (Boston, Houghton Mifflin, 1960), p. xiv. Subsequent page numbers are given in the text.
15 John Steinbeck, *The Grapes of Wrath* (London, Pan, 1975), p. 126. Subsequent page numbers are given in the text.
16 Cook, op. cit., p. xiv.
17 ibid., pp. 160–1, 168–9, 183.
18 Hulbert, op. cit., p. 25.
19 William Adams, 'Natural virtue: symbol and imagination in the American farm crisis', *The Georgia Review*, XXXIX, 4 (Winter 1985), p. 707.
20 Hulbert, op. cit., p. 26.
21 ibid., p. 26.
22 ibid., p. 26.
23 ibid., pp. 26–7.
24 ibid., p. 30.
25 See Fred A. Shannon, *American Farmers' Movements* (Princeton, New Jersey, D. Van Nostrand, 1957), p. 91.
26 Bobbie Ann Mason, *Shiloh and Other Stories* (London, Chatto & Windus, 1983), p. 207. Subsequent page numbers are given in the text.
27 See Ted Solotaroff, 'Writing in the cold', *Granta* 15 (1985), pp. 271–3, and Douglas Unger, *Leaving the Land* (London, William Heinemann, 1984).
28 Unger, op. cit., p. 8. Subsequent page numbers are given in the text.
29 Raymond Carver, *The Stories of Raymond Carver* (London, Picador, 1985), pp. 418, 421–2, 426, 433.

3 Sam Shepard's cowboy mouth: representing masculinity

1 Chris Peachment's interview with Sam Shepard, *Time Out*, 731 (23–9 August 1984), p. 17.
2 Sam Shepard, *True West* (London, Faber & Faber, 1981), p. 29.
3 *Theatre Quarterly* interview in Bonnie Marranca (ed.), *American Dreams: The Imagination of Sam Shepard* (New York, Performing Arts Journal Publications, 1981), p. 193.
4 Shepard, 'Language, visualization and the inner library', in ibid., p. 214.
5 *Theatre Quarterly* interview in ibid., pp. 188–90.
6 ibid., p. 193.
7 Guatam Dasgupta, 'Interview with Spalding Gray', in ibid., pp. 183, 177.
8 Patti Smith in Shepard, *Angel City, Curse of the Starving Class and Other Plays* (London, Faber & Faber, 1978), pp. 242, 245, 244, 243.
9 Bonnie Marranca, 'Alphabetical Shepard: the play of words', in Marranca, op. cit., pp. 30–1.
10 ibid., p. 29.
11 Florence Falk, 'Men without women: the Shepard landscape', in ibid., pp. 90–1.
12 Marranca, ibid., pp. 20–1.
13 Shepard, *Motel Chronicles and Hawk Moon* (London, Faber & Faber, 1985), pp. 140–1.
14 Shepard, *Operation Sidewinder* in *Four Two-Act Plays* (London, Faber & Faber, 1981), p. 153.
15 Jack Gelber, 'The playwright as shaman', in Marranca, op. cit., p. 46; also printed as the introduction to *Angel City . . .*, op. cit.
16 Falk, op. cit., p. 95.
17 ibid., p. 101.
18 Shepard, *The Tooth of Crime*, in *Four Two-Act Plays*, op. cit., p. 106.
19 ibid., p. 81.
20 Shepard, *Angel City . . .*, p. 36.
21 Stanley Kauffmann, 'What price freedom?' in Marranca, op. cit., p. 105.
22 Shepard, *Angel City . . .*, p. 107.
23 Shepard, *Geography of a Horse Dreamer* in *Four Two-Act Plays*, p. 149.
24 ibid., pp. 127, 128.
25 Shepard and Smith, *Cowboy Mouth* in *Angel City . . .*, p. 199.
26 Shepard, *True West*, p. 54.
27 William Kleb, 'Worse than being homeless: *True West* and the divided self', in Marranca, op. cit., p. 112.
28 Shepard, *True West*, p. 63.
29 ibid., pp. 22, 24–5, 34.
30 See Kleb, op. cit., p. 124.
31 Falk, op. cit., p. 101.
32 Shepard, *Curse of the Starving Class*, p. 67. Subsequent page numbers are given in the text.
33 Harold Beaver, *The Great American Masquerade* (London and Totowa, New Jersey, Vision Press and Barnes & Noble, 1985), p. 11.
34 C. W. E. Bigsby, *David Mamet* (London, Methuen, 1985), p. 111.
35 Shepard, *Motel Chronicles*, pp. 44–5.

36 Shepard interviewed by Stephen Fay, *The Sunday Times Magazine*, 26 August 1984.
37 *Theatre Quarterly* interview in Marranca, op. cit., p. 208.
38 Shepard, *Fool for Love* (London, Faber & Faber, 1984), pp. 26–7. Subsequent page numbers are given in the text.
39 A useful introduction to ideas of deconstruction and difference can be found in Barbara Johnson, *The Critical Difference: Essays in the Contemporary Rhetoric of Reading* (London, 1980).
40 Reyner Banham, *Scenes In America Deserta* (London, Thames & Hudson, 1982), p. 228.
41 ibid. For these themes see pp. 10, 21–2, 37, 159, 62, and 224–6.
42 For an account of the role of Lacanian concepts in film theory, see Stephen Heath, 'On suture', *Questions of Cinema* (London, Macmillan, 1981), especially p. 90 for a discussion of the way in which 'cinema is not the mirror-phase'.
43 Stephen Heath's analysis of *Touch of Evil*, 'Film and system' Part II, *Screen*, vol. 16, 2 (1976), p. 93.
44 Interview with Wenders by Melinda Camber Porter, *The Times*, 26 January 1984, p. 9.
45 Interview with Wenders by Saskia Baron, *City Limits*, 151, 24–30 August 1984.
46 *Theatre Quarterly* interview in Marranca, op. cit., p. 199.
47 ibid., p. 198.

4 'Things fall apart': loss in recent American fiction

1 Robert Dallek, *Ronald Reagan: The Politics of Symbolism* (Cambridge, Mass. and London, Harvard University Press, 1984), pp. 105, 102.
2 Jayne Anne Phillips, 'Fast Lanes', *Granta* 19, 'More dirt: new writing from America' (1986), p. 49.
3 Anne Tyler, *Earthly Possessions* (London, Chatto & Windus, 1977), p. 47.
4 ibid., p. 72; Phillips, op. cit., p. 58.
5 Phillips, op. cit., p. 52.
6 Jayne Anne Phillips, 'Rayme – A Memoir of the Seventies', *Granta* 8, 'Dirty realism: new writing from America' (1983), pp. 39, 41.
7 Jayne Anne Phillips, 'El Paso', *Black Tickets* (London, Allen Lane, 1980).
8 Phillips, 'Country' in ibid., p. 172.
9 Raymond Carver, 'Where he was: Memories of my Father', *Granta* 14, 'Autobiography' (1984), pp. 20–1, 24. The piece is also contained in Carver, *Fires* (London, Picador, 1986).
10 Phillips, 'Fast Lanes', *Granta* 19, pp. 58, 60.
11 Tyler, op. cit., p. 71; Phillips, 'The Heavenly Animal', *Black Tickets*, p. 117; Elizabeth Tallent, 'Keats', *In Constant Flight* (London, Chatto & Windus, 1983), p. 58; Bobbie Ann Mason, 'Still Life With Watermelon', *Granta* 8, pp. 111, 109, 118–19; Richard Ford, 'Rock Springs', *Granta* 8, pp. 45–6; Richard Russo, 'Fishing with Wussy', *Granta* 19; Robert Olmstead, 'The Contas Girl', *Granta* 19; Joy Williams, 'Escapes', *Granta* 19.
12 Raymond Carver, 'Night School', *The Stories of Raymond Carver* (London, Picador, 1985), p. 76.
13 Carver, 'Jerry and Molly and Sam' in ibid., pp. 115–16.
14 Carver, 'Mr Coffee and Mr Fixit' in ibid., p. 195.

15 Mary Pat Kelly, *Martin Scorsese: The First Decade* (Pleasantville, New York, 1980), p. 18.

16 Carver, 'Will you please be quiet, please?', *The Stories*, pp. 177, 180.

17 Carver, 'A small good thing' in ibid., p. 346.

18 Carver, 'The compartment' in ibid., pp. 322–30.

19 Carver, 'Feathers', in ibid., pp. 291, 293, 306–7.

20 Ted Solotaroff, 'Writing in the cold', *Granta* 15, 'The fall of Saigon' (1985), p. 266.

21 Diane Johnson, *New York Review of Books*, vol. 32, 17 (7 November 1985), pp. 15–17.

22 Carver, 'How about this?', *The Stories*, pp. 136–7.

23 Bobbie Ann Mason, *In Country* (London, Chatto & Windus, 1986), p. 163.

24 ibid., p. 200.

25 See Elizabeth Tallent, 'Swans', 'In Constant Flight', 'The Evolution of the Birds of Paradise', in *In Constant Flight*.

26 Frederick Barthelme, 'The Browns', *Moon Deluxe* (Harmondsworth, Penguin, 1984), p. 74; see also *Second Marriage* (London, J. M. Dent, 1985), p. 22.

27 Barthelme, *Second Marriage*, p. 40.

28 Barthelme, 'Monster Deal', *Moon Deluxe*, pp. 188, 194; see also *Granta* 8.

29 Tallent, 'Natural Law' in *In Constant Flight*, p. 78.

30 ibid., p. 80.

31 Tallent, 'Asteroids' in ibid., p. 16.

32 Richard Ford, 'Empire', *Granta* 19, p. 18.

33 C. W. E. Bigsby, *David Mamet* (London, Methuen, 1985), p. 44.

34 See Susan Sontag, *On Photography* (London, Allen Lane, 1978).

35 Philip D. Beidler, *American Literature and the Experience of Vietnam* (Athens, Georgia, University of Georgia Press, 1982), p. 3.

36 ibid., p. 16.

37 See Richard Ford, 'Empire', pp. 22–3; Tobias Wolff, 'The Poor Are Always With Us', 'Desert Breakdown, 1968', in *Back in the World* (London, Jonathan Cape, 1986), pp. 76–7, 143. See also 'Soldier's Joy' in the same collection for a character's nostalgia for Vietnam.

38 Phillips, 'South Carolina', *Black Tickets*, p. 154; see also Richard Russo's 'Fishing with Wussy', *Granta* 19, for a post-World War Two veteran who comes back intent on drinking, whoring, and playing the horses.

39 Phillips, *Machine Dreams* (London, Faber & Faber, 1984), pp. 305, 130.

40 Mason, *In Country*, pp. 235, 237.

41 Solotaroff, op. cit., pp. 275–6.

42 Phillips, quoted in Bill Buford, 'Editorial', *Granta* 8, p. 5.

43 Wolff, 'The Barracks Thief' in ibid., p. 169.

5 American crime: 'Debts no honest man could pay'

1 Publicity slogan for Sylvester Stallone's film, *Cobra*.

2 Interview with Michel Foucault, trans. Mollie Horwitz, 'The politics of crime', *Partisan Review*, vol. 43, 3 (1976), p. 456.

3 David Mamet interviewed by Christopher Bigsby, quoted in C. W. E. Bigsby, *David Mamet* (London, Methuen, 1985), p. 111.

4 David Mamet, *American Buffalo* (London, Methuen, 1984), pp. 74–5; see Bigsby's discussion of this passage, ibid., pp. 74–5.

5 Garry Wills, *Inventing America: Jefferson's Declaration of Independence* (New York, Doubleday & Company, 1978), pp. 19–20.

6 George V. Higgins, *A Choice of Enemies* (London, Secker & Warburg, 1984), pp. 275–6.

7 ibid., p. 149.

8 See George V. Higgins, *A City on the Hill* (London, Secker & Warburg, 1975); the phrase continues to reverberate through American political culture. Ronald Reagan has used it in speeches and Frances Fitzgerald chose it as the title for her excellent survey of contemporary communities, *Cities on a Hill* (London, Picador, 1987).

9 Ross Thomas, *The Porkchoppers* (Harmondsworth, Penguin, 1985), pp. 111, 43.

10 Ross Thomas, *The Mordida Man* (Harmondsworth, Penguin, 1983), p. 30.

11 Robert B. Parker, *The Widening Gyre* (New York, Seymour Lawrence, 1983), pp. 5, 147, 148.

12 Elmore Leonard, *LaBrava* (Harmondsworth, Penguin, 1985), pp. 17–18.

13 Hunter S. Thompson, *Fear and Loathing on the Campaign Trail* (London, Allison & Busby, 1974), p. 135; 'Jimmy Carter and the Great Leap of Faith', *The Great Shark Hunt* (London, Picador, 1980), p. 505.

14 Upton Sinclair, *The Brass Check* (Long Beach, California, revised edition, 1928, first published, 1920), p. 222.

15 Richard Stark, *Point Blank* (Lonson, Allison & Busby, 1986).

16 Denis Johnson, *Angels* (Harmondsworth, Penguin, 1985), pp. 109–10.

17 Elmore Leonard, *Stick* (Harmondsworth, Penguin, 1984), pp. 192–4.

18 ibid., p. 153.

19 ibid., p. 195.

20 Mamet in *National Theatre Study Notes*, quoted in Bigsby, op. cit., p. 78.

21 Mamet in the *New York Times*, quoted in ibid., p. 73.

22 Mamet in the *Dictionary of Literary Biography*, vol. 7 (1981), quoted in ibid., p. 66.

23 Mamet, *National Theatre Study Notes*, quoted in ibid., p. 116.

24 See Bigsby's interview with Mamet, ibid., p. 111.

25 David Mamet, *Glengarry, Glen Ross* (London, Methuen, 1984), 'Author's Note'.

26 Bigsby, op. cit., p. 114.

27 Mamet, *Glengarry, Glen Ross*, p. 42.

28 Mamet, *New York Times*, 15 January 1978, quoted in Bigsby, op. cit., p. 72; for Bigsby's discussion of the critics see pp. 82, 84–5.

29 ibid., p. 84.

30 ibid., p. 85.

31 ibid., p. 64.

32 Mamet, *American Buffalo*, p. 7.

33 Bigsby, op. cit., p. 73.

34 Mamet, *American Buffalo*, p. 86.

35 ibid., p. 35.

36 Elmore Leonard, *Swag* (Harmondsworth, Penguin, 1984), p. 23.

37 George V. Higgins, *Kennedy for the Defense* (London, Abacus, 1986), p. 3.

38 K. C. Constantine, *Always A Body to Trade* (London, Allison & Busby, 1986), p. 28. Subsequent page numbers are given in the text.

39 George V. Higgins, *The Patriot Game* (London, Secker & Warburg, 1982), pp. 51, 54, 55.

40 Michel Foucault, *Discipline and Punish*, trans. Alan Sheridan (Harmondsworth, Penguin, 1979), pp. 234, 264, 272.
41 George V. Higgins, *The Judgment of Deke Hunter* (London, Robinson, 1986), p. 256.
42 David Mamet, *Sexual Perversity in Chicago* (New York, Grove Press, 1978), p. 18.
43 ibid., p. 50.
44 Mamet interviewed by Bigsby, in Bigsby, op. cit., p. 124.
45 See Elmore Leonard, *City Primeval* (London, Star, 1982), pp. vii–xii; *LaBrava*, pp. 30–3.
46 For example, Higgins, *Kennedy for the Defense*, ch. 20; *The Patriot Game*, ch. 7.
47 Higgins, *The Rat on Fire* (London, Secker & Warburg, 1981), p. 4; *Imposters*, (London, André Deutsch, 1986), p. 178.
48 For an interesting introduction to Austin see Terry Eagleton, *Literary Theory* (Oxford, Basil Blackwell, 1983), pp. 118–19.
49 Bigsby, op. cit., pp. 66, 113–14.
50 Leonard, *Swag*, p. 45.
51 Leonard, *Stick*, p. 174; *Glitz* (Harmondsworth, Penguin, 1986), p. 43.
52 Leonard, *Stick*, pp. 228–9.
53 Leonard, *LaBrava*, pp. 7–9. Subsequent page numbers are given in the text.
54 Elmore Leonard, *The Switch* (Harmondsworth, Penguin, 1985), pp. 28, 140.
55 Leonard, *Glitz*, p. 237.
56 Higgins, *A Choice of Enemies*, pp. 107–8.
57 Leonard, *Split Images* (London, Star, 1984), pp. 23, 43.
58 Leonard, *City Primeval*, pp. 19–20, 79.
59 Judith Williamson and Don Macpherson, 'Prisoner of Love', in *Consuming Passions* (London and New York, Marion Boyars, 1986), pp. 154, 158, 159.
60 Bigsby, op. cit., p. 15; Pauline Kael's review appeared in the *New Yorker*, 9 February 1976, reprinted in Mary Pat Kelly, *Martin Scorsese: The First Decade* (Pleasantville, New York, 1980), p. 183.
61 Ian Penman's excellent analysis of De Niro appeared in *NME*, 6 October 1984, p. 16.
62 Mamet, *American Buffalo*, p. 3.
63 Robert Parker, *Valediction* (Harmondsworth, Penguin, 1985), p. 147.
64 Hunter S. Thompson and Ralph Steadman, *The Curse of Lono* (London, Picador, 1983), p. 55.
65 Constantine, op. cit., p. 5; Leonard, *Split Images*, p. 54.
66 Higgins, *Imposters*, pp. 220–1.
67 Mamet, *Glengarry, Glen Ross*, pp. 45, 56–7, 62.
68 Leonard, *City Primeval*, pp. 11, 14–15, 17. Subsequent page numbers are given in the text.
69 Leonard, *Stick*, p. 108.
70 Leonard, *Gold Coast* (London, Star, 1983), pp. 35, 173.
71 Leonard, *LaBrava*, pp. 28, 47, 132–3, 178.
72 Bigsby, op. cit., p. 134.

6 'Are you ready for the country?': tradition and American music

1 Bobbie Ann Mason, *In Country* (London, Chatto & Windus, 1986), p. 138.
2 See Michael Watts, 'The call and response of popular music: *the impact of American pop music in Europe*', in C. W. E. Bigsby (ed.), *Superculture: American Popular Culture and Europe* (London, Elek Books, 1975).
3 Roland Barthes, 'The grain of the voice', *Image – Music – Text*, essays selected and translated by Stephen Heath (London, Fontana, 1977), p. 179.
4 Jason Ringenberg of Jason and the Scorchers in an interview with the group by Cynthia Rose, *NME*, 5 May 1984, p. 13.
5 Reyner Banham, 'Mediated environments *or: You can't build that here*', in Bigsby, op. cit., p. 73.
6 Kate Lynch reprints *Rolling Stone*'s piece about Reagan's and Will's comments on Springsteen in *Springsteen: No Surrender* (London, Proteus, 1984), p. 118.
7 Jason Ringenberg in the Cynthia Rose interview, op. cit., p. 13.
8 Greil Marcus, *Mystery Train: Images of America in Rock 'n' Roll Music* (London, Omnibus Press, 1977), p. 62.
9 ibid., pp. 43–4.
10 ibid., p. 50.
11 ibid., p. 62.
12 ibid.
13 Lynch, op. cit., p. 60.
14 Ellen Gilchrist, 'Music', *Victory Over Japan* (London, Faber & Faber, 1985), p. 28.
15 Sam Shepard, *Motel Chronicles and Hawk Moon* (London, Faber & Faber, 1985), p. 154.
16 Marcus, op. cit., pp. 148, 158.
17 ibid., pp. 159–60.
18 Cited in Lynch, op. cit., p. 13.
19 Oscar Zeta Acosta, *The Autobiography of a Brown Buffalo* (San Francisco, Straight Arrow Books, 1972), pp. 19, 68, 73, 190, 195, 196. See also Hunter S. Thompson, *The Great Shark Hunt* (London, Picador, 1980), which contains 'Strange Rumblings in Aztlan', and Thompson's epitaph for Acosta, 'The Banshee Screams For Buffalo Meat', as well as extracts from *Fear and Loathing in Las Vegas*.
20 Rank and File interviewed by Cynthia Rose, *NME*, 29 October 1983, p. 7.
21 See *Aesthetics and Politics*, with an Afterword by Fredric Jameson (London, New Left Books, 1977), p. 13.
22 'Lukács against Bloch', trans. Rodney Livingstone, in ibid., p. 54.
23 Lynch, op. cit., p. 79.
24 T-Bone Burnett interviewed by Cynthia Rose, *NME*, 7 January 1984, p. 19.
25 Eliot's essay is collected in Claude M. Simpson (ed.), *Twentieth Century Interpretations of 'The Adventures of Huckleberry Finn'* (Englewood Cliffs, New Jersey, Prentice-Hall, 1968), p. 108.
26 Marcus, op. cit., pp. 154, 170.

7 The long reaction: 'Americanization' and cultural criticism

1 Robert Elms, *New Socialist*, 38 (May 1986), pp. 12–14.
2 Elizabeth Wilson in a debate on 'Socialist-feminism: out of the blue', *Feminist Review*, 23 (Summer 1986); extracts from the debate including this passage appeared in *New Socialist*, 38 (May 1986), p. 22.
3 Judith Williamson, 'The problems of being popular', *New Socialist*, 41 (September 1986), pp. 14–15.
4 Cora Kaplan, 'The culture crossover', *New Socialist*, 43 (November 1986), pp. 38–40.
5 C.W.E. Bigsby, 'Europe, America and the cultural debate', in Bigsby (ed.), *Superculture: American Popular Culture and Europe* (London, Elek Books, 1975), p. 6.
6 Quoted in ibid., p. 7.
7 Quoted in F.R. Leavis, *Mass Civilisation and Minority Culture*, and in Q.D. Leavis, *Fiction and the Reading Public* (Harmondsworth, Peregrine, 1979), p. 154.
8 Quoted in Bigsby, op. cit., p. 10.
9 Q.D. Leavis, op. cit., p. 181.
10 Tom Nairn, 'The English literary intelligentsia', in Emma Tennant (ed.), *Bananas*, (London, Quartet, 1977), p. 65.
11 Q.D. Leavis, op. cit., p. 214.
12 Chris Baldick, *The Social Mission of English Criticism 1848–1932* (Oxford, Oxford University Press, 1983), pp. 185–6.
13 Francis Mulhern, *The Moment of Scrutiny* (London, Verso, 1981), pp. 77, 126, 125; see also pp. 241–4.
14 Dick Hebdige, 'Towards a cartography of taste 1935–1962', *Block*, 4 (1981), pp. 40, 41.
15 ibid., p. 42.
16 ibid., pp. 43, 44, 45.
17 Gramsci, 'Americanism and Fordism' in ibid., p. 54.
18 ibid., p. 54.
19 Bigsby, op. cit., p. 27.
20 Hebdige, op. cit., p. 54.
21 Richard Hoggart, *The Uses of Literacy* (Harmondsworth, Penguin, 1958), pp. 190, 193.
22 ibid., pp. 201, 247–8.
23 ibid., pp. 257–60, 263–4.
24 ibid., pp. 266–71.
25 ibid., p. 324.
26 *The Collected Essays, Journalism and Letters of George Orwell*, vol. IV, *In Front of Your Nose 1945–1950* (London, Secker & Warburg, 1968), pp. 98–9.
27 ibid., pp. 100–1.
28 *The Collected Essays, Journalism and Letters of George Orwell*, vol. III, *As I Please 1943–1945* (London, Secker & Warburg, 1968), pp. 212, 216.
29 ibid., pp. 217, 218, 219.
30 ibid., pp. 220–3, 229.
31 Ken Worpole, *Dockers and Detectives: Popular Reading, Popular Writing* (London, Verso, 1983), p. 35.
32 ibid., p. 30.

Notes

33 Jeno Peter Becker, 'The mean streets of Europe: *the influence of the American "hard-boiled" school on European detective fiction*', and Thomas Elsasser, 'Two decades in another country: *Hollywood and the cinéphiles*', both in Bigsby, op. cit.; see also Worpole, op. cit., p. 41.

34 Martin Barker, *A Haunt of Fears* (London, Pluto, 1984), pp. 5, 18.

35 ibid., pp. 21, 23, 25, 26.

36 ibid., pp. 26–7.

37 ibid., pp. 29, 30, 35, 41, 42–3.

38 ibid., pp. 80, 82–3.

39 ibid., pp. 134, 135, 139; see the excellent discussion of 'The Orphan', pp. 160–9.

40 ibid., pp. 170–1, 172, 173, 181, 182, 184–5, 185.

41 ibid., pp. 185–7.

42 Alan Wolfe, 'Sociology, liberalism and the radical right', *New Left Review*, 128 (July–August 1981), p. 27.

43 Richard Sparks, 'Special discretion required', *New Socialist*, 48 (April 1987), p. 23.

44 Simon Watney, 'Babbling at the barricades of pornography', *New Socialist* (June 1986), p. 21.

45 See the essays in Martin Barker (ed.), *The Video Nasties: Freedom and Censorship in the Media* (London, Pluto, 1984).

46 See Jane Root's *Open the Box* (London, Comedia, 1986), for these negative images of television.

47 Ien Ang, *Watching Dallas: Soap Opera and the Melodramatic Imagination*, trans. Della Cowling (London, Methuen, 1985), p. 93.

48 ibid., pp. 2, 3; see also A. Mattelart, X. Delcourt, M. Mattelart, *International Image Markets* (London, Comedia, 1984).

49 Ang, op. cit., pp. 18, 55, 56.

50 ibid., pp. 98, 99, 104–6, 108–9.

51 David Morley, *Family Television: Cultural Power and Domestic Leisure* (London, Comedia, 1986), p. 72.

52 Ang, op. cit., pp. 111–13, 113, 114, 115, 116, 119.

53 Patricia Holland, 'The Page Three girl speaks to women, too', *Screen*, vol. 24, 3 (May–June 1983), pp. 85, 86, 87, 88.

54 ibid., pp. 101, 102.

55 Trevor Blackwell and Jeremy Seabrook, *A World Still to Win: The Reconstruction of the Post-War Working Class* (London, Faber & Faber, 1985), p. 52.

56 Judith Williamson, 'The politics of consumption', *Consuming Passions* (London, Marion Boyars, 1986), pp. 229–32.

57 ibid., pp. 232, 233.

58 Terry Lovell, 'The social relations of cultural production: absent centre of a new discourse', in Simon Clarke (ed.), *One-Dimensional Marxism: Althusser and the Politics of Culture* (London, Allison & Busby, 1980), p. 253; see Jean Baudrillard, *For a Critique of the Political Economy of the Sign*, trans. Charles Levin (St Louis, Telos Press, 1981), for a useful if problematic critique of the concepts of use-value and need.

59 The background of this brief sketch is provided by Richard Kinsey, 'Crime in the City', *Marxism Today* (May 1986); see also Ian Taylor, *Law and Order: Arguments for Socialism* (London, Macmillan, 1981); John Lea and Jock Young, *What is to be Done about Law and Order?* (Harmondsworth, Penguin, 1984).

Conclusion: President Rambo's poodle

1 William Burroughs, 'What Washington? What orders?', *Exterminator!* (London, Calder & Boyars, 1974), p. 110.
2 Paul Weller interviewed by Paolo Hewitt, *NME*, 1 June 1985, p. 28.
3 Colin MacInnes, *Absolute Beginners* (London, Allison & Busby, 1980), pp. 52–3.
4 ibid., p. 85.
5 Julie Burchill, *Love It or Shove It* (London, Century, 1985), p. 107. Subsequent page numbers are given in the text.
6 Julie Burchill, *Damaged Gods* (London, Century Hutchinson, 1986), p. 138.
7 Tom Nairn, *The Break-Up of Britain* (London, Verso, 1981), pp. 29–30; see also Perry Anderson, 'Origins of the present crisis', *New Left Review*, 23 (January–February 1964), and 'Components of the national culture', *New Left Review*, 50 (May–June, 1968); criticism of this position can be found in E. P. Thompson, 'The peculiarities of the English', *The Poverty of Theory* (London, 1978), and Richard Johnson, 'Barrington Moore, Perry Anderson and English social development', *Cultural Studies*, 9 (Spring, 1976).
8 Nairn, op. cit., pp. 45–6.
9 Anthony Barnett, 'Iron Britannia', *New Left Review*, 134 (July–August 1982), p. 57; see also pp. 48–50.
10 ibid., p. 62.
11 ibid., p. 63.
12 Nairn, op. cit., p. 55.
13 ibid., pp. 55, 385.
14 Max Pragnell's interview, 'Mining the red seam', *Sunday Times Review*, 15 June 1986, p. 44.
15 Walter Benjamin, *Illuminations*, ed. Hannah Arendt, trans. Harry Zohn (London, Fontana, 1979), p. 233.
16 Information taken from *Design Classics: Levi's 501 Jeans*, narrated by Jancis Robinson, BBC 2, 1 July 1987.
17 Sam Shepard, *Fool for Love* (London, Faber & Faber, 1984), pp. 16, 43.
18 James Agee and Walker Evans, *Let Us Now Praise Famous Men* (Boston, Houghton Mifflin, 1941), pp. 265, 267.
19 ibid., pp. 268, 269.
20 Trevor Blackwell and Jeremy Seabrook, *A World Still to Win: The Reconstruction of the Post-War Working Class* (London, Faber & Faber, 1985), pp. 66, 68–9, 70.
21 Dick Heckstall-Smith, 'A Private Function', *Guardian*, 16 February 1985.
22 Judith Williamson, 'It's different for girls', *Consuming Passions* (London, Marion Boyars, 1986), pp. 50–2.
23 Kate Lynch, *Springsteen: No Surrender* (London, Proteus, 1984), pp. 101, 113.
24 Nigel Matheson, 'The Deltoid Force', *NME*, 7 June 1986, p. 13; this piece also contains the Schwarzenegger quotation.
25 Barbara Creed, 'From here to modernity: feminism and postmodernity', *Screen*, vol. 28, 2 (Spring 1987), p. 65.
26 Salman Rushdie, *Guardian*, 26 May 1986, p. 7.
27 Mary Kaldor and Paul Anderson (eds), *Mad Dogs: The US Raids on Libya* (London, Pluto, 1986), pp. 55, 80, 136, 130.
28 See Edward Said, *Covering Islam* (London, Routledge & Kegan Paul, 1981).
29 Mary Kaldor, 'Introduction', *Mad Dogs*, p. 3.

30 ibid., pp. 4, 9–10.
31 Jamie Dettmer, 'Europe or America: the British political context', in ibid., pp. 35, 36, 37.
32 ibid., pp. 37, 39.
33 Anthony Barnett, *New Statesman*, 21 October 1983, p. 22.
34 E. P. Thompson, 'Notes on the nature of American blood', *Guardian*, 18 April 1986, p. 16.
35 E. P. Thompson, 'Letter to Americans', *Mad Dogs*, pp. 11, 12, 13, 14, 15.
36 E. P. Thompson, 'The view from Oxford Street', in ibid., pp. 142, 143, 144.
37 Lloyd De Mause, 'The secret psyche of Ronald Reagan', *Guardian*, 29 December 1986, p. 9.
38 ibid.
39 Reyner Banham, 'Detroit tin re-visited', in T. Faulkner (ed.), *Design 1900–1960: Studies in Design and Popular Culture of the 20th Century* (Newcastle-upon-Tyne Polytechnic, 1976), pp. 121, 123, 125, 127, 128, 130, 140.
40 Reyner Banham, 'Representations in protest', in Paul Barker (ed.), *Arts in Society* (London, Fontana, 1977), pp. 64–5.

Index

Aaronovitch, Sam 192
Absolute Beginners (MacInnes) 211–12
Accidental Tourist, The (Tyler) 125–7
Acosta, Oscar 169
actors, commitment 70
Adams, Samuel 136
Adams, William 6–7, 32, 39–40, 67
Agee, James 34, 35, 60–3, 226–8
Agrarians, the 58–9
agribusiness 36, 37, 69
agriculture: crisis in 2, 15, 28, 31–2;
    media coverage 31–2; overproduction
    29–31; *see also* farmers, farming,
    farms
Alabama, tenant farmers 60–3
Alamo Bay (Malle) 73
alternative life styles 130
Altman, Robert 101, 105
Always a Body to Trade (Constantine)
    145–6
American Buffalo (Mamet) 135, 141–4
Americanization: and art 247; and
    British decline 215, 218; and the City
    221; and Communist Party 192–3,
    196, 197; and crime novels 186–91;
    opposition to 181–2, 183–5, 194–5,
    210, 212; as threat 24–5, 173, 175,
    179–86, 191, 193, 194–5, 210, 215–
    16; and US foreign policy 239, 240–5
Anderson, Perry 218
Ang, Ien 199–202, 206
Angel City (Shepard) 92
Arbus, Diane 57, 150
architecture, American, and music 159
Arnold, Matthew 24, 26, 180
Astley, Virginia 159
At Close Range (Foley) 73
Atlantic City (Malle) 139

back-projection image 159
Baldick, Chris 182
Band, The 161–2
Banham, Rayner 106–7, 158, 246–7
Barker, Martin 191–7, 198
Barnett, Anthony 218–20, 240
Barren Ground (Glasgow) 58
Barrett, Michele 174
Barthelme, Donald 3, 93, 116
Barthelme, Frederick 3, 122, 128–9
Barthes, Roland 158, 246
Beans of Egypt, Maine, The (Chute) 56
Beaver, Harold 98
Bellamy, Edward 21–2
Benjamin, Joe 193
Benjamin, Walter 184, 185, 224–5, 246
Bennett, Alan 229
bestsellers 26
Bigsby, Christopher 98–9, 130–1, 135,
    142–3, 150, 154, 179–80
Black Mask magazine 189
Black Tickets (Phillips) 118
Blackwell, Trevor 204, 228
body, the: in crime novels 154–5; in
    jeans advertising 230–1
Boesky, Ivan 221
Brecht, Bertold 177, 181
'Bridle, The' (Carver) 83–4
Bright Bill *see* Video Recordings Bill
    (1984)
Britain: and American farm crisis 31–2;
    American influence 24, 191, 196–7;
    decline 218–20; land, importance 29;
    post-war 228–9; special relationship
    209–10, 214–15
Brody, Neville 174
Bryan, William Jennings 19, 49
Buford, Bill 3–4

Index

Burchill, Julie 212–17
Burke, Edmund 13
Burnett, T-Bone 172
business, and crime 140–8, 221
Byatt, A. S. 48
Byrne, David 165

Caldwell, Erskine 58–9
California, politics 10–11
capitalism, growth 22; and tradition 14, 15
Capra, Frank 16
car styling, American 246
Carver, Raymond 9, 75, 83–4, 119, 121, 122–5, 127–8, 134, 163; language and emotion 122–3
Cash, Rosanne 164
Cather, Willa 16–17, 45–51, 126
Cave, Nick 166
Chandler, Raymond 189–90
characterization, flat 127
Chase, James Hadley 188–9, 191
Children and Young Persons (Harmful Publications) Act (1955) 191
Choice of Enemies, A (Higgins) 136
Chopin, Kate 126
Churchill, Winston 197, 198
Churchillism 219, 220
Chute, Carolyn 56, 57, 58
cinema: and crime 139; and the farm 16, 31, 33, 67–73; macho 231–4; and music 163–4; populist 28; transformed into video 199
City, fraud 221
City on a Hill, A (Higgins) 136–7
City Primeval (Leonard) 152–3, 155–6
Coalminer's Daughter 73
collective action 71
colonization, American 25, 209–10, 213, 215, 216, 242
comics: American 186, 194; horror 191–7
Communist Party, and horror comics 192–3, 196, 197
Connolly, Cyril 192
Conservative Party: populism 175–7, 207; and United States 210; *see also* Thatcherism
conservatives: and Americanization 182–3; divisions within 11; and tradition 13–15; *see also* new right

conspiracy theories 13
Constantine, K. C. 145–6, 149, 151
consumerism 223
consumption, politics of 205–7, 210–11
continuity, in crime fiction 145
Cooder, Ry 163–4
Cook, Robin 221
Cook, Sylvia Jenkins 57–8, 60, 63–4
Coppola, Francis 163
corporate America, and crime 139
Costello, Elvis 25, 170
Cotton (Bethea) 58
Country 68, 69, 70, 71–2, 226
country music 5, 28–9, 165; and American heterosexuality 100; *see also* music
Coward, Rosalind 174
Cowboy Mouth (Shepard) 7, 88, 89, 94
cowboys: and detectives 155–6; in literature 89, 226
Cramps, the 167
Creed, Barbara 232
Crèvecoeur, J. H. St. J. 38–40, 46, 51
crime: and the body 154–5; in corporate America 139; as free enterprise 4, 135, 138, 140–8, 221; professional code 144–5; punishment 147–8; and Thatcherism 207
crime novels: continuity 145; English criticism of 186–91; pleasures of 190; sadism in 186, 188
criminals, and police 146
Cruise missiles 210, 215
cultural identity 199–200
cultural imperialism 25, 193, 199–200
culture: agrarian 28, 191; and emotions 122–3; mass 197–204; minority 181–2, 183; popular *see* popular culture
Curse of the Starving Class (Shepard) 3, 92, 93, 95–8

Dallas 1, 179, 181, 199–201
Dallek, Robert 115
Davis, Mike 10, 12
Day of the Locust, The (West) 8
decay, and British writing 134
Delta Force, The 232, 236
De Mause, Lloyd 243–4
Democratic Party, campaigns 28
De Niro, Robert 5, 154

Desert Hearts (Deitch) 101
desert, images of 107
detectives 137–8, 145, 154; and cowboys
   155–6
Dettmer, Jamie 238–9
Dispatches (Herr) 131
Donnelly, Ignatius 23
Duhamel, Marcel 191
Dukakis, Michael 68
Dylan, Bob 27

economy, shifts in 10–11, 12
Edgar, David 174
Edmond (Mamet) 13, 143
Eliot, T. S. 172, 182, 183
Elms, Robert 174–5
Emerson, R. W. 32–3
emotions, and culture 122–3
Enemies of Promise (Connolly) 182
Englishness 193, 195, 196
environment, conservative policy 14
ethics: of frontier experience 89, 99;
   suspension of 141–2
euphemism in modern warfare 237–8
Evans, Walker 60, 61, 62, 63, 150

Falk, Florence 89, 91, 95
Falk, Richard 234–5
Falklands war 213, 218–19
family: as economic unit 34–5; images
   of 108
famine, and overproduction 30–1
Farm Aid 27, 29, 160, 165, 169
farmers: coalition with labour 20;
   collective action 71; concern for 2, 27,
   28; different types 36; early 38–43;
   and financiers 22, 36, 220; as mythical
   figures 28, 29, 32, 40; overproduction
   29–31; poverty 45; protest 17–18, 41–
   2; radicalization 18–19; solidarity
   72–3
Farmers' Alliance 17, 18, 19, 20, 29, 42
farming: and family 28, 32; and
   femininity 2–3, 33–4; in fiction 52,
   74–84; films 16, 31, 67–8; gender roles
   33–5; labourers 35–7, 59; as work
   32–3
farms, loss of 2, 32
'Fast Lanes' (Phillips) 117, 118, 119
Faulkner, William 58

Fear and Loathing in Las Vegas
   (Thompson) 169
Fekete, John 35, 59
feminism and populism 177, 198
Fender, Stephen 38
fiction, American: compared with films
   69; and the grotesque 57, 58–9; new
   sparseness 116–17; regionalism 3–4,
   43, 46–7, 48
Field, Sally 27, 73
films *see* cinema
Financier, The (Dreiser) 23
First Blood 233, 235
Fitzhugh, George 40
Flaubert, Gustave 48, 126
Fonda, Henry 28, 68
Fonda, Jane 27, 281, 68–9
Fool for Love (Shepard) 101–6, 226
Ford, John 28, 68, 178
Ford, Richard, 120, 130
Foucault, Michel 147–8, 157–8
free enterprise 135
Frith, Simon 200
frontier ethic 89, 99
frontier experience, importance of 21,
   25, 40–1, 51

Gaines, Bill 194
Garland, Hamlin 43–5, 46, 51, 70
Gastonia strike 60
Gelber, Jack 90
gender: division of labour 34–5; and
   landscape 3, 101, 102, 106; and
   national identity 245
George, Henry 21
Gephardt, Richard 217
GIs, opposition to 183, 193
Gibson, Mel 70
Gilchrist, Ellen 165
Glasgow, Ellen 58
Glengarry, Glen Ross (Mamet) 98–9,
   142, 150, 155
Godard, Jean-Luc 25
God's Little Acre (Caldwell) 58
Goldwater, Barry 7–8, 10, 13–14
Goodwyn, Lawrence 18, 19, 20, 36–7,
   41, 42
Gosse, Edmund 180
Gould, Jay 20
Gramsci, A. 184

Index

Granta 3
Grapes of Wrath, The (Steinbeck) 28,
30, 35, 63–7, 68, 118
grotesque, the, in fiction 57, 58–9
Gun Club 167

Hall, Stuart 175
Hamilton, Richard 247
Hammett, Dashiell 189–90
Harris, Ed 73
Hawk Moon (Shepard) 165–6
Heath, Stephen 113
Hebdige, Dick 182–3, 184–6, 193, 224
Heckstall-Smith, Dick 229
heritage, marketing 217, 223–4, 226, 228
Herr, Michael 131
heterosexuality: in Barthelme 129; in
Shepard 100–6, 112, 114; *see also*
masculinity
hick chic 67, 125
Hicks, John D. 16
Higgins, George V. 4, 136–7, 144, 147,
148, 149–50, 151–3
Hill, Walter 163
Himes, Chester 191
Hobson, J. A. 23, 222–3
Hofstadter, Richard 13, 14, 17, 18, 20,
67
Hoggart, Richard 24, 182, 183, 185–7,
190, 193
Holland, Patricia 202–3, 206
home and work 33
homogeneity of American culture 185
Honduras, British 182
Hopper, Edward 163
horror comics 191–7
horror videos 191–2, 195, 198–9
Howarth, Gerald 197
Howells, William Dean 23, 43
Huckleberry Finn (Twain) 118, 172–3
Hulbert, Ann 33, 56, 67–73

identity: British 243, 245; cultural 200
I'll Take My Stand 59
Imposters (Higgins) 154, 156
In Country (Mason) 125, 126–7, 132–3
In the Land of Cotton (Scarborough) 58
individualism 16, 17–18, 35; and
collectivity 71
intellectual, populist images 85–6

Iran scandal 15–16, 244–5
Irish music, links 170
It's a Wonderful Life 16

James, Clive 201
James, Henry 23, 26, 125
Jarmusch, Jim 25
Jason and the Scorchers 29, 162, 167,
168
jeans, marketing 223–8, 229–31
Jefferson, Thomas 39, 40, 136
Jewett, Sarah Orne 48, 117, 126
Johnson, Diane 125–7, 128, 130
journalism, investigative 22–3, 46

Kael, Pauline 154
Kaldor, Mary 237–8
Kaplan, Cora 178–9
Kasdan, Lawrence 132
Kauffmann, Stanley 3, 93
Keal, William 190
Keillor, Garrison 67
King, Horace 193
Kinnock, Neil 174, 176, 239
Kirby, Jack Temple 58
Kissinger, Henry 89, 240
Kroc, Ray 14

labour: in agriculture 35–7; congealed
225; gender division of 34–5; and
ownership 32–3, 34, 36–7
Labour Party: arts policy 207–8; and the
City 221–2; law and order 207; and
populism 174, 175–7, 206; post-war
228–9
LaBrava (Leonard) 149, 150–1, 156
Lacan, Jacques 109
LaGuardia, Fiorello 22, 30
Lamb, William 20
land, the: importance of 2, 28, 29;
literary representation of 48–9, 59,
64–5, 107; and machinery 65;
ownership 36–7
Landau, Jon 164
landscape: and gender 3, 101, 102, 106;
in literature 49
Lange, Jessica 27, 68, 69, 73
language: foul 151–4; and law and order
4, 5, 138, 145, 148–9, 151–4; and
realism 149, 151–3; as rhetoric
149–50

law and order, language of 4, 5, 138, 145, 148–9, 151–4; populism of 204, 206–7
Lawson, Nigel 176
Lease, Mary Elizabeth 17
Leaving the Land (Unger) 75–83, 126
Leavis, F. R. 24, 180, 181, 182, 183
Leavis, Q. D. 24, 180, 181, 182
Lee, Robert Edson 38
Lee Rough Rider jeans 225–6
Leonard, Elmore 4, 138, 140–1, 144, 146–7, 148–9, 145, 151, 152–3, 155–6
Let Us Now Praise Famous Men (Agee) 60–3, 164, 226–8
Letters from an American Farmer (Crèvecoeur) 38–40, 46, 51
levelling down 182–3
Levi jeans 224, 225, 229
Lewelling, Governor 30
Leyland trucks, sale 175–6, 210
Libya, US raids on 231, 234, 236–40, 241
Lindsay, Tim 223, 224
Livingstone, Ken 174
Lloyd, Henry Demarest 23
Long Ryders, The 162, 163
Los Lobos, The 161, 168–9
loss, sense of 4, 116, 117, 134, 138
Lost in America (Brooks) 67
Love Always (Beattie) 67
Lovell, Terry 206
Lucas-Tooth, Sir Hugh 193
Luckham, Robin 234
Lukàcs, Gyorgy 171
Lynch, Kate 164, 171–2

McCarthyism 192, 196
McFarlane, Robert 15–16
McInerney, Jay 128
MacInnes, Colin 211–12
Mad Dog Blues (Shepard) 91, 93
Mad Dogs: the US Raids on Libya (Kaldor, Anderson) 233, 234–5, 237–8, 241–2
magazines, crime 188
Mailer, Norman 1, 7–9, 13, 168
Main-Travelled Roads (Garland) 44–5
Malle, Louis 139
Mamet, David 4, 13, 98–9, 130–1, 135,

141–4, 150, 151, 154, 156; *see also* individual titles
Marcus, Greil 25, 161–2, 166
Marranca, Bonnie 88–90
masculinity: in advertising 230–1, 245; and Americanness 88; in cinema 70–2, 231–4; and culture 3, 70; and law and order 138, 145, 155, 156; and music 163
Mason, Bobbie Ann 9, 74–5, 80, 120, 126, 127, 128, 132–4
mass culture 197–204; ideology of 200, 201, 202, 204
mass reproduction 184–5, 224–5
Matthew, George 192
Mean Streets (Scorsese) 122, 143
Mellencamp, John Cougar 29, 160
Mencken, E. L. 59
mess, and new American fiction 134
Michael, George 24
Mind of the South, The (Cash) 59
Minder 229
minority culture 181–2, 183
Missing in Action (Norris) 231, 232, 235
modern art 202
monetary reform 18–19
monopoly, opposition to 22–3
Mordida Man, The (Thomas) 137
Morley, David 201
Motel Chronicles (Shepard) 99, 113
muckrakers 22–3, 46
Mulhern, Francis 182
music: British–American exchanges 157, 160, 170; and cinema 163–4; criticism 158; Englishness 159; masculinity 163; mixture of old and new 162; new American 158, 161, 162, 168; and oppositions 5–6, 160; ruralism 164–5; and sense of place 29, 158–9, 161–2; and the South 164–8
My Antonia (Cather) 48, 50

Nairn, Tom 15, 218, 220, 222–3
narrative distance 126
nationalism 15, 22, 175–6, 245
naturalism 47, 53
Nebraska (Springsteen) 139, 164
New Critics 59
New Deal 16, 60

Index

New Masses journal 60
new right 9, 10, 11–14, 21; and
    Thatcherism 210
New Socialist 174
New Yorkers, and regional fiction 58–9
Newman, Randy 164
No Orchids for Miss Blandish (Chase)
    188–9
Norma Rae 73
Norris, Chuck 231, 232, 235, 236
Norris, Frank 51–5
North, Oliver 235
nuclear protest 209–10

Obscene Publications Act (1959) 197
obscenity, and crime fiction 151–4
O'Connor, Flannery 57, 172
Octopus, The (Norris) 51–5
Operation Sidewinder (Shepard) 90, 91
O Pioneers! (Cather) 47–9, 51
Orwell, George 24, 182, 183, 187–91,
    193, 211
Otis, John 29
overproduction, agricultural 29–31
Owen, David 220

Paris, Texas (Shepard) 100, 106, 107–
    13, 153
Parker, Robert 137, 151, 154
past, investigation in fiction 119
Patriot Game, The (Higgins) 147
patriotism 175, 176, 213, 245
Peachment, Chris 85
Peele, Gillian 11, 12
Penman, Ian 154
Peoples Party 18, 19, 21, 42, 222
Phillips, Jayne Anne 117, 118–19, 120,
    132, 134
photography, influence on fiction 130–1
Places in the Heart (Benton) 68, 69, 73
pleasure: and American images 200–1;
    of consumption 206, 210–11; images
    of 230–1; and mass culture 202; and
    Thatcherism 204
Point Blank (Stark) 139
police: and criminal, rapport 146; and
    the law 146–7
Political Action Committees (PAC) 11
politics: disillusion with 4–5, 136–7
    138; and populism 5, 42

poor whites, in literature 2, 57–8, 60–3,
    64
pop music: British 157, 159, 160, 161,
    168; and history 169; videos 160–1,
    168
popular culture: and American foreign
    policy 239–40; and Americanization
    198–9; and back-projection image
    159; fears of new forms 198; and the
    left 177–9; manipulative 134
populism: in cinema 28; conflict within
    2; double 204; historical flash points
    2; ideology of 201–2, 204;
    individualist 16, 17–18, 35; and the
    land 37; and nationalism 15, 22; and
    New Deal 16, 18; and the past 15–
    19; and politics 5, 42; and style 174;
    Western 14–15; and workers 20–1
Populist Party 29, 37, 41, 42, 43
Porkchoppers, The (Thomas) 137
post-industrial society 216–17
Postman Always Rings Twice, The (Cain)
    186
poverty 45; and whites 2, 57–8, 60–3, 64
Powell, Enoch 214
Presley, Elvis 165, 166–7
Prince 162
Pringle, Peter 234
prison 147–8
private eyes 137–8, 145, 154
Private Function, A (Bennett) 229
producerism 220, 222
property, and labour 32–3, 34, 46–7
protest: anti-nuclear 209–10; rural 17–
    18, 41–2
Pumphrey, George 194–5
Pynchon, Thomas 163

Raffles 188, 189
Raging Bull (Scorsese) 143, 154
railroads, and farmers 41–2, 53–4
Rambo 232, 233–6; Reagan as 234–5,
    236–7, 238, 240, 242, 243–5
Rank and File 170
Ransom, John 59
'Reagan country' 7
Reagan, Ronald 4–5, 6; foreign policy
    231, 234, 236–45; and media 115;
    populist appeal 6–7, 9, 10–11, 12–13;
    and problems 15–16; as Rambo

234–5, 236–7, 238, 240, 243–5; and
  Senate elections (1986) 28, 69
realism: in crime fiction 149, 151, 189–
  90; and language 149, 151–3; and
  romance, opposition 45, 51; self-
  conscious 145; and Southern images
  58–9
reggae 159
regionalism in fiction 3–4, 43, 46–7, 48
Republican Party: candidates 7–9, 10;
  and new right 12
Reykjavik summit 244
rhetoric 149
Richards, Jeffrey 16, 18
right, American: candidates 10;
  contradictions in 197; see also new
  right
Right Stuff, The (Kaufman) 92–3
River, The 29, 68, 69, 70, 71, 72
rivers, cultural allusions 172
road, myth of 118, 125
rock music 160, 161, 168
Rockefeller, Nelson 10
Rockwell, Norman 125, 126
roots: and music 162, 169–70
ruralism, new 2, 67, 70, 125–6, 127–8
Rushdie, Salman 233, 236–7
rusticity: English 181–2; fashionable 67,
  70
Rydell, Mark 70

Said, Edward 236
Schwarzenegger, Arnold 231, 232, 235
Scorsese, Martin 4, 5, 114, 122, 143,
  151, 153–4
Scrutiny 182
Seabrook, Jeremy 204, 206, 228
Second Marriage (Barthelme) 122, 129
Senate elections (1986) 28
sex-novels 186
Sexual Perversity in Chicago (Mamet) 144
Shannon, Fred 41
sharecropping 58, 62, 164
Shepard, Sam, 3, 7, 70, 85; and
  American heterosexuality 100–6,
  112, 114; background 86–7; cowboy
  in 89, 226; and the land 92, 95–8, 99,
  100; masculinity in 3, 88, 91, 101; and
  mediated communication 111–12;
  sixties-style radical politics 89–90,

101; and the South 165–6; use of
  bricolage 93–4; West, transformation
  through popular culture 99, 100, 101;
  women in 88–9, 90; as writer and
  performer 87; see also individual titles
Shiloh and Other Stories (Mason) 74–5
Short, Clare 198
short story, the 3, 116, 117, 122
Sinclair, Upton 23, 46, 139
single-issue campaigns 12
Single Tax 21
Sister Carrie (Dreiser) 223
Skynyrd, Lynyrd 164
small town fiction 125–6, 127–8
Smith, Patti 88, 89
Smiths, the 212
social issues, and new right 12
Solotaroff, Ted 75, 125
Sontag, Susan 131
South, the: in fiction 57–63; in music
  164–8; representation of 165
Southern Gothic School 58–9, 165
Southside Johnny 169
Spacek, Sissy 27, 68, 69
Sparks, Richard 197
Spillane, Mickey 186
Springsteen, Bruce 5–6, 117, 139, 143,
  157, 160, 164, 168, 171–2, 231
Stallone, Sylvester 232, 233, 236
stars, commitment 70
Steadman, Ralph 138
Steinbeck, John 3; *Grapes of Wrath* 30–
  1, 63–7, 81, 118; *Nation* article (1936)
  35–6; populism 64, 66
Stick (Leonard) 140, 156
streamlining, American 184–5
Stribling, T. S. 59
Style Council 210, 211
success ethic 141, 142
Sun 202–4; double populism 204
surrealism in new fiction 130
Swag (Leonard) 144, 156
swearing, in crime fiction 151–4
Sweet Dreams 73
Switch, The (Leonard) 151

tacky, use of 167
Talking Heads 165
Tallent, Elizabeth 120, 128, 129–30
Tax, Single 21

Index

Taxi Driver (Scorsese) 5, 114, 143, 153–4
Tebbit, Norman 176
teenagers, emergence 184
television, effects of 197–202
tenant farmers *see* sharecroppers; poor whites
Tender Mercies (Beresford) 73
Thatcherism: American influence 1, 209, 213–14; as authoritarian populism 175–6, 177; contradictions within 197–8, 204; and crime 207; and Falklands war 219; and Libyan raids 238–40, 242; and pleasure 204
theme park, Britain as 215, 216, 217
Thomas, Ross 137
Thompson, Denys 182
Thompson, E. P. 241–3
Thompson, Hunter S. 138, 154, 169
Thompson Twins 157
Time of Man, The (Roberts) 58
Tobacco Road (Caldwell) 58, 126
Tooth of Crime, The (Shepard) 87–8, 91–2, 114
Top Gun 232
Trading Places (Landis) 141
tradition; and conservatism 13–15; and music 171, 172–3
transport policy and youth culture 206
travel, in fiction 117–19, 125; and history 119–20
True West (Shepard) 94–5
trusts, rise of 22
Turner, Frederick Jackson 16–17, 21, 25, 40–1, 51
Twain, Mark 118, 172–3
Tyler, Anne 117, 120, 125, 126, 127

Unger, Douglas 75, 126, 128
unisex styles, and women 230
United States: colonization of Britain 25, 209–10, 213, 215, 216, 242; culture 25, 28, 181, 210; influence on Britain 24, 191, 196–7; as monolith 25; and popular culture 25; special relationship 209–10, 214–15; *see also* Americanization

Veblen, Thorstein 23, 141, 182
video: and film, differences 199; horror 191–2, 195, 198–9; nasty 198, 216; pop 160–1, 168
Video Recordings Bill (1984) 197, 198
Vietnam, influence on fiction 130, 131–3
Viguerie, Richard 11, 12

Wade, John Donald 58–9
Waits, Tom 162–3
Walken, Christopher 73
Walker, Alice 56, 57
Wall Street 140–1, 221
Warren, Robert Penn 59
Watney, Simon 198
Watt, James 14–15
wealth and poverty 22–3
Weaver, General 17
Weeds (Kelley) 58
Weller, Paul 24, 159, 210–12, 223
Wenders, Wim 100, 107, 111, 113–14
West, the: in literature 43, 48, 50, 51, 88–9, 94; populism 14–15
West, Nathaniel 8
Westland crisis 175, 210
Whitehouse, Mary 197, 198
Whitman, Walt 50, 124–5
Widening Gyre, The (Parker) 137–8
WIFE *see* Women Involved in Farm Economics
Will, George F. 160
Williams, Raymond 181
Williamson, Judith 153, 177–9, 181, 205, 206, 230
Wills, Garry 39, 135–6
Wilson, Elizabeth 177
Wilson, Harold 219
Witness (Weir) 69
Wogan, Terry 201
Wolfe, Alan 14, 197
Wolff, Tobias 128, 131–2
women: as farmers' voice 28, 33; images of 2–3, 49–51, 69, 71–2, 88, 230; and jeans 230; and opposition 28, 33; role 34, 69, 71–2; strong 16, 33–4, 50, 69, 71–2; Western 50
Women Involved in Farm Economics (WIFE) 27, 28, 33
Woodward, C. Vann 16
work: in fiction 125; *see also* labour
working class, affluence 204–5

Worpole, Ken 190
Wranglers jeans 225, 230–1
writing, as work 86, 125

Yank mags 188
Yardley, Jonathan 67
Yoakam, Dwight 170

York, Peter 217–18
Young, Neil 164
Yuppie left 177–8

Zevon, Warren 164
ZZ Top 162